CADOGAN

W9-AAY-836

St Petersburg

Cadogan Guides
3rd Floor, West End House, 11 Hills Place,
London W1R 1AH
becky.kendall@morrispub.co.uk
Distributed in the USA by
The Globe Pequot Press
246 Goose Lane, PO Box 480, Guilford,
Connecticut 06437–0480

Copyright © Rose Baring 1995, 2000
Updated by Katya Galitzine 2000

Book and cover design by Animage

Cover photographs by Ellen Rooney

Chapter title pages designed by Kicca Tommasi
from material by Rose Baring

Maps © Cadogan Guides, drawn by Map Creation Ltd
Series Editor: Linda McQueen
Editing and Proofreading: Linda McQueen and Kate Paice
Indexing: Isobel McLean
Production: Book Production Services
UK ISBN 1-86011-922-0
A catalogue record for this book
is available from the British Library

Printed and bound in the UK by
the Cromwell Press Ltd

*The author and publishers have
made every effort to ensure the
accuracy of the information in
the book at the time of going to
press. However, they cannot
accept any responsibility for any
loss, injury or inconvenience
resulting from the use of information contained in this guide.*

To Olga Lawrence, who lit the the fire

About the Author

Rose Baring first fell under the Russian spell at the age of 12, in a shoe-box of a classroom known as 'The Kremlin'. Back in the 1970s no one dreamed she would go and live in Russia, so the syllabus aimed at a fluent reading of the 19th-century classics. It wasn't until the 1990s that she acquired the vital domestic vocabulary of a Russian four-year-old and a few useful phrases for older ears only. She has two children and lives in London.

Author's Acknowledgements

This book has grown out of the earlier Cadogan Guide to Moscow and St Petersburg, and thanks are due to many of the same people for their continuing input. Liza Hollingshead is always a fount of inspiration, and although we have not been in St Petersburg together for some time, no book of mine on Russia would be complete without acknowledging my profound debt to Oleg Buryan for sharing his passion for his own culture with me. Nor would my St Petersburg be complete without the friendship and hospitality of Sasha Kisilyov and Nellya Levitskaya. For the second edition, my sincerest thanks go to Katya Galitzine, for agreeing to add her expert knowledge of St Petersburg to the mix, to Linda McQueen for her continuing good humour in the Cadogan office at a difficult time, and to Kate Paice for taking errors of fact and consistency as a personal insult. Also to Barnaby, for persuading me not to cut my nose off to spite my face. Where would I be without him?

About the Updater

Of Russian descent, for the past ten years Katya Galitzine has lived a multi-faceted life in St Petersburg. She has recently published her own album: *St Petersburg—Hidden Interiors*.

Updater's Acknowledgements

Thanks to Rose for letting me touch her Russian baby—and to Nadia who did the boring bits. И Надя Рибиницкая для столько скучные звонки—спасибо!

Contents

St Petersburg: the Walks   65–192

Maps and Plans

St Petersburg is a city of ethereal beauty. Suspended between brimming river water and an endless expanse of sky, it manages to combine the haunting northern qualities of a fairytale with the mainstream pomp and glory of a European capital. The pastel façades of its elegant palaces take their chilly colours from nature—blues and greys from the sky, yellows and greens from the land. Yet their form is so much exuberant artifice.

Introduction

Here a classical pediment in marble recalls the rigorous rules of ancient Rome; next door a baroque curlicue suggests central Europe at its most decadent; while down the street Art Nouveau railings reassert the primary inspiration of nature in their vegetable curves. It is a hybrid city—a place of nature and of nurture—in which the natural curve of its rivers is offset by the arrow-straight certainties of its streets.

This grand and haughty exterior, the creation of an empire at its height, belies a history of turmoil. Just ten years after the first sod was turned in this northern wasteland, Peter the Great declared the ramshackle collection of buildings his capital city. He ordered the court to move from ancient, cosy Moscow to its lath and plaster dampness. In the decades that followed, palaces, churches, academies, government ministries and humble dwellings all emerged more or less willingly from the bog. By the end of the 18th century, the combined determination of Peter and Catherine the Great had dragged Russia from medieval obscurity to the centre of the European political stage with St Petersburg as its figurehead. The scene was set for a glittering 19th century, when the very name of the capital was a by-word for glamour and excess.

1

But, beneath the glitz, all was not well. The assassination of Tsar Alexander II in 1881 in the heart of the city exposed the divisions in Russian society for all to see. Revolution broke out in St Petersburg in 1905 and twice in Petrograd (as the city was then known) in 1917, yet the Bolsheviks rewarded the city when they came to power by returning the capital to Moscow and renaming St Petersburg yet again: Leningrad. And the worst was yet to come. In 1935 Stalin turned his paranoid attention on the city, and it is estimated that in that year alone up to one-quarter of the city's population was arrested. Just six years later it was the turn of Hitler to persecute the city, subjecting it to the longest siege in modern warfare, during which well over half a million Leningraders died of hunger. Few cities can conjure up quite such a roller-coaster of a history in only 300 years of existence.

Hardly surprising, then, that for the Russians the city has a rather ambivalent reputation. It was Pushkin who first identified St Petersburg with the autocracy which had created it, in his magnificent poem *The Bronze Horseman*. Throughout the 19th century the city developed a character of its own in literature, a phantasmagorical, malevolent character which had a largely malign effect on the man in the street. Dostoyevsky and Gogol particularly distrusted it, Tolstoy so much so that he wrote about it as little as possible.

When national politics left the city after the revolution, St Petersburg reinvented itself, with some justification, as the cultural capital of the country. It was here, in the 20th century, that some of Russia's greatest artists lived and worked—Anna Akhmatova, Dmitri Shostakovich, Kazimir Malevich and Joseph Brodsky to name but a few. To this day the city's museums, theatres and concert halls rival and often outperform those of the capital, though no Muscovite would ever admit it.

After the initial euphoria over the death of communism in the early 1990s, which culminated in the 1991 decision to readopt the city's original name, St Petersburg has found itself on the sidelines. All roads, it seems, lead to Moscow, with ninety per cent of financial activity taking place in the capital. Petersburgers were particularly appalled in 1999 when national celebrations to mark the 200th birthday of Pushkin, a quintessential Petersburg figure, took place in Moscow: even their culture is being traduced by the all-encompassing tentacles of the capital.

A city in crisis it might be, but St Petersburg is still a magnificent place for visitors. The historic centre is compact enough for the energetic to walk everywhere and there is beauty on all sides. Except in August, the city's theatres and concert halls entertain you by night, while the White Nights festival around the summer solstice at the end of June fills the city with music. Even in St Petersburg, however, where there is less of the conspicuous consumption that characterizes Moscow, you will doubtless find yourself wondering how you can be sipping champagne and eating *blini* with caviar while the old *babushki* outside the metro stations are begging for survival. Sad though it is to witness, old Russia was ever thus.

Travel

From the UK and Ireland *By Air*

Between them, **British Airways** and the Russian airline **Aeroflot** have at least nine flights a week from London to St Petersburg, mostly from Gatwick. Regular Apex return fares for the 3¾-hour flight are currently around £310. It is always worth booking through one of the specialist travel agents listed on pp.9–10. Indirect flights are often cheaper, particularly with **SAS** (Scandinavian Airlines) or **Lufthansa**, both of which fly several times a week from London to St Petersburg. **KLM** via Amsterdam and **Finnair** via Helsinki are also worth checking out.

Regent Holidays (*see* below, p.9) specialize in arranging cheap fares from regional airports, often flying via Amsterdam on the Dutch airline KLM.

Aeroflot flies direct to St Petersburg from Dublin twice a week, and once a week from Shannon Airport, which has serviced Aeroflot's European fleet for many years. Flights to Moscow are much more frequent from both airports, with connections on to St Petersburg. However it may well be cheaper to take a regular Dublin or Belfast flight to Heathrow and connect with another carrier to Russia. Flights from Dublin are operated by **British Midland**, **Aer Lingus** and **Ryanair**, while **British Airways** and **British Midland** fly to London from Belfast.

In the UK

British Airways	✆ (0345) 222111
Aeroflot	✆ (020) 7355 2233
SAS	✆ (0845) 6072772
Lufthansa	✆ (020) 8750 3500
KLM	✆ (0990) 750900
Finnair	✆ (020) 7409 7334

In Ireland

Aeroflot (Dublin)	✆ (01) 844 6166
(Shannon Airport)	✆ (061) 472299
British Midland (Dublin)	✆ (01) 283 8833
(Belfast)	✆ (0345) 554554
Aer Lingus	✆ (01) 844 4777
Ryanair	✆ (01) 677 4422
British Airways	✆ (0345) 222111

From North America

Aeroflot flies direct to St Petersburg from New York three times a week, and daily to Moscow. They also fly to Moscow and thence to St Petersburg from a number of other cities across the states. Fares to Moscow start at around $700. **Delta Airlines** also flies to St Petersburg from New York, via Zürich, four times a week. Prices start as low as $543 return. Specialist travel agents (*see* below) will be able to advise you of the best deals on European airlines, such as **British Airways** via London, **Finnair** via Helsinki and **KLM** via Amsterdam.

Aeroflot		**Delta Airlines** ✆ (800) 241 4141
USA	✆ (800) 340 6400	
Canada	✆ (514) 288 2125	

Airlines in St Petersburg

To reconfirm your return flight, or for other enquiries, use the phone numbers below. Remember that your hotel will happily do this for you.

Aeroflot (international)	✆ 315 0072	**Lufthansa**	✆ 314 4979
(domestic and CIS)	✆ 311 8093	**KLM**	✆ 325 8989
British Airways	✆ 325 2565	**Finnair**	✆ 315 9736
SAS	✆ 325 3255		

Airport–City

Pulkovo-2, St Petersburg's international airport, is not well served by public transport. Either ask your travel agent in the UK to arrange transport to your accommodation, or be prepared to haggle with taxi drivers. Aim to pay $25 to get into St Petersburg. If you speak Russian, or just feel adventurous and want to get out into the real world, bus no.13 will take you to Ⓜ Moskovskaya.

By Sea

Arriving in St Petersburg by boat is a romantic notion, but sadly ferries no longer ply the route. If you are determined to approach the city by water, call Norvista, 277 Regent St, London W1R 8PD, ✆ (020) 7409 7334, to see if the situation has changed. You can also travel by river (slowly) from Finland to Viborg, and then by train to St Petersburg; call the Finnish Tourist Board on ✆ (020) 7839 4048 for information.

By Rail

From the UK

You can get to St Petersburg by train from London in 53 hours, via Brussels, Cologne and Orscha in Belarus. It is more expensive than the cheapest flights, and currently costs around £345 return, including the price of a couchette. For details of the route and up-to-date ticket prices, call Deutsche Bahn, 18 Conduit St, London W1R 9TD on ✆ (020) 7317 0919. European Rail Travel may be able to find you a cheaper alternative.

Students should call their nearest branch of either STA or Campus Travel for special student offers. **InterRail** passes, which allow those under 26 (or more expensively those over 26) a month's unlimited travel on Europe's train network, are not valid for the CIS or the Baltic States. They currently cost £259 if you are under 26, £349 if you are not. Call Rail Europe on 0990 848848. If Russia is the final destination in a long journey it can be worth buying one and paying the fare from the last major station before the border.

When travelling by train it is vital to check which visas you require, even if you will only be in transit through a country. Phone the embassy for the current situation.

Belarus

6 Kensington Court, London W8 5DL,
✆ (020) 7937 3288
1619 New Hampshire Ave, NW, Washington
DC 20008, ✆ (202) 986 1604

Estonia

16 Hyde Pk Gate, London SW7 5DG,
✆ (020) 7589 3428
2131 Massachusetts Ave, NW, Washington
DC 20008, ✆ (202) 588 0101

Latvia

45 Nottingham Pl, London W1M 3FE,
✆ (020) 7312 0040
4325 17th St, NW, Washington DC 20011,
✆ (202) 726 8213

Lithuania

84 Gloucester Pl, London W1H 3HN,
✆ (020) 7486 6401
2622 16th St, NW, Washington, DC 20009,
✆ (202) 234 5860

Poland

47 Portland Pl, London W1N 4JH, ✆ (020)
7323 4018; Ireland 5 Ailesbury Rd, Dublin 4
✆ (01) 283 0855
2640 16th St, NW, Washington, DC 20009,
✆ (202) 234 3800

Ukraine

78 Kensington Park Rd, London W11 2PL,
✆ (020) 7727 6312
3350 M St, NW, Washington, DC 20007,
✆ (202) 333 0606

From Finland

Trains ply the 6-hour route between Helsinki and St Petersburg twice daily. If you haven't got a Russian visa, head for the Russian Embassy, Vuorimiehenkatu 6, 00140 Helsinki, ✆ 90 66 14 49.

From China

The true Trans-Siberian Railway runs to and from Vladivostok on Russia's far eastern seaboard, but two ersatz routes run to and from Beijing—one via the Republic of Mongolia, the other via Manchuria in Northern China. Trains take 7–8 days depending on the route. To find out more about the trip, phone Intourist or one of the other specialist travel agents listed below (*see* pp.9–10).

By Road

It is now the foolhardy rather than the adventurous who drive to Russia in their own cars. Highway robbery, both by the traffic police (the GAI) and by brigands making a living out of it, leaves many people with few possessions by the time they arrive in St Petersburg. A specialist travel agent may be able to advise you.

From Finland

The road from Helsinki to St Petersburg is said to be alive with highwaymen, but you will be safe on a bus. Both Finnord and Saimaan Liikenne Oy run daily express buses on the 8-hour trip between the two cities. Both operate from the main bus station in Helsinki, ✆ 9 6136 8433 and from Italianskaya Ul. 37, St Petersburg, ✆ 314 8951.

Passports and Visas

Ever since the collapse of the Soviet Union, travel agents have been hoping that Russia would stop requiring all foreign visitors to obtain a visa in advance. So far, their hopes have proved fruitless. If you are going to be in St Petersburg for a while and might want to pop out to Helsinki or one of the Baltic states, bear in mind that you will need a double- or multiple-entry visa. Russian visas come in three varieties: tourist visas, business visas and individual visas. You will get a **tourist visa** if you are going to Russia on a package tour or to stay in a hotel for less than a month. It is issued against your hotel bookings, and lasts as long as they do, so it is of little interest to free spirits. Most independent travellers now travel to Russia on a so-called **business visa**, which is valid for up to two months. To obtain one you need a stamped letter of invitation from a registered Russian business organization, a service which most of the travel agents listed below can offer. This allows you to rent a flat, stay with friends or travel around without having to pre-book your accommodation. **Individual visas** are granted to applicants who can show a letter of invitation from an individual Russian. Getting the letter correctly stamped in Russia can take time, so even if you are going to stay with a Russian friend, save them the hassle by paying the £30–50 or so extra charged by travel agents for providing you with an invitation from a business.

Obtaining a visa yourself entails queueing at your local embassy and is an inordinate waste of time. Any of the specialist Russian travel agents mentioned on pp.9–10 will obtain the visa for you, for a small extra charge. You will need a photocopy of the relevant pages of your full passport, which must be valid for at least 6 months, three passport photographs and the right visa application form. Normal processing time for the visa, which costs £10, can be over two weeks, but if you need it more quickly it can be done, at a price. The visa itself is a separate piece of paper, unattached to your passport, so take care not to mislay it.

Russian Embassies and Consulates Abroad

Canada: 52 Range Rd, Ottawa, Ontario K1N 8G5, ✆ (613) 236 7220

Finland: Vuorimiehenkatu 6, 00140 Helsinki, ✆ (90) 66 14 49

Ireland: 186 Orwell Rd, Rathgar, Dublin 6, ✆ (01) 711633 or 977492

United Kingdom: 5 Kensington Palace Gardens, London W8, ✆ (020) 7229 8027

USA: 1825 Phelps Place NW, Washington, DC 20008, ✆ (202) 332 1483

Registration with OVIR

All foreigners in Russia are required to register with the Visa and Registration Department (OVIR) within three days of arrival. Hotels do this automatically for their guests, but other visitors should trudge to the local office, with the person or a representative of the business that invited you, and wait to be disgorged from the bureaucratic nightmare several hours later. Many simply never register, and threatened fines at the airport on departure don't always materialize. If you lose your visa or wish to extend or alter it to a multiple-entry visa, you will need to apply to OVIR. Call first to check on opening hours for foreigners:

St Petersburg, Ul. Saltikova-Shchedrina 4, © 278 3486.

Customs

You will have to fill out a customs form on entry into Russia, giving details of all the money you are bringing into the country, both in travellers' cheques and cash, and any valuables such as jewellery, lap-top computers, video cameras, etc. There is no restriction on the amount of money you can bring with you. Keep the stamped form throughout your trip. Theoretically you need it to change money, though it is rarely looked at. When you leave the country, customs officials may check it against the new form you fill out, to make sure you have not left—i.e. sold—anything, and that you are not leaving with more money than you brought in.

Leaving Russia, your baggage will be X-rayed. Photographers using slide or other sensitive film should take it out and have it examined by hand. Any works of art prior to 1945 will be confiscated. This includes all icons except the obviously modern. Most icons sold to tourists as old are really fakes, but the average customs officer is no more of an expert than you are. You also need the permission of the Ministry of Culture, Nab. Kanala Griboyedova, to export pre-1960 paintings, and if you have spent a lot of money you should make sure that the artist, shop or gallery obtains this for you. Cheaper canvases seem to make it through, though you can never be sure what mood your officer will be in.

Package Tours or Individual Travel?

During the Soviet era, almost the only way to visit was on a package tour with the Soviet travel agency **Intourist**. Diatribes against the luxurious lifestyles of Russia's 19th-century aristocrats were interspersed with eulogies on Soviet achievement. Today, most people still visit Russia on package tours, but these are now organized by a variety of travel agents. In the off-season (November–March) a weekend break or week-long trip can be enticingly cheap. Even if you intend to be independent when you arrive, you may find it cheaper to book a package tour and abandon the group in Russia. A number of independent companies whose approaches tend to be more idiosyncratic also conduct tours to St Petersburg. The best are listed below.

This book was written specifically for those who want to explore St Petersburg independently. If you don't speak Russian, it won't always be easy making your own way around on your own. The Cyrillic alphabet is less daunting than it at first appears, however, and with the aid of a bilingual metro map (*see* p.314) you should be able to recognize the names of the stops. As well as hotels, specialist travel agents will also be able to arrange home-stays with Russian families and accommodation in rented flats. A handful of the most experienced are listed below.

Specialist Travel Agents and Tour Operators

In the UK

Findhorn Ecotravels, The Park, Forres, Morayshire IV36 0TZ, ✆/✉ (01309) 690995. For a more personal service, call Liza Hollingshead, something of a fairy godmother to Russian independent travel. She can issue an invitation, fix up accommodation in someone's home or even rent you a flat in the centre of St Petersburg. She also has experience with youth exchanges. Ecotravels supports a marvellous community for orphaned children in Russia, so using Liza indirectly benefits some of Russia's most neglected citizens. She also sends volunteers to help in the community.

Intourist, 219 Marsh Wall, London E14 9FJ, ✆ (020) 7538 8600. The old Soviet monolith has cranked itself into commercial gear and, with all its contacts and experience, offers competitive package deals, from long weekends to trips on the Trans-Siberian Railway. Don't expect anything radical.

Noble Caledonia Ltd., 11 Charles St, London W1X 7HB, ✆ (020) 7491 4752, **Voyages Jules Verne**, 21 Dorset Square, London NW1 6QG, ✆ (020) 7616 1000, and **Swan Hellenic**, 77 New Oxford St, London WC1A 1PP, ✆ (020) 7800 2200, are all upmarket tour operators, offering cruises between Moscow and St Petersburg on the inland waterways, passing through the medieval heartland of Russia with its kremlins and churches.

Progressive Tours, 12 Porchester Place, London W2 2BS, ✆ (020) 7262 1676, have long specialized in travels to what used to be the Communist bloc.

Regent Holidays, 15 John St, Bristol BS1 2HR, ✆ (0117) 921 1711, ✉ 925 4866, *regent@regent-holidays.co.uk, www.regent-holidays.co.uk.* A highly informative and helpful agency, with 25 years' experience throughout the length and breadth of Russia. Particularly useful for those flying from provincial airports or wanting to visit the Baltic republics as well as St Petersburg.

Russia Experience, Research House, Fraser Road, Perivale, Middx UB6 7AQ, ✆ (020) 8566 8846, *www.trans-siberian.co. uk,* specializes in all things Siberian and beyond. Their trips on the Trans-Siberian offer excursions to Buddhist monasteries in Buryatia and trekking round Lake Baikal. Neil McGowan, who runs the outfit, is a real expert.

Russlang, 5–6 Fenwick Terrace, Neville's Cross, Durham City, ✆ 0191 386 9578. Irene Slatter and her St Petersburg partner run a business teaching Russian to foreigners in St Petersburg and arranging their accommodation with Russian families. They run courses at Easter and throughout the summer.

Scott's Tours, 159 Whitfield St, London W1P 5RY, ✆ (020) 7383 5353, specialize in travel to Russia and the other countries of the former Soviet Union.

Steppes East Ltd., Castle Eaton, Swindon, Wilts SN6 6JU, ✆ (01285) 810 267, ✉ (01285) 810 693, *www.steppeseast. co.uk.* Operating in Russia since *perestroika*, this fantastically experienced crew offers group and individual travel guides, unusual luxuries and access to hidden gems.

In the USA

GlobalQuest, 170 Old Country Road, Mineola, NY 11501, ✆ (516) 747 8880, ✉ (516) 747 8367, *global@globalquest-travel.com*, organize challenging river journeys all over Russia, including the trip between St Petersburg and Moscow.

Intur Holding USA Inc., 610 5th Ave, Suite 603, New York NY 10020, ✆ (212) 757 3884, books travel arrangements for independent travellers.

Pioneer East-West Initiative, 88 Brooks Ave., Arlington, MA 02174, ✆ (781) 648 2020, has been arranging holidays in the ex-Communist bloc for many years.

Russian Travel Service, P.O. Box 311, Fitzwilliam, NH 03447, ✆/✉ (603) 585 6534, specializes in putting you up with a Russian family for the duration of your stay. Their own agent in St Petersburg can arrange, cars, sightseeing, theatre trips etc. when you arrive.

In Russia

To find the cheapest accommodation, try agencies in St Petersburg. Those below will issue you with an invitation for your visa application and arrange accommodation and sightseeing programmes.

Host Families Association, Tavricheskaya Ul. 5–25, 193015 St Petersburg, ✆/✉ 275 1992, *hofa@usa.net*, organizes accommodation in Russian homes.

St Petersburg International Hostel, 3-aya Sovetskaya Ul. 28, 193036 St Petersburg, ✆ 329 8018, ✆ 329 8019.

Getting Around

The jewel in St Petersburg's transport crown is the metro, which continues to amaze visitors with its efficiency. As the city gets poorer, the number of buses, trams and trolleybuses declines, and those that remain are badly overcrowded. Trying to get on to a bus in the rush hour is worse than a rugby scrum, without a touch of sportsmanship in sight. Foreigners have been reduced to tears by the painful shoving and rudeness. It is, at least, dirt-cheap. If you are staying long, consider the advantages of monthly travel passes, which go on sale in the last week of the month in the metro stations and nearby underpasses. They are still very cheap, and mean you don't need to struggle to buy a ticket or token for each journey. A pass for the metro only is called a Проездной на метро (*proyezdnoi na metro*). A pass for all city transport, a единие (*yediniy*), costs more than twice as much.

By Metro (МЕТРО)

See map opposite inside back cover.

While things on the ground lurch from one pothole to another, the metro system glides swiftly underground. Russians often ponder the anomaly: if they can be so effective underground and in space, why is their life on earth such a shambles? Not only is the metro fast and cheap, it is also an architectural and decorative wonder in its own right. One of Stalin's pet projects, the construction destroyed dozens of historic overground buildings, including churches, and replaced them with underground 'People's Palaces'. Marble halls, bronze torchères, mosaics, chandeliers and statues give an impression of an immensely privileged society, quite out of keeping with the insistent crowds of preoccupied and over-burdened citizens that mill beneath them. But the metro stations are more than just a transport system. In winter, when it is below freezing outside, their many benches serve as meeting points for Russians from all over the city. If you have a rendezvous in the metro and there is more than one line at the station, make sure you know at which platform you are supposed to be meeting.

The metro runs from 5.30am to 1am and can be suffocatingly busy in the rush hour, when trains come every 1–2 minutes. You will recognize the stations by the big **M** lit up in red outside. Before using the metro for the first time, study the dual language metro map on the last page of this book. It is also a good idea to write down your route, in Roman and Cyrillic script, so you know exactly which stations you need to look for as you go. Where two lines meet the station tends to have two names, except at Ⓜ Tekhnologichesky Institut where there are just two platforms for the two lines: one for all northbound, the other for all southbound trains. In this book, you are often told to leave the metro via a particular station and a particular exit. This is because the entrances are often far apart above ground, and you could easily miss the start of a walk.

If you do not have a pass, to enter the system you must buy a token (*zheton*, жэтон) or a magnetic ticket from the ticket desk (касса) inside. The price for one journey will be shown on the window. Insert it in the appropriate turnstile, and walk through the gap to the left when the light goes green. Beware that, although there appears to be no barrier, one will snap down painfully on your knees if you try to walk through without paying. If you have a pass, go and show it to the inspector at the end of the row of turnstiles. There are no maps on the platforms, so if you haven't got a map on you, you should check one before getting on the escalator or once you are in the train.

Station names and signposts are only in Cyrillic, so this is where your facility with the alphabet will be tested. As you step off the long, steep escalator, signs list the stations served by each platform. The caretaker at the bottom will help if you can't find your station. Once in the train there are few signs to tell you which station you are pulling into, so be careful to count the stops, or listen to the announcements as you arrive. As the train is about to leave, you will be politely informed to watch out, the doors are closing, and then told the name of the next station. The announcement goes like this: '*Ostorozhno, dveri zakrivayutsya! Sleduyushchaya stantsiya...*'. When you need to change lines, look for signs on the platform, often accompanied by a blue stick man running up stairs, saying переход на станцию...—*perekhod na stantsiyu...* (change to station...) or переход на...линию—*perekhod na... liniyu* (change to line...) followed by a list of stations. Scour the black Cyrillic for something that looks like yours. If you have arrived at your destination, and are asked to leave by the twin station, you will have to use a *perekhod* again. Otherwise look for the sign saying Выход в город (*vwykhod v gorod*) which means 'exit to the city'. If there is more than one, they will give you a list of the streets served by each exit.

By Bus, Trolleybus and Tram

Stops for buses and trolleybuses are signalled by an А (for *avtobus*) and a Т (for *trolleybus*) respectively, with the numbers of the routes marked beneath. Signs indicating tram stops hang from wires over the tramlines in the middle of the road.

If you haven't got a **ticket**, get on at the front as you need to buy one from the driver. Look for a red sign near the door or behind the driver: it will show the current cost of a single ride. The larger number below is the size of fine you will be asked to pay if you don't have a stamped ticket when an inspector comes round. Hand a note well over ten times the price of a ride to the driver (for some reason ten tickets cost more than ten times the cost of a ride!), or get your fellow passengers to pass it all the way down if the vehicle is crowded. Amazingly, within a stop or two a strip of ten flimsy tickets will arrive back in your hand with your change. Tear off one ticket and stamp it in one of the simple machines distributed on the wall throughout the bus, or again pass it to someone nearer who will do it for you. If you have a large piece of baggage you are expected to stamp a ticket for it too.

Getting out of a crowded vehicle has its own etiquette. Those behind you who want to leave will politely ask you if you are getting off—'*Vwy vwykhoditye?*'— and if they suspect you are not they will begin to push past. Many is the time you get swept off, only to have to fight to get back on the bus again.

By Train

Trains serving nearby destinations, such as those in the **Day Trips** chapter, are known as *elektrichkas*. They always leave from the part of the station known as the suburban hall (Прыгородный зал—*prigorodny zal*), which has its own busy ticket office. Queue up, state your destination and ask for a return ticket by adding '*tudá i abrátna*'. Write down the station's name and the words for return (*see* p.299) if you don't feel confident about speaking. Fares are still extremely low.

Getting on to the right train requires further ingenuity. You will find a chronological list of departures, identified by the station at which they terminate and, somewhere nearby, a schematic map of all destinations. Get on any train that ends further down the line from your station, first checking that it will stop for you: there should be a column listing which stations the train stops at. Otherwise, before getting on board ask the driver or a number of your fellow passengers. They will happily shoo you off if you are about to make a mistake.

By Road

taxis

Official St Petersburg taxis are normally beige or yellow with a chequered pattern sprayed on their side. When you put your hand out to stop one, you may find ordinary citizens pulling over trying to make a bit of extra cash on the side. If the driver is alone, these moonlighters, known as *chastniki*, are usually quite safe, though you should use your common sense and get out the moment you feel uneasy. Tell them or show them where you are going, and settle a price before you get in. For a journey in the centre of town, you will be doing well to pay the rouble equivalent of under US$5.

If you are staying in an hotel, they will be able to organize a car for you. To order a cab to your door if you are living in a flat, call ✆ 312 0022/3297 well in advance.

car hire

Given the availability of taxis it is unnecessary, not to say reckless, to drive in the city, but if you are planning a complicated day trip you may decide to do so. Most of the car-hire firms listed below offer cars with or without drivers. Think carefully about whether a driver wouldn't make the trip more relaxing. To drive yourself, you must be over 21 and will need an international driving licence. You should keep your passport and visa with you at all times (and a wad of roubles for the traffic police, GAI). The rental firm will provide you with insurance. They will also brief you on the Russian highway code. What they probably won't tell you is that the other road users will be more unpredictable than any you may have encountered anywhere else. Never leave anything inside your car—not even a packet of cigarettes—when you park, and remove the radio cassette and windscreen wipers, or you may have to buy new ones. Be careful.

Although they tend to be more expensive, it is well worth hiring a well-serviced car from a reputable company, such as those recommended by the major hotels. There is almost nothing on offer for less than US$60 a day. The best companies in St Petersburg are **Auto-Mobile**, Frunzenskaya Ul. 15, ✆ 293 3727, if you want to drive yourself, or **Interavto-Hertz**, bookable through the Grand Hotel Europe or the Moskva Hotel or on ✆ 277 4032.

It is useful to remember that a number of petrol stations sell fuel by credit card. Try Moskovsky Prospekt 100.

When the Neva is not frozen, St Petersburg's bridges all open for 2–3 hours in the middle of the night, allowing boats to enter and leave the system of rivers and canals which runs to Moscow and beyond. To Petersburgers, evenings finish either before the bridges go up or after they have closed again—normally the latter. Details of opening times of bridges are listed on p.275.

Travelling to Moscow

A busy schedule of Aeroflot and other flights connects Moscow's Domodedovo airport and Pulkovo-1 in St Petersburg (*see* p.5 for airline telephone numbers), and Aeroflot's internal safety reputation is improving. Overnight trains between the two cities are much more popular, however. The romance of speeding through the birch-forested countryside, with snow up to the window level or a barely darkening summer's sky, is accompanied by hot tea provided by the attendant, the *provodnik*. Sharing food is an important part of Russian travel, not to mention sharing vodka.

To book tickets for the train, ask the service desk in your hotel, or set off early in the morning to beat the crowds and do it yourself.The central ticket office is at Nab. Kanala Griboyedova, across the canal from the Kazan Cathedral (Ⓜ Nevsky Prospekt). Turn right inside, and right again where it says Интурист. Up the stairs, you can buy tickets at booths no.103 and no.104. At Moskovsky Vokzal (from where the trains depart) there is a tourist desk, off the main hall, near the sculpture of Peter the Great (*open 8am–8pm*). You choose between two-berth first class compartments, known either as S.V. (pronounced *S Vay*) or *luxe* (as the French would pronounce it), or four-berth second class, known as *koopeyny*. *Luxe* is over four times the price of a *koopeyny*. In both, you will have to pay extra for bedding.

Several trains (the best ones are nos.1–6) leave both cities between 11pm and 1am, all arriving between 7am and 9am. To catch them, head for Moskovsky Vokzal at Ⓜ Ploshchad Vosstaniya. There is also a new service known as the Commercial Train (nos.35/36). It costs more than twice as much as the others, but tickets are more readily available and can be bought from the stations themselves.

Recently, there has been a spate of apocryphal stories about robberies on the overnight trains. You could bring a long chain and padlock to add security to the door locks, though I have never had any problems. Sleep with your money and passport under your pillow, and keep your luggage under the bottom beds. A far greater threat to lone women is the unwanted attention of drunk Russian men, and many foreign residents will not make the journey unchaperoned. Two women together should think seriously about travelling in first class, since they will then have the compartment to themselves. For women alone, a four-berth compartment is probably safer than a *luxe* two-berther.

Practical A–Z

Addresses

Finding Russians who have given you their address can be quite an ordeal. A typical set of instructions might read: Moskovsky Prospekt 7, korp. or stroeniye 2, kv.106. Code 274. Decoded, this means you are looking for house (*dom*) No.7 on Moskovsky Prospekt, which somewhere has a second (and quite possibly a third and fourth) corpus or building (*korpus* or *stroeniye*). The flat (*kvartira*) number is 106, and to get in through the main door to the block you need to press buttons 274 in succession on the entry keypad. Happy hunting!

Children

If you can avoid it, don't bring children on holiday here unless they are small enough to carry for long periods or big enough to enjoy city sightseeing. Baby-sitters can be arranged through your hotel. Here is a selection of things children might enjoy.

The **beach** at the Peter and Paul Fortress is good for a sandcastle and a quick paddle. Don't allow your child to swim however, as the river is very polluted. **Boat trips** along the canals of St Petersburg (*see* p.195) are an enjoyable way to pass a summer's afternoon without tiring tiny legs. Otherwise try **parks**: Tauride Children's Park (Tavrichesky Sad) is the official children's park, though there is nothing much there to show for it. They descend in droves with sledges and skis in winter; rumour has it there are skates for rent (*see* p.149). Letny Sad (*adm*), with its musicians and neoclassical sculptures beneath the leafy canopy, can be fun at weekends in summer (*see* pp.84–5). Tsarskoye Selo has an extensive park where you can play hide and seek, go boating and picnic in summer, or hire skis and sledges in winter (*see* p.231). Yelagin Island is nearer to hand and also offers opportunities to skate and boat on its ponds (*see* p.198). In the Yelagin Palace there are fairytale rooms upstairs, where children are entertained, in Russian only, by storytellers. It is also worth checking at the Anichkov Palace on Nevsky Prospekt to see what children's activities they have going.

Of the city's **museums**, the ones most likely to please are the Naval Museum, Old Stock Exchange, Pushkinskaya Ploshchad 4, Vasilievsky Ostrov, which will be popular with model makers, one entire room being stuffed with model wooden boats and their elaborate rigging (*see* p.76); or the Zoological Museum, Universitetskaya Naberezhnaya 1, Vasilievsky Ostrov, © 218 0112, which has a collection of stuffed animals, an exhibition on the discovery of woolly mammoths in the Siberian permafrost, and, a source of great pride, a new live insect zoo (*see* p.168). The Zoo itself, Park Lenina, Petrograd Side (Ⓜ Gorkovskaya), is not for the soft-hearted, but if you do go, take them to eat at Zebra (*see* p.265) afterwards.

For **shopping**, Dom Leningradskoy Torgovli (DLT), Ul. Bolshaya Konyushennaya 21/3, ℘ 312 2627, usually has a good selection of children's clothes and toys. Look out particularly for the old-fashioned mechanical toys which delight those jaded plastic palates. Detsky Mir, Bolshoy Prospekt 25, Petrograd Side, ℘ 233 5636, also has a wide selection of Russian and foreign-made toys and clothes.

Children enjoy the magic of **circuses** and the **ballet** from a very young age (*see* **Entertainment and Nightlife**, pp.276–7). Other venues of particular interest include: Mussorgsky Theatre of Opera and Ballet, Pl. Iskusstv 1, ℘ 219 1978 (Ⓜ Nevsky Prospekt), where young members of the Vaganova Ballet School often perform to a largely juvenile audience; Puppet Theatre for Children, Moskovsky Prospekt 121, ℘ 298 0031 (Ⓜ Moskovskiye Vorota); Zazerkale Children's Theatre, Rubinstein Ul. 13, ℘ 112 5135 (Ⓜ Dostoyevskaya), opera and ballet for kids; Bolshoi Puppet Theatre, Ul. Nekrasov 10, ℘ 273 6672; but check whether the performance is suitable for the children's age group. Rodina Cinema, Ul. Karavannaya 12, ℘ 311 6131, shows children's films and clown and mime performances.

Climate and When to Go

St Petersburg suffers cold, snowy winters from November to March. Spring is short and miraculous. Within days the bare skeletons of the trees are covered with long-awaited greenery and the parks are full of picnicking groups. Only the unwise venture out in summer without a telescopic umbrella in their bag, for bright sunshine can suddenly be interrupted by half an hour of heavy rain. The chill of autumn makes itself felt from late August, and the golden trees are at their best in late September. While your mobility will be restricted in winter by the temperature, it is an exhilarating, dry cold, providing you are well clothed. Bright blue skies and sparkling snow make it a romantic time to see the city. The only times of year when the weather can be miserable are November and December, and late March to early April, when a mixture of snow and thaw turns the pavements either into skating rinks or a succession of elephantine puddles.

Bear in mind that, because of the city's northerly latitude, the number of daylight hours is limited between November and January. Conversely, around the summer solstice in mid-June the 'White Nights' take place. Even at 3am it isn't truly dark, and for a number of weeks the city never sleeps. Even pensioners take a midnight stroll down to the Neva, while the city's younger generations sing, drink and dance for days and nights on end.

Crime and the Police

A near-hysterical campaign by the western press has tried its best to kill Russian tourism with stories of theft, mugging and general lawlessness in both Moscow and

St Petersburg. The truth is that Russians used to be too frightened to prey on tourists but now, as in any other democracy, they aren't. Things are little worse than in most capital cities in Europe, and certainly not as dangerous as in Rome or Seville. Unless you are intent on business, the closest you will come to the Russian mafia, if you are unlucky, is to sit near a table of them at a restaurant. After ten months living in the city, I haven't a single personal scare story to offer. A few particular observations and guidelines will help you to have an equally hassle-free stay.

As an obvious foreigner, you will be assumed to have money about your person. Dress inconspicuously and don't wear flashing jewellery or chunky, expensive watches. Leave them and other unnecessary valuables, like your passport and ticket, in the hotel safe. Always be aware of where your valuables are (if possible in a zip-up pocket). On Nevsky Prospekt swarms of gypsy children use all manner of diversions to distract you while they pick your pockets and bag. It is easy to prevent them by choosing a safe place to carry money, travellers' cheques and credit cards, and keeping a firm hand on your camera and the opening of your bag.

If you are flagging down a taxi or private car for a lift, never get into one that already has anyone apart from the driver in it. If you are staying with friends, never give your full address or your telephone number to strangers. A taxi driver does not need to know the flat number, and it is easy to find out the address of a telephone number through directory enquiries.

Except during the 'White Nights', don't walk around late at night on your own. It is safe (women alone *see* pp.29–30) to use the metro to get back to your bed at night, depending on how far you have to walk at the other end. If you are unlucky enough to get mugged, don't resist. The gun is probably real, as they are very easy to get hold of. You are asking for trouble by straying into areas of organized criminal activity such as prostitution and drugs. While prostitutes picked up in your hotel may be safe, there are so many stories of punters being drugged and robbed that you should be aware of the risk. Russia is now thought to be the major route to Europe for opiates from the Golden Triangle in Southeast Asia, and the central Asian republics keep the ex-Soviet Union self-sufficient in marijuana. It isn't easy to find out where to get drugs, and if you do you'll find yourself in a violent subculture. Don't do it.

The police (*militsia*) wear a grey uniform with red epaulettes and cap band. Their vehicles are either strident navy blue and white, or a rather insipid yellow and light blue. You are supposed to carry your passport with you at all times in case they stop you, but in practice if you play the innocent they will take it no further.

If you are robbed you will need a statement from the police to claim on your insurance. There is now a 24-hour foreigners-only hotline, © 164 9787, to report crime. If you need to go in person, the office is on the fourth floor of Ligovsky Pr 145.

Electricity

St Petersburg is powered by 220v AC, accessed by round two-pin plugs. Be sure to bring whatever adaptors and transformers you will need, as they may be hard to track down in Russia.

Embassies and Consulates

Foreign embassies are based in Moscow, but many countries (not all) have set up consulates in St Petersburg. If you don't seem to be represented yet, call your embassy in Moscow (code 8–095).

Consulates

United Kingdom, Ploshchad Proletarskoy Diktatury 5, ✆ 325 6036.

Canada, Malodetskoselsky Pr 32, ✆ 325 8448.

United States, Ul. Furshtadtskaya 15, ✆ 274 8689/8568.

Embassies

Australia, Kropotkinsky Per 13, Moscow, ✆ 965 6070.

Ireland, Grokholsky Per 5, Moscow, ✆ 288 4101.

Gay Scene

A fragile sense of identity among Russia's male gay community was fostered by the campaign to repeal Article 121 of the penal code in the early 1990s. Under the code homosexuality, even between consenting adults, was punishable by up to five years in prison. In 1993 the campaign succeeded, and since then homosexuals have been quietly celebrating, though prejudice from their heterosexual compatriots is near universal and often violent. However, many leading figures in the artistic world in St Petersburg are coming out, and at the city's more arty clubs you will find some wonderfully camp characters, as well as transvestites. St Petersburg's premier cruising grounds are the Dumskaya Ul. arcade of Gostiny Dvor and Ploshchad Ostrovskovo. Gay clubs are listed on p.280.

Lesbians are much less conspicuous. The imported word *lesbianka* is used to describe them, and Russians tend to react as if the concept itself is some alien import. The Russian feminist movement has never had a radical, lesbian-feminist wing, and even leading feminists will tell you that lesbianism does not exist. The scene in the city's gay clubs gives the lie to this, however.

Kriliya, St Petersburg's Gay and Lesbian Association, can be reached on ✆ 312 3180 for advice and accommodation suggestions.

Fire	*pozhar*	✆ 01
Police	*militsia*	✆ 02
Ambulance	*skoraya pomoshch*	✆ 03

You are unlikely to contract anything more than a bout of mild diarrhoea during your stay in St Petersburg, but it is vital that you bear a few basic rules in mind. Foreigners are currently advised to be vaccinated against diphtheria, tetanus and hepatitis A and B. There have also been cases of cholera. Don't forget to take out comprehensive travel insurance.

Do not drink tap water in St Petersburg. Until recently, it was thought that water boiled for 10 minutes and left to stand for a day was safe, but now even that causes upset stomachs. The water supply, worsened by the combined flood control dam/road which has been half built across the Gulf of Finland, is alive with the virulent bacteria *giardia*. This will cause severe diarrhoea, the only cure for which is a course of specific antibiotics. Consult a doctor if you think you may be infected.

Though they would probably be available, bring any prescription or other medicines that you need with you. Previously unavailable 'luxuries', such as tampons, are now for sale in most hotels, all foreign supermarkets and most Russian pharmacies as well. All of the medical clinics listed below have pharmacies attached, where a wide range of western drugs are available. It is useful to know the generic name for any drugs you use regularly (such as the contraceptive pill), as they go under different brand names in different countries. If you happen to go to a German-backed clinic, they will be able to prescribe an equivalent drug.

Most hotels have a doctor on call at all times. If you are not staying in a hotel, or have any doubts about your treatment, ring one of the highly professional clinics listed below. Most can arrange air evacuation in the event of an emergency, or will book you into the best equipped Russian hospitals, which used to be reserved for higher Party functionaries only. None of this comes cheap.

medical clinics

American Medical Centre, Serpukhovskaya Ul. 10, ✆ 326 1730.

Emergency Medical Consulting, Izmailovsky Pr. 14, ✆ 112 6510/2

Clinic Complex, Moskovsky Prospekt 22, ✆ 316 6272, has been used by St Petersburg's most privileged citizens and, until the invasion of foreign medical centres, by diplomats and tourists as well. Independent of the state system, it is now private and equipped to near western standards, with disposable syringes, modern X-ray machines, etc.

Homeopathic Clinic, Ul. Prazhskaya 12, ✆ 269 5813. Most Russians take a variety of herbal cures and homeopathic medicines as a matter of course.

Partly due to a lack of availability of many drugs commonly available in the West, the Russians may yet have the last laugh when we turn out to have unleashed a Pandora's box of uncontrollable viruses by our overuse of drugs. If you want to give the natural way a try, you can't do better than this, the oldest homeopathic clinic in the country. It claims to be 10 times cheaper than similar treatment in the West.

dental clinics

The **American Medical Centre** and the **Clinic Complex** offer dental treatment. Otherwise try **Dental Palace**, Millionnaya Ul. 10, ✆ 314 1459.

oculists and opticians

Vision Express, Ul. Lomonosova 5, ✆ 310 1595, for glasses and contact lenses.
24-hour Eye Trauma Clinic, Lityeiny Prospekt 25, ✆ 272 0503.

chemists

Damian Pharmacy, Moskovsky Prospekt 22, ✆ 110 1744, is attached to Polyclinic No.2, and fully stocked with western drugs.
Homeopathic Pharmacy, Nevsky Prospekt 50.

The Internet

It is possible to buy an adaptor for your modem to plug into the Russian telephone socket, but you will need to find a specialist electronics shop (try TeleAdapt in London, ✆ (020) 8233 3000). Alternatively, buy an American lead and wire it into a Russian telephone plug (available at electronics shops across the city).

To pick up e-mail, call your regular service provider and ask their advice. If you want to register with a local provider try Nevalink on ✆ 310 5442 or e-mail *info@nevalink.ru*.

If you haven't got your computer with you but want to check on your e-mail or surf the web, head for one of Nevalink's two public access spaces: in the Central Ticket Agency, Nab. Kanala Griboyedova 24, ✆ 168 6734, or in Moskovsky Station, Pl. Vosstaniya 2, ✆ 277 2517.

Because of poor media and communications in general, the Russians have made extensive use of the Internet and have web pages galore. To read them you will need a Russian Language Kit of some kind. If you are a Mac user, bear in mind that Macintosh has made almost no inroads into Russia.

Libraries

If you are looking for material in English on St Petersburg, or general reading material, head for the well-appointed Galitzine Library (Biblioteka Golitsyna) at Nab. Reki Fontanki 46, ✆ 311 1333.

Media

The best place to find newspapers from home is in the city's main hotels. By far the best of the local English language press is the *St Petersburg Times*, a twice weekly venture with good cultural listings in the Friday edition and extensive business coverage in both. Look out also for *Pulse*, a monthly magazine with good reviews of cultural events. By comparison, *Neva News* is little more than a curiosity. All are available free in the major hotels, restaurants and western supermarkets.

television

There are four main TV channels in St Petersburg: the national channel, ORT; TV St Petersburg for more localized news and chat shows plus films; *Rossiya* channel for sport and news as well as dubbed American and Mexican soaps; and lastly the Russian University channel. Most hotels and many bars and cafés subscribe to a cable network, offering CNN, the BBC, or more popularly MTV and Sky.

radio

St Petersburg's radio is almost exclusively Russian-language (except for the BBC World Service on 1260kHz/238m). Try Europa Plus (100.5 FM) or Radio Rox (102 FM) for rock and pop, or Radio Klassica (106 FM).

Money and Banks

local currency

The rouble became Russia's national currency in 1534. Since the time of Peter the Great it has been divided into 100 kopeks. In these days of desperate inflation the rouble is known derisively as 'wooden' money, since it has as good as no metallic or real value. What the Russians now value is *kapusta* (cabbage), the slang for US dollars. For several years, dollars worked as an alternative currency, but since 1 January 1994 all transactions in Russia must, legally, be carried out in roubles.

The highest denomination rouble note currently in circulation is the 500, with 100, 50 and 10 rouble notes below it. 1, 2 and 5 rouble and 50, 10, 5 and 1 kopek coins are also available. Any indication of prices in this book is made in dollars, since the financial crisis of August 1998 sent rouble inflation rocketing once again.

what money to take

The easiest currency to exchange—in banks, at kiosks on the street, in exchange bureaux, with friends—are US dollar bills. Make sure your bills are in pristine condition. There have been a lot of forged dollar bills in circulation, so everyone is very wary, and if they doubt the authenticity of a bill they just won't accept it, even if it is your last. Most major European currencies will also be accepted. Remember always to take your passport, visa and your customs form with you when changing money in any form. Banks are usually open Mon–Fri 9am–6pm, longer in hotels, and your receptionist will always be able to point you in the way of a 24-hour facility. You can use ATM machines, for roubles only, if your card shows a Cirrus or Mastercard symbol.

Always change money at a legitimate exchange bureau, of which there are hundreds in each city. Don't be tempted by anyone loitering nearby offering a better rate. They *will* rip you off, probably in a big way, by sleight of hand.

Hotel exchange bureaux and some banks will change travellers' cheques. You will be safest with American Express since they are the best known. There is also an American Express office where you can buy travellers' cheques in the Grand Hotel Europe, Mikhailovskaya Ul. 1/7, © 329 6060. You can also use major credit cards in smart hotels, restaurants and shops (take your passport), but never rely on it; you should always have enough cash on you to cover your expenditure. Visa and MasterCard are the most widely accepted. To report your card lost call:

Eurocard/Mastercard/Visa: © 312 6012.

Museums and Opening Hours

Museum opening hours are infinitely variable, and are specifically quoted in the text of this guide. The only generalizations are that they are often closed on Mondays (or Tuesdays), and that most stick to the tradition of a *sanitarny dyen* (a 'hygiene' day) once a month, usually in the first or last week of the month.

Shops in Russia tend to stay open until 8 or 9pm, though many close for a lunch hour some time between 1 and 4pm. They are mostly closed on Sundays except for the western-style supermarkets, most of which are open seven days a week. Kiosks are the late-night godsend, selling everything from vodka to toothpaste.

National Holidays and Festivals

With the death of the Soviet Union, which loved to celebrate milestones in the Communist year with national holidays and vast parades, the holiday situation has become rather confused. Die-hard Communists and those yearning for the stability of the old days still turn out on 7 November, the anniversary of the Bolshevik Revolution. New holidays have been added, commemorating the historic events of *perestroika* and the Yeltsin era, and the main religious holidays have been reinstated as national holidays. If you are here for Russian Easter or Christmas, go to one of the all-night services which start at midnight and go on until the small hours. At Easter the miracle of Christ's resurrection is celebrated each year by the lighting of a multitude of candles and the incantation 'Christ is risen!' (*khristos voskres*), to which the reply is 'Truly He is Risen!' (*voistinu voskres*).

The only regular festival that impinges on tourists is the White Nights (*Byeliye Nochi*) when the long hours of daylight bewitch the city into all-night revels. Pop concerts on Palace Square and musical events of all sorts on Yelagin Island punctuate the drinking and dancing which accompany the raising of the bridges across the Neva in the early morning.

New Year's Day	1 Jan	**Victory in Europe (VE) Day**	9 May
Orthodox Christmas	7 Jan	**Russian Independence Day**	12 June
International Women's Day	8 March	**White Nights Festival**	c. 21 June–
Orthodox Easter	March/April		11 July
International Labour Day	1 May	**Revolution Day**	7 November
Spring Day	2 May	**Constitution Day**	12 Dec

Packing

It rarely gets very hot in St Petersburg, so even if you are coming at the height of summer bring a jersey or coat for the evening. A light mackintosh and a telescopic umbrella are also useful to combat the summer showers. In winter, with temperatures dropping as low as –20°C, you need warm clothing, including gloves, a hat, a scarf and thermal underwear. Since Russian interiors, including museums, are very well heated, it is best to dress with plenty of layers so that you can take off as many as you need to make yourself comfortable.

At all times of the year except the summer, the most important item in your Russian wardrobe will be a good pair of boots. Not only should they be warm for the winter, they must also have good grips so that you have a chance of standing upright on the icy pavements. In early spring and late autumn, it is vital that they are waterproof too, since puddles of thawing snow reach gigantic proportions and are often unavoidable. Most boots fail this test on one count or another, but perseverance in finding the right pair will pay rich rewards in warm dry feet.

So as not to waste time, you should bring everything you think you may need, including your own toiletries and photographic supplies, although all can be bought in Russia. A miscellany of things you may find particularly useful include a plug for the basin, which isn't always supplied, some laundry detergent to do your own washing, a torch for badly lit streets and stairwells, toilet paper and insect repellent to fight off vicious mosquitoes, which seem to breed somewhere in the city all through the year, but are particularly virulent in summer and autumn. If you go out in the countryside at this time of year, you will not be able to avoid them.

The Russians are great present-givers, so if you are going to be making friends think about packing some gifts that are redolent of home. Things like tights, which used to make great presents, are now easy to get hold of in Russia, so you will need to be rather more imaginative. Think in terms of tapes (not CDs) of quintessentially English/Scottish/Irish/American music, good picture books showing your native land, curiosities like Edinburgh Rock, or books of native poetry for those who speak English. If you know people well enough, and winter is drawing in, a good supply of multi-vitamins and minerals is always pounced upon.

Photography

Flash photography is often forbidden in museums and churches, although they don't object to people using fast film and natural light. It is best to bring your equipment with you but both slide and print film, VHS cassettes and, to a lesser extent, Super-8 cassettes are available.

Post Offices

The main post office (*Glavpochtamt*) in St Petersburg is open 8am–8pm Mon–Fri with slightly shorter hours on Sundays. It is at Pochtamtskaya Ul. 9 (Ⓜ Nevsky Prospekt) in St Petersburg.

Russia's postal service is appalling. Incoming mail from abroad is often waylaid, opened for any valuables and dumped in ponds near the airport. Outgoing post takes weeks, and even that sometimes goes astray, though postcards are generally reliable. Slightly more expensive but thoroughly reliable are the services (via the Finnish postal service) offered by Post International, Nevsky Prospekt 20, ✆ 219 4472 (open Mon–Fri 10am–7pm, Sat 11am–4pm) and Westpost, Nevsky Prospekt 86, ✆ 275 0784 (open Mon-Fri 10am–8pm, Sat and Sun 12 noon–6pm). Call the following numbers for information about courier services:

DHL: Nevsky Palace Hotel, Nevsky Pr. 57 ✆ 325 6100, ✉ 325 6116.

Federal Express: Ul. Mayakovskovo 2, ✆ 279 1287, ✉ 273 2139.

Religious Services

The 'when in Rome' principle works particularly well in Russia, since the services of the Russian Orthodox Church, with their moving chants, elaborate vestments and opening and closing of doors in the iconostasis, are a spectacular mystery. If you choose well, the packed, standing congregation will be overlooked by icons of transcendent beauty, the faces of all illuminated by a thousand candles. Try the **Cathedral of St Nicholas** (Nikolsky Sobor) on Nikolskaya Ploshchad.

If you want to worship in your own denomination during your stay, consult the Friday edition of the St Petersburg Times or call:

Catholic: St Catherine's Church, Nevsky Prospekt 32/4, ✆ 311 5795.

Jewish: Choral Synagogue, Lermontovsky Prospekt 2, ✆ 114 0078.

Muslim: Mosque, Kronverksy Prospekt 7, ✆ 233 8918.

Sports and Activities

With pompous, straight-faced slogans such as Stalin's 'trained muscles and bodies have military uses', a cult of sport was encouraged during the Soviet period. Team sports took place under the auspices of the workplace; footballers playing for Spartak, for example, received their salary from the aviation industry.

Today there is a plethora of sporting activities on offer. Particularly fun for visitors are the winter opportunities for cross-country skiing and skating. Retailers of sports equipment are listed in the chapter on shopping (*see* p.287).

banyas

Not strictly a sport, but central to the Russian body beautiful, is the tradition of visiting the bathhouse or *banya*. Foreigners either love it or hate it—being stark naked and beetroot-red in front of countless other members of their own sex. The routine is simple. Take your own towel, wash things, creams and, if you want, a pair of flip-flops (you can often hire these there). Before entering the building, look around for someone selling bundles of birch and oak twigs, complete with leaves. Do the most traditional thing and buy a switch of birch (*veniki*) and then enter and pay the fee. Undress in the changing room and give any valuables to the attendants. In the washing room find a bowl (*tazik*), fill it with very hot water and soak your *veniki* for several minutes while you shower or slosh yourself with water. With your switch, head for the steam room (*parilka*) where the sight of piles of rolled flesh surmounted by woolly hats awaits: the heat is not supposed to be good for exposed hair. There is usually a staircase leading to an infernal balcony. Sit or stand as high as you can bear, flicking yourself and your friends gently with the *veniki* once the pores begin to open. Go in and out of the heat, relax for a while with a cup of herbal tea in the changing room, and give yourself a really good scrub before leaving.

Nevskiye Bani, Ul. Marata 5/7, ✆ 311 1400, is a large modern complex with banyas for both sexes.   Ⓜ Mayakovskaya

Gay banya on Ul. Dostoyevsky—an unmarked address but you'll find it if you're determined. Beware, though, of unprotected sex, as AIDS is rife here.

boating

Yelagin Island, near the bridge over to the Buddhist Temple. Rowing boats for rent on the lake.   Ⓜ Chyornaya Rechka and bus 411 or 416 to Lipovaya Alleya

Neva Yacht Club, Martinova Nab. 94, Krestovsky Ostrov, ✆ 235 2722 or Kostya Klimov, captain of the Argus, on ✆ 166 0222. Yachts sleeping 6–8 can be rented for the weekend at rates of around $100–$150 a day including crew and catering.   Ⓜ Petrogradskaya, plus tram 17 or 18

flying

Baltic Air, ✆ 104 1676, offers 15-minute helicopter rides round the city from the Peter and Paul Fortress at weekends. Bring ID. Hot-air balloons are offered by **Aerotour Balloons**, ✆ 265 5018 or **Oparin Balloons**, ✆ 264 6358.

ice skating

Tauride Park, ✆ 272 6044, is designated for children, who ski, sledge and skate here in winter in great numbers. **Kronwerk Canal**, behind the Peter and Paul Fortress, is a great place to head if you have your own skates. If not, go to the lake on **Yelagin Island**, near the Buddhist Temple, ✆ 239 0911 (*see* **Boating** above). In summer you can skate on the rink at the **Letny Sportklub**, Naberezhnaya Reki Fontanki 112, ✆ 292 2081/2128.

riding

Prostov-Park, Krestovsky Ostrov 20, ✆ 230 7873, offers riding in nearby Primorsky Park as well as lessons in dressage and show-jumping. **Olgino Motel and Campsite**, ✆ 238 3671, is the only place used to renting horses on a regular basis. They can arrange troika rides in winter. Elektrichka from Finlandsky Vokzal to Olgino station.

skiing

Among the best places to ski in the vicinity of St Petersburg are **Tsarskoye Selo** (*see* p.231) or **Pavlovsk** (*see* p.240). You can rent skis and sledges from an office in the semi-circular wing of the main Catherine Palace at Tsarskoye Selo.

swimming pools

Health certificates from a Russian doctor are required before you can use most municipal pools, so check before you go. The same does not apply to club pools.
Dinamo Sports Centre, Dinamo Prospekt 44, ✆ 235 2944, has a huge pool among its many facilities. *Open 6am–12pm.* Ⓜ Krestovsky Ostrov
Delfin, Ul. Dekabristov 38, ✆ 114 2054, contains a pool (*open 6am–12pm*).
There are also tiny pools in the **Hotel Pribaltiskaya** and **Hotel St Petersburg**.

tennis

There are tennis courts at the **Lawn Tennis Club**, Pr Metallistov 116, ✆ 540 1886, and at two locations on Krestovsky Ostrov. Phone ✆ 235 2077 to reserve a court in **Primorsky Park Pobedy**, or ✆ 235 0407 for one at the smart **Tennis Club** at Konstantinovsky Proezd 23. Both lie on bus route 71a from Ⓜ Krestovsky Ostrov. The **Pulkovskaya Hotel**, Pl. Pobedy 1, ✆ 123 5122, also offers tennis courts.

spectator sports

Ice hockey: The city's best team, SKA St Petersburg, play at the Yubileiny Sports Palace on Petrograd Side, ✆ 119 5615, and Kirov Stadium, ✆ 235 4877.

Telephones

Pay phones are located throughout the city, and are designed to take either phonecards, which can be bought from kiosks, the post office or metro stations, or metro tokens (*jetons*). The later are only for local calls. There are also plenty of both to be found at the Central Telegraph Office on Ul. Bolshaya Morskaya 3–5, ✆ 314 0140 (open 9am–9pm daily).

For long distance calls in Russia dial 8, wait for the uninterrupted tone, and then dial the code and number. To make an international call you will need at least 100 units on your phonecard. Dial 8, wait for the change in the tone, then dial 10, followed by the country code and the telephone number, omitting the 0 from the beginning of the area code. Country codes are as follows:

Australia	61	Ireland	353	Sweden	46
Canada	1	New Zealand	055	United Kingdom	44
Finland	358	Norway	47	USA	1
Holland	31				

If you have trouble getting through, the number for the international operator, many of whom speak English, is ✆ 315 0012. You can also book an international call on this number. If you are ringing from someone else's phone, they will happily ring you back and tell you how much your call cost if you ask.

Hotel telephone charges are astronomical, whether you go through the reception desk or use the business centre. Always check the rates before you call, as there is nothing more deflating after a phone call home than to be faced by a bill that makes you feel you have been taken for a ride. Both business centres and the central telephone and telegraph offices listed above will send faxes for you. The difference in the price is considerable.

The best telephone book is the *Traveller's Yellow Pages* to St Petersburg, which should be available at your hotel bookshop.

Time

St Petersburg is 3 hours ahead of Greenwich Mean Time and 11 hours ahead of Eastern Standard Time. Since the clocks go forward and back at around the same time as in the UK (last Saturday of March and last Saturday of October), they remain 3 hours ahead for most of the summer as well.

Tipping

Everybody loves a tip, but the practice is by no means obligatory. A lot of the time you will be charged over the odds for the service in question (e.g. in taxis) so don't even think of tipping. In restaurants good service should be rewarded as a much-needed incentive, since it is in such short supply. Some restaurants have started adding a service charge, so check before deciding on the size of your tip.

Toilets

Russian public conveniences are not for the faint-hearted. Most have recently been privatized (some have even been turned into shops) and conditions are marginally better than they used to be. You pay as you enter and will be given some toilet paper, though it is safest to keep some with you at all times. Even smart restaurants sometimes run out. If you are choosy, use the toilets in the smart hotels.

Tourist Information and Tours

There is no such thing as a tourist information booth in St Petersburg. Most visitors end up booking a personal guide or joining a tour through their hotel. If you are not staying at a hotel, the most convenient way to book yourself a place on the regular schedule of tours is to visit the Astoria Hotel, Issakievskaya Ploshchad. If you want help in getting to somewhere even remotely unusual, you will have to hire a guide. With the emergence of a number of new independent companies specializing in tourism, this need not be as expensive as it sounds, and their approach is often more flexible and interesting than that of the traditional school of statistic-spouting.

Service Desk, Grande Hotel Europe, Ul. Mikhailovsksaya 1–7, ✆ 312 0072, ext. 6242. At very short notice this well-organized hotel will provide you with an English-speaking guide for sightseeing trips.

Ost-West Kontaktservice, Ul. Mayakovskovo 7, ✆ 279 7045, 🖅 327 3417, will give you reliable information and maps, set you up on an English-speaking tour or find you a personal guide.

Women

During the day Moscow and St Petersburg appear to be almost entirely free of sexual harassment, but at night, after the appearance of the vodka bottle, you may well find yourself prey to unwelcome attention. The good thing is that most of the men are too drunk to be any great threat, so that walking briskly away will leave them trying to focus and wondering where you have gone. Drunks in restaurants may pester you for a dance, but with luck the waiters will help to keep them away. As a woman alone you will feel conspicuous in most Russian restaurants, so it is best to stick to your hotel at night. Even when dining with another woman make sure you choose your restaurant well. Mafiosi haunts and casinos are hopping with prostitutes and men on the prowl. If you have a long way to walk at the other end of your journey, don't take the metro at night, and don't flag down a car on your own at night either. Most Russian men will insist on seeing you home, and if you know they can't afford it you can suggest paying for the taxi to take them back home after dropping you. It is normally just as easy to say 'no' to a Russian friend who becomes amorous at the end of the bottle as it is to say 'yes'.

The *Matrioshka* Society

Women can do everything; men can do the rest

For decades, the most popular Russian souvenir has been a nest of wooden *matrioshka* dolls. There is an uncanny and doubtless subconscious symbolism in this pleasing and ubiquitous toy. Time and again you will hear Russian women likening their husband to another child, only more demanding: on top of her own job, she must not only wash, cook and clean for him, but she is also expected to capitulate to his late-night, vodka-sodden advances. Divorce rates are soaring, and Russian women are learning to live without men. The all-female family, a mother bringing up a child, often living with her own mother, is increasingly common.

For despite the complaints, Russian society is still remarkably male-centric. The Soviet Union may have been the first society to emancipate women officially, but, while 90% of children's doctors are women, they make up only 6% of Russia's surgeons, and less than 2% of the prestigious Academy of Sciences. Women themselves are often accomplices in the male conspiracy to keep them in their place, bringing up their boys to behave just as the husband they despise. Even intelligent, high-achieving Russian women tend to think feminism is a western disease, the product of a bourgeois society which turns women into power-hungry vamps.

In a recent survey, only 6 per cent of married Russian women claimed to be satisfied by their sex life. There is almost no sex education in Russian schools. Family planning services, though gradually improving, betray a societal lack of respect for the female body. The main method of contraception is still abortion; most clinics have no private operating theatres, and eight women may undergo abortions at the same time in one large room. Anaesthetic is not normally on offer and after-care extends to lying down on a bed for a couple of hours. The average Russian woman undergoes 12 abortions in her lifetime.

Things are gradually improving. If you can pay for it, family planning now offers pills and cervical smears, and *glasnost* has certainly brought sex out of the closet, most visibly in the form of pornography. It is interesting to speculate whether the advent of male *matrioshka* sets will augur in a new, nurturing Russian man, willing to do more than pay lip-service to old-fashioned gallantry.

History

Until 1 February 1918, Russia followed the
Julian calendar, which was 13 days ahead of
the Gregorian calendar then used by the rest of
Europe. Throughout this book, history has been
aped, so that only dates from February 1918
are given in the Gregorian calendar.

31

St Petersburg's beginnings were extraordinary. Founded almost overnight at the beginning of the 18th century, in less than 10 years the city became capital of a country stretching as far as Vladivostok on the Sea of Japan. It was, wrote Diderot, like putting your heart in your little finger. Only a man possessed, a tyrannical autocrat, could have done it.

Peter the Great

By the time Peter I became sole Russian ruler at 24 in 1696, Russia had been governed from Moscow for over 200 years. Peter was a ferociously energetic giant of a man, over 2m tall, with a lifetime of political experience. He spent much of his teens in Moscow's foreign community, where he developed an insatiable interest in western know-how and technology. His admiration for things foreign was matched by his deep distrust of Russia's conservative, scheming society. As a ten-year-old he had seen the assassination of several members of his close family during a military uprising in Moscow. He loathed the old capital and its medieval ways.

Yet no one could have anticipated the revolution he was to unleash on his nation. By the time Peter died in 1725 Russia, for the first time in history, was a force to be reckoned with in Europe. He created a modern professional army and navy from scratch, and defeated the Ottoman Empire and the hitherto omnipotent Swedes. He built a new capital for the country on its European border and introduced a host of new ideas, fashions and technological innovations. Many of these he picked up during his travels to Europe, where he laboured beside his courtiers learning skills and engaged professionals—architects, boatbuilders, gardeners and other craftsmen —to return with him to Russia and disseminate their knowledge. On his return he personally shaved the beards off the boyars who came to see him, and hung models of European-style clothing from the gates of Moscow for anyone to copy.

Yet his legacy is far from straightforward. Argument has raged ever since between the 'westernizers' and those who believe that his reforms were contrary to Russia's Slavic heritage. Even in Peter's day, many of his subjects believed him to be a changeling sent back from Europe to destroy Holy Russia and all that she held dear.

The Foundation of St Petersburg

With his surprise defeat of Sweden, the tsar achieved access through the Baltic to the open seas. Once he had captured the Swedish fort on the River Neva in 1703, he began to build the Peter and Paul Fortress. Though he was not yet thinking of a new capital, he was mindful of his need for a port, and made a heroic gesture of confidence in staking a claim to the sea route when all surrounding land was in Swedish hands. But he was right. Russia's time had come. In 1709 the Russians inflicted irreparable damage on the Swedes at the Battle of Poltava in the Ukraine and, though Sweden didn't make peace until 1721, she never seriously threatened Russia again.

During the early years of St Petersburg's construction, 40,000 peasants and captured Swedish soldiers were conscripted to sink piles into the marshy ground. They were hampered by the lack of daylight, the absence of local building materials and frequent flooding when the ground was not frozen. Wolves, disease, cold and the lack of a local supply of food contributed to the mortality rate among the labourers, whose skeletons made a considerable contribution to the foundations of the city.

In 1710 the imperial family and the government were moved from their cosy Moscow palaces to the chilly northern city. In 1712 Peter declared St Petersburg his capital, and by the end of his life what had been the humblest of fishing hamlets had become the fulcrum of a society excitedly exploring new ideas in science and the arts, government and social life. In summer, high society retired to summer palaces which stood proud in landscaped parks round the city. They dined in pavilions where tables disappeared through the floor between courses, delighted in ingenious series of fountains and passed the White Nights in lantern-filled glades. How far they had come from Moscow. By dint of his own furious energy, Peter had managed to rid himself altogether of the capital he so distrusted.

Once in St Petersburg, Peter rationalized his government into ministries known as colleges, and institutionalized a meritocracy with his Table of Ranks of the Russian Empire. From now on all men of talent, whatever their birth, would be able to join one of the three branches of state service, the military, civil and court, and make their way up its 14 official ranks. Peter's own government was conspicuously full of new men of talent, like his prime minister Alexander Menshikov. Peter's second wife and appointed successor, Catherine, was born a Lithuanian peasant. Her good looks had been noted by Peter's loyal commander Peter Sheremetev during his campaign against the Swedes, and she had been taken into his household. From there she became the mistress of Menshikov, who later introduced her to the tsar.

Great emphasis has rightly been placed on Peter's reforming zeal. However he also left behind him an autocracy strengthened by a powerful secret police, a legal system that rewarded informers, and a legacy of cruelty. Peter's most repellent act of personal violence was the killing of his own son. As early as 1707 Alexei, Peter's only child by his first wife, found himself championed by the tsar's enemies. The boy grew up so terrified of his father that he tried a number of times to renounce his succession and retreat to a monastery. By 1717 he was so afraid that he ran away to Vienna and thence to Italy, only to be coaxed back by Peter's envoy. On his return, he was forced to renounce his right to the throne, and four months of interrogation began. Peter used Alexei as an excuse to wipe out his obvious enemies, for the young man was so scared that he would confirm the treachery of anyone the tsar suggested. After he had been sentenced to death, Alexei died in his cell in the Peter and Paul fortress, probably from wounds inflicted during torture. Rumours at the time even placed responsibility in the hands of the tsar himself.

The Petticoat Period

After Peter's death, men occupied the throne for only ten of the remaining 75 years of the century. This was the first and last time that women were to hold paramount power in Russia. It is a period remembered for its advances in the fields of architecture, the arts and sciences, and had great impact on the St Petersburg we see today.

Thanks to Peter's tinkering with the succession, the years after his death were fraught with changes. His wife Catherine was succeeded by Peter II (son of the ill-fated Alexei) who chose to live in Moscow. In 1730 Empress Anna forced the court back to St Petersburg, and set about taming its wild northern spirit. The strong Germanic influence of Anna's advisors, brought with her from Kurland where she had been married, was resented by the Russians, and stability only really returned with the accession of Empress Elizabeth, Peter's only remaining daughter, in 1741.

Elizabeth was a strong but contradictory character. She loved to drink, hunt and dance, and only fell asleep around dawn. Yet from time to time she would disappear into a convent, giving the court a break from her incessant 'metamorphoses', balls at which guests had to cross-dress. The future Empress Catherine put this obsession down to Elizabeth's shapely ankles, which could only be fully admired in men's clothing. Matters of statecraft the attractive and energetic Elizabeth left to able ministers, but her deep interest in the arts is still felt in St Petersburg today. Some architects and patrons were made for one another, and this is gloriously true of Bartolomeo Francesco Rastrelli and Elizabeth. Between them they built three of the city's most memorable monuments: the Winter Palace, the Catherine Palace at Tsarskoye Selo and the Smolny Cathedral and Convent. In each of these buildings, Rastrelli's florid rococo embellishment of essentially simple, harmonious, rhythmical structures seems to mirror the character of the empress.

Catherine the Great and the Expansion of the Empire

Elizabeth's choice of successor, her petty-minded nephew Peter III, was surprising, though her choice of his wife, the minor German princess Sophia of Anhalt-Zerbst, was inspired. Sophia was baptized into the Russian church before her wedding and took the name Ekaterina (Catherine) for her Russian identity. Soon the marriage turned into a prison sentence for both parties, with Catherine alleging that it had never been consummated and Peter seeking refuge in the arms of his mistress. By the time Peter came to the throne in 1761, Catherine had borne a son, Paul, and a daughter who had died, but neither can reliably be thought to have been Peter's offspring, and many surmise that the true Romanov dynasty stopped here.

An intelligent and cultured woman who worked hard to learn the language and culture of her new country, Catherine could be forgiven for overthrowing Peter III, who preferred drilling toy soldiers to government business. He signed only one major piece of legislation in his seven-month reign, and that was largely drafted by

Elizabeth. When he threatened to divorce Catherine and send her to a convent in 1762, her allies acted. Within days he was dead and Catherine II ruled Russia.

Immensely well read, Catherine admired the philosophers of the Enlightenment and wanted their approval as a modern ruler. She became a regular correspondent with Voltaire and Diderot, who visited her in Russia, bringing back glowing reports of her intelligence and humanity. Between her words and her deeds, however, an ever-widening chasm opened as she confronted the realities of ruling Russia.

In 1773, the success of a peasant uprising led by the Cossack Emilian Pugachev, in which land- and serf-owners were murdered around the River Volga, took her by surprise. It was quashed in 1774 and Pugachev executed. Catherine was shaken by the vehemence of feeling against her and, though she opposed serfdom, she did nothing to improve conditions. Alarmed by the American War of Independence and genuinely appalled by the regicide of the French Revolution, she backtracked so far as to ban Diderot's celebrated Enlightenment text, the *Encyclopédie,* after 1789. Her 1785 Charter of Nobility enshrined the aristocracy's right not to pay tax, and by the end of her reign courtiers were even speaking a different language from their serfs: while the peasants spoke Russian, the nobles now spoke French.

The most notorious feature of Catherine's reign was her series of lovers. Given her isolated position as lone ruler in a foreign country, it is hardly surprising she sought intimate friendship. Rumours of her voracious sexual appetite were exaggerated by her enemies in Europe who were disturbed by Russia's advances against the Turks. While it was normal for kings to have mistresses, a woman who had gobbled up her incompetent husband before assuming the throne herself needed to be kept in her place. As for the rumour that she died trying to satisfy herself with a stallion...

The tsaritsa's mania for building transformed St Petersburg. She marshalled rivers and canals between granite embankments, built neoclassical palaces for her lovers and schools for the daughters of the gentry. She enlarged the Winter Palace to hold her private art collection, and bought treasures from all Europe to fill it. She added breathtaking wings to the palace at Tsarskoye Selo, helped the building of Pavlovsk by lending the project her favourite architect, Charles Cameron, and encouraged the landscaping of the magnificent parks round the out-of-town palaces.

Catherine earned the encomium 'the Great', as Peter had done, for foreign policy successes. The partitions of Poland that she engineered with Austria and Prussia brought hundreds of thousands of square miles and millions of new subjects into the Russian Empire. During two successful wars with Turkey the balance of power in the Balkans swung in favour of Russia. She acquired new lands in southern Ukraine and round the Sea of Azov, as well as trading concessions on the Black Sea and the Bosphorus. In 1783 Catherine's lover, Prince Grigory Potemkin, annexed the Crimea, gaining a fertile agricultural belt and a plethora of sea-ports. By the end of Catherine's reign, Russia was poised to take up her position as a world power.

The Emperor Paul

Paul never had an easy relationship with his domineering mother. During a lonely youth he had a brilliant education, allowing him to shine when he visited Versailles, but, as Peter III's putative son, he was courted by Catherine's enemies. During his 34-year wait for the throne, Paul became embittered and deluded. He was happiest in self-imposed exile at Gatchina, his military state-within-a-state, obsessively drilling his troops. His accession in 1796 was greeted with dread because of his draconian capriciousness: exiling officers to Siberia for wearing their caps at the wrong angle, banning the word 'snub-nosed' out of embarrassment at his own features.

St Petersburg society tolerated Paul until 1801 when, in admiration for Bonaparte, he reversed Russia's anti-French policy. Leading figures, including Catherine's last lover, Zubov, and the governor of St Petersburg, acted quickly. The conspirators consulted his son and heir Alexander, who is thought to have agreed to his father's deposition on condition that he not be harmed. In the event Paul was smothered in Mikhailovsky Castle on 24 March, for which Alexander never forgave himself.

The Napoleonic Wars and the Triumph of Alexander I

Paul's eldest sons had been educated by the best tutors that Europe could provide. When Alexander ascended the throne at 24, it looked as if Enlightenment ideas might finally take root in tradition-bound Russia. In the early years of his reign his leading advisor was Mikhail Speransky, who went as far as suggesting that Russia should elect a parliament (*duma*). But as the threat from Napoleon grew, Speransky was overshadowed by the conservative, aristocratic inner circle and Alexander's domestic policies were entirely eclipsed by the war with France. Though experienced commanders advised caution, Alexander was determined to ride the surge in Russian patriotism and engage the enemy. Russia fought with Austria and Britain against Napoleon, receiving a crushing defeat at the battle of Austerlitz in December 1805. The price of Alexander's inexperience was 11,000 Russian dead.

By the time Napoleon invaded Russia with his Grand Army, at 600,000 the largest army ever, in June 1812, she had had time to recover. Napoleon's campaign was uncharacteristically badly planned. The French advanced to Moscow, arriving after their Pyrrhic victory at Borodino in September 1812. Relying for provisions on the countryside they passed through, they had not bargained on the peasants' patriotism, and by the time they reached Moscow the army had dwindled to little over 100,000. The Russians abandoned Moscow and set fire to much of the city: Alexander's commander-in-chief, General Kutuzov, judged that the vastness of the Russian countryside alone would defeat the invaders. Napoleon and his troops occupied the Kremlin, horrified at the destruction of the city around them, and tried to contact Alexander in far-off St Petersburg to begin negotiations. Napoleon waited for a month, but the Russian court refused to respond, and with the onset of winter the French army was forced into hasty retreat. Bowed down by booty, they made easy targets. The Cossacks recovered almost all the country's treasures, and many weakened, freezing stragglers were picked off by the peasantry. By the time they crossed the Russian border at the River Niemen, as few as 5,000 French soldiers remained. The Russian army followed the French to Paris, taking part in the allied campaign that led to Napoleon's abdication in 1814. At the Congress of Vienna, Russia took her place as one of the five great European powers.

New, grand Empire-style palaces and public buildings in St Petersburg trumpeted Russia's blossoming self-confidence over the next 20 years. Yet Alexander was haunted by guilt for his father's murder. In the autumn of 1825, the tsar's wife fell ill and the two went to Taganrog, a spa on the Sea of Azov. In November the tsar died of an unspecified illness; by the time his body arrived back in St Petersburg it was too decomposed to identify. Rumours abounded that Alexander had not died, and had substituted a soldier's rotted body for his own. The tsar is widely believed to have lived on for half a century in Siberia, as a holy hermit, Fyodor Kuzmich. Bolshevik investigators opened his sarcophagus but only deepened the mystery; they found that Alexander III had substituted another coffin for the original, lending credit to the belief that the original body was not the tsar.

Nicholas I: 'Orthodoxy, Autocracy, Nationality'

Alexander's death without an heir was the first moment of imperial weakness to be exploited by democrats. The rebels, who became known as the Decembrists, were led by army officers who wanted to establish a constitutional monarchy. When Alexander's youngest brother Nicholas was declared tsar, the officers roused their men in defence of his elder brother Constantine, who unknown to them had renounced the throne. The rebels made their doomed stand on what is now Decembrists' Square, having persuaded only half of the garrison to turn against the new tsar. After a day-long stand-off, troops loyal to the tsar broke up the ice on the Neva to prevent their quarry escaping, and mowed down several hundred rebels before the Decembrists surrendered. The five leading figures were hanged, after personal interrogation by Nicholas I, and over a hundred were sent to Siberia.

Nicholas I, the 'Iron Tsar', never swerved from this unforgiving course. He instituted strict censorship and established a new secret police. University syllabuses were monitored by the state and students forced into uniform. No one was allowed abroad to study, as Nicholas tried to stifle dissent under the slogan 'Orthodoxy, Autocracy, Nationality'. After the European revolutions of 1848, repression was stepped up even further. Though everyone recognized the iniquity of serfdom, Nicholas was afraid to dismantle it for fear of the unknown. Yet threats to the autocracy never came from that quarter; it was always the intelligentsia, chattering away in their drawing rooms in Moscow and St Petersburg, from whom the tsar had most to fear. The most famous revolutionary group infiltrated by the police under Nicholas I was the St Petersburg Petrashevsky Circle, exposed in 1849. Fifteen of its leading participants, including the young Fyodor Dostoyevsky, were subjected to a mock execution, pardoned at the last second, and sent to Siberia.

Paradoxically, Nicholas' reign is also the Golden Age of Russian literature, during which Pushkin, Lermontov and Gogol established a modern literary tradition that blossomed into the next century. Poetry became a national obsession, with Pushkin as its undisputed tsar. New periodicals appeared regularly, and Russians came to express their opposition to the autocracy in literature, albeit in veiled terms. Nicholas I censored Pushkin's work personally, and when the poet died in a duel fomented at court (*see* p.101), blame was partly laid at the feet of the autocracy.

Nicholas's greatest error was to threaten Turkey. Since the Napoleonic Wars, Russia had appeared worryingly invincible, so in 1854 Britain, France and Austria rallied to Turkey's defence in the Crimean War. The mirage of Russian strength vanished, for, though most of the fighting took place on her back door in the Crimea, she found herself embarrassingly ill-equipped. While the rest of Europe had built railways and strengthened the military on the back of massive industrialization, Russia had stagnated because the vast majority of her population was tied to the land by serfdom. Nicholas died in despair of the course of the war in 1855, leaving his son Alexander II, who had advised against it, to oversee its humiliating conclusion.

Alexander II: Reform and Assassination

Alexander II, described by the French ambassador as 'not a great intellect but…a generous soul', is the most tragic 19th-century tsar. Praised as the 'Tsar Liberator' for his emancipation of the serfs, he died by a revolutionary terrorist's bomb. Alexander undertook reform with genuine enthusiasm, determined to abolish serfdom rather than wait for rebellion. He developed some genuine local government and a modern legal system, including trial by jury. The universities were allowed to teach philosophy and literature, pupils were encouraged to study abroad, and secondary education was extended to new sectors of the population.

Yet these reforms merely encouraged a rush of further demands. Calls for a *duma* (parliament) received ardent support from the universities and other educated sectors of society. The Edict of Emancipation, passed in 1861, was riddled with problems. The tsar could not afford to alienate the land-owning aristocracy, so the serfs were not given land, but had to buy it over a period of years. The price was so high that most peasants quickly fell behind with their payments and were no better off than before, working for the same landowners to pay off their debts.

The turning point in Alexander II's reign, when fear again became the prime motivation of government, came in 1866 with the first attempt on his life, just outside the Summer Garden on the banks of the Neva. Even before this, one of the seminal texts of the Russian revolutionary movement had been written from a jail cell in the Peter and Paul Fortress. Nikolai Chernyshevsky's *What is to be Done?*, passed by two censors, each of whom thought the other was supposed to suppress it, was published legally in 1863. Lenin claimed that it converted him to the revolution.

The revolutionary lead was taken by 'People's Will' (*Narodnaya Volya*), a group that believed in political assassination to advance the cause. After several attempts, in 1881 they killed the tsar on the very day that he was considering proposals for a *duma* and for disbanding the secret police. A bomb thrown at his carriage failed to explode and the tsar climbed out to confront the would-be assassin, only to have his legs torn off by a second bomb. Within two hours he was dead. Today, the altar of the Cathedral of the Saviour on the Blood marks the spot where the tsar, whose reign began so promisingly, was defeated by the clash of reform and autocracy.

The cycle of fear intensified with the accession of Alexander's son Alexander III. His first act was to execute all the leaders of People's Will he could, and for the rest of his short reign he lived in such fear of assassination that he was rarely seen in public. His government was dominated by Konstantin Pobedonostsev, a devotee of autocratic Orthodox Russia and enemy of the 'great falsehood' of parliamentary democracy. The clampdown on liberal reforms inevitably provoked assassination attempts. One would-be killer, Alexander Ulyanov, was executed in 1887— another milestone on the road to revolution for his brother, Vladimir Ilich Lenin.

To deflect criticism from the increasing repression, Alexander III and Pobedonostsev encouraged the impoverished peasantry to take their anger out on local Jewish bankers. From 1881–2 pogroms against the Jews, to which local police were largely instructed to turn a blind eye, were commonplace, culminating in a spate of attacks in 1891–2 and in Pobedonostsev's decree expelling the Jews, except for those with certain qualifications, from Moscow and St Petersburg.

Still, Russian industry made rapid progress. An unprecedented period of peace in Europe was seized on by Russia's industrialists, many of them members of a new middle class who built family empires from modest beginnings. The government's industrial policy was masterminded by the brilliant Sergei Witte, son of a railway official and much derided by others in government. He encouraged home-grown entrepreneurs and foreign investment and funded 'state capitalism'. Between 1881 and 1900, Russia's railway network more than doubled in length. In the 1890s the Baku oilfields made Russia the second largest producer of oil in the world, and by the early 20th century she challenged France for the position of fourth industrial producer in the world. By 1914, the outskirts of St Petersburg were peppered with factories. New areas of the city, such as the Petrograd Side, were developed and covered with the Art Nouveau villas and apartment blocks of the new middle class. Architects such as Fredrik Lidval developed a uniquely Petersburgian synthesis of this architectural movement, known in Russia as *Style Moderne*.

Yet living conditions amongst factory workers were hellish. In bachelor barracks workers only got a bed in shifts, so that employers could pay for half as many beds as workers. In small factories families sometimes lived where they worked, bringing up babies next to noxious chemicals and sleeping on planks laid down over the filthy floor. Other families lived in corners of rooms with crumbling plaster, holes in the walls, cockroaches, piercing cold and precious little hygiene. Rather than improve the lot of the working class, industrialization did little more than bring large numbers of discontented workers together and amplify the divide between rich and poor. And it did nothing to answer the resounding demands for political modernization which were rising from almost every corner of society.

Nicholas II: Last of the Romanovs

Alexander died unexpectedly in 1894, leaving his gentle, credulous 26-year-old son Nicholas in power. Largely educated by Pobedonostsev, Nicholas II absorbed the reactionary lessons of his mentor and had no initiative to bridge the growing rift between people and tsar. Ill omens for the reign began at the coronation in Moscow in 1896, where 1,300 people were accidentally trampled to death. Nicholas compounded the tragedy by attending a ball thrown in his honour that evening by the French ambassador, instead of declaring a period of mourning as his instinct suggested. Russia was scandalized by his heartless behaviour.

Alexandra, Nicholas's wife and a granddaughter of Queen Victoria, was feverish in her converted zeal for Russian Orthodoxy and an unquestioning believer in the autocracy. As the troubled reign wore on, the isolated couple retreated to the Alexander Palace at Tsarskoye Selo, spending as little time as possible in the city. They clung to a belief in the Russian peasants' unswerving loyalty to the tsar, a belief strengthened between 1905 and 1916 by their infamous friendship with the extraordinary peasant 'holy man' Rasputin (*see* pp.58–60). As well as the healing powers he seemed to exert over the haemophiliac heir to the throne, Tsarevich Alexei, Nicholas and Alexandra came increasingly to believe his comforting words and even to follow his advice on the appointment of ministers. The tsarevich's disease was a closely kept secret, and the outside world was unable to understand, and deeply suspicious of, Rasputin's intimacy with the family.

Industrialization had quadrupled St Petersburg's population in the last half of the 19th century, and caused confusion amongst Russian Marxists, most of whom lived in exile abroad. Some believed Russia could leapfrog the stage of fully fledged bourgeois capitalism straight to Marx's socialist workers' state. Others followed Marx's theories to the letter and believed that they would have to bide their time before the revolution could take place. This argument came to a head at the 1903 Congress of the Social Democratic Workers' Party of Russia, the leading Marxist body. The orthodox Marxists (the *Mensheviks*, 'Men of the Minority') split from

Lenin's followers (the *Bolsheviks*, 'Men of the Majority') who believed that the dictatorship of the proletariat would have to be brought about by an élite party that would direct the politically unprepared workers. Living abroad, mostly in London, Lenin propagated his ideas through his newpaper *Iskra* ('The Spark') which was read by Russia's left-wing expatriates and smuggled back to the motherland.

The extension of Russia's influence at the Far Eastern end of the new Trans-Siberian Railway, meanwhile, antagonized Japan. The ensuing Russo-Japanese war (1904–5) was disastrous. News of Russian defeats reached a population demoralized by an industrial slump, and by 1905 strikes were rapidly spreading through the factories. On 9 January, Father Gapon, a priest in charge of a workers' association, organized a massive march of striking Petersburg workers to present a petition to their 'little father', the tsar. Government paranoia turned an event of potential reconciliation into the beginning of the end. As the marchers, carrying icons and images of the emperor and empress, converged peacefully on the city centre, the Imperial Guard opened fire. Estimates of the dead range from 100 to 1,000, and the image of an indivisible tsar and people was shattered once and for all. 'Bloody Sunday', as the event was known, was a disastrous watershed in Russian history. It set off strikes throughout the country, naval mutinies and even peasant uprisings.

The unrest, which became known as the 1905 Revolution, was exacerbated when the Japanese sank the Russian fleet at Tsushima. Nicholas was forced to accept constitutional reform and a limit to his autocracy. The October Manifesto of 1905 set out plans for a bi-cameral legislature (the state *duma* and the state council) elected on wide male suffrage, but the tsar retained a veto over legislation. By the time the *duma* sat at St Petersburg's Tauride Palace, the tsar had reversed a number of these concessions, and right up until 1917 he treated the parliament with contempt, dissolving it by force whenever it brought up unpalatable subjects.

The liberal bourgeoisie, who would have been satisfied by a genuine constitutional monarchy, banded together in the *duma* to form the Constitutional Democratic (Kadet) Party. The St Petersburg Soviet of Workers' Deputies gave a more radical alternative. Elected directly by the workers, the soviet briefly became a vital arm of local government, giving working people a taste of power for the first time.

The First World War and the 1917 Revolutions

The pageantry of the 300th anniversary of the Romanov dynasty in 1913 and the burst of patriotic fervour that greeted Russia's entry into the First World War merely papered over the deep divisions in the country. To give it a less Germanic ring, St Petersburg was renamed Petrograd.

By 1915, the early Russian advances into East Prussia and Galicia had been reversed. Rasputin's influence looked all the more suspicious when he and the empress were left alone in the capital while Nicholas, foolishly in view of his inexperience, took over command of the army headquarters at Mogilev. In 1916 another offensive, led by General Brusilov, was initially successful, but crumbled in the face of enormous casualties. In the midst of this demoralizing see-saw, Rasputin was murdered in December 1916 in the Yusupov Palace (see p.112). While the imperial family went into mourning, the population rejoiced. After a while, however, it must have dawned on many that Rasputin was not the cause of Russia's malaise but merely one of the symptoms.

By the end of 1916 some 3½ million Russian soldiers had been killed, wounded or captured, and the troops' morale had all but collapsed. The Germans had to move piles of corpses before being able to advance. On civvy street there was little to celebrate either. Provisioning the army took precedence over feeding civilians. The lack of bread in the cities was becoming serious, particularly in Petrograd. In February 1917, strikes and bread riots were backed by a mutiny of the huge garrison of new recruits in the city. To curb the growing anarchy, the state *duma* arrested the tsar's government and established a provisional committee. Realizing that he had no loyal troops, let alone a government, on 2 March the tsar abdicated in favour of his younger brother Mikhail. The following day Mikhail followed suit, and the Romanov dynasty came to an abrupt end. Within days the entire family were placed under house arrest in the Alexander Palace at Tsarskoye Selo.

The soldiers and workers in the city took advantage of the situation to set up soviets of workers and soldiers deputies along 1905 lines, most important of which was the Petrograd Soviet of Workers' and Soldiers' Deputies. Lenin returned to Russia in April, given safe passage in a sealed train by the Germans who saw him as a virus that would weaken their enemy. Despite his winning slogans of 'Peace, Bread and Land' and 'All Power to the Soviets', his Bolshevik party had failed to win over the soviets, who stuck to their moderate policy of working with the government. As 1917 progressed, the provisional government, led from July by Alexander Kerensky, failed to reverse the course of the war or to solve the food shortages. In an incident known as the July Days, people took to the street demanding that the soviets overthrow the government. But the soviets were unprepared, and the provisional government put down the troubles. Leaders of the soviets such as Leon Trotsky were arrested, and Lenin fled into exile again, this time in neighbouring Finland. By October, however, the Bolsheviks had taken control of the Moscow and St Petersburg soviets, and decided on an armed seizure of power.

The ground was just right. Soldiers had started deserting in huge numbers and the country became increasingly ungovernable. Early on the morning of 25 October, Red Guards trained by Trotsky occupied key buildings in Petrograd in the name of soviet power. The battle to arrest the provisional government in the Winter Palace began late that night with a blank shot fired by naval mutineers from the cruiser *Aurora*. On Palace Square gunfire was exchanged for a number of hours, but the fight was never the heroic event filmed by Eisenstein for his film *October*. The government's only defenders were a few officer cadets and a regiment of women soldiers, and at 2.10am all except Kerensky, who had escaped in a car provided by the American Embassy, were arrested. Petrograd, cradle of the century's greatest revolution, escaped with remarkably little bloodshed.

Lenin, the Civil War and the New Economic Policy

Lenin, who had returned to St Petersburg a couple of weeks before the final showdown, now took control. One of his first decrees did at a stroke what the majority of Russia's population had wanted for over 150 years—legitimized the seizure of land by the peasants. Yet the Bolsheviks were faced with massive difficulties: out of the whole country, the soviets only controlled Petrograd and Moscow. Russia's allies in the West, France, Britain and particularly America, were venomous about the coup, and enraged by the new government's intention to abandon the war. In November 1917, a Constituent Assembly was elected by near universal suffrage in the first and only free election in Russia until 1990. The Socialist Revolutionaries got almost twice as many votes as the Bolsheviks, who only won a fifth of the seats. The assembly sat for just one day in the Tauride Palace before the Bolshevik Red Guard shut it down. To combat counter-revolution, Lenin set up the Cheka, the prototype KGB, under the ruthless command of 'Iron' Felix Dzerzhinsky. In March 1918 Lenin, who saw the city as the embodiment of the tsarist state and distrusted its liberal intelligentsia, moved the government to Russia's old capital Moscow and into the Kremlin. Petrograd, which became capital of the nation because of the prejudices of one ruler, was thus demoted by the prejudices of another.

To fulfil the Bolsheviks' promise of peace and bread, Trotsky agreed to the punitive German terms of the Treaty of Brest-Litovsk in March 1918, by which the Russians surrendered the Baltic Republics and Poland and recognzied both the Ukraine and Finland as independent states. Even before the cessation of hostilities, however, new battle lines were drawing themselves within Russia. Diverse groups of anti-Bolsheviks were coming together under the leadership of a handful of 'White' army generals in the south and east, while an allied naval force landed at Murmansk in the north in March. By 1919 the Civil War was in full swing. The Red Army was fighting off attacks from General Kolchak and the White Cossacks in Siberia, General Denikin from the Ukraine and by the Finns, Balts and the Allies in the north. One rallying point for the Whites was the Romanov family, who had been exiled to the Urals. In July 1918, as White armies drew closer, the tsar, his entire family and their small retinue were taken down into the basement at the Ipatiev House in Yekaterinburg and shot. DNA testing recently carried out on the bodies has finally laid to rest the story that Anastasia, the youngest daughter, had escaped. Intriguingly, it is the body of the haemophiliac Alexei that has not been found.

It was a difficult time for Petrograd, whose population fell to only a third of its pre-revolutionary level. Unemployment increased after the capital moved to Moscow, and the city was riddled with real poverty. Horses, dogs and even rats were torn apart for food, and furniture was burned to keep the population from freezing.

That the nascent Red Army managed to repel the enemy on all fronts by 1921 is more a measure of the lack of communication between the various White forces than brilliant tactics on the part of the Reds. The Allied force in the north withdrew in 1919; their deployment, after the end of the First World War, was extremely unpopular at home. As the Whites were pushed back into a tiny enclave in the Crimea, those who wanted to flee the Bolshevik regime made their way south, through a land devastated by war and famine, to where French and British ships evacuated the last of the Whites to Constantinople and beyond.

The Civil War took a disastrous toll on the already tattered economy, and it is estimated that over five million people died of starvation in 1921–2. Lenin's economic policy, known as War Communism, by which food and armaments were simply requisitioned from peasants and factories, had been extremely unpopular. Many of those who had fought for the Revolution in 1917 became disillusioned by the Bolshevik terror. A mutiny of the previously loyal naval base at Kronstadt in 1921 was accompanied by large-scale industrial strikes. The mutiny was put down ruthlessly; troops stole across the ice to the island in the middle of the Gulf of Finland in white suits, and Trotsky did not rest until all the 'heretics' had been shot.

At the 10th Party Congress then in progress, Lenin introduced the 'New Economic Policy', a form of state capitalism by which the state would continue to support heavy industry, banking and finance, while some private business would be encouraged. The peasants would be taxed in kind, but would be free to sell excess produce from their own plot of land on the open market, and small businesses were allowed in towns. At the same time, however, all who opposed the Bolsheviks were imprisoned and killed, and the political model that was to serve the Soviet Union so badly for the next 70 years was instituted. All power resided in the (Bolshevik) Communist Party. Political power struggles were confined to the ladder of the party hierarchy. In 1922 Josef Stalin found himself a convenient rung from which to launch his bid for the top, as Secretary General of the Communist Party. In 1922–3 Lenin suffered a series of strokes; he died in January 1924. Stalin masterminded Petrograd's second change of name that century, to Leningrad.

Stalin, Collectivization and the Purges

Stalin, a Georgian whose real name was Joseph Vissarionovich Djugashvili, had been educated in a religious seminary. In a time of explosive rhetoric, his secretary described the quiet, pipe-smoking man as using 'words to conceal his thoughts'. He was sly, obsessed by power and paranoid that everyone was conspiring to deprive him of it. Many blame his violent, drunken father for setting him on the road to terror. By 1929 he had used the party mechanism to promote his supporters, and had picked off all the old Bolsheviks who might in any way threaten his position. In 1925 Leon Trotsky, the fiery proponent of continuous international revolution, was removed from office by the triumvirate of Stalin, Zinoviev and Kamenev, who favoured the policy of securing 'socialism in one country'. In 1927 Stalin ganged up with Bukharin, Rykov and Tomsky to turn on Zinoviev and Kamenev, and in 1929 he turned on his new allies and dismissed them from office. By the end of that year, Stalin was the only member of Lenin's Politburo still in power.

In 1927 the 15th Party Congress had adopted Stalin's first Five Year Plan for the economy, reversing the liberalization of Lenin's New Economic Plan, and in 1929 Stalin decided to radicalize it further. Instead of the voluntary collectivization of agriculture, peasants were forced to give up their land, livestock and tools to the local collective or state farm, where they would work, and from which they would receive salaries. Those who rebelled by burning their supplies and killing their live-stock, particularly the richer peasants known as the *kulaks*, were killed or exiled to Siberia. Allied to bad harvests in 1931 and 1932, the forced collectivization caused a famine in which between 5 and 10 million lives were lost. In Kazakhstan alone, 1½ million peasants, one third of the population, died during collectivization, a process which destroyed their traditional nomadic system of agriculture.

In industry too, Stalin implemented rapid reform. New mines in the east provided raw materials for huge new heavy industry plants, whose main purpose was to ser-vice the weapons industry. Each factory's annual programme and unrealistic output targets were set by Gosplan, a vast central bureaucracy, and all private initiatives were shut down. Within months of the first annual plan, factory managers were cooking the books to show that they had achieved the targets set, and a chain of institutional lying was set in place. From the start, central planning was a farce. By the time it was publicly challenged for the first time in 1988, one respected econo-mist reckoned it would take 30,000 years and full computerization, which Gosplan didn't have, to draft a thorough and workable annual economic programme.

At the 1934 Party Congress, delegates expressed their reservations about Stalin's policies by voting the Leningrad Party leader, Sergei Kirov, on to the Central Committee by many more votes than Stalin. As a result, most of them would be dead or in labour camps by the time of the next Congress five years later.

On 1 December 1934 Sergei Kirov was assassinated at his office in the Smolny Institute. Although Stalin was behind his death, he fixed the blame on a terrorist cell which he claimed also aimed to assassinate him. He then began to arrest hun-dreds of people who might conceivably be against him, though most of his victims were loyal party members. Leningrad suffered particularly badly, with some 40,000 citizens arrested in the immediate aftermath of Kirov's death. In August 1936, at the first of the Moscow Show Trials that shocked and fascinated the world, he rid himself of his old enemies Zinoviev and Kamenev. By means of systematic interrogation by the NKVD (forerunner of the KGB), they were forced into confessing to the murder of Kirov and were shot.

The worst period of the terror, known as the *Yezhovshchina*, was heralded by the appointment of Nikolai Yezhov as head of the NKVD in September 1936. Hundreds of thousands of loyal party members were arrested, and jails all over the country were filled to overflowing. The same methods of interrogation were used over and over to get people to confess to being guilty of anti-Soviet sentiments and to force them to implicate their colleagues. The 'guilty' were dispatched by the trainload to camps in the permafrost of Siberia, where they were forced to build railways or labour in mines and forests with little food and few clothes, in ceaseless sub-zero temperatures. They died by the thousand.

In June 1937 the purge of the Red Army began, a policy that was to have devastating consequences when Nazi Germany invaded five years later. There was no evidence of any military plot, but Stalin dreaded a challenge to his power from such a powerful body and took preventative action. After the trial and execution of eight leading generals on charges of spying and treason, a further 40,000 army officers (three quarters of the total) were purged. There was no way the army could make up that loss of experience before the war. The Great Purge came to an end when Beria took over the NKVD in December 1938, by which time 12 to 15 million people had been arrested and at least a million executed.

The Great Patriotic War, the Blockade and Stalin's Last Years

Not long after this self-inflicted bloodbath, the Soviet Union found itself embroiled in what Russians call the Great Patriotic War (the Second World War). In the course of it 20 million Russians died, 7 million of them in the military, the rest during the Nazi occupation of the country. Because losses were so large, the war remains a tangible scar on the Russian psyche to this day.

Stalin thought that the Nazi-Soviet Non-Aggression Pact signed in August 1939 would safeguard the Soviet Union from invasion. It divided central Europe into German and Soviet spheres, and in 1939–40 the Soviets made the most of it, marching into Eastern Poland (now Belorussia), Lithuania, Latvia and Estonia, and attacking Finland. Then, in June 1941, Hitler invaded the Soviet Union without a declaration of war. Though his intelligence had been warning him of such a move, Stalin was so shocked he was temporarily incapacitated. His voice was not heard on the radio, and it took several days for him to recover.

The Germans moved quickly. By September 1941 Leningrad was almost surrounded. The siege of Leningrad, known to Russians as the Blockade, was only lifted in January 1944. Hitler had given the order to destroy the city completely.

Without running water or electricity and almost without food, the inhabitants of the city manned a spirited defence against continuous shelling by the surrounding Germans. The only supply route, known as the 'Road of Life', saw trucks crossing the treacherous ice of Lake Ladoga to the city in winter. In summer every square foot of earth in the city was planted with food, but even this was pitifully inadequate. At its worst, tales of cannibalism were rife. Though an accurate figure is hard to find, in the '900 Days', some 670,000 citizens are thought to have died. In winter, when it was too cold to dig graves for the dead, frozen corpses lined the streets waiting for collection.

Those hoping for a reprieve after their war heroism were in for a shock. Returning prisoners of war and other soldiers thought to have been exposed to 'foreign' ideas, including Alexander Solzhenitsyn, were sent straight to labour camps in Siberia. In 1948 the purge of 'cosmopolitans', a thinly disguised code for Jews, was launched, while Andrei Zhdanov harangued and imprisoned the country's artists and writers into political orthodoxy. Once again Leningrad was singled out for particular opprobrium, and what should have been a period of rebuilding and pride in the city was clouded by yet more arrests. The city's intellectuals were particularly disturbed by the abuse heaped on their greatest living poet, Anna Akhmatova.

Despite the poisoned atmosphere, Leningrad set to work restoring some of its most treasured buildings. In the days before the Nazis' arrival the most important treasures from the great palaces and museums had been packed off to the Urals, while others were buried and stored in cellars. After the war it was discovered that most of the out-of-town palaces had been almost completely destroyed. The curators set to work immediately to restore them down to the last door-handle. This extraordinary feat continues to this day, and the palaces are the pride of Russia.

When Stalin died in March 1953, the people of the Soviet Union wept in their millions at the news although, as the poet Yevtushenko observed, those tears were tinged with fear of the unknown. Stalin had been in power for almost 30 years, and was seen to have led the country in her finest, most painful hour—victory in the war. In the economic sphere, Stalin's achievements seem impressive at first glance. At the time of Lenin's death in 1924, the country had barely recovered from the Civil War; by the time Stalin died in 1953 the Soviet Union had become one of the two great powers. To achieve this, however, Stalin showed a pathological disregard for human life, and his economic development, predicated on the rapid growth of Soviet military might, entirely neglected the domestic needs of the population.

Krushchev and the Thaw

On Stalin's death, Lavrenti Beria, the sadistic and powerful head of the NKVD, seized power, only to be shot dead by his peers at a meeting of the Politburo. They were now free to pursue much-needed economic and social reforms, raising the standard of living by concentrating industrial resources on the production of consumer goods such as fridges, washing machines and cars. By 1955, Nikita Khrushchev had consolidated his power base in the party and, as General Secretary, assumed overall control of government. A far cry from Stalin, Khrushchev was friendly and open. The greatest physical changes to Leningrad during his leadership were the massive new housing developments that began to spread out on the edges of the cities. Known derisively as *khrushchoby*, a pun on the leader's name and the Russian word for a slum, these box-like flats nevertheless helped to ease the urban housing crisis, made critical by wartime devastation and continuous migration from the countryside.

Though perhaps best remembered in the West as the only leader to take his shoe off and bang it on the table to express disapproval at the UN, Khrushchev is remembered by his fellow countrymen as the man who led the onslaught on the memory of Stalin. At the 20th Party Congress in 1956, Khrushchev delivered a blistering six-hour condemnation of his former boss in closed session to the shell-shocked delegates. Some eight million victims of Stalin were rehabilitated, some posthumously, others in time to flood home from the camps in Siberia. In 1961 Stalin's embalmed body was moved out of Lenin's mausoleum and buried with other Soviet leaders beneath the Kremlin Wall behind it. In 1962, Krushchev, who is said to have read the manuscript personally, gave the go-ahead for the publication of Alexander Solzhenitsyn's *One Day in the Life of Ivan Denisovich*, an unflinching fiction based on the author's eight-year internment in the Siberian gulag. Yet all was not roses. Boris Pasternak, whose novel *Doctor Zhivago* criticized the still hallowed Bolsheviks of the Revolution and Civil War, was published abroad. The author was not permitted to travel to receive his Nobel Prize for Literature, and was expelled from the Writers' Union. It was under Khrushchev too that the despicable practice of sentencing dissidents to psychiatric hospitals began.

Foreign policy was Khrushchev's most turbulent area. While in 1955 he was preaching peace with the West, in October 1956 Soviet troops were sent into Hungary to crush the revolt against Soviet control. Krushchev was not about to sacrifice the satellite Communist states of East Europe, the Soviet Union's *cordon sanitaire*, which had been hard-won in the Second World War. A brief thaw in relations with the West, during which Khrushchev made his successful trip to the United States, was followed by increased confrontation. In 1961 the Berlin Wall was erected by the East Germans, providing a tangible symbol of the opposition between the two world systems. When Soviet missiles were discovered in Fidel Castro's newly Communist Cuba the following year, the world came to the brink of nuclear war. Last-minute negotiations between Kennedy and Khrushchev averted a confrontation; the Soviets dismantled their arms on Cuba and a few months later America quietly stripped its own missiles from Turkey and Italy.

Khrushchev's attitude to the economy is summed up by his statement that 'we must help the people to eat well, dress well and live well. You cannot put theory into your soup or Marxism into your clothes'. Sadly, the results were not as promising. To cure the perennial agricultural shortages, Khrushchev instituted the 'Virgin Lands' policy, which provided a new irrigated area the size of Canada's arable land in Siberia and Kazakhstan. The dry soil was not suitable for cultivation, however, and severe erosion soon made it unproductive. There was still a massive lag between supply and demand for most consumer items as well. In the course of his flamboyant premiership, Khrushchev managed to alienate many of the interest groups within the Soviet élite. In 1964, the Presidium agreed to overthrow him. Khrushchev was told to retire 'on grounds of ill-health'.

Stagnation

Khrushchev was succeeded as General Secretary of the Communist Party by Leonid Brezhnev, whose 18-year premiership divides roughly in two. The first 10 years are remembered as a time of relative plenty. Thanks to incentives in agriculture and increased investment in the manufacture of consumer products, the average Soviet salary fed you, clothed you and provided a modicum of home comforts if you were prepared to queue. With inadequate infrastructure for the service or repair of domestic machinery, and the lack of spare parts, a 'second economy' began to flourish with a black market in scarce goods and services. By the early 1980s, this was estimated to account for up to 20 per cent of GNP, and even within state factories any spare capacity after the fulfilment of their quota was often used to work secretly *nalevo* ('on the left'). The agricultural crisis of 1975 and a sudden scarcity of goods put an end to this idyll, and suggested that, far from solving the country's problems, the relative hard work of the past decade had simply hidden them for a while. People began to doubt the constant exhortations that the Soviet Union was catching up with and about to overtake the economic achievements of the United States. Daily reports on the radio of this or that collective farm exceeding its agricultural targets just didn't square with empty fridges.

Brezhnev's support came from Party *apparatchiki*, whose tenure had been secured by his administrative reforms. For most of them, life was good. Their perks included the right to shop at special shops where imported goods were available at subsidized prices; they also enjoyed better housing, holidays and hospital treatment. Corruption became endemic, with Brezhnev himself, and infamously his daughter Galina and her husband, receiving the lion's share. The Leningrad party secretary Grigory Romanov thought nothing of borrowing the priceless Frog Service from the Hermitage for his daughter's wedding banquet. When, after Brezhnev's death, corruption in Uzbekistan was investigated, every single member of the local hierarchy—from party to trade unions—was implicated.

While his cronies quite literally got away with murder at times, Brezhnev took a tough stand on Jews who wished to emigrate and on political dissidents. After Solzhenitsyn was stripped of his citizenship and sent into exile in 1974, dissident activity increased, with the formation of underground groups reporting on human rights abuses, as well as an increase in the volume of *samizdat* (self-published) literature. But after the surge of protest that greeted the Soviet Union's war with Afghanistan in 1979, Brezhnev once again jammed foreign broadcasts in Russian and arrested many leading dissidents, including Andrei Sakharov, who was sent into internal exile in Gorky (now Nizhny Novgorod again). Brezhnev was right to be scared. Afghanistan turned out to be the beginning of the end.

Brezhnev was incapacitated by his first stroke in 1976, but such was the inertia of his government that he remained in power until 1982. A well-known Russian anecdote graphically characterizes this period of his leadership. Stalin, Khrushchev and Brezhnev are travelling together in a train when it grinds to a halt. Stalin orders the train driver and his crew to be taken out and shot and, not surprisingly, the train stays still. Khrushchev orders their rehabilitation, but to no effect. Brezhnev then pulls down the blinds on the windows, and exhorts his fellow passengers to pretend they are moving.

Brezhnev's successor Yuri Andropov was suspect in the eyes of the West as former head of the KGB, but his premiership saw a crackdown on corruption in which 40 out of 150 regional party secretaries were dismissed. He also tried to stem the national addiction to alcohol that was so costly in terms of lost working hours and health. But the aged Politburo was still trying to prevent the younger generation taking power. When Andropov died after just 15 months in office, his chosen successor, the sprightly 53-year-old reformer Mikhail Gorbachev, was passed over in favour of Konstantin Chernenko. The 72-year-old reactionary, already dying of chronic emphysema, survived for little more than a year.

Gorbachev and the Second Russian Revolution

The pace of change under Gorbachev left the Soviet Union and the world gasping for breath. The first Soviet leader since Lenin to have been to university, Gorbachev recognized that he had inherited a regime in crisis, and that radical measures were needed to avert disaster. However, not even he realized the extent of popular disillusionment. He might never have announced his famous twin policies of *glasnost* (openness) and *perestroika* (restructuring) in 1985 had he realized that he, the Communist Party and the Soviet Union itself would be swept away by them.

At first, change was slow in coming. When one of the nuclear reactors at Chernobyl blew up in April 1986, it took Gorbachev three days to remember about *glasnost* and admit that the radiation clouds detected over Scandinavia were the result of a nuclear disaster at the plant near Kiev. Gradually, discussions opened on the subject that still haunted the country—Stalin's terror. In 1986 *Doctor Zhivago* was published for the first time in Russia and, at the end of the year, Andrei Sakharov and his wife Elena Bonner were released from internal exile in Gorky—a sign of true change. In 1987, splits began to appear in the traditionally united face of the Communist Party; as well as the hardliners, there was also a spirited radical group who called themselves the Democratic Union. Even now Gorbachev showed his loyalty to old ways by banning them from meeting. Boris Yeltsin, who made a name for himself exposing the privileges and corruption of the party, resigned from the Politburo and was sacked as head of the Moscow Communist Party.

1989 turned out to be a momentous year in European history. The new era was heralded by the March elections to the Congress of People's Deputies, in which, for the first time, a real element of choice existed. Both Yeltsin and Sakharov were elected with overwhelming majorities, though at the rowdy first session of the Congress Gorbachev tried pathetically to turn the clock back by switching off the microphone as Sakharov railed against the system. In July, striking miners managed to wring real concessions out of the government, and in the autumn, sensing the disintegration of the monolith, the satellite states of Eastern Europe one by one declared the end of the Communist dictatorship and independence from the Soviet Union. Soviet troops on their soil were ordered by Moscow not to move; the motherland was too tired and bankrupt to continue policing her massive empire.

After the dismantling of the Berlin Wall, secession movements in the republics of the Soviet Union received a further boost with the widespread success of nationalist candidates and parties in the 1990 local elections. In Leningrad, the reforming figure of lawyer Anatoly Sobchak, a stalwart supporter of further freedoms, took over the mayors' office. On May Day the traditional march of Communist glory turned into a protest, and Gorbachev was jeered off the podium on Lenin's mausoleum. Shortly afterwards Yeltsin declared Russian independence from the Soviet Union and in July, in front of TV cameras at the Party Congress, he tore up his membership card. By the end of the year, two million other members had followed suit. In reaction to the threatened anarchy, Gorbachev and the hardliners retrenched. Eduard Shevardnadze's prophetic warning of a coming dictatorship as he resigned in December was borne out by the brutal violence used by Soviet troops trying to quash the nationalist uprisings in the Baltic Republics in January. But the tide of history was behind the secessionists, and by May 1991 Estonia, Latvia and Lithuania had all reestablished their independence. The following month, the people of Leningrad asserted their own identity by voting to restore the city's original name, St Petersburg.

It was the overwhelming victory of Yeltsin in the June elections for President of the Russian Republic, making him the first Russian leader ever to be elected, that gave him the confidence and authority to overturn the Communist system in the wake of the August coup attempt against Gorbachev. While Gorbachev was away on holiday, the country found itself under the 'protection' of a group of hardliners who had formed the 'State Committee for the State of Emergency in the USSR'. It was a shoddily planned coup, for while Gorbachev was under house arrest in the Crimea, the plotters' real enemies, the radical reformers, were never captured. Yeltsin made his way clandestinely to the White House, seat of the Russian parliament on the banks of the River Moskva, and led a three-day vigil against the threat of encroaching troops. By the second night, protective barricades were manned by upwards of 100,000 people, and the bewildered young soldiers in the surrounding tanks had been persuaded not to act. That evening three young men were crushed to death beneath the tracks of a tank on the nearby Garden Ring, but by the next day most divisions had come over to the democrats. In St Petersburg the military stayed off the streets, though a crowd of pro-democracy supporters rallied round Anatoly Sobchak to defend the Mariinsky Palace. On the third day, the coup attempt collapsed. Some of the plotters responded in time-honoured Russian fashion by drinking themselves into a stupor; another committed suicide.

Gorbachev returned within hours, ashen-faced, as if to a new planet. Two days later, he was demolished on live television by Yeltsin, who forced him to sign a decree declaring the Communist Party, of which he was still a loyal supporter, illegal. The Russian flag flew for the first time since the Revolution, in place of the hammer and sickle. During the rest of the year, the Soviet Union disappeared as the Ukraine, Belarus, Georgia and other republics declared their independence, only to ally themselves loosely with Russia again in the new Commonwealth of Independent States. Gorbachev, the emperor without an empire, resigned on Christmas Day 1991.

The Trials Begin

The rest of the 1990s have been an exhausting emotional and economic roller-coaster for Russia and her people. The immediate attempt to transform the command economy to a market economy with a short, sharp shock was wishful thinking. No infrastructure existed for the mechanisms of the market—no banking system, no legal safeguards, an inadequate distribution network—and most of Russian industry was so far from competitive that it needed completely rebuilding, not privatising.

1992 saw a 500 per cent rise in the price of some foodstuffs and rocketing inflation. Savings that would have kept a couple in comfortable retirement for over 20 years were suddenly worth US$40, and providing a safety net for the millions of Russians living below the poverty line became a political imperative. The dynamic young monetarist Prime Minister Yegar Gaidar was replaced by the Soviet-era industrialist Viktor Chernomyrdin, who turned out to be less of a hardliner than many feared.

Fighting between the executive and legislative arms of government has been one of the defining political battles of the 1990s. Newly entrusted with the right to oppose, parliamentarians have ignored calls for consensus at a time of national emergency, and have used their rights to the full. For its part Yeltsin's executive has not broken entirely with Russia's totalitarian past and has sometimes made high-handed use of its executive powers, seeking to increase them wherever possible. The most serious conflict came in October 1993 when Yeltsin disbanded the unruly parliament and its leaders, Ruslan Khasbulatov and Alexander Rutskoi, occupied the White House, while troops loyal to Yeltsin beseiged the building from the outside. The parliamentarians' supporters, a strange mixture of old-guard Communists and Slavic nationalists known as the Red-Brown coalition, stormed the nearby mayor's office and went on to try to take over the state TV and radio network at Ostankino in the north of the city. After a long stand-off, early on 4 October government troops finally moved into action. The confrontations, particularly at Ostankino, were violent, and in the course of 24 hours 62 people died. Shelling of the White House set the building on fire, and at 6pm Khasbulatov and Rutskoi gave themselves up.

The results of the December 1993 elections surprised everyone with the strength of the vote for the erroneously named Liberal Democratic Party led by Vladimir Zhirinovsky, who attempted to capitalize on Russia's natural xenophobia. He ranted against the ungrateful republics who had seceded from the former Soviet Union, and vowed to rebuild Russia's military strength and solve her economic problems. With the powers invested in him by the new Constitution however, Yeltsin was largely able to continue the business of government unhampered.

A poor turn-out in St Petersburg's local elections in 1994 left the city without a legislative assembly for most of that year, during which Mayor Sobchak capitalised on his reputation for extravagant entertaining, hosting both the Goodwill Games and visits by two members of the British royal family, Prince Charles and the Queen. Little was done, however, to improve the lot of the average Petersburgers, who began to resent the lifestyle of their elected leader.

War in the secessionist republic of Chechnya began in December 1994, putting further pressure on Russia's limping economy, while the Russian body count alienated many of the government's supporters. Parliamentary elections in 1995 gave the Communists a leading position and their candidate, Gennady Zyuganov, was widely tipped to beat Yeltsin in the presidential elections of spring 1996. However, by now real power in Russia lay in the hands of an oligarchy of financial-industrial tycoons who had made millions during the privatization of Russia's assets and were not about to have their fortunes jeopardized by mere politicians. Putting the might of their extensive media empires behind President Yeltsin, they swung the election in his favour with their biased coverage.

Yeltsin co-opted one of his opponents, General Lebed, to end the bloody war in Chechnya, which he duly did, only to be rewarded with his own dismissal.

St Petersburg and the Millennium

In the summer of 1996 St Petersburg dismissed its mayor, replacing him with his deputy Vladimir Yakovlev who, in the reorganization of the local administration, became governor of the city. After an indecisive start, Yakovlev took the radical step of reducing state subsidies in such crucial areas as housing, provoking an outcry from both the local legislative assembly and his own voters. On the back of his balanced budget however, he managed to float a Eurobond issue for the city, which did wonders for St Petersburg's self-confidence and led to a rash of repairs and construction projects.

It wasn't until the assassination of Yakovlev's deputy, Mikhail Manevich, in August 1997, that the bubble burst. The true extent of the city's corruption and escalating crime wave could no longer be ignored, with ex-mayor Sobchak already under investigation, rumours circulating about the business activities of Yakovlev's family and figures for assassination and kidnapping lending credence to the city's reputation as a mafia stronghold. Assassinations continue to this day, one of the saddest being the death in November 1998 of Galina Starovoitova, a far-sighted member of the Russian parliament and early champion of human rights in post Soviet Russia. Police officers, members of the security services and even members of the St Petersburg government have all been arrested in connection with violent crimes.

Since the catastrophic financial crisis of August 1998 that led to the devaluation of the rouble, St Petersburg's confidence has been further diminished. Like Sleeping Beauty, the city slumbers while real life continues in Moscow, the only place in Russia where there are still jobs and money aplenty. Symbolic of the current nadir of St Petersburg's power was the fact that celebrations to mark the 200th anniversary of Pushkin, the city's beloved poet, were largely hijacked by Moscow in the summer of 1999.

For the visitor, the city's beauty remains undiminished and the appalling level of crime is rarely visible. The markedly democratic spirit of her current legislature is inspiring, but for the majority of her citizens life is hard. Savings were wiped out by the 1998 devaluation, pensions, student stipends and state wages are still paid several months in arrears and nothing gets cheaper. On top of the destabilizing effect of the millennium, Russia faces the end of the Yeltsin era in the year 2000, with the mayor of Moscow, Luzhkov, as the front-runner to replace him. How that will help St Petersburg in the run-up to her 300th birthday in 2003 remains to be seen.

Topics

Vodka

In 988, when Prince Vladimir was casting round for a religion for his people, he was forced to reject Islam because he knew that its prohibition on alcohol was an impossible condition. Since their earliest contacts with Russia, foreigners have remarked upon the symbiosis of the Russians and their tipple. In *The Travels of Olearius in Seventeenth Century Russia*, the Holsteiner Adam Olearius remarked that 'the vice of drunkenness is prevalent among this people in all classes, both secular and ecclesiastical, high and low, men and women, young and old... None of them anywhere, anytime, or under any circumstances lets pass an opportunity to have a draught or a drinking bout.' Foreign embassies were horrified to find that unless guests were made insensible from alcohol the host was not considered to have done his duty. During the reign of Peter the Great, the Danish Ambassador became so liverish that he offered to finance the building of an entire monastery if the Tsar would only stop forcing him to drink himself into a coma. Old habits die hard, as you will doubtless find out. Bear in mind the wisdom of Anton Chekhov, who remarked that though 'Vodka is white...it paints your nose red and blackens your reputation'.

For centuries, the Russians' favourite tipple has been vodka (literally the 'little water'), a distilled grain spirit which is said to have been invented by monks in the 15th century. The most common brands today are Moskovskaya or Stolichnaya, though if you know where to look you can also find *limonnaya* (lemon), *pertsovka* (red chilli) and *zubrovka* (bison grass) vodkas. Since a bottle of the real thing is often beyond the reach of the average Russian purse, home-brew, known as *samogon*, now finds its way on to the market, packaged as the real thing, only cheaper. To be sure that your purchase is genuine vodka you will have to take advice from an experienced local who will be able to tell from a number of pointers, including the speed at which bubbles travel through the liquid. Those who know they can't afford the national tipple slake their indigenous thirst on a variety of 100% proof colourless liquids known generically as 'spirit' (*spirt*). As living proof that it won't kill you, my only advice is to make sure that your shots are watered down.

Invitations to drink are often signalled by flicking the neck with your middle finger off your thumb. This is said to originate from a brilliant soldier whom Peter the Great rewarded with a tattoo beneath his beard. At the sight of the tattoo, any publican was obliged to serve the soldier as much vodka as he wanted for free. Vodka should be drunk freezing cold, though no self-respecting Russian would wait if the bottle in question happened not to be. Otherwise, the etiquette varies little. The vodka is poured into small glasses, filled almost to the rim. Diluting it with tonic or orange juice is sacrilege. A toast is proposed, the shortest and most common of which is *na zdoroviye*, 'good health'. The assembled company raise their glasses and down the fiery spirit in one, followed by a *zakuska* or snack—a piece of pickled fish or mushroom, a slice of cucumber or at the very least a piece of bread.

The Mafia

You can't talk about Russia today without referring to the cabals of men and women who have hijacked the most profitable areas of business and run them as their private fiefdoms. Known collectively as the mafia, they are not one cohesive group but a myriad of power bases, best defined by their organized and illegal business practices, and the violence with which they protect their turf. They vary in size and importance from a small ring of criminals running prostitutes in a regional hotel to the networks that control Russian politics and the media. The mafia is so rampant that there is barely a business in the country that isn't involved, if only by paying protection money.

The mafia is not simply a result of the official changeover to capitalism and the market economy. Just as prohibition created its own very profitable market in alcohol in the United States in the 1930s, so the empty shelves of the old Soviet Union hid a vast network of profitable markets in hard-to-obtain consumer goods, in the party membership that was vital for promotion beyond a certain level and in taboo luxury items. Unlike the 'private' mafia structures in the capitalist world, because of the centralized structure of production the extensive Soviet mafia inevitably included state officials who were bribed to procure sought-after items. In the largest exposé of public corruption, the so-called 'White-gold' cotton scandal unearthed in Uzbekistan in the 1980s, every single party and *komsomol* member, state and trade union employee and economic manager in the republic was shown to be implicated. They could not all be jailed and, as elsewhere, their fraternities of mutual advancement lived on, well-placed to exploit the privatised possibilities of the new post-Soviet era.

Ironically, the widespread, secretive corruption of the Soviet mafia, which included high-ranking, die-hard Communist Party members such as General Secretary Leonid Brezhnev, was partly responsible for the demise of the Soviet system. By milking the already tottering state, weakened to a point of near political and economic bankruptcy, the mafia hastened the advent of Gorbachev's *perestroika*. The directors of new businesses continued to exploit their 'friendship' with state officials, and began to exploit the new opportunities thrown up by the changing situation. State money which had been salted away in Swiss bank accounts found its way back into the country as the foreign contribution to joint-venture companies. Those in charge of the privatization of state assets, ignoring the obvious illegality of insider trading, have put profitable business the way of their friends and associates at knock-down prices. Protection rackets in St Petersburg feed on new private businesses; unprotected by the ever-changing laws, the fledgling enterprises are easy prey. The contraction of the Russian armed forces and their withdrawal from the countries of the former Warsaw Pact has given rise to rampant profiteering and the sale of weapons and equipment by disillusioned officers. Journalist after journalist has paid for their investigations into high-level corruption with their life, while in 1997 even St Petersburg's deputy governor was assassinated.

As a tourist, you are very unlikely to come across the mafiosi, except in the cities' smarter restaurants where you may unwittingly rub shoulder pads. When shopping in the fruit and vegetable markets, you are inevitably dealing with the protected business of the southern republics who produce the goods—the Georgians, Azeris and Uzbeks. Beware of prostitutes, who are often controlled by groups intent on profiting from your wallet without any services rendered. The Russian mafia is now thought to play a major role in the trafficking of opiates from the Golden Triangle in Southeast Asia to Europe and USA, so you should also steer well clear of drug deals.

The wealth of the Russian mobsters is now legendary and international, with court cases brought against Russian godfathers in New York. An adversary of a mafia group from the breakaway republic of Chechnya has been murdered in North London, and estate agents in nearby ritzy Hampstead have reputedly been inundated by requests for million-pound pads, paid for with ready cash in suitcases.

Rasputin

Born in a village in Siberia in about 1862, Grigory Efimovich Rasputin's life ended with his murder in St Petersburg in 1916. The strange story of his rise from peasant wagoner to royal confidant is one of the best known in Russian history, and yet one of the most widely misunderstood. To call him the first Bolshevik, as did his murderer Yusupov, is only the most absurd of the myriad theories. His success can only be understood in the light of age-old Russian traditions, linked to the political climate of the early 20th century and to the specific characters involved in his drama.

Since the Middle Ages there has been a tradition of holy fools and wandering holy men, known as *startsi* (singular—*starets*), in Russia. Some have exerted a purely local influence, wandering from village to village dispensing wisdom and advice, whilst the fame of others has reached the ears of the highest in the land. In the 16th century Ivan the Terrible built St Basil's Cathedral over the tomb of a holy fool, Basil the Blessed, whose prophesies he had found so accurate. Even closer links between royalty and the *startsi* were forged in the 19th century. To this day there is currency in the rumour that Tsar Alexander I did not die at Taganrog but faked his demise so as to retire in solitude to Siberia. Alexander is said to have become a holy hermit in repentance for his part in the murder of his father Tsar Paul I (*see* **History**, p.36).

When tales of Rasputin's wisdom began to circulate in St Petersburg, it is hardly surprising that he was introduced to the devout royal couple. By 1907 Rasputin was a well-travelled 45-year-old, who had spent time in the monasteries of Mount Athos as well as the Holy Land. What is more, he was said to have powers of healing and, unbeknownst to the general population, the royal household was in dire need of such help. After the birth of four daughters, Alexandra had finally borne a son in 1904, only to discover that he had inherited the life-threatening blood-disorder haemophilia. In 1907, when Rasputin was first called to minister to the young boy, Nicholas II noted in his diary that 'Alexei was saved from certain death by his [Rasputin's] prayers'. For the next nine years, Rasputin acted as a fairy godfather to the boy, soothing him with his words and hands, and kneeling in a vigil of prayer beside his bed in times of danger. In 1912 when doctors feared for the tsarevich's life after a fall, a telegram was dispatched to Rasputin in Siberia. As soon as his reply was received the boy began to recover. 'The illness is not as dangerous as it seems,' the telegram read; 'don't let the doctors worry him.' Whether you believe in such powers, or whether the holy man's effect had more to do with the family's desire to believe in his powers, there is little doubt that Rasputin did save the tsarevich on a number of occasions.

What is equally undeniable is how strange all this must have looked from outside the royal circle. Knowing little of the tsarevich's illness or the *starets'* effect upon it, the gossip of St Petersburg was Rasputin's debauched behaviour, the other side of the 'saintly' character which the tsarina so admired. At gypsy restaurants Rasputin was frequently reported leading the way in binges of feasting, drinking and dancing, foul-mouthing members of the aristocracy and the government and crawling drunk into his carriage on the arm of at least one if not two voluptuous women. The list of women hypnotized into his bed by his staring green eyes and knowing looks is legendary. His flat at Gorokhovaya Ul. 64 was constantly watched by the police. His last telephone number was St Petersburg 64646, not far removed from 666—the Number of The Beast.

At the beginning of the First World War, the German tsarina's popularity dipped to an all-time low. When Nicholas went off to the front, she was left in the company of the holy man, whose advice in matters of politics she passed on faithfully to the tsar, who often took it. By the end of 1916, when reverses at the front were met by starvation at home, there was a clamour to end his backward-looking influence. The ruling classes found it impossible to attack the tsar directly, and vented their anger on this strange figure who had captivated the tsar and tsarina to the point where ministers were chosen on his whim.

Vladimir Purishkevich was a member of the Duma (parliament), and held extreme monarchist beliefs. On 18 November he delivered a stinging appeal to his fellow parliamentarians to save the tsar from the 'dark forces' threatening him. Listening from the public gallery was Felix Yusupov (*see* p.112). The following day he rang Purishkevich, inviting him to join him in killing the 'holy man'. Yusupov lured Rasputin to his palace on the banks of the Moika Canal (*see* pp.111–13) on the pretext of a party. He and his fellow conspirators—Purishkevitch, the tsar's cousin Grand Duke Dmitry, an army doctor called Lazovert and an officer named Sukhotin—attempted to poison the *starets*. When this failed, they tried shooting him. Then, with the connivance of the police, who shot a dog to account for the blood, Rasputin's body was taken to the far side of town and thrown under the ice of a tributary of the Neva, where it was found three days later, his hands clinging to the supports of a bridge. Where poison and four bullets had failed, drowning eventually succeeded. Yet Rasputin's death solved nothing. The licentious holy man was only a symptom of the real cause of the people's misery—the stubborn conservatism of the autocracy itself. Within months the February Revolution had dethroned the tsar and swept away the monarchy.

Icons and Iconostases

In the Orthodox church an icon is a religious painting, depicting Christ, the saints, or an episode from the holy texts. The name derives from the Greek word *eikon*, meaning image. Unlike Western European religious art, icons are more than mere images. They are venerated by worshippers, who address prayers to them in the belief that they will be heard and acted upon by the particular saint in heaven.

The tradition of icon-painting finds its earthly roots in the earliest painted portraits, found around the Egyptian town of Fayum and dating to the time of Christ. They are lively, intimate portraits, painted on wooden boards and buried with the deceased they represent. The idea of portable images attracted an early Christian following, since the icons could be carried away by the believers during periods of persecution. The spiritual roots of icon painting are more complex, beginning with the legends of the portraits St Luke is said to have painted of his contemporaries. A great icon should reflect the perfect harmony of the eternal world, and to prepare themselves for this mystical task, icon-painters would often fast and go through long rituals of physical and spiritual cleansing before beginning an icon. In this aspect icons can act as the focus of meditation on the nature of the holy. Mirroring the belief that Jesus was God's incarnation on earth, icons are also an incarnation of the unknowable and invisible. They should act as a window on the transcendant reality of Christian beliefs. And because of the reverse perspective used by icon painters, instead of being independent of the image, the viewer or worshipper is pulled into the picture. He finds himself standing at the point of infinity, playing a vital role in the spiritual matrix which defines the boundaries of the image.

The iconostasis or wall of icons in which icons are traditionally hung in a church is like a cosmological diagram. The bottom row is known as the **Local Tier**, and contains icons with a specific relevance to the church—such as icons depicting the saints after whom it is named and after whom its patrons were named. At the centre of the Local Tier you will find the **Royal Gates**, normally decorated with panels showing the four apostles and the Annunciation. Above this comes the most important **Deesis Tier**, where full-length representations of the saints intercede on behalf of humanity, with Christ enthroned at the centre of the tier. To the left and right of Christ you will always find the Virgin Mary and St John the Baptist respectively, often flanked by the Archangels Michael and Gabriel. The rest of the tier is usually made up of disciples, apostles and local saintly bishops. Above the Deesis Tier comes the **Festival Tier**, in which the great feast days of the Orthodox Church are celebrated. At a minimum, these normally include scenes of the Birth of the Virgin, the Presentation of the Virgin in the Temple, the Annunciation, the Nativity, the Presentation of Christ in the Temple, the Baptism, Christ's Entry into Jerusalem, the Crucifixion, the Descent into Hell, the Ascension, the Old Testament Trinity and the Dormition of the Virgin. The **upper row** depicts the patriarchs and prophets of the Old Testament leaning towards a central icon of the Virgin Mary.

By the time Russia adopted Orthodoxy from Constantinople in the 10th century, strict rules had been drawn up governing the painting of icons. Since many of the early icons were said to have been painted by St Luke himself, they were holy relics. Just like any reproduction of the Bible, icons were not intended as original works of art but copies, and it was out of the question to change any detail of the original. The composition of each image had been carefully studied and given a name, depending on the exact position, dress and pose of its subject. Most of the earliest icons surviving in Russia were either imported from elsewhere or painted by foreign masters who had come to answer the needs of the new Orthodox nation. In the 15th century Russian icon painting came into its own, with a brief, superb flowering begun by a foreigner known as Theofan the Greek and continued by two native masters Andrei Rublyov and Dionisy. The best examples of their works are to be found now in the Tretyakov Gallery in Moscow, the Russian Museum in St Petersburg, and in the iconostases of the Cathedral of the Annunciation in the Kremlin, and the Cathedral of the Trinity at the Trinity Sergius Monastery in Sergeyev Posad. Very little is known of the lives of any of these celebrated painters, but those with a serious interest should watch Tarkovsky's film *Andrei Rublyov* for its evocation of the spirit of medieval Russian icon painting.

Until the Revolution, an icon hung in the corner of almost every room in the land, known as the Red Corner (*krasny ugol*). Very often these were directly replaced by cheaply reproduced images of Lenin, Marx and Engels, prophets of the new religion, but today you will again find small lamps burning before icons in many a home.

Superstitions

There are few more superstitious people in the developed world than the Russians. Every day on national television, after the evening news and weather, a serious man or woman in a donnish gown reads the nation's horoscopes to a devoted audience. Even Russian literature is said to have been saved by superstition. In 1825, as Alexander Sergeyevich Pushkin set out from his country estate to join the Decembrist Uprising in St Petersburg, a hare crossed his path in an unlucky omen. The poet and father of Russian literature returned home, and lived on to write his most important works including the epic poem *Eugene Onegin*.

To avoid a terrible *faux pas*, you may find it useful to bear the following in mind when visiting Russians. It is considered bad luck to shake hands or kiss across a threshold, and also bad luck to give even numbers of flowers, on any occasion except at a funeral. Walking around in bare socks in a flat is thought to bode a death in the family, so always accept the offer of a pair of slippers (*toofli*) that will be made. You may think it a blessing, but bear in mind that as a woman if you sit at the corner of the table it is said that you will not marry for seven years. When there is a silence in the conversation, the Russians think nothing as optimistic as that there is an angel flying overhead. To them, it means another policeman has just been born. Before you leave the house on a journey of any length, you should sit down for a minute on your bags. If you leave something behind, it is said to be bad luck to return for it.

Fabergé

Few words conjure up the opulent world of *fin de siècle* Europe so vividly as the name of the Russian pre-Revolutionary court jeweller Carl Gustavovich Fabergé. Of French Huguenot origin, the Fabergé family had fled persecution in 17th-century France, but it was not until the mid 19th-century that they entered the jewellery business. Gustave Fabergé opened a small shop in the Imperial capital, St Petersburg, in 1842, and four years later his son Carl, the genius of the family, was born.

Carl Fabergé studied with a leading German goldsmith and travelled to the great centres of craftsmanship in Italy and France before taking over the family business in St Petersburg in 1870 at the age of 24. Carl was gifted with a brilliant, naturalistic talent for design, incorporating and to a certain extent anticipating the trends of the Arts and Crafts and Art Nouveau movements towards an interest in materials for their own sake and not merely for their monetary value. Fabergé used rock crystal and semi-precious marbles as well as diamonds and precious metals, and even the boxes they came in, hand crafted from polished holly-wood with white silk linings, were works of art.

It comes as no surprise that the most famous jeweller of all time should have lived and worked in turn-of-the-century Russia, a land abundant with precious and semi-precious stones and metals. The first 30 years of Carl's 47-year supremacy coincided with the greatest economic boom in Russian history. In 1885 Carl became court jeweller to the Romanov dynasty, and though it is estimated that the income of Nicholas II, the last of Russia's tsars, was less than 25 per cent that of the British royal family at the time, the Russian royals were conspicuous spenders. As well as personal presents for friends and relatives, Fabergé designed and produced decorations and official gifts. Fabergé's fame, however, stems from the fabulous, bejewelled Easter eggs which they made for the tsars.

In 1885, Alexander III was casting round for a present for his homesick Danish wife when he commissioned Carl Fabergé to copy an egg, containing a jewelled hen, from the Danish royal collection. So pleased was the tsarina with her gift that Alexander continued the tradition every year, allowing Fabergé complete freedom of design and finding his family enchanted by the imaginative results. When his son Nicholas II ascended the throne, he ordered two eggs to be made every year—one for his mother, the Dowager Empress, and one for his wife. The design was a complete secret, always incorporating an element of surprise and often taking some topical event, such as the coronation or the inauguration of the new Trans-Siberian railway, as its theme. The eggs would be presented by a member of the Fabergé family in person, an occasion which came to be the focus of enormous anticipation. Of the 54 eggs crafted for the Romanovs, 47 survive. Ten are still in the Kremlin collection, the rest scattered throughout the world. The Imperial Fabergé egg record holder is the collection of the now-deceased American publishing mogul Malcolm Forbes, which includes 11 of the Imperial creations. However Fabergé also created eggs for other royal families and extravagant individuals. Anyone wanting to purchase an egg should bear in mind that the last one to come onto the market sold for US$5.5 million in November 1994. A cheaper alternative would be to visit the showroom of Fabergé's aesthetic heir, the jeweller Ananov, in the Grand Hotel Europe on St Petersburg's Nevsky Prospekt.

Tapochki

Any definition of these infuriating felt over-shoes, designed to protect the ubiquitous parquet in Russian palaces, would be incomplete without mention of their secondary, unintentional effect on their wearer's dignity. You will find yourself forced into them in most museum lobbies, and from the moment you begin to try to find a pair the right size, the battle begins. The felt is matted and grimy to the touch, the elastic looks as if it has been borrowed from pre-war knickers and if you are lucky enough to get a pair with ties, there will probably only be one of them.

Having negotiated your boots or shoes into them, you will then discover that *tapochki* have a life of their own. One way or another, when it comes to going up or down stairs your pair of pedal gloves will be lagging behind or ahead of your feet, catching themselves on the steps in a determined effort to trip you up. There is no alternative to suffering this indignity, though it may be helpful to remember the floor-polishers of yesteryear whose entire working life was spent encased in these wretched contraptions. Carrying the tools of their trade with them, they would be called to aristocratic palaces before parties to skate up and down the parquet of the ballroom, shining it with their custom-built, polish-sodden *tapochki*. As Eugenie Fraser recalls in her book *The House by the Dvina*, 'crossing one arm behind his back each man skated over the floor, the leg with the attached brush swinging back and fore in a wide sweep while the other dragged behind twisting and hopping' until 'their damp shirts clung to their backs'.

Walking has been a pastime in St Petersburg ever since foreigners first came here in the 18th century. After midday, Nevsky Prospekt, the main thoroughfare of the city, would be thronged with citizens and strangers alike, some on foot, others in speeding carriages. As well as shopping, people promenaded to flirt, pick up the latest gossip, and simply to be seen. Even today, there is nothing more characteristic of the city than this seething showcase of humanity. Housewives go about their business with grim-faced determination, while choleric would-be politicians harangue their opposition, artists woo potential sitters and children pick the pockets of unwary tourists. Walking the length of the street is left to you, for, though a number of these walks cover parts of Nevsky Prospekt, they concentrate on leading you off into the less obvious nooks and crannies of the city. You will be able to recognize the entrances to the many art galleries, 19th-century department stores, basement bars and cafés that punctuate the ground-floor façades.

The Walks: Introduction

For a calmer summer introduction to the 'Venice of the North', there could be nothing better than a boat. In a city built on no less than 44 islands, the waterways once constituted an important method of transport. Just as in Venice, all of the smartest St Petersburg palaces faced a canal or river, and their liveried barges could be seen dodging the delivery vessels of Nevsky Prospekt's major retailers right up until the Revolution. Today, activity on the water is less frenetic, largely confined to the occasional tourist boat (*see* p.195). If you want to be sure of an English-language guide, or to organize something out of the ordinary, call ✆ 325 2954.

Before setting out on any of the following itineraries, there are a few vital things to bear in mind. Make sure that your sightseeing is not going to be scuppered by the dreaded *sanitarny dyen*, particularly if you are here in the first or last week of the month: every museum and gallery is closed one day a month for what is supposed to be a thorough clean; these days are noted in the text.

If it is cold or wet, take taxis or public transport (though St Petersburg's is unbearably crowded) between the highlights of each walk. These are asterisked with a snowflake on the title page of each excursion. In winter it gets dark at about 3pm, so you must start in good time in the morning. Many of the city's cultural monuments are closed on Mondays and Tuesdays. However, **Walks I and II** are ideally suited to the first day of the week, and the labyrinthine Hermitage (**Walk VII**) is also open on Tuesdays.

If you get lost and have trouble making yourself understood, refer to the list of changed street names on pp.293–4. Your helpful Petersburger may be more familiar with the old names than new.

A Taste of St Petersburg

Imperial Splendour in the **Winter Palace** and at the **Catherine Palace** in Tsarskoye Selo.

Waking the Sleeping Beauty: St Petersburg's musical heritage is best appreciated at the **Mariinsky Theatre** or in the **Shostakovich Philharmonia**.

In search of Crime and Punishment: Dostoyevsky's creations haunt **Haymarket Square** (Sennaya Ploshchad), while the man himself can be found at the **Dostoyevsky Flat Museum**.

Beastly Bridges: walk between gold-winged griffons on **Bank Bridge** (Bankovsky Most), open-mouthed lions on **Lion Bridge** (Lviny Most) and rearing stallions on **Anichkov Bridge**.

Dive back into a bright new future. Make your way to the **Russian Museum** for avant-garde art from the turn of the century and some of the earliest abstract work in the world.

Suspended between Heaven and Earth: at the **Cathedral of St Nicholas** or the **Buddhist Temple**.

Soviet Sensations at the **Museum of Russian Political History**, the **Cruiser Aurora** and before **Lenin's Statue** outside Finland Station.

Pursuing the Petersburg Poets: Search for the site of Pushkin's fatal duel at **Chyornaya Rechka** and experience the chill outside the **Kresty Prison** where Anna Akhmatova spent hundreds of hours queuing for news of her son during the Great Terror.

Heroism and Hunger during the Siege: the **Piskarovskoye Memorial Cemetery** and the **Monument to the Defenders of Leningrad**.

Retail Therapy: **Kuznechny Market** for fresh or dried mushrooms and divine Siberian honey, **Yeliseyev's** for the Soviet equivalent of the Harrods Food Halls and **Gostiny Dvor** for souvenirs and browsing.

Nocturnal Ramblings: anywhere during the **White Nights**, but particularly the banks of the Neva and the Summer Gardens. Step back in time in the cobbled alleys of the **St Peter and Paul Fortress** by lamplight.

Start: *Decembrists' Square (Ploshchad Dekabristov),* Ⓜ *Nevsky Prospekt/Gostiny Dvor. Leave via Nevsky Prospekt, using the Canal Griboyedova* (Канал Грибоедова) *exit. Turn right and walk down Nevsky Prospekt until you see trees stretching away to the left. Turn left on to Admiraltyesky Prospekt and right at the back of St Isaac's Cathedral. Through the trees ahead rears the horseback statue of Peter the Great on Decembrists' Square. From Nevsky Prospekt, trolleybuses 5 and 14 will take you to St Isaac's Square, on the other side of the cathedral, and bus 22 goes to Admiraltyesky Prospekt.*

Walking Time: *3½ hours. Start after 10.15am or you may be too early for the fortress.*

I: The Founding Father

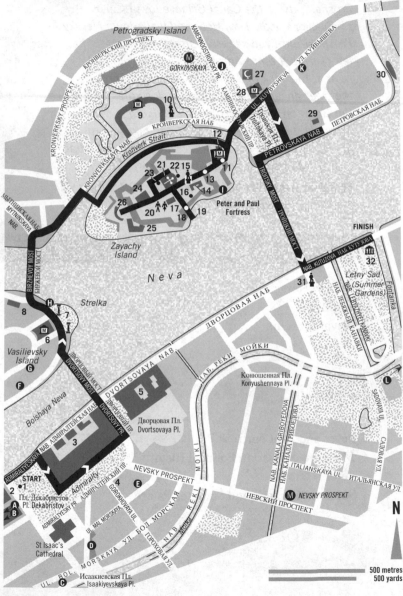

Sites

1 The Bronze Horseman
Medny vsadnik
Медный всадник

2 Senate and Synod Building
Zdaniye Senata i Synoda
Здание Сената и Синода

3 Admiralty
Admiralteystvo
Адмиралтейство

4 Cheka
Чека

5 Winter Palace (Hermitage)
Zimny dvorets (Ermitazh)
Зимний дворец

6 Stock Exchange/Naval Museum
Birzha/Voyenno-Morskoy muzei
Биржа/Военно-Морской музей

7 Rostral Columns
Rostralniye kolonny
Ростральные колонны

8 Pushkin House (Institute of Russian Literature)
Pushkinsky dom
Пушкинский дом

9 Artillery Museum
Voyenno-Istorichesky muzei artillerii
Военно-Исторический музей артиллерии

10 Decembrists' Monument
Pamyatnik Dekabristov
Памятник Декабристов

Sites inside Peter and Paul Fortress

11 Ivan Gate
Ivanovskiye vorota
Ивановские ворота

12 Museum of the Gas-Dynamics Laboratory
Muzei Gazodinamicheskaya Laboratoria
Музей Газодинамическая Лаборатория

13 St Peter's Gate
Petrovskiye vorota
Петровские ворота

14 Engineers' House
Inzhenerny dom
Инженерный дом

15 Sculpture of Peter the Great
Statuya Petra Velikovo
Статуа Петра Великого

16 Main Guardhouse
Gauptvakhta
Гауптвахта

17 Commandant's House
Ober-Komendantsky dom
Обер-Комендантский дом

18 Neva Gate
Nevskiye vorota
Невские ворота

19 Commandant's Pier
Ober-Komendantskaya pristan
Обер-Комендантская пристань

20 Toilets
Tualety
Туалеты

21 Cathedral of SS Peter and Paul
Petropavlovsky sobor
Петропавловский собор

22 Grand Ducal Burial Vault
Usypalnitsa
Усыпальница

23 Boathouse
Domik Botika
Домик Ботика

24 Mint
Monetny dvor
Монетный двор

25 Trubetskoy bastion
Трубецкой бацион

26 Alexeyevsky Ravelin
Алексеевский равелин

27 Mosque
Mechet
Мечеть

28 Museum of Russian Political History
Muzei russkoy politicheskoy istorii
Музей русской политической истории

29 Cabin of Peter the Great
Muzei domik Petra I
Музей домик Петра I

30 Cruiser Aurora
Kreiser Avrora
Крейсер Аврора

31 Statue of Suvorov
Statuya Suvorova
Статуя Суворова

32 Summer Palace
Letny dvorets
Летний дворец

Restaurants and Cafés

A Bistro 'Le Français'
Бистро 'Le Français'

B Crocodile Bar
Бар Крокодил

C Nikolai
Николай

D Hotel Astoria
Gostinitsa Astoria
Гостиница Астория

E Sevillia
Севиллиа

F The Old Customs House
Staraya Tamozhnya
Старая Таможня

G Academia
Академия

H Café
Кафе

I Austeria
Остерия

J Grand Café Antwerpen
Гранд Кафе Антверпен

K Café Fortetsia
Кафе Фортеция

L Café Ambassador
Кафе Амбассадор

On one side the sea, on the other sorrow,
On the third moss, on the fourth a sigh.

the court jester, on the site of nascent St Petersburg

Were it not for one man possessed by a single-minded vision of his country's future, there would be no city at all here today. Peter the Great is one of the colossi of history, a controversial and pivotal figure in the development of his nation. To some he is a demi-god, to others the Antichrist. Some see his dictatorial programme of Europeanization—forcing the boyars to invite women to their parties and to introduce their children to their prospective spouses six weeks before the wedding day—as a civilizing influence. Others point to his murder of his own son, his enjoyment of torture and his encouragement of denunciation to argue that Peter was just another link in a chain of despotism reaching from the mists of medieval Muscovy to Stalin's purges. What is incontrovertible is his effect on Russia's subsequent history, of which his madcap scheme to build a new capital city here, and its exquisite, timeless result, is a symbol.

This itinerary noses out the few varied buildings, dotted around the city centre, which survive from Peter's pioneering days. You will find as many Petersburgers enjoying their unique waterfront as tourists, and a clutch of buskers enlivening their patch of turf. There's jazz and violins in the Peter and Paul Fortress, which lay at the heart of the early settlement. The floor of its Baroque cathedral bristles with the sarcophagi of the Romanovs from Peter onwards, including the last tsar, only recently laid to rest. Peter's first home in the city, a two-room log cabin of archetypal Russian design, faces his European-looking Summer Palace built a decade later.

The once hard-line Museum of the Revolution has metamorphosed into the Museum of Russian Political History, though it is still the best place to see good Soviet memorabilia. Private dealers do a roaring trade in tackier Soviet souvenirs on the banks of the Kronverk Strait. At noon on Fridays the exotic turquoise mosque, one of the most northerly on earth, brings out the city's hidden Muslim population. Avoid this walk on Tuesdays, Wednesdays and the last Monday of the month. Sadly, the Summer Palace is also closed from 11 November to 30 April.

lunch/cafés

A **Bistro 'Le Français'**, Ul. Galyernaya 20, ✆ 315 2465; *open 11am–1am*. A corner of Paris tucked away behind the Senate and Synod building at the start of the walk—try the gungy onion soup with a crust of melted cheese, followed by *steak frites* or salmon.

B **Crocodile Bar**, Ul. Galyernaya 18, ✆ 314 9437; *open 12–3*. Lunchtime bar with good food and a lovely atmosphere.

C **Nikolai**, in Dom Arkhitektorov, Bolshaya Morskaya Ul. 52, ✆ 311 1402; *open 12 noon–11pm, closed weekends*. The Architects' Union is a professional club that responded to the economic squeeze by opening its doors to all comers. The food is predictable—soups and cold *zakuski* followed by a meat or fish dish with potatoes—but the joy of the place is its panelled dining rooms and quiet, mixed-sex clubby atmosphere. There's also the **Matador** bar downstairs.

D **Hotel Astoria** and **Hotel Angleterre**, Bolshaya Morskaya Ul. 39, ✆ 210 5757; *open 9am–12 midnight*. The best place to get a coffee to set you up for the walk is in one of the two ground floor hotel café/bars here. Sit down with a frothy cappuccino or an espresso and a slice of cake. The **Winter Garden Restaurant** serves good, if formal, *à la carte* lunches to the tinkling of a piano.

E **Sevillia**, Malaya Morskaya Ul. 7, ✆ 315 5371. Spanish restaurant close to Nevsky Prospekt, serving delicious food, with an authentic Latin feel to the décor. The Spanish dancing in the evenings costs more.

F **The Old Customs House (Staraya Tamozhnya)**, Tamozhenny Per 1, ✆ 327 8980; *open 1pm–3am, credit cards accepted*. For a real splash, this five-star restaurant serves European cuisine in a high-class setting—make sure you look the part.

G **Academia**, 1st Birzhevoy Proezd, ✆ 327 8949; *open 12 noon–5am, with disco 9pm–12.30am; credit cards accepted*. Huge trendy delicious pizza restaurant.

I **Austeria**, Peter and Paul Fortress, Ioannovsky Ravelin, ✆ 238 4262; *open 12 noon–midnight*. Very good Russian cuisine and live music in the Petrine interior of this restaurant in the fortress (taxis can drive in to drop you there). Larger groups are well catered for, but it's worth booking in advance. There is a cheaper bar, **Kazenat**, attached to the restaurant, done up to look just like the inside of the prison that stands next to it; the bar also serves food.

J **Grand Café Antwerpen**, Kronverksky Prospekt 13/2, ✆ 233 9746; *open 1–11pm*. This sparkling clean restaurant is a good lunch option with Russian-European food, and a **café** next door for snacks (*open 12 noon–12 midnight*). There are tables outside in summer, and live music from 7pm.

K **Café Fortetsia**, Kuybysheva Ul. 7, Petrograd Side, ✆ 233 9468; *open 12 noon–11pm*. In this red velour, brothel-style interior, dishes from the extensive Russian menu are carefully prepared and cooked from fresh ingredients. Avoid the fish options; try steak with mushroom sauce and chips instead, after a steaming bowl of *borshch*.

L **Café Ambassador**, Nab. Reki Fontanka 14, ✆ 272 9181; *open 1pm–5am*. Cosy, chintzy and gauzy, this small café prepares its large main courses attentively with plenty of fresh vegetables. The succulent stuffed peppers and tomatoes are a treat. Some of the friendly young staff speak English, and there is always some form of alcohol. Service can be a bit slow. Next door the smarter **Club Ambassador**, *open 1pm–12 midnight*, ✆ 272 3791, serves a very expensive menu in a mock-medieval candle-lit cavern.

71

*There is no better place to begin your acquaintance with St Petersburg here in **Decembrists' Square**, by the banks of the River Neva and Russia's most famous sculpture.*

Looking out over the broad flat waters to the watercoloured palaces beyond, it is hard to imagine the site as Pushkin describes it, before the horseback emperor ever clapped eyes on the place:

> *...here and there,*
> *On moss-grown, boggy shores a rare,*
> *Ramshackle hut loomed dark, the dwelling*
> *Of a humble Finn.*

Yet at the end of the tsar's reign in 1725, some 22 years later, there were 40,000 people, including all of Russia's leading families, living in stone houses on this flat marshland. Propping them up were many more, the skeletons of serfs, Swedish prisoners of war and convicts who died sinking piles into the unstable, disease-infested marsh.

In celebration of that double-edged achievement an admiring Catherine the Great, Peter's granddaughter-in-law, commissioned this equestrian **sculpture** from the French sculptor Etienne Falconet. By that time, the westernizing trend begun by Peter had reached such heights that Catherine consulted Diderot and Voltaire on her choice of a sculptor. Unveiled in 1782, it shows Peter firmly in control of his mount, Russia, her back hoof squashing the snake of Treason, his free hand out-stretched over the landscape he so brutally tamed. The two inscriptions, in Russian and Latin, state simply 'To Peter I from Catherine II 1782'. The wave-like granite base that bears them comes from a favourite hill of Peter's some kilometres from the city, known as Thunder Rock. This bit is said to have been split off by lightning, and it took an entire year for its bulk to be manhandled into its present position.

The sculpture towers above mere mortals much as the tsar did in his day. Peter was well over 6' 6" tall, and from early childhood his body had been spasmodically racked by terrifying physical convulsions, so that, while gracious and majestic of mien, he could seem severe and wild. Overall, says the Duc de Saint Simon, his 'manner announces wit, intelligence and grandeur and is not without a certain grace'. The head of the sculpture, more wild than gracious, was sculpted by Falconet's future daughter-in-law, Marie Collot.

Known as the **Bronze Horseman** (Myedny Vsadnik), the sculpture's importance was dramatically increased when it starred in Pushkin's 1833 epic poem of the same name. The poem's human protagonist, poor Yevgeny, loses his fiancée and his mind in the terrible 1824 flood of the city, and is chased through the ravaged and empty streets of his imagination by the terrifying, clattering sculpture, symbol of the autocratic state and of the destructive potential of Peter's unnatural city:

> *Across the empty square*
> *Yevgeny ran and seemed to hear*
> *Great, swelling, mighty peals of thunder*
> *And feel the pavement quaking under*
> *A horse's heavy hoofs. For there,*
> *Behind him, to the darkness wedded,*
> *Lit by the moon's pale ray and slight,*
> *One hand in warning raised, the dreaded*
> *Bronze Horseman galloped through the night...*

Yevgeny is the first of the now-familiar small men of Russian fiction, hounded by the whims of tsar and state. In Pushkin's nightmarish vision of St Petersburg there seems even to be a hint of the Revolution.

Until 1925, the square was known as Senate Square, after the ordered neoclassical **Senate and Holy Synod building** which still surrounds the arch to the west of the Bronze Horseman. It was built in 1829–32 by Carlo Rossi, a distinctly serious and formal building with sculptural and architectural details picked out in white, including the staples of classical architecture: porticoes, friezes, pediments and mythical bas-reliefs. The Senate, the supreme court of appeal and the body responsible for tax collection, occupied the northern end of the building; the ecclesiastical administration the other. Both institutions were originally created by Peter. The Senate governed while he was away fighting, while the Holy Synod replaced the office of the Patriarch, which he abolished in 1700, bringing the Church directly under his control. Today the building contains the State Historical Archives.

In 1925, however, the name was changed to commemorate Russia's first, unsuccessful revolution, the Decembrist Uprising of 14 December 1825, which took place on this square. A group of army officers used uncertainty over the succession after the death of Alexander I to persuade their soldiers to take up arms and press for a constitutional monarchy. The new tsar, Nicholas I, made short shrift of the rebels. The ice on the Neva was broken by heavy artillery to cut off their escape and soldiers fired straight into the crowd of 3,000. The five ringleaders were hanged and 130 others exiled to Siberia. Thus was choked 'the first cry of Russian freedom' beneath the steadfast gaze of Peter who, though revolutionary in his own way, disapproved strongly of such attempts to interfere in the God-given task of government.

> *Opposite the Senate and Synod building across the square, the similarly coloured walls of the Admiralty are obscured by trees. Walk into the* **Admiralty Gardens,** *away from the river.*

In summer, local beer companies set up small open-air cafés around here: look out for open parasols with beer slogans. Nearby, a Bactrian camel crouches beneath a bust of Prezhvalsky, the Russian Asiatic explorer best known to us for his discovery of the small wild horse named after him. Better known in Russia is the fact that he looks exactly like Stalin: there have been many attempts to put the explorer and the tyrant's mother in the same place at the appropriate time. The only certainty is that Prezhvalsky was in the same country at Stalin's conception. Such wicked speculations have an edge to them here, in the land where the poet Osip Mandelstam died in prison, arrested for likening Stalin's moustache to a cockroach.

In front of the main arch of the Admiralty, surrounding a large round fountain, are statues of the writers Lermontov and Gogol, and the composer Glinka, and in the garden beyond one of the Romantic poet who inspired Pushkin, Vassily Zhukovsky.

Appropriately the main thoroughfares of Nevsky Prospekt, Gorokhovaya Ulitsa and Voznesensky Prospekt radiate out from the **Admiralty Building**, as they did then. For one of Peter's main reasons for founding the city on the Neva was its proximity to the open sea. Peter was determined to create a navy, and was so successful that less than 70 years later, under Catherine the Great, the Russians defeated the veteran Ottoman sailors at the battle of Chesme. The exemplary neoclassical building that stands here today was built in 1806–23 by the architect Andreyan Zakharov. Its 218ft gilded spire, topped by a sailing ship weathervane which has become a symbol of the city, replaced an earlier spire rising from the single-storey admiralty and shipyard built here by Peter (1704–11). The original building was designed in the shape of the Russian letter Π (P) for Peter, and opened on to the Neva. Arcaded workshops surrounded the central slipways on which the early Russian fleet was built. Peter, who had himself studied ship-building in the Dutch yards of Zaadam and Amsterdam and at Deptford on the Thames, felt perhaps most at home in this tough labouring environment. He had travelled abroad incognito with a seal which stated only that 'I am in the ranks of the pupils and require instruction', and is often called the 'carpenter tsar'. When he came to dine here with the Lords of the Admiralty, he would insist on eating only naval rations of smoked beef washed down with beer, to the accompaniment of fife and drums playing in the tower. This was the tsar's most attractive quality—his ruthlessness and cruelty were equalled by his dogged humility in the face of his own ignorance, and he was always willing to labour next to any man in order to learn and encourage others to learn.

When the Admiralty was rebuilt in the early 19th century, it kept the same Π-shaped plan, merely adding a second Π inside the first and separating them by a canal. From the embankment this original plan has been completely obscured, as the last ship was built here in 1844 and buildings have taken over the central shipyard. However the garden façade of what is now the Dzerzhinsky Higher Naval Engineering Academy, founded in 1925, is little altered. The relief above the tall central arch depicts Neptune in his shell vessel, handing his trident, symbol of mastery of the seas, to Peter I (*The Establishment of the Russian Fleet*). Despite the fact that the Russian Orthodox Church demanded the removal of a number of 'pagan' statues in 1860, the corners of the attic are crowned with classical heroes: Alexander the Great, Achilles, Ajax and Pyrrhus. Above them, surrounding the tower, a perfectly proportioned portico supports 28 allegorical statues connected with the navy—the elements, seasons and muses of astronomy among them.

Opposite the Admiralty, the grey and white building at Admiraltyesky Prospekt 6 was the headquarters of the Bolshevik secret police, the Cheka, from December 1917 to March 1918 when it moved, with its boss 'Iron' Felix Dzerzhinsky and the rest of the government, to Moscow. It might seem an unlikely job for a Polish nobleman, but Dzerzhinsky got there by sheer dedication, going as far as to have his mother executed for counter-revolution. You can go in: the building is now a specialist **branch** of the **Museum of Russian Political History** (*see also* p.83; *open Mon–Fri 11–6*), with three small rooms displaying exhibits on the Cheka.

*Continue along the façade in the garden and turn left at the far corner of the building, beneath the decorative portico. The square ahead is Palace Square (Dvortsovaya Ploshchad, see p.93), with the Winter Palace and Hermitage on the left, the General Staff building on the right. Tear yourself away and go on to **Palace Bridge (Dvortsovy Most)**, over the Neva.*

During the White Nights festival in June (*see* p.276), this stretch of the Neva is at the centre of the all-night walkabout that possesses the city as the bridges go up. Looking right from the bridge, you see the river at its widest. The right bank here became the city's smartest, and perfectly illustrates the secret of St Petersburg's architectural aesthetics. Generations of architects sought to make their mark on the flat site by a judicious and rhythmical use of vertical lines—pillars, spires and statues arranged like so many musical notes on the page. It is a far cry from the traditional cities of medieval Muscovy, which centred on a fortified hill-top Kremlin, with houses looking into a central courtyard rather than out. It seems that the very size of the Neva demanded a new form of grandeur, its glassy mirrored surface crying out for the narcissistic splendour of long façades. This was no organic creation, rather—as Dostoyevsky described it—a most 'premeditated city'.

In order to establish a capital here, where there was little daylight, no local building stone, a regularly flooding river and little local food supply, Peter press-ganged some 40,000 labourers a year. Thousands died of typhoid, starvation and cold, or were taken by the wolves who roamed the streets. For 20 years it was forbidden to build in stone anywhere else in Russia, and for 56 years every carriage, boat or barge coming into the city had to bring a toll in building stone. Peter's first director of building, Domenico Trezzini, designed three standard plans for the houses of the capital, which were made available to those who gradually found themselves forced to leave Moscow. In 1710 an imperial *ukaz* or dictat ordered the imperial family and government to move to this cold northern wasteland. In 1712 Peter ordered that 'one thousand of the best families of the nobility, etc. are required to build houses of beams, with lath and plaster, in the old English style, along the banks of the Neva from the Imperial Palace' (*i.e.* this bridge) to a point way beyond what the eye can see. Opposite, the merchants and traders were to build wooden houses for themselves. Because these buildings were all erected in such a hurry, none lasted long, including the first two Winter Palaces built on the site of today's Hermitage. Foreigners visiting at the time describe drunken parties in rooms where the wind whistled through open roofs and water cascaded down the walls.

> *Palace Bridge leads on to **Vasilievsky Ostrov** (St Basil's Island), which Peter originally intended to be his city centre.*

Since there were no bridges in those days, this scheme stood little chance. Standing on the north side of the Neva, the island was completely inaccessible from most of Russia in autumn and spring, when the ice formed and melted, making the river impossible to navigate. By 1719 the city sensibly radiated out from the Admiralty.

The tip of this island, the largest in the Neva delta, is called the *strelka* (the arrow) and from the 1730s to the 1880s it served as the city's main harbour. Today, it's used for fishing and for newlyweds to have their photo taken with the Peter and Paul Fortress as a backdrop. Directly behind the point of the island, which divides the Neva into the Bolshaya (Large) and Malaya (Small) Neva, stands the neoclassical **former Stock Exchange**. It is a copy of the famous Greek temple at Paestum in Italy, and its stocky Doric colonnade contrasts with St Petersburg's overriding use of the more ornate Corinthian order. The exchange began its life as a wooden building in the area known as the Dutch market; it was here that all negotiations for trading wares were agreed. Barges would draw up along the neighbouring embankments and prices for the goods were decided before trading on land commenced; the Stock Exchange grew up from this arrangement. In 1805–10 the present building was designed by Thomas de Thomon to house the increasingly sophisticated Exchange, and the great terracotta **rostral columns** in front were erected to balance the ensemble. These too are classical, being copies of columns used by the Romans to commemorate naval victories. Ships' prows project from the columns, and fires on top once lit the harbour shore. The four figures at the bottom of the columns represent Russia's four great rivers, the Neva, the Volga, the Dnieper and the Volkov. Despite the return of capitalism, the **Naval Museum** (✆ 218 2502, for a tour map ✆ 328 2502; *open 10.30am–4.45pm; closed Mon, Tues and last Thurs*) is still in the Stock Exchange. Along with the Kunstkamera and some of the zoological exhibits, this museum houses some of the earliest exhibits in the city. Have a look at the main hall with its finely made model boats, including Peter the Great's first childhood launch, the so-called 'grandfather of the Russian fleet'.

The two identical porticoed buildings flanking the Exchange were built some 15 years later and originally used as warehouses. To the north is now the Museum of Soil Science, to the south the Zoological Museum (*see* p.213).

Walk on to the bridge across the Malaya Neva, passing the **Institute of Russian Literature** (*© 328 0502; open by arrangement Mon–Fri 10–5*), *a run-down yellow neoclassical building topped by a drum and dome.*

Known as **Pushkin House**, this is the repository of some of the country's most valuable literary material, including most of the poet's surviving manuscripts. It seems only right that they should remain in the literary capital, a city whose extraordinary origins and 'premeditated' quality have provoked so many authors to make it an almost tangible character. It is hard to imagine Dostoyevsky, Gogol or Akhmatova without St Petersburg; even Tolstoy, who loathed the place, needed its social whirl as an object for his disapproval. From the way Russians talk about their city on the Neva, you could be forgiven for imagining that the physical city is merely a mirage, and that what it stands for, its metaphysical self, is the reality.

Once over the bridge, turn right and follow the banks of the river to the bridge over on to Zayachy (Hare) Island, and the **Peter and Paul Fortress** (Петропавловская Крепость).

Peter and Paul Fortress

© 238 4540; open 11am–5pm and until 4pm on Tues; cathedral closed Wed and last Tues of month.

The fort, one of the best-preserved examples of its type in Europe, is an irregular hexagon of massive walls, sloped against artillery attack and defended by bastions at each corner. If you are here around midday, be prepared for the single noon cannon-shot, which has sounded every day (except during the siege) since a similar salute proclaimed the end of the Great Northern War on 4 September 1721.

Resist entering the fortress and turn left along the shore. On the other side of the Kronverk Strait, the canal that separates the fortress from the Petrograd Side, you'll see a three-storey brick horseshoe-shaped building.

Designed in part by Nicholas I, the **Arsenal** was completed in 1860 to house the bulk of the Russian army's weapons, and its courtyard contains tanks and artillery pieces. Though it never had a true defensive purpose, the building roughly followed the lines of the earlier *kronverk*, a series of earthwork fortifications built to protect the fortress on its most vulnerable side. Today it houses the **Artillery Museum** (*© 233 0382; open Wed–Sun, 11am–5pm*). Beyond it, a small granite **obelisk** commemorates the hanging place of the five leading Decembrists in 1826.

Continue on round the fortress until you arrive at the **Ivan Gate**, *a simple rusticated triumphal arch whose date celebrates the completion of the*

The Peter and Paul Fortress, part of the *raison d'être* of Peter's city, never faced a full-scale attack. It was started in 1703, at the height of the Great Northern War, but was well protected by the island forts of Kronstadt and Kronschlott in the gulf. From an earthworks built hurriedly in one year, it progressed first to wooden and then to stone buildings and battlements. By the time of its completion in 1740, the war had been over for 19 years and Russia's northern borders secured. The greatest threats to the fortress were the 1917 October Revolution and the siege of Leningrad. In the first, it went over to the Bolsheviks early on and served as the revolutionary field headquarters, where the attack on the Winter Palace was masterminded. During the siege, the spire of its central cathedral was camouflaged and damage to the fortress during the bombardments was limited to shell fragments. The food shortage in the siege was such that the men who were to camouflage the spire had to be given extra rations for several days to build up enough strength to scale it.

But if the fortress was never militarily important, it was the symbolic centre of political power, taking over from the Kremlin as the government prison and the burial place of the tsars. Peter hated Moscow; when he was ten, he had stood in the Kremlin and watched as many of his supporters, including his uncle, were torn limb from limb by a bloodthirsty, chanting, drum-beating mob of soldiers. When it came to the building of the Cathedral of SS Peter and Paul in the fortress, he insisted that its spire be taller than the Ivan the Great Belltower in Moscow.

Before progressing into the body of the fortress, the mysteriously named **Gas-Dynamics Laboratory Museum** *may be of interest. It is tucked into the outer defences beyond the ticket office; open 11–5, Tues till 4, last tickets one hour before, closed Wed.*

The museum commemorates a laboratory that worked on space rockets on the site in the 1930s. Much of it is taken up with a dull photographic record of scientists of 'Gas-Dynamic' fame in Soviet style, but the last exhibit, the round Soyuz command capsule, is staggering. That a man should travel so far in so little and survive!

You enter the fortress itself through **St Peter's Gate**, *a Baroque triumphal arch decorated with a wooden bas-relief.*

The relief, a survival from the earlier gate, was a charm, protecting the city with an allegory from the life of its patron St Peter. When Simon Magus attempted to prove his pagan superiority over St Peter by flying, a prayer from the saint scattered the demons assisting him and the sorcerer plummeted to the ground. Should anyone be so foolish as to challenge the city, the implication goes, such will also be his fate. The central building represents the city, with Peter the Great dressed as a Roman officer to the right. Falling from the heavens is the winged figure of Simon, and the Holy Spirit appears in the tympanum above. Beneath is the double-headed eagle of the Russian Empire, which has captured the ancient coat of arms of Moscow, St George and the Dragon, and brought it to the new capital. The statues in the niches are later and represent either the lovers Mars and Venus (with her vanity mirror) or the goddesses of war, Bellona, and wisdom, Minerva (with her snake).

The gate was built in 1707 and redecorated in 1717–18 by Domenico Trezzini, director of building in 1704–13, the first of a series of foreign architects invited by Peter to leave their cosmopolitan mark. It gave the finishing touch to the walls which he had recently built in brick, and could be closed with a portcullis.

> *Before getting to the cathedral, the main avenue passes a yellow building on the left, a rare if undistinguished example of 1740s military architecture known as the **Engineers' House**. It houses changing exhibitions from the collection of the St Petersburg History Museum.*

Beyond it, set behind a lawn which was once the military drill ground, the **Main Guardhouse** was neoclassicised as late as 1907–8, and it shows. What was formerly a single storey building now has two and supports a tacked-on portico, its four pillars bunched in pairs unceremoniously to the sides. On this side of the lawn a **sculpted Peter the Great** sits comfortably on a chair, where during his reign soldiers were made to sit on the knife-edge spine of a big wooden horse for several hours as a punishment. The sculpture, by Michael Shamyakin, shows Peter life-size, with no hair, a small, bullishly determined face on a thick neck and immense attenuated hands, legs and feet. It's a far cry, artistically and symbolically, from the heroic Bronze Horseman, and is based on Carlo Rastrelli's contemporary wax effigy. Yet at a stroke it sends up the Russian (and Soviet) tradition of monumental civic sculpture, identifies the pomposity that is so much a part of the official city and wrests the place from its inhuman autocrats to return it to mortal inhabitants.

> *Turning left at the end of the lawn leads down the side of the pink and white **Commandant's House**.*

The fortress commanders lived here until 1917, enlarging it until it attained its present size in the 1890s. The first commander, true to Peter's desire to modernize his country by importing know-how, was a Scotsman, General James Bruce. He died in 1720 and is buried in the Commandant's Graveyard by the cathedral, beneath a sadly unreachable slab showing a soldier mourning with his horse. The trials of the Decembrists and the Petrashevsky Circle were held in the building, near to the prisons in which the accused were held. Among those tried here was the young Dostoyevsky, a natural conservative who was nevertheless not immune to the revolutionary fever that infused the city from 1825 onwards.

*At the end of this walkway the **Neva Gate** pierces the curtain wall and leads on to the handsome **Commandant's Pier**, which was clad in granite in 1787 along with the rest of the city's riparian banks.*

As you pass through the gate to survey the palatial embankment opposite, spare a thought for those killed in the flood-tides recorded to the right. Each plaque records a particular flood, the highest marker recording the terrible 1824 inundation when all of the fortress, Vasilievsky Island, the Petrograd Side and the mainland almost as far as the Moscow Station were drowned. This is the flood so tragic for poor Yevgeny in Pushkin's *Bronze Horseman*. Pushkin sees Peter's bloody-minded determination to build a city on this unsuitable marsh as yet another example of the autocratic despotism that the Russian people, personified by Yevgeny, are fated to endure.

In good weather, tourists on the pier are serenaded by mellow jazz. It's a measure of the 'mafia' extortion in the city that even the buskers pay protection money. The island's main beach is to the right of the pier, round the bastion. In winter watch out for 'walruses', the hardy citizens who meet up for a dip in holes they make in the ice. And whatever the air temperature, if the sun is shining you may well catch someone sunbathing, sheltering from the wind in the corners of the fortifications.

*Go back along the walkway to the **Cathedral of SS Peter and Paul**.*

The cathedral stands on the site of an earlier wooden Church of St Anne, and was designed by Trezzini in 1712. In the Russia of that time, where churches were almost exclusively squarish, topped by a forest of cupolas and with separate bell-towers, its Baroque silhouette and long, thin basilica shape would have seemed outrageously foreign. The eastern façade, minus the sculpture that once rose from it, still bears traces of the worn 19th-century fresco of SS Peter and Paul with Jesus. The vaulted building beside the cathedral, adorned with a mosaic of the Virgin and Child, is the **Grand Ducal Burial Vault**, where members of the Romanov family were buried between its consecration in 1908 and the Revolution, and again in the 1990s. In 1991 the angel that holds a golden cross on the spire was brought down for repairs, and two time capsules were discovered within. One dated back to the last known ascent for repairs in 1859, and contained information on the history of the cathedral's building works; the second had been left in a bottle by some trick-sters in 1957, leaving a message saying simply 'to the next ascenders'.

Before entering, note the western façade. Just 23 years after it was completed in 1733, the cathedral was struck by lightning. A massive fire broke out, and roof, cupola and belltower were destroyed. The restoration that followed was less than sensitive. The original volutes on either side of the belltower had been elegant and flowing, with a smooth downward line; their replacements were snub-nosed and painfully undecorated. At the attic level, a triangular pediment concealed the base of the next level of the belltower, so that it seemed to rise from behind the façade. This was replaced by a second pair of volutes, completely spoiling the effect.

Beneath the soaring painted vaults within, white marble sarcophagi contain the bodies of all Russia's emperors and empresses after Peter, except for the murdered Ivan VI and Peter III. Peter the Great's body, which lay waiting here in a sealed coffin for years until his cathedral was ready, is up near the iconostasis on the right, his tomb bedecked with commemorative medals and flowers. Mystery surrounds the coffin of Alexander I (*see* p.37). Above them, the ceiling is borne aloft by eight massive square piers, marbled to match the coloured sarcophagi of Alexander II and his wife, carved from green jasper from the Altai and rhodonite from the Urals.

The theatrical gilded iconostasis, with wooden carved curtains drawn back and massive Royal Gates (*see* p.61), was designed by Ivan Zarudny in the 1720s and carved in Moscow, where the 43 icons were painted. Previously, iconostases were an almost solid wall of paintings, whereas here the palanquin over the communion table beyond is visible above the royal doors, themselves an unusual architectural fantasy showing the disciples coming to the Last Supper, with the Virgin Mary, the Holy Spirit in the form of a dove and the Archangels Michael and Gabriel above.

In the passage that leads into the Grand Ducal Burial Vault, and the rooms off it, are exhibitions on the restoration work and the mint (*see* p.81). The vault itself is a sepulchral white dome. It was designed by David Grimm, Anton Tomishko and Leonty Benois, and is something of a victim of history. Designed to accommodate some 60 members of the Romanov family, its purpose was cut short by the Revolution at only 13, though three of the Grand Dukes killed by the Bolsheviks in 1919 are now here, as well as the heir to the Romanov dynasty, Grand Duke Vladimir, who died in 1992. The reburial of the last tsar and his family, who were killed at Ekaterinburg in 1918, took place on 17 July 1998, exactly 80 years after their murder. The service was attended by European royals from all over the world, presided over by Boris Yeltsin (who formerly, when governor of Ekaterinburg, had ordered the destruction of the house where they died to prevent it turning into a place of pilgrimage). Not enough money was available to make marble gravestones, so cement blocks were used instead, covered in marbled sticky-backed plastic.

Leave the complex through Leonty Benois' fine wrought-iron fence, inspired by the famous fence at the Summer Gardens. You now come face to face with a Baroque **boathouse**, *marooned in a sea of pebbles. It was built to house the 'Grandfather of the Russian Fleet' which is now in the Naval Museum.*

The **Mint** (built in 1800–2 and inscribed Монетный Двор) brings to mind an apocryphal story about Russia's tin-based currency. One particularly cold winter, when temperatures fell below –86°, the entire coinage turned to white powder, as tin does under such conditions. Russia's currency was produced in the fortress from 1724, though the present building only produces centenary and other medals: popular collector's items which stand up against inflation far better than the rouble.

The **Trubetskoy Bastion** beyond the Mint and the **Alexeyevsky Ravelin**, an outer fortification, tell of the grisly side of the fort's history—as a prison. Saddest of all is the story of Peter's son Alexei, who became the focus of opposition to Peter. The monarch had sensitive memories of treason within the royal family and reacted with hideous ferocity. On Peter's orders—perhaps with his participation—the terrified 28-year-old was interrogated and tortured from February to June 1718. He was condemned to death, and died in his cell in the Trubetskoy Bastion on 26 June. Whether it was Peter who struck the final blow is not known, but the irony of a reforming monarch bringing the bloodiest tradition in Russian history, royal infanticide, to his new Westernized capital is not lost. Peter also struck off a law that had made unfair denunciations of others a punishable offence, thus laying the foundations for the sneaking that became such a part of the Soviet system.

Between benighted Alexei's time and 1872, when a new prison was built in the Trubetskoy Bastion, enemies of the state were held in the 'Secret House', a prison in the Alexeyevsky Ravelin. The leading Decembrists were executed from there. When three of the five nooses failed to work the first time round, one of the prisoners, Muraviev Apostol, muttered mournfully, 'Poor Russia. She cannot even hang decently.' Dostoyevsky was also imprisoned there before a terrifying mock execution, but received a last-second pardon from the tsar.

The **Trubetskoy Bastion** (*open 10–6; closed Wed and last Tues; tickets from Ioannarsky Ravelin or Boat House*) has been a prison museum since 1924, though it covers only the history of the building in tsarist times. As well as members of the 'People's Will' faction who assassinated Alexander II, and the radical writer Chernyshevsky (*see* p.39), Kropotkin, Trotsky and Gorky were also imprisoned here. After the Revolution several members of the Romanov family were kept here before their execution. The cells have been returned to their sombre 19th-century condition, and you can learn the code with which the prisoners communicated with one another. There is a fantastic view from the bastion's roof.

> *Return to St Peter's Gate and leave the fortress via the wood and stone **bridge** leading to the Petrograd Side.*

It was built in 1738–40, and embellished with period street lamps and iron railings in 1953. The pedestrian's death-trap ahead, **Trinity Square** (Troitskaya Pl.), was the heart of the city in its first few years of existence. The square once contained the Triumphal Osteria of the Four Frigates, an inn that Peter the Great frequented happily alongside merchants, architects and officers. His tipple was vodka with cayenne pepper. During Soviet times it was known as Revolution Square because it was a place of demonstration in the revolutionary years 1905 and 1917. On Bloody Sunday, 9 January 1905, a crowd of workers marching to petition the tsar for a living wage was fired upon by troops, killing some 48 demonstrators. At least 150 more died elsewhere, and what had been intended by its coordinator as a peaceful reconciliation of proletariat and tsar catapulted the country into its first revolution.

Today, trees and the traffic on Kamennoostrovsky Prospekt distract attention from St Petersburg's only **mosque** (*open daily 12.30–2pm, busy on Fridays*). Given to the city by the Emir of Bokhara, it was built in 1910–14, its roof modelled on Tamerlane's mausoleum in Samarkand. It has been under restoration for some years, the brilliant turquoise roof now dull concrete. The **Museum of Russian Political History**, Kuybysheva Ul. 2/4 (*© 233 7052; open 10–5; closed Thurs*) is suffering from an unsurprising identity crisis: until 1993 it was the Museum of the October Revolution. The building is an expansive example of *Style Moderne*, distinguished by the use of different textures of building materials, fluid metalwork fantasies and coloured glass. It was commissioned by the highly successful ballerina Mathilda Kshessinskaya, who had an affair with the future Tsar Nicholas II and married his cousin, Grand Duke Andrei. One of the last survivors of the old days, she lived in Paris, teaching ballet to future stars including Margot Fonteyn, and only died in 1971 at the age of 99. In March 1917 the Bolsheviks requisitioned the house as their headquarters; when Lenin returned to Russia in April he came here from the Finland Station to address the crowds from the balcony facing the square.

As well as exhibitions on Russian history, and the life of Kshessinskaya, there's a souvenir and art shop and a waxworks exhibition, entitled *Terror or Democracy*, with 29 figures all on one or other side of the tenuous line dividing those who furthered democracy in Russia and those who suppressed it with terror, including figures as diverse as Dostoyevsky and Fanya Kaplan. An English-language guide is available. Pop into the building to take a look at the resplendent revolutionary red stained-glass windows in the main hall and for a drink in the courtyard café.

Walk straight towards the River Neva, and turn left on the embankment.

Some 100 yards down the embankment a landing flanked by a pair of Chinese Shih-Tze statues heralds Peter the Great's first home in the city. Brought back from Manchuria in 1907, these pug-like creatures are traditional temple guardians, though this humble wooden hut must seem a comedown for them. Though he founded a city that became a byword for extravagant splendour, Peter himself was a man of simple tastes. Opposite the statues, the pairs of young people you may see are queuing to register their marriages at the Palace of Weddings, formerly the Palace of Grand Duke Nikolai Nikolaevich.

Peter's Cabin

Open 10am–5.30pm; closed Tues.

Hidden in a wooded garden beyond a bronze bust of Peter, the **Cabin of Peter the Great** (Домик Петра I), Petrovskaya Naberezhnaya 6, was encased in the present brick and stone superstructure by Nicholas I in 1846. The central log cabin is the oldest surviving structure in the city and was built for the tsar in three days in 1703. He lived in it, when here, until 1708. Originally it would have been plastered on the outside and brightly painted. The internal door surrounds preserve traces of plastered floral decoration. It has been furnished with period pieces of simple beauty and some of the tsar's personal possessions, such as his icon of the Redeemer, but the overall impression is one of extreme puritanism and discomfort, especially as Peter was a tall man and would have had to stoop to avoid the low roof. The boat on display beside the house was supposedly used by Peter to save a group of fishermen on Lake Ladoga in 1690, and the exhibition explains the events of the Great Northern War. As you leave the building, straight across the river at the edge of the Summer Gardens is Peter's next home, the Summer Palace.

> *Retrace your steps to Kamennoostrovsky Prospekt and cross the Neva on the city's most beautiful bridge, the **Trinity Bridge** (Troitsky Most).*

It was built at the end of the 19th century to a French design, to celebrate the silver wedding anniversary of Tsar Alexander III and Marie Feodorovna. Its gentle curve is divided down the middle by a series of fine *Style Moderne* crucifixes from which the trolleybus lines are suspended. At the far end the bridge gives on to the Field of Mars (*see* p.97), introduced by a statue of Field Marshal Suvorov (1730–1800) whose skeletal face is unmistakable beneath his disguise as the Roman god of war.

> *Turn left along the embankment, walk over the Swans' Canal (Lebyazhya Kanavka) and enter the **Summer Gardens** (Letny Sad) through the gate in Velten's iron palisade.*

Summer Gardens and Summer Palace

> *Gardens small adm; free Sun. Palace ✆ 314 0456; open 11am–6pm; closed Tues and last Mon of the month, and from 11 Nov–30 April. Tickets can be bought at the Tea Pavilion.*

Peter the Great always had magnificent gardens in mind here, though what you see today is largely the product of Catherine the Great's more sober classical tastes. The delicate railings were erected to a design by Yuri Velten in 1770–84, at the same time as the embankment of the Neva was clad in granite and the gardens separated from its banks. Their identical sections of golden-tipped spears, divided by granite pillars topped with urns and two gates, tap into the secret of St Petersburg architecture, rhythm, yet give it a strict classical twist. Peter modelled his gardens on a grand reverie of Versailles, and brought in the French architect Alexandre Jean-Baptiste Leblond in 1715. They sang to the splashing of 50 fountains, fed by waters in a tank on the banks of the thus-named Fontanka River. Formal topiary set off marble and limestone sculptures imported from Italy, and were themselves framed by aviaries and orangeries. There was a grotto in which the 3rd-century

Roman Tauride Venus (now in the Hermitage) presided, and even a miniature boat in which Peter's favourite dwarf rowed amongst the swans on Lebyazhy Canal.

When the 1777 floods destroyed the complex water system that fed the fountains, the present grove was laid out, and only the large Carp Pond at the far end of the gardens was left. Beside it, in the early 19th century, a vast, inappropriate porphyry vase, a present from the king of Sweden, was erected. Many of the more valuable sculptures were taken away, leaving the largely 19th-century assortment now here. In summer the park is St Petersburg's favourite, where busking musicians enliven the air with the ethereal sound of pipes, while nearer the Neva a brass band turns an honest rouble striking up a national anthem at the merest whiff of a tourist.

Near the corner where the Neva meets the Fontanka are two 1820s exhibition halls, the **Tea and Coffee Pavilions**, and a large bronze of **I. A. Kryllov**, which attracts children like the Peter Pan statue in Hyde Park. He wrote animal fables, and the plinth is decorated with bas-reliefs illustrating the stories. The 1855 statue was by Pyotr Clodt, who seems to have sculpted almost every animal in the city.

For its first 100 years, the garden was only accessible to courtiers. Here one of history's most intriguing meetings, between the equally highly sexed Casanova and Catherine the Great, took place. Their chaste conversation about sculpture and the king of Prussia is a dire disappointment, and Casanova rather uncharacteristically remarked, 'who can resist making such speeches to a monarch, and, above all, a monarch in petticoats.' After it was opened by Nicholas I to all 'decently dressed people' the Whit Monday marriage fair took place beneath the impassive gaze of the sculptures on the central alley. Bachelors and prospective brides would line up backed by their families, who bargained over their matrimonial fate.

Peter's **Summer Palace** (Letny Dvorets), built by Domenico Trezzini, in 1710–14, is grander than his wooden cabin but still little more than a family house and a far cry from later gargantuan palaces. Despite its simplicity, it is one of the most satisfying buildings in the city, with its Dutch-influenced outside and period interior.

The walls are divided by pale terracotta bas-reliefs hinting at Peter's naval mastery over the Swedes in the Great Northern War. They are almost the only works in the city by Andreas Schlüter, a German architect whom Peter poached from Berlin to take over from Trezzini in 1713. He was one of Peter's few mistakes in his foreign recruitment drive. After his Berlin Mint fell down, Schlüter went rather mad, and he died within a year of arriving in Russia. After the Peace of Nystadt in 1721 Peter commissioned the sculpture of Peace and Plenty in his garden. It shows Victory placing a laurel crown on Russia, who tramples the defeated lion of Sweden.

Within, the palace has been restored as near as possible to its original decoration. Peter lived and worked on the ground floor, while his family were secreted up the staircase hidden behind the carved oak figure of Minerva in the hall. The Admiralty Chair, whose dimensions were measured for Peter himself, presides in the corner reception room. The portraits are of the tsar's contemporaries, among them Peter's right-hand man, Prince Alexander Menshikov, who was a barefoot pie-seller when Peter first met him. Yet by the end of his reign Menshikov's intelligence and energy had been rewarded with the greatest fortune in the land and unparalleled power.

In Peter's bedroom, the ceiling depicts Morpheus, god of sleep, scattering the poppies of oblivion. In his workshop are the lathes that the tsar used, and a massive instrument for measuring the strength and direction of the wind which, connected to the weather vane, works to this day. It was here, as the Danish ambassador witnessed, that Peter often conducted his affairs of state 'dressed in a leather jerkin like a workman, operating a lathe... During my visit, he from time to time left the lathe, walked to and fro, and discussed the most important affairs.' Peter's fascination with science and technology was another aspect of his interest in progress.

The palace dining room is a family affair, for Peter left Menshikov to arrange all official state banquets in his grander palace on Vasilievsky Island (*see* pp.164–5). The neighbouring kitchen was the latest thing, with the only internal tap in the city, and a hood over the fires, covered in finest Dutch tiles. The Green Study, the finest in the house with its trove of marquetry, is fitted with built-in glass-fronted cupboards where Peter originally displayed his collection of oddities, the Kunstkamera, most of which is now in the Museum of Anthropology and Ethnography (*see* p.212). The elaborate hunting scene carved in walnut above the mirror in the pink ballroom was at least partly the work of the tsar himself. In this suite Peter's second wife Catherine brought up her children including the future tsarina Elizabeth. Here you will find the boat-shaped cradle in which she soothed her babes to sleep.

Considering his volatile temper, Peter and Catherine's marriage was a happy one, a fact that you can almost sense from the building. Menshikov first met the future empress when she was a prostitute following the Russian army. After she had been his mistress for a while he introduced his peasant girl to the tsar, who fell immediately for her dark intelligent charms. At first he kept their marriage a secret to protect her from the snobbish Russian court, and only crowned her empress a year before he died. Yet it was said that he was unable to refuse her frequent requests for clemency for others, so that if he really wanted to execute someone he would schedule it for while she was away. He once offered a victorious general anything he chose as a reward 'except Moscow and Catherine'. After Peter's death in 1725, with the help of the former pie-seller, the former prostitute ascended the throne.

You may want to sit for a while in the gardens, and ponder the disparate and talented group of characters who laid the foundations of the city we see today. To get back to **M** *Nevsky Prospekt/Gostiny Dvor, walk through to the far end of Letny Sad, turn right outside and walk 20m or so to Ulitsa Sadovaya. Either walk left along it or catch any tram a stop or two to Nevsky Prospekt itself.*

Start: Ⓜ *Nevsky Prospekt/Gostiny Dvor*

Walking Time: *2 hours*

II: The Imperial City

Sites

1   Lutheran Church and Peterschule
    Lyuteranskaya Tserkov/Peterschule
    Лютеранская Церковь/Петершул

2   Dutch Church
    Gollandskaya Tserkov
    Голландская Церковь

3   Stroganov Palace
    Stroganovsky dvorets
    Строгановский дворец

4   House with Columns (Barrikada cinema)
    Kinoteatr barrikada
    Кинотеатр баррикада

5   Main Staff Building
    Zdaniye glavnovo shtaba
    Здание главного штаба

6   Alexander Column
    Alexandrovskaya kolonna
    Александровская колонна

7   Winter Palace (Hermitage)
    Zimny dvorets (Ermitazh)
    Зимний дворец (Эрмитаж)

8   Guards' Headquarters
    Shtaba Gvardyeskovo Korpusa
    Штаба Гвардейского Корпуса

9   Small Hermitage
    Maly Ermitazh
    Малый Эрмитаж

10 New Hermitage
    Novy Ermitazh
    Новый Эрмитаж

11 Hermitage Theatre
    Ermitazhny teatr
    Эрмитажный театр

12 Marble Palace
    Mramorny dvorets
    Мраморный дворец

13 Field of Mars
    Marsovo polye
    Марсово поле

14 Former Barracks of Pavlovsky Regiment
    Kazarmi Pavlovskovo Polka
    Казармы Павловского Полка

15 Mikhailovsky Castle
    Mikhailovsky zamok
    Михайловский замок

16 Mikhailovsky Palace/Russian Museum
    Mikhailovsky dvorets/Russky muzei
    Михайловский дворец/Русский музей

17 Church of the Saviour on the Blood
    Tserkov Spass na Krovi
    Церковь Спас на Крови

18 Former Imperial Stables
    Konyushennovo Vedomstvo Zdaniye
    Конюшенного Бедомстба Здание

19 Pushkin Flat Museum
    Muzei-kvartira A. S. Pushkina
    Музей-квартира А. С. Пушкина

20 Glinka Kapella
    Khorovaya kapella im. M. I. Glinka
    Хоровая капелла им. М. И. Глинка

Restaurants and Cafés

A   Stroganov Yard
    Stroganovsky Dvor
    Строгановский Двор

B   Taleon Club
    Клуб Талеон

C   Sevillia
    Севиллиа

D   House of Scholars Café
    Kafé v dome Uchenikov
    Кафе в доме Учеников

E   Grocery
    Produkti
    Продукты

F   Café
    Кафе

G   Café Ambassador
    Кафе Амбассадор

H   Le Chandeleur
    Ле Шанделер

I   Restaurant Sankt Peterburg
    Ресторан Санкт Петербург

J   Sakura
    Сакура

K   Tchaika
    Чайка

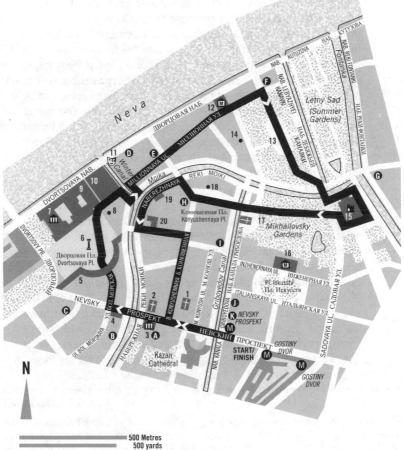

N

500 Metres
500 yards

Once the Romanovs had established their new capital, they lost no time in beautifying it. Within 70 years of a foundation stone being laid for the Peter and Paul Fortress on the muddy banks of the Neva, fortune-seeking architects, craftsmen, painters, choreographers, theatre directors, set designers, pâtissiers, milliners and dress designers were flocking to the city from Paris, Rome and London. This itinerary explores the most fashionable quarter of the city, where palaces, castles and extravagant barracks were built throughout the 18th and 19th centuries. The architecture mirrors the changing society, from the light decorative touch of the 'petticoat period', when women reigned for 65 out of 70 years, to the celebratory Empire style following the victory over Napoleon and beyond. Since 1917 most of the buildings have been colonized by offices or museums, though some were converted into communal flats. With the advent of capitalism, foreign companies and Russia's home-grown *nouveau riche* have recognized the potential value of this real estate, and palatial apartments are once more gracing the ground and first floors.

Though this walk passes through Palace Square, the interior and collections of the vast Hermitage Museum in the Winter Palace are discussed separately in Walk VII. Moseying down between the palaces on Millionaire Street we find the Marble Palace, which Catherine the Great built for her lover Grigory Orlov and which now houses exhibitions of Russian art from the immense collection of the Russian Museum. Royal assassinations loom large at the Mikhailovsky Castle on the far side of the immense Field of Mars, and at the nearby Church of the Saviour on the Blood. Continuing the theme, the walk finishes with a visit to the flat in which the great poet Pushkin breathed his last. To follow this itinerary on a Tuesday would be a big mistake, and bear in mind that the Pushkin Museum is also closed on the last Friday of the month.

lunch/cafés

Ⓐ Stroganov Yard (Stroganovsky Dvor) in Stroganov Palace, Nevsky Prospekt, ℰ 311 7297 (*open 10am–2am*). One of the latest trendy eating establishments, with an outdoor bar and tables surrounded by Baroque architecture and marble statues. The service is charming but can be slow; there's a crèche for babies, and in spring and autumn you are serenaded by music from the turn of the century as you dine.

Ⓑ Taleon Club, Nab. Reki Moiki 59, ℰ 315 7645; *open noon–6am (bar), 3am (restaurant)*. The fantastically restored Eliseev House has become St Petersburg's most expensive restaurant, the haunt of the city's élite, with great wine and food.

C Sevillia, Malaya Morskaya Ul. 7, ✆ 315 5371. Spanish restaurant close to Nevsky Prospekt, with delicious food and an authentic Latin feel to the décor. There's Spanish dancing in the evenings.

D House of Scholars Café, Dvortsovaya Naberezhnaya 26, to the left of where Zaporozhsky Pereulok comes down to the embankment. Enter through the glass and wood porch of this great Florentine Renaissance palace of Grand Duke Vladimir and cross the sombre hall with its magnificent Chinese pots to find the cosy café beyond the staircase.

E One of the best **grocers** (Продукты) in town is on the corner of Ul. Milliónnaya and Zaporozhsky Pereulok. On a good day you could find smoked salmon and champagne, though you will have to queue at different counters for them. There is always cheese, butter and sausage. Almost opposite is a **bread shop** (булочная).

G Café Ambassador, Naberezhnaya Reki Fontanki 14, ✆ 272 9181; *open 1pm–5am*, is not far off the walk by the Mikhailovsky Castle (*see* p.71).

H Le Chandeleur, Ul. Bolshaya Konyushennaya 1, ✆ 314 8380 (*open 11am–midnight*). French-style crêperie with salads.

I Restaurant Sankt Peterburg, Kanal Griboyedova 5, ✆ 314 4947 *open 12 noon–4am*. This is a slick establishment set up with tour groups in mind. There are small intimate tables, though at night you can't avoid the somewhat dubious floor show which ingeniously manages to mix semi-nudity with Russian history. Its English-language menu is inventive but expensive. The attached café round the corner (*open 4–9pm*) serves good, ordinary Russian food, which you can choose by pointing at the samples laid out on the counter.

J Sakura, Kanal Griboyedeva 12, ✆ 315 9474 (*open 12noon–11pm*). Japanese restaurant.

K Tchaika, Kanal Griboyedeva 14, ✆ 312 4631 (*open 11am–3am*). German beer cellar. Between this and the Sakura, above, is also an Italian ice-cream bar.

Leave **M** *Nevsky Prospekt via the Kanal Griboyedova* (Канал Грибоедова) *exit and turn right down Nevsky Prospekt, over the Griboyedov Canal to pass the outstretched arms of the Kazan Cathedral (see p.117) on your left.*

After the first street on the right, you see the plain yellow façade of the **Lutheran Church of St Peter**, Nevsky Prospekt 22–24, which for a time masqueraded as a municipal swimming pool, though the city has now given the building back to its communicants. It was built in the 1830s, but is flanked by two 18th-century buildings which date back to the earlier Lutheran church on this spot. Behind the building is one of Petersburg's oldest schools, the mid-18th-century Peterschule, which still teaches its syllabus in two languages, German and Russian. 'Special' schools like this existed throughout the Soviet period, preparing citizens for work with Intourist and the Foreign Ministry, but with the collapse of the Iron Curtain they have become still more popular. Those who can afford it are even sending their children to private 'gymnasiums', modelled on their 19th-century predecessors, where Latin and Greek have been reintroduced into the curriculum. Until the Revolution the seemingly secular green building at Nevsky Prospekt 20 hid the **Dutch Church** behind its portico; it is now a gallery selling unremarkable Russian art.

Since the foundation of the city, the banks of the River Moika ahead have been one of its smartest addresses. In 1752–4 the Stroganov family commissioned Empress Elizabeth's pet architect Bartolomeo Rastrelli to build the green and white **Stroganov Palace**, which still overlooks the river on the far side of Nevsky Prospekt. Toning down his favoured Baroque extravagance, which he lavished on his imperial palaces, Rastrelli designed this private house with masterly control, though it was originally painted bright orange. Pillars are used to emphasize the plain entrance arch on Nevsky Prospekt and the centre of the façade on the Moika, and rhythm injected into the building by the orderly use of stucco ornament around the windows. Admire the interiors by Rastrelli, and those designed later by the Stroganovs' genius serf-architect Andrei Voronykhin. The Russian Museum funds the restoration of its halls and uses them for exhibitions.

The Stroganovs, who lived here until 1917, were fabulously wealthy. 'Richer than the Stroganovs' was an expression used to describe the impossible. From the 15th century onwards they were awarded vast tracts of the Ural Mountains by the tsars, where they extracted salt and iron, felled timber and traded in the abundant animal furs. In the 16th century it was the Stroganovs, not the inhabitants of the Kremlin, who hired an army of Cossacks to drive the Tartar Khan from Siberia. Having supported the Romanov claim to the throne in the 17th century, they never looked back, as titles and offices were heaped upon successive generations.

For an idea of just how fashionable the Moika was, the Stroganov palace looked directly across the water towards that of their close friend the Empress Elizabeth, whose own Rastrelli palace was not finished until the 1760s. The tall pink building that now stands there, the **House with Columns** (occupied by the Barrikada Cinema) originally served as the home of St Petersburg's Chief of Police.

> *Nevsky Prospekt crosses the Moika River over the earliest iron bridge in the city, known as **Police Bridge**. If the weather is perfect, you may be tempted to hire one of the flotilla of small boats moored down to the right (see p.195). If not, over the bridge it is worth diving into Staraya Kniga, Nevsky Prospekt 18, on the right, to admire the elegant mahogany shop fittings and sniff out a bargain. Turn right just after the shop.*

While most of Ul. Bolshaya Morskaya presents a unified 19th-century façade, the high grey granite building on the left, now the Long Distance Telephone Exchange, was designed as the headquarters of the Azov–Don Commercial Bank by St Petersburg's greatest *Style Moderne* architect, Fyodor Lidval, in 1908–9. The curiously angled double arch of the **Main Staff Building**, which lies ahead, acts as an exhilarating triumphal entrance to Palace Square (Dvortsovaya Ploshchad), hiding until the last minute the immense, sea-green façade of the Winter Palace.

Palace Square and the Winter Palace

For 230 years the sculptures that decorate the roof of the palace have looked down on the square, bearing indulgent witness to the follies of mankind. Nineteenth-century diplomats describe freezing on the balconies as the imperial family derived their increasingly false sense of security from another four-hour parade of soldiers. By 1879 even the square was sometimes unsafe for them, and a member of the 'People's Will' terrorist group made an attempt on the life of Alexander II as he rode through it. But it was troops opening fire on a peaceful demonstration of workers on 9 January 1905, killing and wounding hundreds, that propelled the revolutionary movement into top gear and precipitated the 1905 Revolution. Ironically, the gathering had been organized by a monarchist, Father Gapon, who sought to prove that the tsar still had the well-being of his people at heart by allowing him to listen to and act upon their grievances. It was here too that a decisive four-hour gun battle ended with the arrest of the last members of the provisional government in the palace at 1.50am on 26 October 1917 and ushered in the rule of the Bolsheviks. John Reed, the American journalist famed for his eye-witness account of the Revolution, captures the spirit of hope that accompanied it when he wrote that, that night, 'on Palace Square I watched the birth of a new world.' To many Russians today, those events are known simply as the *catastroph*.

Standing in Palace Square, it is easy to understand how such a theatrical forum could encourage myths in an already mythomanic regime. In 1920 the third anniversary of the Revolution was celebrated with a dramatic reconstruction of the storming of the Winter Palace, in which thousands of extras rushed across the square in a heroic charge that had never taken place. Eisenstein's film *October*, shot in 1928, immortalized the image. For the first few years after 1917, May Day and 7 November (the anniversary of the October Revolution after the adoption of the Gregorian calendar in 1918) were greeted by Constructivist and Futurist canvases thousands of metres long hung from the palace roof. Impressive though the procession of the proletariat that accompanied them was, it often owed more to the promise of an extra bread ration than revolutionary fervour.

Even today Palace Square is the pulse of the city, the place where people go to hear the news. During the events of August 1991, the city's Mayor Sobchak came here from his barricaded office on St Isaac's Square to address the protesting crowd. More recently it has been the White Nights pop concerts on the square which attract the largest crowds, while strange bedfellows still congregate on the traditional Communist holidays calling for a return to the ways of sobriety—elderly die-hard reds, hard-faced Russian nationalists and hard-line Orthodox believers—

the so-called red-brown coalition. At other times gypsy beggars, tourists and even massed processions of Hari Krishna devotees occupy the space.

The Winter Palace itself, now part of the world-renowned Hermitage Museum, was the last of the six winter homes built for the imperial family in the first 60 years of the city's history. It was commissioned by the Empress Elizabeth and built by Bartolomeo Rastrelli in 1754–62, at the same time that he was building the Catherine Palace for her at Tsarskoye Selo. With these two buildings he created a new style to express 'the glory of all Russia', a product of his distinctive hybrid genius. Born in Italy, Rastrelli spent ten formative years from the age of 16 in Russia with his sculptor father before going abroad again to study. He used the exuberance of the Italian and French Baroque tradition in a way uniquely suited to Russia's colourful building tradition and her flat, never-ending landscape.

Here, the long low façade feels surprisingly light, thanks to his use of repetition and change in the decorative motifs, which are highlighted in white. In between the attached porticoes, where two-storey composite columns stand on single-storey Ionic arrangements, the windows are made to dance by slight alterations in the entablature and bronze-painted decorative flourishes. Crowning all, the bronze statues and urns on the roof, oxidized to appear organically connected to the building, add an unlikely touch of the surreal. Once, as the Victorian traveller Augustus Hare was told, they shared the roof with servants, who worked, among other tasks, 'to keep the water in the tanks from freezing during the winter by casting in red-hot cannon-balls—[they] built themselves huts between the chimneys, took their wives and children there, and even kept poultry and goats who fed on the grass of the roof. It is said that at last some cows were introduced.' The central portico, surmounted by its pediment, is the only vehicular entrance into the palace's inner courtyard, which once echoed to the staccato clatter of hooves and the roll of royal carriage wheels.

While the Winter Palace symbolizes Russia's emergence on to the European stage as a power to be reckoned with, the **Main Staff Building** opposite marks another decisive moment in the development of the superpower mentality. Commissioned within five years of Alexander I's defeat of Napoleon in 1812–14, its architect Carlo Rossi was entrusted with a whole series of architectural ensembles in the city, each one of which uses a neoclassical idiom to express the confidence and imperial ambitions of post-Napoleonic Russia. As in contemporary France, the style became known as Empire (*ampir*) or Alexandrine Classicism. Thanks to its graceful softening curve, the regular yellow and white edifice does not overpower the Winter Palace opposite. In the none-too-subtle allegory used in many capitals of the western world, the building is surmounted by a sculpture of Victory riding forward, triumphant, in a chariot drawn by six racing horses. To underline the point, the Alexander Column at the centre of the square was erected by his brother and successor, Nicholas I, and bore the inscription 'To Alexander I from a grateful Russia'. The column is one of the tallest ever erected, a single piece of granite on a tall plinth topped by an angel whose face is modelled on that of the victorious emperor. It took two years to carve the 600-ton granite column from the rock face and a year to transport it to the city. Since 1834 it has stood on its plinth without pegging or mortar, balanced only by its own immense weight.

The third side of Palace Square is filled by a relatively small yellow and white classical building, designed as the **Guards' Headquarters**. It was built in 1837–43, the visible tip of a whole series of barracks and army staff buildings beyond.

> *Leave the square via the street between the Guards' Headquarters and the Winter Palace, Millionnaya Ul.*

As its name suggests, this is St Petersburg's Millionaire's Row. In the early days, Peter I settled his many foreign friends and advisors here and it became known as the German quarter. However, during the second half of the 18th century the Winter Palace expanded further up the street, and other members of the royal family, courtiers and even court architects took up residence here.

Adjoining the Winter Palace you will find the **Small Hermitage**, built for Catherine the Great in 1764–5 by Vallin de la Mothe, and beyond it the **New Hermitage**. Commissioned by Nicholas I as Russia's first purpose-built art gallery, this solid, Renaissance-inspired building, whose niches are set with statues of artists of the Renaissance and classical period, was entered via the monumental carriage porch held aloft by ten marble atlantes. Today the entire palace complex is a museum and the main entrance is on Dvortsovaya Nab., overlooking the Neva (*see* **Walk VII** for the interior of Hermitage Museum). Opposite the carriage porch, at the end of the 19th century, a Renaissance fortress was erected to house the royal archives, though since the Soviet period it has contained the naval archive.

> *Millionnaya Ul. crosses the Winter Canal (Zimnaya Kanavka), leaving the Imperial Palace behind. If you look left, you will see a covered bridge near the Neva embankment which leads to the **Hermitage Theatre**, built for Catherine the Great by Giacomo Quarenghi in the 1780s.*

The gateways on the left of the street were originally the back entrances to the great palaces that line Palace Embankment (Dvortsovaya Naberezhnaya), whose façades are best appreciated from the other side of the river (*see* p.80). If you stroll through the arch at No.29, you will find yourself in the service courtyard of the Palace of the Grand Duke Vladimir, now the **House of Scientists**. The central block, much older than his palace or the surrounding courtyard, once served as stabling for his 36 horses and 40 carriages, whose coachmen were amongst the smartest in the city in their scarlet or green uniforms, trimmed with raccoon fur.

As you walk down the street, there are a couple of pretty 18th-century buildings (No.22 and the former Main Pharmacy at No.4) but it is in the undistinguished 19th-century beige palaces that events of historical importance took place.

At Millionnaya Ul. 10, on 3 March 1917, the Romanov dynasty finally relinquished the throne of Russia in the aftermath of the February revolution. The day before Nicholas II had abdicated in favour of his brother, Grand Duke Michael, who took just one day to follow his example. The pink and white house next door, with its delicate stucco moulding, was built by the prolific German architect Stakenschneider for himself, and acted as an important international cultural salon in the mid-19th century.

*At the far end of this prestigious street, at Nos. 5/1, the **Marble Palace** (Mramorny Dvorets) stands in splendid isolation, its first storey camouflaged in plain grey granite.*

Marble Palace

✆ 315 9196; open 10am–5pm; closed Tues.

The palace owes its name to the multi-coloured marble-clad façade above. Here in 1768 Catherine the Great ordered the hitherto Baroque architect, Rinaldi, to build a palace for Grigory Orlov, her lover of eight years and the father of her son Alexei Bobrinsky, using the recently discovered deposits of coloured marbles from the Urals and Siberia. She wanted to thank Orlov for his and his brothers' leading role in the 1762 coup against her husband which put her on the throne, and her generosity to her lovers was well known. Not even Catherine herself had a stone palace, and indeed at the time of its completion this was the only one in the capital. Rinaldi realized that marble was too classic a material for his beloved, curvaceous Baroque, so he built Russia's first neoclassical building instead. The handsome but severe regularity of its façades is alleviated in the portico of the courtyard entrance, where rounded columns support a pediment with a clock surrounded by garlands and swags.

Inside, the banisters and doorways are decorated in grey-blue marble. Walking up the main stairwell is like travelling through a Wedgwood pot; the powder-blue walls offset white plaster bas-reliefs on a martial theme, although many of the niches gape sadly, their statues missing. Until August 1991, such holes were filled with Lenin memorabilia, for this was a branch of the Central Lenin Museum. In a grand gesture of sweeping change, one of the first exhibitions installed by the Russian Museum, which now uses the space, was of pre-Revolutionary official portraiture—royalty, aristocrats, lawyers, government ministers and patriarchs. In the palace's Great Hall, Rinaldi's decorative genius exploited the colourful properties of the more valuable marbles to fine effect. The white marble eagle is a play on the name Orlov, which means just that in Russian.

Field of Mars

Depending on the time of year, you will either want to linger among the lilac of the Field of Mars (Marsovo polye), or scurry across it wishing that the eternal flame at the centre of the central Monument to Revolutionary Fighters were a bit more accessible.

The Field of Mars is a vast open grassy space, but ever since a frail nonagenarian Petersburger described how she was taunted and dive-bombed by a German pilot as she made her solitary way across it during the siege, it's seemed eerie and haunted to me. Beneath the paths, shrubs, benches and the heroic granite walls of the monument lie Bolshevik victims of the 1917 revolutions and the Civil War. Some 800,000 citizens are said to have shown their support for the February Revolution by massing for the first burial of 184 of its victims in late March 1917. The granite monument adorned with quotations from Commissar Lunacharsky was erected two years later and the eternal flame lit in their memory in October 1957, the 40th anniversary of the Revolution.

This open space has been used as a place of amusement and public activity since its marshy soil, the source of both the Moika River and the Griboyedov Canal, was first drained by Peter. Its character turned predominantly martial (hence the name, after Mars, the Roman god of war) under Paul I, who obsessively drilled his troops here, and his son Alexander I, who had V. P. Stasov build the immense classical Barracks of the Pavlovsky Regiment to frame its western side. Paul I had founded this regiment, which was named after himself, and not the least of his psychological quirks was to recruit for it only men whose snub noses matched his own. The sandy parade ground, known as the Petersburg Sahara, was transformed into a garden in 1920, by 16,000 workers taking part in the Soviet institution known as a *subbotnik*, a Saturday devoted to voluntary labour. As municipal governments have less and less money to spare on cleaning their cities, so a fond longing for the days of *subbotniki* stirs in the breasts of their older citizens. A far-away look glazes their eyes as they remember when Pioneers (the Soviet equivalent of the Boy Scout and Girl Guides) were marched out to clean the city's ponds after the thaw in spring.

*Aim for the tall spire diagonally opposite the Marble Palace across the Field of Mars. It rises above the church in the **Mikhailovsky Castle** (Mikhailovsky zamok) on the other side of the Moika.*

Mikhailovsky Castle

The sad tale of Paul I's life culminates in the Mikhailovsky Castle. Paul chose to believe that he was the only legitimate son and heir of Peter III and Catherine. As a child he saw almost nothing of his mother, and when he was eight she and her lover Grigory Orlov plotted the coup which was to end in the death of his father. Rather than act as regent during Paul's minority, Catherine then usurped the throne. In the meantime, Paul's second marriage had turned out to be surprisingly happy and loving. As the Count and Countess of the North, he and Maria Fyodorovna made a European tour in 1781–2. The bright, brilliantly educated Paul was the darling of Versailles.

Catherine's reign was a long one, however, and Paul was 42 by the time he reached the throne. The 34 years of waiting, tainted by gossip surrounding his mother's successive affairs and rumours about his own legitimacy, had taken their toll. Vengeful and filled with hatred towards his mother, Paul compensated by drilling regiments of soldiers to immaculate standards. Vestiges of the sentimental idealism which had made him a loving husband remained, though they took such quaint forms that he became the laughing stock of Europe. On one occasion, in order to spare the populations of Europe the pain of war, he issued an invitation to all the crowned heads of Europe, published openly in the newspapers, to solve disagreements by personal combat in the form of duels.

Given the circumstances of his life, the dream that convinced Paul to build his home here seems like a subconscious urge to wipe out his early memories and replace them with something safe. The Archangel Michael appeared to him and told him to build a church on the site where he was born, legitimizing the destruction of Rastrelli's gay-looking Summer Palace, built for the Empress Elizabeth, where he was snatched away from his mother when only a few hours old. In its place Paul ordered Bazhenov to design him a fortress, and Vincenzo Brenna to build it. The site was already protected on two sides by the Fontanka and Moika Rivers, and the other two he dug to form a moat. A drawbridge which was raised at dusk protected the sleeping inhabitants.

Tragically, it was in this monument to emotional and physical security that Paul met his brutal death. His behaviour had become so unpredictable that a St Petersburg cartoon showed him holding a paper marked 'order' in one hand, another marked 'counter-order' in the other, and with 'disorder' written on his forehead. He was so sensitive about his nose that he refused to have his profile on the coin of the realm and even banned the use of the word 'snub-nosed'. Most dangerously of all, he distrusted the nobility and, ignoring their traditional exemptions, had them flogged in public and exiled on a whim. On 11 March 1801, just 40 days after taking up residence, Paul was smothered in his bedroom by a group of men including his mother's last lover and his own closest advisor, the Governor-General of St Petersburg.

The elegant earthy-pink square building surrounds an octagonal courtyard, entry to which is through a massive granite gateway on the south side of the building. Over the gate a pediment relief depicts the Triumph of Russia. Both on the obelisks that flank the gate and all round the inner courtyard you will see plaques bearing Paul's cipher, which, in his insecurity, he insisted on having inscribed some 8,000 times around the building. Outside the gateway, Paul erected the bronze horseback statue of Peter I, which had been cast by Carlo Rastrelli, father of the architect, and rejected by Catherine, with an inscription directly aping his mother's on the Bronze Horseman in Decembrists' Square: 'To great-grandfather, from great-grandson'. Inside, the building was originally furnished with pieces confiscated from the homes of his mother's many lovers.

Extensive restoration work is taking place here, and it is used for exhibitions by the Russian Museum (*see* **Walk IV**, pp.125–34). The handful of rooms currently open, to the left as you enter the castle, exhibit a selection of prints about the history of the building. After Paul's death, no member of the royal family would inhabit the place, and it was eventually given over to an Academy of Military Engineering in 1823. The academy's most unlikely alumnus was Fyodor Dostoyevsky. Though he passed out third in his class, Dostoyevsky's heart was never really in his profession. 'What idiot drew this?' snarled the tsar of a fortress Dostoyevsky had inadvertently drawn without doors. Today, despite the restorations, part of the building is still occupied by the naval library.

On the third floor, through a labyrinth of corridors and staircases, you will find the New Academy, a contemporary art gallery and studio space for fans of the school of academic classicism begun by art guru Timor Novikov. This currently holds fortnightly exhibitions on Thursdays at 4pm; call ✆ 272 8222 to check.

A walk round the castle shows how each side differs. Facing the Fontanka the building is at its most secretive, screened by trees. Only on the northern façade is there a break in the unyielding walls—overlooking the Field of Mars and the Summer Garden a first-floor terrace, supported by pillars, stands above a broad flight of steps leading to the ground.

Returning to the church staircase, a gate in the railing allows you to cross Sadovaya Ul. and enter the **Mikhailovsky Gardens** *directly opposite.*

These belong to the slightly later Mikhailovsky Palace, visible on the far left of the gardens. This now houses the superlative collection of native painting and crafts that makes up the Russian Museum (*see* **Walk IV**, pp.125–34). On the banks of the Moika, which borders the gardens to the right, the Rossi pavilion, named after the architect who designed both the palace and the Main Staff Building we saw at the start of the walk, stands reflected in its waters. The far end of the gardens, dense with trees even in winter, is delineated by an exceptional early *Style Moderne* railing, florid and plastic, its floral bracts and full-blown blooms transforming themselves into all manner of imaginings at the whim of the beholder.

You can't miss the Church of the Resurrection, the fantasy pseudo-Russian confection that soars colourfully towards the sky between the gardens and the Griboyedov

Canal. Better known as Spass na Krovi, the **Saviour on the Blood** (*open daily 11–6;*
© *315 1636*), it was built between 1887 and 1907 to mark the spot where
Alexander II was mortally wounded by a bomb thrown by a member of the 'People's
Will' revolutionary movement on 1 March 1881. The canal has been narrowed so
that the altar stands exactly where the royal blood stained the pavement.

The church manages to combine all the hallmarks of 17th-century Russian church
architecture, with its use of brick, the tent-roofed central tower, *kokoshniki* gables
and eight further domes including the gilded belltower. Its twisting, multi-coloured
domes refer blatantly to the icon of touristic Russia, St Basil's Cathedral in Red
Square. It's entirely out of place in St Petersburg, but fun.

The 7,000 square metres of mosaics, both on the exterior and in the interior, were
designed by some of the greatest artists of the late 19th century, when a movement—similar to William Morris's Arts and Crafts movement in Britain—sought to
revive Russia's heritage. The interior, which has been undergoing restoration since
the 1970s, shimmers with mosaic religious scenes on walls, piers and vaults,
designed by Vasnetsov, Nesterov and Vrubel among others. Transfiguration, crucifixion and resurrection scenes adorn important parts of the exterior.

Opposite the church is St Petersburg's main open-air tourist market. As well as
massed *matrioshkas* and swathes of floral scarves you may be lucky enough to find
old musical instruments and other antiques.

> *Beyond the Griboyedov Canal, passing round the Saviour on the Blood on
> your left, Stable Square (Konyushennaya Ploshchad) opens up with what
> was the **Imperial Stables**, the vast pink and white building, on the right.*

As the internal combustion engine superseded the horse, the Leningrad Taxi
Transport Company took over this early 19th-century building during the Soviet
period. The taller domed section in the centre is accessible as its upper floors are a
recently reopened, and hence very bare, church. Its greatest moment of glory took
place between 1 and 3 February 1837, when the body of Alexander Sergeievich
Pushkin, Russia's greatest poet, lay here following his death in a duel. He was
brought from his last home, just round the corner at Naberezhnaya Reki Moiki 12.

> *To get there continue straight along beside the stables to the banks of the
> River Moika. Turn left and walk along the embankment until you reach
> No.12, the **Pushkin Flat Museum** (Dom-muzei A. S. Pushkina).*

Pushkin Flat Museum

> © *314 0006; open 11am–5pm; closed Tues and last Fri of the month. If
> you happen to be here on 10 Feb (the date of Pushkin's death according to
> the calendar adopted by the Bolsheviks in 1918), the place will be teeming
> and readings will begin shortly after the time of death, 2.45pm.*

Situated on a graceful curve of the river just behind Palace Square, the museum complex occupies buildings round a peaceful courtyard, which is rarely empty of Pushkin fans here to commune with him and his muse. It is hard to describe just how dizzy a position Pushkin holds in the estimation of the Russians, but it is certainly not adequate to describe him as Russia's Shakespeare. Here Pushkin flows with the last glasses of vodka, whether you are with factory workers, artists or politicians. For Russians, poetry has been the voice of freedom through the centuries of oppression and Pushkin's death, to which he was driven partly by the contemptuous attitude of courtly society, has made him something of a martyr.

The building at the back of the courtyard was once the stable of a 1730s house built here for the Empress Anna's German favourite Biron, and predates the house in which Pushkin lived by some 65 years. The first floor gallery always has some kind of literary exhibition going on, and even if you don't read Russian they are often gloriously visual, tracing, for example, one period in Russia's unparalleled history of book illustration. The point of the visit is to see Pushkin's flat, reconstructed in the 1920s to a plan of the flat drawn when the poet died by his friend, the poet Vasily Zhukovsky. Many of the poet's possessions, and copies of his paintings, litter surfaces and walls. If you hire an English-language cassette guide, which for once is quite good, you avoid having to be conducted in a Russian-language tour.

Pushkin lived here for the last four months of his life, from September 1836, renting the flat from Princess Volkonskaya, whose brother Sergei had been exiled to Siberia for his part in the Decembrist uprising. A visit to the flat begins backwards, at the servants' door, where a copy of the last note posted to keep enquirers informed of the poet's deteriorating condition reads: 'The patient is in an extremely dangerous condition'. The irony of his death is that had Pushkin had his way and lived:

> '...in family love
> contented, easeful, peaceful, quiet,
> ageing by our fathers' graves,
> at home on patrimonial lands...'

as he longs in one of his unfinished poems, he would have escaped so pointless an end. However, Tsar Nicholas I, who barely trusted him but recognized his talent, threatened to withdraw his research rights in the state archives if he retired from the capital. So Pushkin's beautiful wife Natalia was here to provoke idle rumours about her relationship with one D'Anthès, a young French cavalry officer. In the malicious, introverted society of St Petersburg, it wasn't long before anonymous letters arrived, calling Pushkin 'the historiographer of the Order of Cuckoldry'. Two months later Pushkin challenged D'Anthès to a duel at Chornaya Rechka, then outside the city. D'Anthès fired first and his bullet lodged in Pushkin's stomach, but the poet nevertheless managed to take his shot and wound the Frenchman in the hand. This was at 5pm on 27 January, and until he died two days later crowds flocked to his door for news. After that, 'multitudes of people of all ages and ranks kept gathering in crowds about his coffin—women, old men, children, schoolboys, common people in sheepskins...' and his funeral mass was packed, despite decrees ordering all staff and students of the university to attend their lessons throughout the day.

Upstairs the flat centres on Pushkin's study, as it did in his day, the second to last room in the tour. In the second room, the sitting room, you will find portraits of Pushkin and his close friends Vyazemskoy, Zhukovsky and Odovsky, and in the next, Natalia's room, a copy of the famous watercolour of her by Bryullov. After the room in which one of Natalia's sisters stayed comes the nursery where the couple's four children worked and played. It is now devoted to memorabilia of his death, including the 'cuckold' letter, the waistcoat and a glove he was wearing, and candles from his funeral.

Pushkin's study is still dominated by his library of over 4,000 books, here seen in replica. His desk is strewn with papers. The inkstand, decorated with an Ethiopian, was one of his favourite objects as it reminded him of his great-grandfather Abram Hannibal, who had been brought to Russia as a gift for Peter I and became not only his friend but also his chief military engineer. The metal travelling box belonged to Hannibal, while the letter knife, walking sticks, Turkish sabre and pipe were all Pushkin's own. The clock in this room reminds visitors eternally of the moment of his death. The last room in the flat contains the poet's death mask beside a portrait of the deceased by Kozlov and a lock of his hair, which Pushkin's valet had cut off for the budding novelist Ivan Turgenev at his request. The table opposite holds a copy of the Lermontov poem on the death of Pushkin which had him exiled to the Caucasus.

> To return to Ⓜ Nevsky Prospekt, continue along the banks of the Moika, to the Glinka Kapella which was once the home of the Court Choir (No.20). Worming your way through to Bolshaya Konyushennaya Ul. via the courtyards of the Kapella, you will find yourself in archetypal Petersburg. Warrens of courtyards like this, each overlooked by the blank staring windows of a score of flats, are hidden behind even St Petersburg's most glamorous façades. Turn right along the avenue, and left when you hit Nevsky Prospekt. The station is just beyond the Griboyedov Canal.

III: A Clutch of Cathedrals

Walking Time: *2½ hours. Try to include the interior of the Yusupov Palace by phoning ℂ 314 8893 to arrange a tour in English, and set off an hour before your appointment. This will add a further ¾ hour to the itinerary.*

> **Start:** Ⓜ *Sennaya Ploshchad (Ploshchad Mira)/Sadovaya*

III: A Clutch of Cathedrals

600 metres
600yards

N

Neva 100 m

NEVSKY PROSPEKT НЕВСКИЙ ПРОСПЕКТ

АДМИРАЛТЕЙСКИЙ ПРОСПЕКТ ADMIRALTYESKY PROSPEKT

УЛ. МАЛ. МОРСКАЯ
УЛ. БОЛ. МОРСКАЯ
ГОРОХОВАЯ УЛ.
GOROKHOVAYA

L

14

Isaakiyevskaya Pl.

K

13

J

КОННОГВАРДЕЙСКИЙ БУЛЬВАР
KONNOGVARDEYSKY BULVAR

10 **12**
УЛ. СОЮЗА СВЯЗИ

11

УЛ. ТРУДА УЛ. ТРУДА
УЛ. ЯКУБОВИЧА UL. YAKUBOVICHA
УЛ. СОЮЗА СВЯЗ UL. SOYUZA SYYAZI
УЛ. БОЛ. МОРСКАЯ

ПЕР. ГРИВЦОВА PEREULOK GRIVTSOVA

УЛ. ПЛЕХАНОВА

15

I

БОЛЬШАЯ МОРСКАЯ BOLSHAYA MORSKAYA
РЕКИ МОЙКИ REKI MOIKI
Moika
16 **17**

F

H

НАБ. КАНАЛА ГРИБОЕДОВА NAB. KANALA GRIBOYEDOVA

7

НАБЕРЕЖНАЯ NABEREZHNAYA

8

9

УЛ. ПЛЕХАНОВА UL. PLEKHANOVA

G

SADOVAYA

M

НАБЕРЕЖНАЯ РЕКИ МОЙКИ REKI MOIKI

D **E**

УЛ. ДЕКАБРИСТОВ

START

M SENNAYA PLOSHCHAD
Сенная Пл. Sennaya Pl.

УЛ. ГЛИНКИ UL. GLINKI

4

ГРАЖДАНСКАЯ УЛ. GRAZHDANSKAYA UL.

НАБ. КАНАЛА ГРИБОЕДОВА NAB. KANALA GRIBOYEDOVA
Griboyedov Canal

UL. DEKABRISTOV

5 **C**

6

РЕСНАТНИКОВ
УЛ. СОЮЗА ПЕЧАТНИКОВ
UL. SOYUZA PECHATNIKOV

Театральная Пл. Teatralnaya Pl.

ПРОСПЕКТ РИМСКОГО-КОРСАКОВА
PROSP. RIMSKOVO-KORSAKOVA

B

ВОЗНЕСЕНСКИЙ ПРОСП.

САДОВАЯ УЛ.

МОСКОВСКИЙ ПРОСПЕКТ MOSKOVSKY PROSPEKT

НАБ. КАНАЛА КРЮКОВА NAB. KANALA KRYUKOVA

Никольская Пл. Nikolskaya Pl.

3

БОЛЬШАЯ УЛ. BOLSHAYA UL.

1

2

НАБЕРЕЖНАЯ РЕКИ ФОНТАНКИ NABEREZHNAYA REKI FONTANKI

SADOVAYA UL.

РОДЧАСКАЯ ПОДЪЯЧЕСКАЯ

VOZNESENSKY PROSP.

ФОНТАНКИ FONTANKI
Fontanka

A

NABEREZHNAYA
NABEREZHNAYA

Restaurants and Cafés

A Old Café
   Staroe Café
   Старое Кафе

B Russkiye Samovary
   Русские Самовары

C Bakery-patisserie
   Bulochnaya-Konditerskaya
   Булочная-Кондитерская

D The Noble Nest
   Dvorianskoye Gnezdo
   Дворянское Гнездо

E Shamrock Pub
   Пуб Шамрок

F Idiot Café
   Кафе Идиот

G 1913

H Adam Ant
   Адам Ант

I Nikolai
   Николай

J Kochubey
   Кочубей

K Hotel Astoria
   Gostinitsa Astoria
   Гостиница Астория

L Café
   Кафе

M Federico Fellini
   Федерико Феллини

N Sakura
   Сакура

O Tchaika
   Чайка

P Grand Hotel Europe
   Gostinitsa Yevropeiskaya
   Гостиница Европейская

Q Nevsky 40
   Невский 40

R Café
   Кафе

Map labels:

ITALIANSKAYA UL. ИТАЛЬЯНСКАЯ УЛ.

M N O P
21
M NEVSKY PROSPEKT
FINISH
Q R
M
GOSTINY DVOR M
20
LUZHSKAYA UL. DUMSKAYA UL.
SADOVAYA UL. САДОВАЯ УЛ.
18
UL. LOMONOSOVA УЛ. ЛОМОНОСОВА
19
SADOVAYA UL.

SENNAYA LOSHCHAD

Sites

1 Children's Park (Yusupov Garden)
Yusupovsky sad
Юсуповский сад

2 Yusupov Palace (on the Fontanka)
Yusopovsky dvorets (na Fontankye)
Юсуповский дворец (на Фонтанке)

3 St Nicholas's Cathedral
Nikolsky sobor
Никольский собор

4 Rimsky-Korsakov Conservatoire
Konservatoriya im. N. A. Rimskovo-Korsakova
Консерватория им. Н. А. Римского-Корсакова

5 Mariinsky Theatre
Mariinsky teatr
Мариинский театр

6 Synagogue
Sinagoga
Синагога

7 New Holland
Novaya Gollandiya
Новая Голландия

8 Vallin de la Mothe Arch
Arka
Арка

9 Yusupov Palace (on the Moyka)
Yusupovsky dvorets (na Moyke)
Юсуповский дворец (на Мойке)

10 Nabokov's House
Dom Nabokova
Дом Набокова

11 Statue of Nicholas I
Statuya Nikolaya I
Статуя Николая I

12 Former German Embassy
Byvshoye nemetskoye posolstvo
Бывшое немецкое посольство

13 Manezh (Central Exhibition Hall)
Manezh (Tsentralny vystavochny zal)
Манеж (Центральный выставочный зал)

14 St Isaac's Cathedral
Isaaktyevsky sobor
Исаакиевский собор

15 Flood Marker

16 Blue Bridge
Sinny most
Синий мост

17 Mariinsky Palace
Mariinsky dvorets
Мариинский дворец

18 Bankovsky Bridge
Bankovsky most
Банковский мост

19 Former Imperial Bank
Byvshy assignatsionny bank
Бывший ассигнационный банк

20 Kazan Cathedral
Kazansky sobor
Казанский собор

21 Dom Knigi
Дом Книги

105

Less than fifty years separate the building of the two cathedrals, both by Russian architects, that begin and end this walk. The earlier St Nicholas's Cathedral was designed at the height of Russia's whimsical Baroque, expressing the country's new-found confidence in a Europeanized and gilded version of Russian traditions, while the Kazan Cathedral is in the mainstream of European architecture. It consciously mimics St Peter's in Rome, ignoring the eastern roots of Orthodox church architecture and announcing Russia's emergence as a great European power. In between, Catherine the Great, with her studious energy and encouraging self-confidence, had pummelled, negotiated and codified Russia out of adolescence.

Yet, beneath this architectural gilding, something of St Petersburg's mythic ambivalence should be gleaned from today's contrasting locations. The walk starts in the depths of Dostoyevsky's city: Haymarket Square. In 1992 Russian men and women came back on to the streets here to drink, trade and socialize, just as their fictional forebears did between the covers of Dostoyevsky's novels. A steady stream of milling shoppers carries you past palatial gardens and across the leafy Griboyedov Canal into the relative quiet of St Nicholas's and the musical theatre district, bordered on three sides by canals. From here, the Moika River sweeps back through the official 19th-century city, past mounted tsars, former embassies, grand hotels and ill-conceived monumentalities to the echoing brilliance of the Kazan Cathedral, until recently the Museum of the History of Religion and Atheism. You can walk it in a matter of hours, and yet in the 19th century you sense that people rarely crossed the bridges between these two worlds.

To make the most of the itinerary, follow it on Thursday–Saturday.

---

lunch/cafés

Ⓐ Old Café, 108 Nab. Reki Fontanka, ✆ 316 5111; *open noon–11pm*. A tiny, atmospheric Russian restaurant with only a few tables, so book in advance if you can.

Ⓑ Russkiye Samovary, opposite the Yusupov Palace Gardens on Ul. Sadovaya, is a cheap drop-in in which *blini* and *kefir*, a longevity-promoting yoghurt drink, are the standard fare.

Ⓒ The **Bakery/Pâtisserie** (Булочная/Кондитерская) overlooking the Mariinsky Theatre sells the best iced rum babas in town, in the crowded stand-up café in the left side of the shop. Queue first at the till opposite, praying they have not run out, and ask for 'kófye ee room bába' (кофе и рум баба). Then present your receipt at the café, repeat the request and give extra roubles if you want sugar (sákhar/сахар).

D **Dvorianskoye Gnezdo (The Noble Nest)**, Ul. Dekabristov 21, ✆ 312 3205; *open 12 noon–12 midnight*. Top-class, five-star, hugely expensive European restaurant inside the Yusupov orangerie.

E **Shamrock**, Ul. Dekabristov 27, ✆ 219 4625; *open 12 noon–2pm*. A Russian take on the Irish pub.

F **Idiot Café**, Nab. Moiki 82, ✆ 315 1675. A student hangout, popular with expats for brunch. Russian vegetarian food.

G **1913**, Ul. Dekabristov 2/13, ✆ 315 5148; *open 12 noon–1am*. Air-conditioned Russian restaurant with reliably good food.

H **Adam Ant**, Nab. Moiki 72, ✆ 311 5575; *open 1pm–midnight*. European cuisine for smart post-*perestroika* Russians.

I **Nikolai**, Dom Arkhitektorov, Ul. Bolshaya Morskaya 52, ✆ 311 1402; *open 12 noon–11pm; closed Sat and Sun*. Ten out of ten for décor, less for the food (*see* p.260).

J **Kochubey**, Konnogvardeysky Bulvar, ✆ 210 9615; *open 1pm–midnight*. Good German-style food.

K **Hotel Astoria**, Isaakiyevskaya Ploshchad. You will find a café/bar inside the entrance closest to the cathedral and the Winter Garden restaurant, which serves good *à la carte* meals for lots of roubles, inside the other.

M **Federico Fellini**, Ul. Malaya Konyushennaya 4/2, ✆ 311 5078; *open 12 noon–1am*. St Petersburg's first and only cinema restaurant: each room is decorated in a different cinematic theme, with the waiting staff dressed accordingly.

N **Sakura**, Kanala Griboyedova 12, ✆ 315 9474 (*open noon–11pm*). Japanese.

O Q **Tchaika**, Kanala Griboyedova 14, and **Nevsky 40**, Nevsky Prospekt 40, are both German joint ventures, more bars than restaurants, though both offer an adequate microwaved menu to their often foreign clientèle.

P **Grand Hotel Europe**, Ul. Mikhailovskaya 1–7, with its restaurants, bar and café, is not far from the Kazan Cathedral at the end of the walk (*see* p.117).

If you arrive at **O** *Sadovaya, change stations below ground to leave via* **M** *Sennaya Ploshchad. As you come out on to the mess of Sennaya Ploshchad (Haymarket Square), half building site, half market, note that we will be leaving it via Sadovaya Ul., the road to the right with tramlines running along it.*

When free trading on the street was legalized, with a certain historical inevitability **Haymarket Square** became St Petersburg's foremost flea-market, where petty salesmen and women traded everything from secondhand locks to caviar. Until the Revolution, when it assumed the pompous name Peace Square, it had been the centre of the city's most notorious slums, an inferno of cheap lodgings, brothels, sawdust-and-spittle alehouses, moneylenders, madmen, vagrants and animals. Here, not surprisingly, the cholera epidemic of 1831 spread triumphantly from one household to another, and here too Dostoyevsky chose to house the oppressed yet proud hero of *Crime and Punishment*, Raskolnikov. Those with a particular interest might want to see where authorities on the book reckon he lived—Ul. Grazhdanskaya 19—and where he killed the moneylender (*see* below).

The Church of the Saviour, for 200 years the square's central feature, was demolished in 1961 to make way for the first metro station. Now the building of the extension of the metro below ground has further destroyed the integrity of the square, with one small, porticoed early 19th-century Guard House clinging ever more tenuously to its life, surrounded by corrugated iron and metal kiosks.

Leave Sennaya Ploshchad via Sadovaya Ul. After a few hundred metres the **Yusupov Garden** *opens up behind railings on the left.*

Once the private garden of the pretty but crumbling Yusupov Palace to the south, it opened to the public after the family moved out in the 19th century. It was here, on the 18th-century ornamental ponds, that Russian figure-skating modestly began; here that several future Olympic champions etched their first figures of eight into the ice. Today it is designated a children's park, and is still a popular venue for skating in winter.

Almost opposite the entrance to the gardens, Ul. Rimskovo-Korsakova, named after the composer, leads at a diagonal over a quiet stretch of the Griboyedov Canal. Cast an eye over Naberezhnaya Kanala Griboyedova 104, which Dostoyevsky used as the model for the home of the old moneylender Aliona Ivanovna in Crime and Punishment, *before continuing to* **St Nicholas's Cathedral** *(Nikolsky sobor).*

St Nicholas's Cathedral

With its five gilded domes and cupolas floating above a pale blue building, this is one of the most popular churches in the city. Open throughout the Soviet period, including the blockade, it was chosen for her funeral in March 1966 by Anna Akhmatova, the poet whose works became a mantra for opponents of the regime.

Built in 1753–62 on the site of a naval parade ground, it has always been known as the 'Sailors' Church', and on Sundays the surrounding shady garden bristles with their uniforms. The architect was Savva Chevakinsky, one of St Petersburg's first successful Russian architects, who had worked with the Baroque genius Rastrelli both on the Winter Palace and at Tsarskoye Selo. Here he effortlessly fuses the characteristics of European Baroque architecture with the liturgical needs of the Orthodox Church, in which the faithful are free to walk around, praying to the various icons and before the iconostasis (*services daily,* © *114 0862 or 114 6926*). Particularly fine is the bright upper chapel and its gilded iconostasis (*not always open*), while the dark and atmospheric lower chapel is open throughout the week. To the west of the church on the banks of the Kryukov Canal (Kanal Kryukova) rises its four-tiered Baroque belltower.

Theatre Square and Mariinsky Theatre

*Due north of the cathedral, tramlines run down the centre of Ul. Glinki and into **Theatre Square** (Teatralnaya Ploshchad), which, since the middle of the 18th century, has been a centre for public amusement.*

In its early days the square was known as Carousel Square and resounded to the music of the fairground. Today it offers the more highbrow charms of performances in the opera studio of the Conservatoire or the Mariinsky Theatre of opera and ballet, two of Russia's most prestigious musical establishments. The Rimsky-Korsakov Conservatoire was built in 1896 to house the educational institute founded by the pianist and composer Anton Rubinstein in 1864. Its illustrious graduates include Tchaikovsky, Prokofiev and Shostakovich. A statue of Rimsky-Korsakov, who was the director of the Conservatoire for many years, sits on its left, and one of Glinka, whose *A Life for the Tsar* was the first Russian opera, on its right. It was in the Bolshoi Theatre on the site of the Conservatoire that this and other early Russian operas were first performed.

Opposite is the home of what has been better known in our era as the Kirov Opera and Ballet Company, from whose rigorous training the West was fortunate to receive the dissident stars Rudolf Nureyev, Natalia Makarova and Mikhail Baryshnikov. It has recently taken back the name that it was given at its foundation in 1859, the **Mariinsky Theatre** (*Mariinsky Teatr*), after the reigning Tsarina Maria Alexandrovna, wife of Alexander II. The ungainly green and white exterior hides one of the prettiest auditoriums in the world, decorated in a refined blue and gold. The Revolution transformed this splendid 1,800-seat theatre into a People's Palace, the French Ambassador noting that within six weeks of the tsar's abdication in March 1917 'all the imperial coats of arms and all the golden eagles have been removed. The box attendants had exchanged their sumptuous court liveries for miserable, dirty grey jackets'. The Royal Box on that night was filled with revolutionaries recently freed from Siberia and other, closer prisons. After a German bomber hit the building during the siege, children, many of them orphans recruited to learn the skills that would be needed to restore the city after the war was over, set to work on the ceiling in November 1943. For many of them, it was the first concrete restoration they had worked on in a life that was to be devoted to the struggle to preserve St Petersburg.

The splendidly louche stage curtain continues to punctuate performances, and the golden eagles and royal insignia have now been reinstated on the Royal Box and two Grand Ducal boxes. While you are passing the theatre, bargain with the touts who hang around the door for tickets to the performances. Try to make sure they don't sell you one with a restricted view. Pat yourself on the back if you manage to get a seat for $15, and go to it expecting a spectacle in the old-fashioned sense, not the innovative cutting edge of production. Though the Mariinsky is currently considered better than its rival, the Bolshoi in Moscow, the need to earn hard currency to keep the theatre going means the main company is often on tour abroad. Don't miss the charming round poster-holders on either side of the theatre entrance, with their own coolie hats to keep off the rain and snow.

Kolomna and New Holland

The area behind the Mariinsky Theatre to the west was known as **Kolomna**, and housed many of the city's Jewish families at the turn of the century. Most Russian Jews were confined to a pale of settlement in Belorussia, the Ukraine and western Russia, and only those with higher education or useful professional qualifications were allowed to live in the city. During the reigns of Alexander III and Nicholas II, both of whom were markedly anti-semitic, legislation curbing Jewish freedoms of movement and ownership was accompanied by attacks on Jews and their property to which the administration largely turned a blind eye. Many Jews took part in the Revolution, and the early Soviet period was a time of unprecedented freedom, with access to higher education freely available for the first time. After the Second World War, during which many Ukrainian and southern Russian Jews had been killed by Hitler, Stalin also turned his paranoid attention towards them. With the foundation of the state of Israel in 1948, the label Zionist became synonymous with treachery, and Jews made up a disproportionate percentage of the gulag population. For the remainder of the Soviet period, they were persecuted by a restriction on their freedom to emigrate, and by discrimination in education and at work. Nowadays, most of those who wish to leave have done so, and some are even returning, preferring the indisputable anti-semitism of Russia to their isolated lives in Israel. Sadly, with the freeing up of Russian society, anti-semitism is rampant, and long-supressed theories of the Revolution as a Jewish conspiracy, led by prominent Communist Jews like Trotsky, Lenin, Zinoviev, Kamenev, Sverdlov and Radek, are too. You can visit the pseudo-Moorish **Synagogue**, Lermontovsky Prospekt 2, once you have secured a skull-cap from the visitor's shop.

*Walking north on the banks of the Kryukov Canal, you come to the Moika River, on the far side of which lies **New Holland** (Novaya Gollandia).*

This site, secreted behind tall brick walls, was originally used to store and season ship's timbers during Peter the Great's reign, and is still occupied by the Russian navy. A short distance to the left along the canal, you come upon the stone and brick arch built by Vallin de la Mothe in the 1760s–70s to give access to its internal canals. Though it is only a small industrial project in a city abounding in flamboyant palaces, this arch is one of the most satisfying and perfect. Its proportions are lofty but excellent, the combination of materials bold and the fluid use of stone highly original. Look particularly at the graceful stone drapes over and around the arch and at the roundels between the pairs of side pillars. This inspired French architect had been recruited to head the architecture department at the new Academy of Arts in 1759 and during his 16 years here had little time for private commissions.

> *If you retrace your steps to the Kryukov Canal and continue along the south bank of the Moika, you come to Vallin de la Mothe's only major piece of private work, the **Yusupov Palace** (Юсуповский Дворец— Yusupovsky Dvorets), Naberezhnaya Reki Moiki 94, currently occupied by the Union of Teachers.*

Yusupov Palace

> *© 314 8893; open daily; groups must pre-book; individuals can just turn up or join the guided tours at 12, 1, 2 and 3, plus also 11 in summer. There is a cassette player guide, or come with your own translator. Unless you join the guided tour (see p.204) you will see nothing of the interior or the cellars in which the drawn-out murder of Rasputin began. Concerts are held in the miniature theatre between October and May.*

The Yusupovs, who at the time of the Revolution were the richest family in Russia, built no fewer than seven palaces in St Petersburg, the back of one of which we have already seen on this walk. These were just the visible tip of the iceberg—they had 37 estates strung out across the country, some of which were literally covered in a film of crude petroleum, and in 1917 their wealth was estimated at $350–$500 million (a barely imaginable sum in those days).

This palace began life as the home of the Shuvalov family. Prince Yusupov bought it in the mid-18th century and invited de la Mothe to enlarge it. It was his plan that the palace should announce itself, as it does today, with a six-column portico. The ornate carved wooden door echoes the Yusupov coat of arms plastered on the pediment of the building. Several decorative alterations and extensions to the building were made in the 19th century, particularly under Prince Nikolai Yusupov in the 1830s, and then at the end of the century with the addition of a theatre.

The Yusupovs emigrated at the time of the Revolution, unable to take a fraction of their renowned collection of pictures, sculpture and furniture with them. In the post-revolutionary chaos, the house briefly sheltered the embassies of a handful of European states before they moved with Lenin's government to Moscow. It then became a museum until finally, in 1925, most of the collection was transferred to state museums and the palace given over to use as a cultural club for teachers.

The tour of the interior comes in two parts. First, in the rather humble bachelor apartments of Felix Felixovich Yusupov, the son and heir, the characters, circumstances and events surrounding the prince's part in the assassination of Rasputin (*see* pp.59–60) are recounted. With the aid of photographs, including one of the dead monk, and a disturbing Madame Tussaud's-type installation, that dark evening of 16–17 December is brought vividly to life.

Monky Business

Felix Yusupov was an unlikely assassin. Born to a beautiful mother longing for a daughter after the birth of three sons, he spent the first five years of his life dressed as a girl, a habit he seemed loath to give up once he began to dress himself. He regularly went out dressed as a woman, and loved eliciting the attention of other men including, on one occasion in Paris, King Edward VII of England. When he went up to Oxford University, his household included a chef, a chauffeur, a valet, a housekeeper and a groom. He returned to Russia in 1914 to marry the tsar's niece Irina, though the French ambassador describes him as 'rather too prone to perverse imaginings and literary representations of vice and death...his favorite author is Oscar Wilde...his instincts, countenance and manner make him much closer akin to...Dorian Gray than to Brutus.'

Felix only conceived the mission to kill Rasputin after partying with the dissolute holy man in the most dubious dives as well as consulting him for his healing powers. He invited the *starets* to his house on the pretext of a party, saying that they would dine first in private. Upstairs were his fellow assassins Dr Lazovert, who had doctored the cakes and wine with cyanide, Grand Duke Dmitry, a cousin of Nicholas II, Vladimir Purishkevich and an army officer called Sukhotin. When Rasputin seemed unaffected by the poison, Felix shot him in the heart. An hour later Felix returned to look at the body, which rose and grabbed him by the throat. Felix struggled free and ran upstairs to alert his conspirators, while Rasputin dragged himself out into the garden. Purishkevich followed and pumped three shots into him. Still Rasputin would not die, and only expired after he was pushed under the icy waters of the river.

The second part of the tour spies on the living quarters of Felix's parents and the palace's public rooms, with a great variety of interiors from the early 19th to early 20th centuries. The white marble staircase was brought in its entirety from an Italian villa. The ground floor has a wooden panelled dining room and a Moorish room with a central fountain—extremely fashionable at the end of the 19th century and, for the Yusupovs, particularly appropriate. There is also a fascinating room with a specially constructed acoustic anomaly incorporated into the apse. Among other aural oddities, if you stand in the middle of the arch at the entrance to the apse and speak directly to the back wall, your voice appears wildly amplified in your ears, but not to anyone else standing about. Upstairs the public rooms begin with an enfilade of drawing rooms decorated in the Empire manner for Prince

Nikolai Yusupov, the most successful of all his line. The final columned rotunda was created to show off the lush turquoise ceramic vases he was given by Louis XVIII during his ambassadorship in Paris. The chandelier in the ballroom is one of the finest in the city, while those in the massive hall next door are made of papier mâché, as the suspended ceiling couldn't take the weight of bronze and crystal. The late 19th-century enfilade of rooms leading back to the jewel-like rococo theatre of the same date housed the pride of the family art collection. Though he was not alive when this theatre was built, the successful Nikolai Yusupov was famous for his antics in his theatre near Moscow. With one wave of his stick the entire cast would appear on the stage naked. Since they were all chosen for their talent from among his serfs, his wish was their command.

A little beyond the palace, Pochtamtsky Bridge over the Moika is tangibly suspended. Bounce across it and turn right along Ul. Bolshaya Morskaya one of the most fashionable streets in old St Petersburg.

Ul. Bolshaya Morskaya 47 was the home of the Nabokovs, now a **museum** (*© 315 4713; open 11–5, closed Mon, Tues*). In this turn of the century house, with its *Style Moderne* ironwork and high floral mosaic featuring overblown lilies, the future author Vladimir Nabokov (1899–1977) was brought up. His aristocratic father, V. D. Nabokov, was a liberal member of the *duma* and a minister in the 1917 Provisional Government. When Nabokov was 20, the family emigrated to Berlin and he and his brother were sent on scholarships to Cambridge. Writing first in Russian and then in English, Nabokov published his first novels in Berlin in the 1920s, under the pseudonym V. Sirin. In 1940 he moved to America where he taught and also made his mark as a lepidopterist. Butterflies and moths were an interest that began in childhood: early photographic portraits of Nabokov by St Petersburg's leading photographer, Karl Bulla, show him delicately handling a book of butterfly plates. With the success of *Lolita*, his tale of sexual obsession which was published in 1959, he was able to devote himself solely to writing. Admired for his stylized use of language in both English and Russian, he is also well known for his translations—of Pushkin's *Eugene Onegin* and of Lewis Carroll's *Alice in Wonderland.*

The far end of the street, beyond St Isaac's Square, was one of the most fashionable pre-revolutionary shopping streets, and china eggs with the name on still hang above the entrance to No.24, the original Fabergé shop (*see* pp.62–3).

St Isaac's Square and St Isaac's Cathedral

First however comes monumental St Isaac's Square (Isaakiyevskaya Ploshchad), which was named after St Isaac of Dalmatia, upon whose saint's day Peter the Great was born and to whom he built a small wooden church here. A monumental square was first mooted in 1760 though none of the large buildings today are that old, the cathedral being the fourth church on the spot, completed in 1858.

The equestrian statue of Nicholas I in the centre was erected a year after the completion of the massive cathedral, by which time the Mariinsky Palace (1839-44) behind it was already in place. The military-loving monarch is portrayed in cavalry uniform, his prancing steed defying gravity on its two back legs. The female figures surrounding the biographical bas-reliefs on the pedestal are portraits of his three daughters and his wife, who commissioned the statue, representing Faith, Wisdom, Justice and Might. It was sculpted by Pyotr Klodt, Russia's first specialist equestrian sculptor, whose four powerful *Horse Tamers* decorate the Anichkov Bridge over the Fontanka on Nevsky Prospekt.

Moving clockwise round the triangular square, you pass the forbidding red granite columned building of the former German Embassy (1911–12), now the Dresdner Bank and St Petersburg Tourist Company offices. Strange but true, the young Mies van der Rohe, who went on to head the Bauhaus and build some astonishing modern buildings in America, was involved in the building when he was working for its Berlin-based architect Peter Behrens. The distinctly cleansed use of period references was dubbed 'scraped classicism'. In July 1914 (according to the old Russian calendar), following the German declaration of war on Russia, a crowd of patriotic Petersburgers attacked the embassy.

*Continue heading towards the Neva down the pavement beside the cathedral until you come to Isaakiyevskaya Ploshchad 1, the **Central Exhibition Hall** (open 10am–6pm when there is an exhibition on; closed Thurs). It occupies a former riding manège where cavalrymen were put through their paces.*

Fronted by a fluteless Doric portico, it was built in 1804–7 by Giacomo Quarenghi. The aspirations of the horseguards within were symbolized by the pair of sculptures without—they show the Dioscuri, the heavenly twins of Leda and Zeus, who were thought of as the protectors of the state. The Holy Synod, which sat nearby, felt that the two naked twins were intentionally baring their bottoms at the clergy of St Isaac's: the statues were removed in 1840 and only replaced in 1954. The hall shows occasional exhibitions of contemporary art.

*Though religious services are once again held in **St Isaac's Cathedral** (Исаакевский Собор—Isaakiyevsky Sobor), it is still a museum, ℂ 315 9732; open 11am–6pm; closed Wed; you can climb to the colonnade (kolonnada) surrounding the dome for a panorama of the city between 11am and 4pm. Tickets are for sale in the kiosk to the right of the entrance on St Isaac's Square.*

Official tours of the cathedral drown you in a sea of numbers, for St Isaac's indulges the Russians' instinctive awe of vastness. A pompous building, the epitome of an imperial cathedral, it cost over 23 million silver roubles to build. In 1818 one of the young French architect Auguste de Montferrand's 24 suggested plans was commissioned by Alexander I to replace the existing cathedral. Such was its scale that it was only finished in the year of Montferrand's death, 1858, long after the tsar and even his successor had died. Serfs laboured to sink wooden piles into the marsh for foundations. The massive granite columns for the porticoes, each weighing nearly 114 tons, were transported from their quarry in Finland on specially designed ships and a small railway built for the purpose. The dome, decorated by fire-gilding, claimed the lives of many workmen who died inhaling mercury vapour. A host of sculptors worked on the external pediments' bas-reliefs, each surmounted by one of the evangelists, on the angels at each corner and on the classical figures that surround the dome. The relief over the entrance portico depicts the Adoration of the Magi, and on the far side it shows the Resurrection. The east and west pediments depict scenes from the life of St Isaac.

The areas to concentrate on are the paintings in the dome and the iconostasis. The dome was decorated by Karl Bryullov, the first Russian painter to gain international fame, winning the Grand Prix at the Paris Salon in 1834 for a painting entitled *The Last Days of Pompeii*, now hanging in the Russian Museum. Portraits of the apostles and evangelists are surmounted, above the windows of the dome, by the Virgin Mary in heaven with saints and angels. Recessed in the very top of the cupola, and lit by yet more natural light, hovers a white dove, symbol of the Holy Spirit. The marble iconostasis, studded with mosaic icons, is gaudy but impressive. Vertically divided by 10 massive malachite-veneer columns, the monumental royal gates are flanked by two smaller columns covered with lazurite. From behind the gates stares a wide-eyed stained glass representation of Christ Resurrected, very unusual for Russia and in fact made in Munich. The mosaics were only created between 1851 and 1914, to replace oil paintings which were disintegrating quickly in the cold, wet environment. *Smalti* (mosaic pieces) of over 12,000 different shades, all made in St Petersburg, were used to recreate the effect of a painting. The painstaking lime-wood model of the cathedral was sculpted over 11 years by a serf, M. Salin, who was given his freedom for these labours.

On the third side of St Isaac's Square is the **Hotel Astoria**.

It occupies both its original *Style Moderne* building (1910–12) on the corner with Ul. Bolshaya Morskaya, and the Angleterre Hotel, a cheaper wing, which continues down Ul. Malaya Morskaya. The 1988–9 campaign to save the former building, by one of St Petersburg's greatest *Style Moderne* architects Fyodor Lidval (though it's not his best), was one of the first examples of an open citizens' protest after *perestroika*. Though redevelopment has stripped the interior of much of its original atmosphere, the protest made its mark, if only in the collective psyche. In the 1989 election that followed, the entire slate of high Party and city officials was rejected, and reformers like ex-mayor Anatoly Sobchak, a professor of law at the university, were given their first taste of power.

*The **Mariinsky Palace**, which dominates the far end of the square, is approached across the Blue Bridge over the Moika. This is the city's broadest bridge, wide enough to carry a bewildering number of lanes of traffic. If you feel up to it you could risk negotiating them to marvel at the hideous heights the Neva has managed to reach in its periodic floodings of the city, recorded on a cast iron flood-marker beside the river.*

The palace, built for Maria Nikolayevna, daughter of Nicholas I, in 1839–44, is the seat of local government. It is closed to tourists, but were one able to penetrate its rather dour exterior, over-dominated by the high central attic, one would find the Rotunda Hall in which the artist Ilya Repin recorded the centenary of the State Council (1901) in his painting now hanging in the Russian Museum. In 1917 it housed the short-lived Provisional Government.

Turning left as you look at the palace, walk a little way along the south bank of the River Moika before turning right up Pereulok Grivtsova (Переулок Гривцова). The buildings become increasingly residential as the street reaches Griboyedov Canal, which always seems rather quiet.

Overlooking the junction, to the right, is a fine example of what is jokingly referred to as 'too-late' (i.e. Stalinist) Classicism. The 1952 building shows a hideous disregard for classical geometric proportions, with its tall, thin, broken portico and an absolutely vestigial use of sculptural decoration.

Turn left along the northern banks of the Griboyedov.

Just after the embankment crosses busy Gorokhovaya Ul., on the far side of the canal a mid-18th-century Baroque palace is crumbling behind its dirty terracotta and white coat of paint. Many old buildings in the centre of town were communalized after the Revolution, with several families, each living in their own, often tiny, room, sharing a bathroom and kitchen with each other. Bulgakov wrote that 'only someone who has lived in a *kommunalka* can know the meaning of true hell'. As successive Soviet governments struggled to build housing in the suburbs, especially after the damage done during the siege, many people accepted rehousing on the outskirts in their own, albeit tiny, flat. There were never enough flats for all, however, and many of those who remain in the centre of the city still live communally, the conditions inside little better than those outside. With the government's privatization scheme, those who can are buying their neighbours out and applying to privatize whole flats, though by and large it is the rich coming in from outside who are buying up the city's prime real estate.

Walking on along the canal you come to Bankovsky Bridge, suspended from the mouths of gold-winged griffins, who according to classical mythology stand guard over gold.

The bridge leads to the back of what was the Imperial Bank, whose classical façade faces Apraksin Dvor on Sadovaya Ul. (*see* p.142). Today it is one of the most popular institutes of higher education, the University of Economics and Finance.

Kazan Cathedral

*As you continue round the bend in the canal, the immense yellow stone colonnade and then the green ribbed dome of the **Kazan Cathedral** (Kazansky sobor) come into view. Entrance to the **Museum of the History of Religion** within is down the steps into the basement on the canal side of the building (© 311 0495; open 11am–5pm weekdays, 12.30–5pm weekends; closed Wed).*

The variegated stone was quarried nearby and was so soft it could be sawn into blocks when just excavated. On prolonged contact with the air it has become rock-hard. Inside, you can hire an English-language cassette (poor quality), if you want. First impressions on emerging into the main cross-shaped body of the cathedral are of immense space, marble and a forest of pillars. Indeed, when it was completed in 1811, it was the third largest church in the world. Beneath the dome, an Escher-like mosaic of marble covers the floor, and to the right of the altar as you look at it is the marble-veneered Tsar's Box, where he would attend services. Over the side doors are bas-reliefs. That on the left shows Peter, sword drawn, protecting Christ from the soldiers in the garden of Gethsemane, while on the right is a depiction of Christ carrying the Cross to Calvary. Also to the right of the altar is the precious silver iconostasis containing mostly 19th-century icons. The main icons, from left to right, portray the Russian saint Sergei Radonezhsky, Mary Magdalene, the Birth of Mary (particularly fine), Jesus Christ, St John the Theologian and St Catherine.

In the north chapel is the grave of Field Marshal Mikhail Kutuzov, who led the Russian army to victory against Napoleon in 1812 and whose spirited and sympathetically modest character leaps from the pages of Tolstoy's *War and Peace*. Buried in June 1813, he lies behind a fence adorned with his family crest and beneath the icon that he always carried into battle with him. The painting gives a clue as to why the cathedral's full name is the Cathedral of Our Lady of Kazan. It shows the victory march in Moscow following the defeat of the Poles by Prince Pozharsky in 1612, led by the protecting icon, Our Lady of Kazan. It was to glorify that icon that Paul I built this cathedral, installing what few people realized was merely a copy. Until 1904 the icon was safely in a monastery in Kazan, but it then disappeared, only to resurface in West Europe after the Second World War. It is now owned by the Russian Orthodox Church in the USA.

A series of exhibits occupies the main nave. Here you can see 19th-century painted monks' habits, torturous metal devices worn to challenge ascetics and a host of valuable silver and bejewelled church vestments and relics. More interesting is the small selection of artefacts relating to traditional Russian folk beliefs, to the right of the door as you look at it. There is a mask made from birch bark for frightening evil spirits, a doll's coffin, with which spring was encouraged, and Easter eggs, traditionally dyed a life-giving blood red, also to encourage the season of growth.

Leave the building via the basement and make your way to its front.

An elaborate double-columned semi-circular colonnade sweeps into the deep central portico, from whose pediment radiates a striking asymmetrical gilded sunburst. This is a show church, so much so that the Orthodox convention of having the altar in the east was entirely superseded by the need for a prestigious entrance on Nevsky Prospekt. It was Paul I, who had incidentally been to the Vatican, who set a competition for its design, and chose that of Prince Sheremetev's talented serf-architect Andrei Voronikhin. Its main doors are copies of Ghiberti's gates of the Baptistry in Florence, which are meant to have ushered in the Renaissance, yet the sculptures on either side of them have a distinctly Russian flavour—from left to right they portray St Vladimir, the first Christian king of Kievan Rus, St Andrew, John the Baptist draped in fur and Russia's warrior saint Alexander Nevsky. In the garden in front of the cathedral are statues of field marshals Kutuzov and Barclay de Tolly, who also fought Napoleon. This space has long been associated with popular politics, and in February 1917 the square was at the centre of the demonstrations that led to the abdication of the tsar.

Before returning to the metro on Nevsky Prospekt, beyond the canal, or visiting a local eatery, take a look at the Style Moderne *building opposite.*

Built as a Singer sewing-machine factory and now St Petersburg's biggest book store, **Dom Knigi**, its rounded fluidity is in complete contrast with the decorative and deeply-carved classicism of the cathedral. The globe at the top of its round tower used to light up at night, and seamstresses sat working on the marvellous American machines at the windows to encourage trade.

IV: On and Off the Nevsky

Start: Ⓜ *Nevsky Prospekt, leave via the Griboyedov Canal* (Канал Грибоедова) *exit*

Walking Time: *2 hours, plus another two to do justice to the Russian Museum*

Sites

1 Church of St Catherine
Kostyol sv. Yekateriny
Костел св. Екатерины

2 Duma Tower
Dumskaya bashnya
Думская башня

3 St Petersburg Philharmonia
Peterburgskaya Philharmonia
Петербургская Филармония

4 Mussorgsky Maly Theatre
Maly teatr im. M. P. Mussorgskomu
Малый театр им. М. П. Мусоргскому

5 Mikhailovsky Palace/Russian Museum
Mikhailovsky dvorets/Russky muzei
Михайловский дворец/Русский музей

6 Museum of Hygiene
Muzei Gigieni
Музей Гигиены

7 Winter Sports Stadium
Zimny stadion
Зимний стадион

8 St Petersburg Circus
Tsirk
Цирк

9 Church of SS Simeon and Anna
Tserkov sv. Simeona i Anny
Церковь св. Симеона и Анны

10 Sheremetiev Palace/
Museum of Musical Instruments
Sheremetyevsky dvorets/
Muzei Muzikalnikh Instrumentov
Шереметевский дворец/
Музей Музикальных Инструментов

11 Catherine Institute
Yekaterinsky institute
Екатеринский институт

12 Anna Akhmatova Museum
Muzei Anny Akhmatovy
Музей Анны Ахматовы

13 Beloselsky-Belozersky Palace
Beloselsky-Belozersky dvorets
Белосельский-Белозерский дворец

14 Galitzine Library
Biblioteka Golitsina
Библиотека Голицина

15 Anichkov Palace
Anichkovsky dvorets
Аничковский дворец

16 Yeliseyev's (Gastronom No 1)
Yeliseyevsky magazin
Елисеевский магазин

17 Russian National Library
Rossiskaya Natsionalnaya Biblioteka
Российская Национальная Библиотека

18 Alexandrinsky Theatre
Alexandrinsky teatr
Александринский театр

19 Museum of Theatre and Musical Arts
Muzei teatralnovo i musikalnovo iskusstva
Музей театрального и музыкального искусства

20 Vaganova Ballet School
Khoreograficheskoye Uchilishche im. A. Ya. Vaganovoi
Хореографическое Училище им. А. Я. Вагановой

21 Bust of Lomonosov
Byust Lomonosova
Бюст Ломоносова

22 Apraksin dvor
Апраксин двор

23 Former Imperial Bank
Assignatsionny bank
Ассигнационный банк

24 Vorontsov Palace/Suvorovsky Academy
Vorontsovsky dvorets/Suvorovskoye Uchilishche
Воронцовский дворец/Суворовское Училище

25 Gostiny dvor
Гостиный двор

26 Armenian Church
Armyanskaya tserkov
Армянская церковь

Restaurants and Cafés

A Grand Hotel Europe
Gostinitsa Yevropeiskaya
Гостиница Европейская

B Café Ol
Кафе 01

C Kavkaz Café
Кафе Кабказ

D Milano
Милано

E Metekhi Café
Кафе Метехи

F Ket
Кет

G Graf Suvorov
Граф Суворов

120

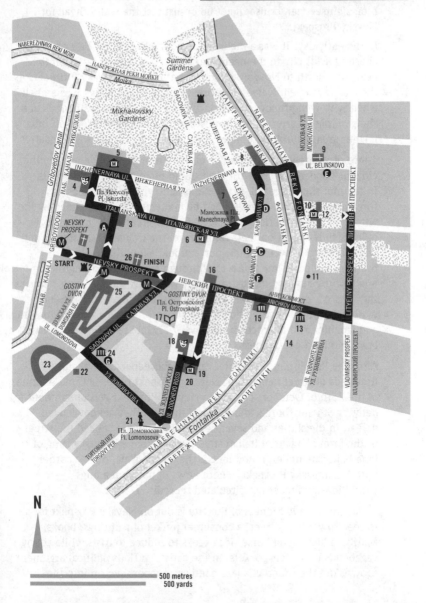

N

500 metres
500 yards

It is hard to think of another city in which one street is as dominant as St Petersburg's Nevsky Prospekt. If you want to shop, take in a play or film, sightsee, eat, cruise, meet up or just test the water, head for Nevsky Prospekt.

In the early days it was a lifeline connecting the centre Peter had chosen for his city to the nearest existing road, which ran from the pearl-rich north to Novgorod, along what is now Ligovsky Prospekt. As the city developed, Nevsky's impressive 3km perspective was embellished with well-proportioned palaces, theatres, hotels, cathedrals and shops. From its arterial flow a network of smaller streets led off into further architectural ensembles: more palaces, museums and theatres.

There was barely a public edifice elsewhere in the city, and daily the citizens flooded Nevsky with their 'rapid phantasmagoria' (Gogol). In the morning resentful, lowly clerks scurrying to the office in threadbare overcoats were soaked by meltwater puddles aimed by the wheels of their superiors' carriages. Governesses with their charges, officers showing off on their return from the Caucasus, husbands and wives dressed as well as their purse would allow them, all promenaded past shop fronts and through gardens, gleaning the mood of the city and its gossip as they went. Brushed by their hems as they passed, drunks, beggars and madmen scrounged an existence while prostitutes hovered down side streets. As well as entertainment and laughter, the microcosm on Nevsky Prospekt bred resentment, envy and hard-heartedness.

After the Revolution, the Soviet regime succeeded in changing hundreds of street names, but Nevsky Prospekt never became Avenue of the 25th of October. To abolish Nevsky Prospekt was tantamount to denying St Petersburg's identity, and in 1944 they acknowledged defeat. In the sixties and seventies subtle rebellion stalked the street in the form of a pair of Italian shoes, a line from a Vysotsky song or long hair. The underground met at the Saigon Café, on the corner with Vladimirsky Prospekt, where news of poetry readings, exhibitions and meetings circulated secretly.

Today the joy and sadness of the city is out on Nevsky Prospekt for all to see. Towards the river, a consumer junket of paintings, books, Marlboro kiosks and horse rides seeks to seduce tourists while young vagabonds pick their pockets. In the centre, furious political argument drowns out the sound of a jazz band as shoppers swarm into the nearby department stores. Near the Moscow station on Ploshchad Vosstaniya, drunks and the benighted former inmates of mental hospitals, which have been closed on a massive scale because of lack of funds, grub around for a living on the street. Gogol would notice little difference.

Surprisingly, many of the buildings on this walk still serve the same purpose for which they were built: the Grand Hotel Europe, the Alexandrinsky and Mussorgsky Theatre of Opera and Ballet (formerly the Maly), the public library and the circus. Others have been turned into museums. The collection of Russian paintings in the Russian Museum is as rich and vibrant as that of the Tretyakov in Moscow, hanging in rooms overlooking peaceful palace gardens. The Museum of Theatre and Musical Arts gives a colourful lightning guide to Russian drama, while sombre greys dominate the museum devoted to the life struggle of the 20th-century poet Anna Akhmatova.

To make the most of this itinerary, with its shopping and cultural possibilities, walk it on Thursday–Saturday. As long as you don't start too early, you could also follow it on a Wednesday, when the Museum of the Theatre and Musical Arts opens at 1pm. My advice would be to give yourself two hours in the morning, have lunch after the Russian Museum and continue the rest of the walk in the afternoon.

lunch/cafés

A **Grand Hotel Europe**, Ul. Mikhailovskaya 1/7, ✆ 329 6000. From 7am to 11pm you will find somewhere to graze in this top-of-the-range hotel. An Italian restaurant, a Chinese restaurant, a café in the atrium and the quick ever-changing menu at Sadkos are all good daytime possibilities.

B **Café 01**, Karavannaya Ul. 7; *open 12 noon–4pm, 5–11pm*. Cosy and very popular, this is an ideal place to drop in for a bowl of spiced soup to keep you going. Sadly, you may find it is full.

C **Kavkaz**, Karavannaya Ul. 18, ✆ 315 3900; *open 10am–1pm*. Bar/café/restaurant serving reliable Georgian food.

D **Milano**, Karavannaya Ul. 8, ✆ 314 7348; *open 12 noon–midnight*. Italian restaurant run by a charming Milanese.

E **Metekhi Café**, Ul. Belinskovo 3; *open 11am–9pm*. The better of the two adjacent Georgian cafés, Metekhi caters well for vegetarians with grilled cheese, *sir sulugumi*, and *lobio* (bean stew), beside meaty soups and entrées.

F **Ket**, Karavannaya Ul. 24, ✆ 315 3900; *open 12 noon–11pm*. Clean basement café-restaurant, popular with locals. Russian-European food with good sauces.

G **Graf Suvorov**, Ul. Lomonosova 6, ✆ 315 4328; *open 12 noon–2am*. Five-star cuisine at one of the best small restaurants.

*Leave ⓜ Nevsky Prospekt via the exit marked Canal Griboyedova (Канал Грибоедова), emerging from an unlikely blue and white 19th-century façade opposite the Kazan Cathedral (see **Walk III**). Turn left.*

Up Nevsky Prospekt on the left, the cream façade of the **Church of St Catherine** (1762–83), set back from the road, provides the backdrop for a vibrant art market. Hundreds of paintings, suspended from makeshift stands, wait for passing tourists. The church was one of a clutch of foreign denomination churches on Nevsky Prospekt which earned it the name the Street of Tolerance. Designed by Vallin de la Mothe, and now under restoration, it was the hub of Catholic St Petersburg.

Next to the church is the Grand Hotel Europe, and opposite rises the ungainly red tower of what was the town *duma*, surmounted by a coppice of aerials. Built in 1804 as a fire watchtower, it was later used to signal to the royal palaces outside the city. In the building beneath it, which runs at right angles to Nevsky Prospekt along Dumskaya Ul., the elected city council became the focus for anti-Soviet sentiments after the Revolution, but was only closed down in October 1918. Today Dumskaya Ul. is the unlikely cruising ground for the city's homosexuals. Still a beleaguered minority, until the repeal of Article 121 of the penal code in 1993 they faced up to five years' imprisonment for sexual activity. The arcade beneath the tower on Nevsky Prospekt used to house rows of jewellers in the Serebryaniye Ryady (Silver Rows), but is now a mediocre art salon. The entrance is besieged by cartoonists and portrait painters. Paintings and a few antiques, as well as theatre tickets, are for sale in the delicate yellow and white classical portico, the Portik Rusca, that stands alone beyond the Duma Tower.

Turn left round the corner of the Grand Hotel Europe (Gostinitsa Yevropeiskaya) into Mikhailovskaya Ul.

Though built in 1873–5 the hotel owes its character (what is left of it after its deluxe Swedish refurbishment) to the facelift it was given by the city's most talented Art Nouveau architect, Fyodor Lidval, in 1908–10. On the other side of the street stands one of the city's most important classical music venues, the **St Petersburg Philharmonia**. In tsarist times this building was the Nobles' Club, but from the mid-19th century its main hall became best known for the concerts held by the Russian Musical Society. In 1893 Tchaikovsky conducted the premiere of his Sixth Symphony here before dying a few days later from cholera. At the turn of the century Isadora Duncan, the American dancer, made her Russian debut on this stage. But the Philharmonia's proudest moment took place on 9 August 1942, during the siege. With guns pounding just 13km away, the orchestra, depleted by conscription and starvation, gave the first performance of Shostakovich's Seventh, the 'Leningrad' Symphony, partly written in the besieged city. The heroic concert was beamed across the Soviet Union by radio, a broadcast that still brings tears to the eyes of those who lived through the blockade.

As Mikhailovskaya Ul. opens out into **Ploshchad Iskusstv,** *Square of the Arts, one is struck by a sense of harmony.*

The whole ensemble was designed to go with the Mikhailovsky Palace, which stands straight ahead. It formed part of Alexander I's architectural celebration of Russia's triumph over Napoleon, coordinated by the talented neoclassicist Carlo Rossi. Such was Rossi's favoured status with the emperor that there were rumours that Rossi was the offspring of a liaison between his Italian mother and Paul I. The severe classicism of the square's façades is tempered by the large central garden, which focuses on a statue of Pushkin by the post-war sculptor Mikhail Anikushin.

The main building on the left-hand side of the square is the **Mussorgsky Theatre of Opera and Ballet.** *The first building on the same side (No.5) was the site of the famous basement club known as the* **Stray Dog.**

In its heyday in 1913 the Stray Dog was one of the world's great bohemian clubs, for at that time there was nothing more radical than a gathering of St Petersburg's poets and painters, who were challenging the boundaries of their arts at every step. They would sit sipping coffee, or slump drunk over a table, occasionally woken from their reveries by the impromptu recitation of a few lines or a loud blast from the piano. One of its stars was the willowy poet Anna Akhmatova, who numbered herself among its 'heavy drinkers' and 'women of loose morals'. Surveying its fatalistic decadence with what Brodsky calls a 'note of controlled terror' in her voice, she seemed to prophesy imminent catastophe and the downfall of the avant-garde. Nineteen months later, Russia was at war with Germany, and the stage set for the Revolution, which ultimately and fatally rejected the daring avant-garde in favour of the saccharine platitudes of Socialist Realism. Many of the Stray Dog's habitués ended their lives in exile abroad if they were lucky, in the Siberian gulag if not.

Walk round the square and into the front courtyard of the Mikhailovsky Palace, now the **Russian Museum** *(Gosudarstvyenny russky muzei).*

Russian Museum

✆ 314 3448; open 10am–5pm; closed Tues. You enter the museum by a basement door, to the right of the portico. The ticket office, cloakrooms and a café are all to be found in the labyrinth of corridors that leads to the stairs into the main hall. On either side of the grand double staircase you will find the museum shop, selling high-quality postcards.

The palace was built in 1819–25. The piers of its gates are surmounted by mock trophies of war, and the sumptuous classicism of its full-blown Corinthian portico, heroic frieze and heavily stuccoed pediment suggest an empire in the ascendancy. Inside, however, the Mikhailovsky Palace has more to do with culture than imperial ambition. Grand Duke Mikhail's wife Elena, 'a blaze of beauty and health and cheerfulness', infused it with cultured, intelligent enthusiasm, bringing together artists, musicians and scientists in her 'salon'. The pianist Anton Rubinstein used its rooms as a music school before founding the St Petersburg Conservatoire in 1864, and the Grand Duchess even established the country's first observatory, out at Pulkovo. It was a time when the fabulous fortune of the royal family was fortuitously linked with good taste, and even the balls at Mikhailovsky were an artistic event. The Marquis de Custine, who attended one in 1839, recalled:

> *The interior of the grand gallery in which they danced was arranged with a marvellous luxury. Fifteen hundred boxes of the rarest plants, in flower, formed a grove of fragrant verdure... It might have been supposed that these strange plants, including large palms and bananas, all of whose boxes were concealed under a carpet of mossy verdure, grew in their native earth, and that the groups of northern dancers had been transported by enchantment to the forests of the tropics. It was like a dream; there was not merely luxury in the scene, there was poetry.*

The palace was sold to Nicholas II in 1895 to create the Russian Museum. His father Alexander III, a great collector, had decided to create a public gallery of Russian art after visiting Moscow's Tretyakov Gallery, founded by two rich merchant brothers. If they could do it, he certainly should too. However, Alexander died before realizing his plan, and it was left to Nicholas to found it for him, calling the museum he opened here in 1898 the Russian Museum of Alexander III.

The Russian Museum owes much of its wealth to the nationalization of private collections after the Revolution, and to the museum's appropriation of an estimated 40,000 icons from churches that were shut down or destroyed during the Soviet period. It competes with the Tretyakov for the best collection of Russian painting, though at any one time only a fraction of its collection is on show.

> *The following itinerary gives a chronological history of Russian painting, and to a lesser extent sculpture, weaving through the three interconnected buildings of the museum. After the main palace, it passes through the Rossi Wing and up to the first floor of the Benois Building, where paintings from the 20th century are displayed. The applied and folk art collection on the ground floor of the Rossi Wing is sometimes open. Temporary exhibitions are usually hung on the ground floor and part of the second floor of the Benois Building.*

Begin by taking the palace stairs, which sweep up to a gallery of Russian 18th- and 19th-century sculpture beneath a soaring ceiling decorated with sumptuous *grisaille* murals, painted in various tones of grey and white in imitation of plaster reliefs. When Rossi built the palace he had access to a fabulous circle of craftsmen and decorators, attracted to St Petersburg by the imperial building craze. Many of the murals, including these, were executed by members of the Italian Scotti family.

*Turn left at the top of the stairs and you will find yourself in the spiritual world of Russian **icon painting**, Rooms 1–4 (see pp.60–61).*

The museum's collection of sacred images begins with a few surviving icons from the 12th to the mid-14th century. The small, intense *Golden-Haired Angel* (12th century), whose peaceful, dreamy gaze bears witness to God's tenderness, was once part of a panel that showed Christ flanked by two such guardians. Also in this room is a refined mid-14th-century depiction of the first Russian martyrs, *Princes Boris and Gleb*. The sons of Prince Vladimir of Kiev, who brought Christianity to the people of Kievan Rus in 988, they were murdered by their older brother Svyatopolk, 'the accursed'. Whatever their spiritual credentials, they are depicted in worldly 14th-century Russian clothing, rendered in minute detail.

Room 2 is devoted to the two great centres of icon painting from which abundant examples survive: the northern cities of Novgorod and Pskov, which were never sacked by the Mongols. The Novgorod School, represented by an icon of St George killing the dragon, and another showing the siege of Novgorod by the city of Suzdal, is characterized by bright colours, exaggerated outline shapes and a greater sense of movement. The three Pskov icons here are rigid, hieratic and formal by comparison. To appreciate the difference, compare the Novgorod and Pskov icons of the Harrowing of Hell hanging opposite one another. Both depict the moment when Christ, after His death on the cross, descended into hell to bring Adam and Eve and the godly women and men of the Old Testament with him into heaven.

Russian icon painting reached its apex in the late 14th and early 15th centuries, as the country emerged from Mongol domination. In Room 3 are two immense thin panels from the Cathedral of the Assumption in Vladimir, by **Andrei Rublyov**, arguably the greatest ever icon painter. Depicting the *Apostles Peter* (left) *and Paul* (right), they are not in very good condition, but do show Rublyov's definitive traits. The figures are traced with masterly linear simplicity, while their faces are a picture of gentle wisdom. Rublyov's talent lies in saturating his images with a sense of inner godliness. Also by Rublyov is the *Presentation of Jesus at the Temple*, which concentrates with a touching and fragile intensity on the figure of Christ, a tiny ray of hope clutched tenderly in the arms of the typically elongated, Rublyovian priest. The beautifully composed icon of *St John the Evangelist* receiving the word of God and dictating it to his pupil on the rocky, surreal landscape of Patmos dates from the 16th century, in the style of the Moscow School which Rublyov founded.

Work by **Dionysy** in Room 4 marks the end of the heyday of icon painting. Here the sense of intense spirituality disappears, replaced by a concentration on physical detail and story-telling. One's attention is grabbed by the ribbons in an angel's hair or an overpowering use of gold. The miniature icons in the octagonal display case, by masters of the Stroganov school, are fine examples of this later tendency.

From Room 5, English labelling makes it easier to find your way around.

As you pass through the door you find yourself expelled from the spiritual world of medieval Russia. The transition to the worldly portraits of the 17th and early 18th century is cushioned by the fact that early Russian portraiture, known as *parsuna*, borrowed many techniques from the only indigenous art form. The portrait of Y. F. Turgenev in Room 5 is a good example, with its sharply defined, iconesque blocks of colour. This was soon to change. Peter the Great's infatuation with western Europe encouraged him to invite western painters here, and to send talented Russians to study abroad. Within decades painters such as **Ivan Nikitin** (*c*. 1688–1741) were producing works like the wonderfully informal portrayal of the strong but troubled Hetman, his collar undone and the whole picture painted at an angle.

Rooms 6–10 follow the development of Russian art after Peter's death. A vogue for mosaic portraits (Room 6) ran parallel to the development of factories, set up with western know-how, producing decorative materials such as glass, tapestries and ceramics for all the new palaces. Note how the chandeliers develop from simple bronze in Room 5 to the delicate bronze, coloured glass and crystal affairs from the heyday of Imperial Russia. In Room 7 the walls are lined with tapestries from the St Petersburg factory set up with the help of Dutch masters. In the centre of the room is a finely cast bronze of Empress Anna Ivanovna, a remote, immovable, bejewelled mass beside her delicate black slave, by **Carlo Bartolomeo Rastrelli** (1675–1744). The main enfilade of the palace begins here, overlooking the garden.

Room 8 is dominated by the talents of **F. S. Rokotov** (1735–1808), a serf-artist trained in St Petersburg and the first Russian portraitist to try to build some psychological depth into his portraits. Room 9 sees the beginnings of a trend that was to dominate Russian painting for almost 100 years. The foundation of the Academy of Arts in St Petersburg in 1757 encouraged a strict adherence to the principles of classicism, and portraiture lost ground to the painting of historical, biblical and mythological scenes. Coupled with the development of a proud national consciousness, this could be stultifying. One of its earliest exponents was the Ukrainian **Anton Losenko** (1737–73), here depicting Prince Vladimir of Novgorod, who, rejected by Rogneda, determines to take her by force. But having killed her father and brothers, and destroyed her native Polotsk, Vladimir is beset by remorse when he finds Rogneda weeping in her room. Despite its emotive subject matter, the picture inhabits an emotional limbo because, for the painter, the subject is purely an intellectual exercise. Room 10, in contrast, represents the peak of 18th-century portraiture. A lyrical series by **Dmitry Levitsky** (1735–1822) depicts the first graduates of Catherine the Great's Smolny Institute, a boarding school for noble girls, painted at the empress's request. As well as the three Rs, the girls were encouraged to develop their musical and dramatic talents, and often took part in performances at the royal palaces. The best loved of the portraits shows Khovanskaya, playing the part of a boy, courting her schoolfriend Khrushcheva, the shepherdess, chucking her under the chin with cheeky playfulness. Levitsky also painted the full-length allegorical portrait of Catherine the Great as Legislator at the Temple of Justice, an official work intended to emphasize Catherine's fairness as a ruler. At the height of Bolshevik madness in 1918, the city's Arts Committee had to fight a tricky battle to prevent the portrait being taken and its canvas used for a revolutionary work.

Room 11, the most sumptuous in the palace, is known as the White Hall. Its perfect white scagliola walls were the envy of the world; George IV asked for the secret, only to discover that it lay in a particularly fine white alabaster excavated near Kazan. The powdered alabaster is fixed to the wall with gesso, heated, and the hardened surface polished. The paintings on them were executed by Vighi. Like all the original fixtures and fittings, the pale blue and gold suite of furniture, and the strange smoky blue smalt console tables were part of Rossi's master design.

Most of the rest of the first floor is devoted to the romantic classicism taught by the Academy of Arts. A brief respite is afforded by the virtuoso portraits by **Vladimir Borovikovsky** (1757–1825), another Ukrainian, in Room 12. Two of the massive canvases in Room 14 by **Grigory Urgiumov** (1764–1823) illustrate turning points in Russian history. The first depicts the *Tartar Submission to Ivan IV* in 1552 at Kazan, the second the *Coronation of Mikhail Romanov* in 1613, which brought the Time of Troubles to an end. Room 15 is shared by two giants of Russian 19th-century painting, **Ivan Aivazovsky** (1817–1900) and **Karl Bryullov** (1799–1852), who won the Grand Prix at the Paris Salon in 1834 for the dramatic *Last Days of Pompeii*. Gogol and Pushkin were among those overcome by the painting, though today it is hard to appreciate what all the fuss was about. Bryullov's talents seem better used in the many portraits also hanging in this hall. On the wall opposite the theatrical melodrama of Pompeii rolls the meditative calm of Aivazovsky's extraordinary luminous seascapes. Aivazovsky, who lived in the Crimea on the banks of the Black Sea, is said to have painted over 6,000 seascapes.

There is more light relief from the pomposity of the Grand Academic Halls in the intimate landscapes in Room 16, many painted by Russian emigrés, and the portraits by the serf-artist **Orest Kiprensky** (1782–1836) in Room 17. His vision of romantic nobility is best expressed here in the full-length portrait of Evgraf Davidov dressed as a colonel in the Hussars. The tousled-haired hero's resplendent uniform stands out from the moody shadows, one effete hand resting informally on his hip.

> *If the first floor belongs to portraiture and the nobility, the **ground floor** is the preserve of 19th-century genre painting concerned with the lives of the peasantry and Russia's burgeoning middle classes.*

By the mid-19th century, the Academy of Art's proclamation that 'art must aim at revealing virtue, at immortalizing the deeds of the great men who deserve the nation's gratitude' was patently out of date. The Napoleonic Wars had shown that it was not only 'great men' who defended the country, but also millions of peasants who had both fought and harassed the enemy out of Russia. The fight was on to free the serfs, and urban sophisticates began to patronize genre painting focusing on the charms of the Russian countryside. **Alexei Venetsianov** (1780–1847), whose paintings hang in Room 18, was the first to take painting back to the village. He depicts peasants, whether *Cleaning the Sugar Beet* or simply resting in the fields, in a moment suspended in time; there is no attempt at narrative or psychological depth. This natural realism was popular enough for the artist to set up his own school in the countryside, in competition with the Academy. Venetsianov anticipated the move away from this institution, although it was by no means a steady flow. Such was the fickleness of artistic fashion that, when Bryullov won international approval for *The Last Days of Pompeii* in 1834, many pupils deserted Venetsianov to return to the Academy. In Room 19 you will find works by some of Venetsianov's pupils, the most talented being the tragic serf-painter **Grigory Soroka** (1823–64). His works, particularly *The Fishermen*, are saturated with a sense of the unchanging tasks of the Russian peasant and the peaceful rhythm of their environment. Despite his talent, Soroka was unable to free himself from serfdom as a gardener, and became increasingly rebellious. Ironically, it was after the abolition of serfdom made him a free man that he was accused of taking part in peasant disturbances; rather than face a public flogging, he committed suicide.

Vasily Tropinin (1776–1857), also born a serf, was one of the first Russian portraitists to take an interest in the urban middle classes. Room 20 abounds with faces from Tropinin's own milieu, Moscow's mercantile Zamoskvarechye district.

The works of **Alexander Ivanov** (1806–58) displayed in Rooms 21 and 22 amply illustrate his incredible technical virtuosity and his obsessiveness. Accepted by the Academy at the age of 11, Ivanov was at first taught by his academician father Andrei. In 1831 he went to Italy on a scholarship, and only returned shortly before his death. The effect that Italy, and particularly its Renaissance painting, had on him can easily be discerned in the form and colour of his works. In 1832 Ivanov conceived the idea for his great life's work, *The First Appearance of Christ Among the People*. He worked on the painting for some 25 years, making sketch after sketch. Room 21 has a clutch of these sketches, and an early version of the final painting. The almost identical 'original' is in Moscow. Other paintings by the faithful Ivanov include *Jesus' Appearance to Mary Magdalene*. He also painted secular works, including the Italianate landscapes that can be seen in Room 22.

Under the tsars' censorship, Russian art was slow to express social criticism and satire. Vasily Perov's anti-establishment attitude may well have had personal roots in his father's exile to Siberia. His canvas *Monastery Refectory* in Room 23 reveals his view of 19th-century Russia. Red-faced, pot-bellied monks ingratiate themselves with grandees while ignoring the beggar woman trying to catch their attention. Not surprisingly, several of Perov's pictures were banned by the authorities. Room 24 contains a number of canvases by the talented landscape painter **Alexei Savrasov** (1830–97), one of the first to depict the Russian landscape. When first exhibited, his *The Rooks Have Returned* (in the Tretyakov), a clump of rook-strewn birches in a dirty spring landscape, caused an eruption of nationalist pride.

The determination to create a truly Russian school of painting, after 200 years of pervasive foreign influence, led to the most important moment in Russian 19th-century art. Two years after the emancipation of the serfs in 1861, the Academy set yet another mythological subject for its annual Gold Medal competition. Disgusted by the irrelevance of the theme, 14 students led by Ivan Kramskoy left to set up their own association. They became known as the *Peredvizhniki*, Wanderers, and were quickly joined by others including Savrasov. Some penetrating portraits in Room 25 shows **Kramskoy**'s talents (1837–87). A strange sense of empathy between sitter and artist draws you into the picture. The radiant portrayal of Mina Moiseyev, a picture of assured, dignified peasanthood, shines out above the rest.

Nicholas Ge (Gay), another founder member of the Wanderers, experimented with different genres before settling, under the influence of Alexander Ivanov, on biblical themes. In Room 26 is his marvellous portrait of the great novelist Lev Tolstoy at work, with his permanently knitted brow. Nearby hangs a painful historical scene, *Peter the Great Interrogating Tsarevich Alexei*, which captures the mutual distrust that characterized their relationship and the atmosphere of doom that hung over the event (*see* p.33). Ge's dramatic portrayals of biblical events are represented by the eerie, moonlit *Jesus arriving at Garden of Gethsemene*.

The best loved landscape painter of the second half of the 19th century was without doubt **Ivan Shishkin** (1832–98). His arboreal hymns to his native land hang in Room 27, and seem to tug at the heartstrings of most sentimental Russians. His portrait by Kramskoy a few rooms back shows a wild-haired man with subtly smiling eyes. Shishkin was known as 'the poet of the Russian forest', and his interest was so exclusive that if ever it was felt he should include a man or animal in his pictures, he would invite another artist to paint them for him.

Rooms 28–32 contain a range of lesser late 19th-century canvases including genre scenes by **Vladimir Makovsky**, who champions the underdog in his *Doss House* and *Bankruptcy*, and **Karl Savitsky**'s highly charged set-piece *To the War*.

An expensive shop in Room 29 sells reproduction Russian jewellery, including the much-copied Fabergé enamel eggs.

One of the most beloved Russian painters of all time was **Ilya Repin** (1844–1933), who came to be best known as a portraitist, though the paintings that first made him popular were bold canvases on social and historical themes. Repin arrived in St Petersburg the very year the Wanderers boycotted the Academy. Although he studied at the Academy, he soon came to think of Kramskoy as his teacher. Dominating Room 33 is his *Barge Haulers on the Volga*, which depicts a team of ragged men struggling at every step of their backbreaking life's work. As well as betraying moral outrage at the reality of their life-threatening, medieval drudgery, the painting also works on a subliminal level. The older men, particularly the man lagging at the back, have no chance of escape except death, but the younger recruit at the centre of the group, lit by a benevolent burst of light, is already kicking at the traces. Hope for a better future is invested in him. When he first saw it, Dostoyevsky read it as a reminder of each man's duty to his fellow men.

Rooms 34 and 35 are devoted to Repin's portraits from the-turn of-the-century art world: his *Lev Tolstoy*, a Whistleresque full-length portrait; the critic *Vladimir Stasov*; the pianist *Anton Rubinstein*; and the composer *Alexander Glazunov*. The ebullient picture of the *Zaporozhian Cossacks Writing a Mocking Letter to the Turkish Sultan* depicts a perhaps mythical episode of the 17th century, when the cossacks of the Zaporozhian Republic rejected the sultan's offer to enter his service.

> *To find the other Repin* chef d'œuvre *on show, the* Ceremonial Meeting of the State Council, 7 May 1901, *you must pass downstairs through Room 39 (see below) and turn right into Room 54.*

Some of the sketches for this official commission, portraits of individual councillors, are loaded with character despite their hurried, impressionistic execution. Note Councillor Pobedonostsev, Chief Procurator of the Holy Synod and high priest of the systematic repression and retrenchment that took place under Alexander III.

Room 39, to which we must return, is alive with **Filip Maliavin**'s exuberant red swirl of a peasant woman dancing. A peasant himself, Maliavin (1869–1940) became a monk in the Russian monastery on Mount Athos at the age of 14, and stayed for six years until his talent was recognized by a visiting academician who persuaded him to return to St Petersburg to study fine arts. The academy was unable to tame Maliavin's innate Russian love of colour, and though he did paint portraits it is these effusive paintings which fully express his painterly genius.

Rooms 40–41 herald another important development in late 19th-century Russian painting, another step along the path beaten by the Wanderers and their Slavophile supporters. The wealthy industrialist Savva Mamontov set up an artistic commune and encouraged an Arts and Crafts movement similar to those flowering in Europe to develop. Its roots lay in traditional Russian skills and the belief that the essence of Russia lay in her medieval history, literature and folk tales. **Alexei Ryabushkin** (1861–1904) and **Victor Vasnetsov** (1846–1926) devoted their energies to conjuring up this world in all its doom-laden, violent and colourful variety.

> *Walk along the corridor (Room 49) and up the stairs on to the first floor of the Benois Building.*

Encouraged by Abramtsevo's multi-media approach to decorative and applied arts as well as painting, the talents of one of Russia's most individual painters, **Mikhail**

Vrubel (1856–1910) flourished. Vrubel was a ceramicist and mural painter, and the fractured images of his paintings in Room 66 have a tactile quality normally associated with mosaics and tiles. He returned again and again to the themes of beauty and immortality that can be seen in paintings such as *The Flying Demon* and *The Six-Winged Seraphim*. The gap between his craving for these qualities and the reality of his life became unbearable, and Vrubel ended his life blind and confined to an insane asylum.

Another attempt to capture the essence of Russia was made by **Mikhail Nesterov** (1862–1942), whose religious mysticism is shown on the walls of Room 67. 'I love the Russian landscape,' he wrote. 'Against its background the meaning of Russian life and the Russian soul can be felt better and more clearly.' Alongside this search for a truly Russian school other painters had a more international attitude to the arts. 'Art for art's sake' was the credo of the World of Art (*Mir Iskusstva*) group, whose works hang in Room 68. Their patron was the aesthete and impresario Sergei Diaghilev, who organized exhibitions of foreign art in St Petersburg and published a *World of Art* magazine. The artists in this group, who included Leon Bakst and Alexander Benois, worked on the set designs for Diaghilev's Ballet Russe, which toured Europe with great success from 1911. Their canvases are flamboyant and theatrical, strongly influenced by Art Nouveau, called in Russia *Style Moderne*.

Room 69 contains the eerie works of the unhappy **Victor Borisov-Musatov** (1870–1905), whose cool perception of the world around is explained by his withdrawn existence. 'When I am frightened by life I rest in art...sometimes it seems to me that I am on a deserted island. And it is as if reality does not exist.' The contrast with **Valentin Serov**'s worldly portraits in Room 70 could not be more marked. Among his clients were the richest of Russia's pre-Revolutionary nobility: Zinaida Yusupova (the mother of Felix Yusupov who helped to assassinate Rasputin) and the Countess Orlova. Serov, originally trained at Abramtsevo, also became involved with Diaghilev. In Room 71 you can see his famous sketch of the ballerina Anna Pavlova for the poster of the Russian Season in Paris, and his nude portrait of Ida Rubinstein, who also danced for Diaghilev. Seeing her as a 'living bas-relief', Serov painted her in the faintly monochrome style of an Egyptian stone carving.

Rooms 72 and 73 give an overview of other contemporary styles: the impressionistic landscapes of **Konstantin Korovin** (1861–1939), early Impressionist still lifes by **Mikhail Larionov** (1881–1964), and **Boris Kustodiev**'s colourful canvases imbued with the primitive influences of folk traditions. The distinctive landscapes of **Nikolai Roerich** in Room 74, charged with his own pantheistic perception of the world, are as happy in the New Age of the late 20th century as they were in pre-Revolutionary Russia. Roerich's idealism was typified by the campaign he began to press the League of Nations to sign a clause protecting cultural monuments in times of war—a clause eventually enshrined in the treaty of the United Nations.

Rooms 75–79 romp through the avant-garde, one of the most important periods in the history of Russian painting, and the only one to rival the 15th-century icon painters for creative innovation. Although the avant-garde had a greater impact on world art than any other group of Russian painters, thanks to Stalin they are thinly represented here. From the mid-1920s, the only form of art encouraged by the state was Socialist Realism, which replaced the heady atmosphere of experiment with an endless stream of paintings glorifying the Revolution, the Party and the People. Until the advent of Gorbachev, the Russian Museum's exhibition of 20th-century painting followed that credo. In its cellars however, it was protecting thousands of avant-garde canvases, and the new hanging is continually evolving. That many avant-garde painters welcomed the Revolution and saw themselves as revolutionary painters creating a new art for the new times is all the more ironic.

Appropriating foreign artistic movements such as Cubism and Futurism as a spring-board, the Russian avant-garde was propelled by its national traditions and by the Revolution to create a whole series of -isms of its own. While the works of **Pavel Kuznetsov** (1878–1968) in Room 75, **Kuzmin Petrov-Vodkin** (1878–1939) in Room 76 and **Natan Altman** (1889–1970) in Room 77 are broadly figurative and clearly emerge from the movements that preceded them, many of the works in Room 79 seem completely fresh. **Natalia Goncharova** (1881–1962) and her partner **Mikhail Larionov**, who lived abroad from 1915, were at the forefront of Russian Primitivism before Larionov branched out into what he called Rayonism. **Liubov Popova** (1889–1924) and **Vladimir Tatlin** (1885–1953) were leading exponents of a specifically Russian style known as Constructivism which, inspired by the industrial age, owed as much to architecture and stage design as it did to painting. For the moment, the museum's permanent collection of Russian art ends on this explosive note. A wealth of paintings by Suprematist **Kazimir Malevich** (1878–1935), the indefinable **Pavel Filonov** (1883–1941), Agitprop painters and photographers **Mayakovsky** (1893–1930) and **Rodchenko** (1891–1956) and the cream of the Socialist Realists have yet to emerge from the reorganization.

To leave the museum, retrace your steps back into the main palace and down through the basement.

Walk diagonally to the left across Ploshchad Iskusstv and turn up Italianskaya Ul., passing the Kommisarzhevskaya Drama Theatre on the right. Cross Sadovaya Ul. and continue into Manezhnaya Ploshchad.

Just before the square opens out, the light blue and white 18th-century palace on the right contains an institute and museum of hygiene (*see* p.213). On the left side of the square, beyond the fenced garden, stands the yellow and white edifice of the former Mikhailovsky Manezh, a riding-school that now hosts an amusement arcade. Rossi's resculpting of this area, to go with the Mikhailovsky Palace, extended as far as this building, whose neoclassical exterior echoes those on Ploshchad Iskusstv. During the Revolution the building was used by the Bolsheviks' Armoured Car Detachment. The best repertory cinema in St Petersburg lies within the impressive granite building at the far end of the square. It is the House of Cinema, a club primarily for members of the Petersburg film industry.

> *Turn left out of the square by the cinema and walk up to Inzhenernaya Ul. Facing you are the guard houses of the* **Mikhailovsky Castle** *(Mikhailovsky zamok), which Rossi also adapted.*

This was constructed on the site of Empress Elizabeth's summer palace to protect the paranoid Emperor Paul I (*see* p.98); the few rooms open to the public contain exhibitions that are a further part of the Russian Museum collection (*© 210 4173; open daily 10–5, closed Tues; best to book a tour*).

> *Turn right; as the road bends round to the right, the porch of the late 19th-century green and white St Petersburg Circus building (*closed August*) looms on the far side of the street. Cross the bridge ahead, Most Belinskovo, over the broad, calm reaches of the Fontanka River, which once fed the fountains in the Summer Gardens to the left.*
>
> *Stand with the bridge behind you and look around.*

The **Church of SS Simeon and Anna** straight ahead, whose single dilapidated dome rises from decorative Corinthian pilasters, is one of the oldest in the city, built in 1731–4. The entrance, beneath the three-storey classical belltower, leads into a plain green and white stucco interior, only recently reopened.

The waterfront in both directions is lined with 18th- and 19th-century palaces of the nobility, as far as the eye can see. The finest, with its yellow Baroque façade hidden behind elaborate railings on the bank to the right, belonged to the Sheremetiev family (*see* below). The classical portico beyond that heralds the former **Catherine Institute**, now a library. The building was commissioned from Quarenghi by Catherine the Great to serve as a school for young noblewomen.

> *Walking right, you can admirie the beautiful railings and 19th-century gates of the palace by Duc Corsini more closely. Go through the gates into the Sheremetiev Palace, now the* **Museum of Musical Instruments** *(Muzei musicalnykh instrumentov), © 272 4074; open 12 noon–6pm; closed Mon and Tues.*

This little-known treasure of a museum holds one of the largest collections in the world. The instruments come in birch bark and ivory, inlaid and painted, bejewelled and enamelled. There are tiny violins for keeping in pockets, known appropriately as *pochetti*; Glinka's Fischner piano made in St Petersburg; and a beautiful 17th-century painted harmonica; as well as two vast horn orchestras used by the tsar's troops, and early Russian and gypsy instruments, often accompanied by prints that show them in use. Acres of balalaikas culminate in one decorated by Prokofiev. There are also collections of instruments from the Eurasian landmass, stretching from Istanbul through Persia (Iran) to Japan.

> *Leave the palace from the rear, or if you haven't visited the museum simply walk through it or around it to the gardens behind. On the right-hand side, in a large hidden courtyard, is the **Anna Akhmatova Museum** (Muzei Anny Akhmatovy).*

Anna Akhmatova Museum

✆ 272 2211; open 11–5; closed Mon and last Wed.

The attentive, craggy profile of Anna Akhmatova (1889–1966) is an icon of her time. Writing with deceptive simplicity, she had already become one of Russia's most popular poets by the outbreak of the First World War. Her early poems have been sifted for prophetic utterances to show that she was always destined to be the voice of her people. Her life supplied ample material—close friends and a husband were killed, her son was imprisoned for the 'sins' of his parents, other friends fled into exile, her poetry was repressed for two long stints and she often had little more than two kopeks to rub together.

Anna was born on the Black Sea, but moved almost immediately with her family to Tsarskoye Selo, the town surrounding the tsar's summer palace outside St Petersburg. Her family name was Gorenko, but before the publication of her first poem her father suggested that she should not bring the shame of poetry on his respectable upper middle-class family. Anna's choice of surname shows a well-tuned poet's ear. Akhmatova was a name shared by her great-grandmother and the last Tartar khans to threaten Moscow. Where they left off with swords, she carried on with words—words that so threatened Stalin that he banned them.

Akhmatova came to live here, in the servants' quarters of the Sheremetiev Palace, with her lover Nikolai Punin and his wife and child in 1924. She continued to live in the apartment until 1941, and again from 1944–54, always with Punin's first family. The museum is on the second floor. It traces Akhmatova's life story through photographs, manuscripts, editions of her poetry, sculpture and personal effects.

Room 1 deals with Akhmatova's childhood, her courtship by fellow poet Nikolai Gumilev, their marriage and travels in Italy and France. They founded a new poetic orientation, Acmeism, seeking clarity and rejecting the prevailing Symbolist obfuscation. There are also photographs of the in-crowd at the Stray Dog cabaret.

In Room 2, tragedy surfaces with the First World War, the Revolution, which she watched only half in horror, and the Civil War. Gumilev and Akhmatova had been drifting apart, he travelling the world while she stayed at home. In 1918 she asked him for a divorce. In 1921 Gumilev was shot for his alleged part in an anti-Bolshevik conspiracy. Akhmatova steadfastly refused to emigrate, but from 1925, when for 15 years her poetry was not published, life became increasingly hard.

The sparse, dramatic intensity of Room 3, with its icon *Do Not Weep For Me Mother* and sculpture entitled *Akhmatova—Poems*, is dedicated to her great poem *Requiem*, composed in these rooms from 1940–41. To write it down could have led to the death sentence, so she would pass each fragment to a friend who memorized and then burnt it. At the heart of the poem lies her son Lev's arrest in 1935, and his disappearance into the gulag in 1939. It was while queueing to give him a food parcel that the events she describes in the preface to the poem occurred. A woman in the queue behind her whispered, 'Can you put this into words?'

> *'And I said:*
> *—I can.*
> *Then a ghost of a smile slipped across*
> *what had once been her face.'*

Room 4 is dedicated to Leningrad in the late 30s and 1940, and to those poets who died or were persecuted for their art. Amongst the exhibits are collections celebrating the lives of Akhmatova's first husband Nikolai Gumilyov, another Acmeist poet Osip Mandelshtam who died in the gulag in 1938, and Marina Tsvetaeva who committed suicide shortly after her return from exile in Paris in 1940.

Room 5, in which Akhmatova lived from 1938 to 1941, when she was evacuated from the besieged city and went to live in Tashkent, contains many of her personal possessions. Above the desk is a Modigliani drawing of her, done in 1911 in Paris. Until a recent exhibition when a Russian friend of mine recognized four more in the series this was thought to be the only one to survive. While her husband travelled, Akhmatova and Modigliani whiled away enjoyable hours sitting on park benches, reciting Verlaine. One day, Anna went to his studio to give him a bunch of flowers but the painter was not there. Finding a narrow crack of window open, she threw them in, one by one. Later Modigliani asked how she had managed to get in. He refused to believe that she hadn't arranged the way they had fallen with her own two hands. Whether they were lovers will probably never be known.

Room 6 is devoted to her epic and complicated *Poem without a Hero*, written and amended in 1940–62. Dedicated to dead colleagues, friends, Leningrad during the siege and Isaiah Berlin, it is also a portrait of European literature and of the role of the poet. Accompanying it are pictures of Leningrad during the blockade, and of Tashkent where Anna spent most of the war. The part Isaiah Berlin played in Anna's life is a perfect illustration of its ironic drama. Berlin was visiting Leningrad in 1945. In a secondhand bookshop on Nevsky Prospekt he bumped into a literary critic and quietly asked if Akhmatova was still alive. The critic phoned Akhmatova and the pair set off for this flat. 'We climbed up one of the steep dark staircases to an upper floor and were admitted to Akhmatova's room…' as Berlin describes it. 'A stately, grey-haired lady, a white shawl draped about her shoulders, slowly rose to greet us. Anna Andreevna was immensely dignified, with unhurried gestures, a noble head, beautiful, somewhat severe features, and an expression of immeasurable sadness. I bowed—it seemed appropriate, for she looked and moved like a tragic queen—thanked her for receiving me, and said that people in the west would be glad to know that she was in good health, for nothing had been heard of her for so many years.' They had not been there long when, to his horror, Berlin heard an English voice in the courtyard, shouting his name. Randolph Churchill (Winston's journalist son) had been told by Berlin's travelling companion where he was, and wanted to know if Berlin would act as his interpreter. Everyone in the building was now aware that Akhmatova was receiving foreigners. Berlin left, but Akhmatova was brave enough to invite him back later that night, and the two spent all night and well into the following morning talking. It is thought that the 1946 decree vilifying her for being 'too remote from socialist reconstruction' and Zhdanov's disgusting rantings against the poet as 'half nun, half whore' were partly a result of Churchill's blunder. The decree was only annulled in 1988, although from the 1950s until her death in 1966 Akhmatova was published again, and even travelled to Taormina and Oxford to receive prizes and honorary degrees.

Leave the garden from the top left corner and go on to Lityeiny Prospekt. Since the 1930s Lityeiny has meant the institutional thuggery of the KGB, who meted it out from their 'Bolshoi Dom' (Big House) down the street to the left. Turn right and walk to Nevsky Prospekt. The enormous yellow and white neoclassical building on the other side of Lityeiny was built as a hospital by Quarenghi in 1803–4, commissioned by Emperor Paul's kindly widow Maria Fyodorovna, and serves the same purpose today. Turn right on Nevsky Prospekt and walk towards the Anichkov Most.

On the corner of Nevsky Prospekt and the Fontanka River is one of the city's most memorable buildings, the **Beloselsky-Belozersky** palace. Its dusky Pompeian red colour and the vigorous male torsos (atlantes) upholding its balconies are a startling, virile contrast to the delicate pilasters and pastel shades of most of the city. It was built in 1846–8 by Andrei Stakenschneider. From 1884 it was the home of Alexander III's reactionary brother Grand Prince Sergei and his devout wife Elizabeth, whose sister Alexandra went on to become empress. The marriage was not a happy one—he banned *Anna Karenina* from her reading list on the grounds that it would encourage 'unhealthy curiosity and violent emotions'—and ended when Sergei was blown up by a bomb in the Kremlin. Until recently the offices of the local Communist party, it has now become a venue for concerts and cultural exhibitions. Guided tours are also offered, but you need to book in advance on ✆ 315 5236. Even if you don't manage to make it into the garish, much-gilded state rooms, the surreal white hall and staircase will give you a feel of it. Evening concerts are advertised on Nevsky Prospekt, and tickets are sold in the hall.

At No.46 Nab. Reki Fontanki, around the corner, is another red building, which houses the **Galitzine Library** (*open daily*), the only Anglo-Russian library in St Petersburg, with a collection of books covering Russian history of the 20th century as seen from abroad. The house is the family home of Prince George Galitzine, in whose memory the library was set up.

The **Anichkov Bridge** and Anichkov Palace, which faces the Beloselsky-Belozersky across the Fontanka, are named for the colonel and military engineer who built the original wooden drawbridge here at the dawn of the city. For the first few decades it acted as a toll bridge: carts were turned back unless they carried a piece of stone for the building site that was St Petersburg. Rebuilt in 1839–41, it was soon adorned with the rearing fiery stallions sculpted by St Petersburg's resident horse sculptor Pyotr Klodt. Two conflicting tales encourage visitors to examine the animal's nether regions carefully. One professes that the sculptor sketched a profile of Tsar Nicholas I in the veins of one horse's groin, the other that the profile of the vanquished Napoleon can be recognized in another's genitalia.

The **Anichkov Palace** has been rebuilt and added to since it was designed in high rococo style for the Empress Elizabeth's lover, Alexei Razumovsky, whom she is said to have married in secret in 1742. Her daughter-in-law Catherine the Great presented it to her own lover Grigory Potemkin, who had the exterior toned down to the more fashionable classical style. Quarenghi added the bold colonnade down the Fontanka façade, and it was converted into government offices in 1809–10. From 1819 the palace was occupied by the heirs to the throne, until Alexander III decided not to move out after his coronation—it contained his much-loved art collection, later the basis of the Russian Museum. His widow lived here until shortly before the Revolution, counselling her son Nicholas II through his disastrous reign. After retiring to the Crimea, she finally left the country in April 1919. Since 1927 the palace has been given over to educating and entertaining the young, initially as the Palace of Pioneers, the Soviet equivalent of the Boy Scouts and Girl Guides. During the summer, there are concerts by military bands and choirs. Call © 310 4395 to see the restored but bare interior and the beautiful and rare winter garden.

Walking on down Nevsky Prospekt, the glass façade across the road at No.58 contains the Comedy Theatre and, on the ground floor, the Art Nouveau hall built in 1902–3 to house Yeliseyev's grocery shop.

Known officially as Gastronom No.1 but still called **Yeliseyev's** by all, Russia's pre-Revolutionary Fortnum and Mason's is one of the city's best-supplied grocers. The interior is resplendent. Beneath a high gilded ceiling, shoppers mill around the original wood and glass counters, eyeing home-grown and imported produce under chandeliers and lights spraying out from the walls like bunches of flowers.

Cross back over Nevsky Prospekt to admire yet another of Carlo Rossi's remarkable urban set pieces.

Ploshchad Ostrovskovo

Originally named for the Alexandrinsky Theatre, the square now honours 19th-century Russia's most prolific dramatist, A. N. Ostrovsky. Behind railings on the left, the Anichkov Palace gardens are linked to the ensemble by their two pavilions designed by Rossi, one of which is now a Versace shop. This area is a favourite meeting place for the city's outdoor chess enthusiasts. When new pipes were laid beneath the square, rather than abandon their places, players merely perched their chess sets on top of abandoned diggers and their bottoms on concrete drains.

Against the backdrop of the Alexandrinsky Theatre, a building of truly imperial splendour, is the city's only statue of Catherine the Great. Though she did so much to foster the spirit of the city, the statue was not erected until 1873. In an allegory of her reign, the empress stands on a plinth surrounded by the clutch of figures without whom the obscure German princess would never have become Empress of All the Russias. Walking anti-clockwise round the monument you see the field marshals who masterminded Catherine's victories over the Turks, P. A. Rumyantsev and the skeletal A. V. Suvorov, separated by Grigory Potemkin. Her chancellor and foreign minister A. A. Bezborodko is in conversation with fellow-statesman Ivan Betskoi. Beneath her flowing metal cloak are Admiral Chichagov and Grigory Orlov who, with his brothers, masterminded the *coup d'état* that gave Catherine the throne. On the empress's right is poet Gavriil Derzhavin, while another conspirator and President of the Academy of Sciences, Ekaterina Dashkova, reads beside him.

The right-hand side of the square is occupied by the **Russian National Library**, commonly referred to as the '*publichka*'. Established in the reign of Paul I (1796–1801) using Catherine's collection of books (including the libraries of Diderot and Voltaire) as a base, it was extended by Rossi when he built the Alexandrinsky Theatre. The façade sports statues of philosophers by Pimenov and Demut-Malinovsky, ranged beneath the goddess of wisdom, Minerva. Perhaps the library's greatest hour came during the siege, when most of the city's public institutions closed down. Day in, day out, librarians kept their doors open, helping members of the public search their precious treasure to find ways of manufacturing matches, recipes for candles, and clues for converting wood into an edible substance or creating artificial vitamins. If you are interested in consulting its 25 million tomes, take along your passport and a photograph of yourself and pay a small rouble fee. Be warned that this is not a lending library, and reading space is scarce.

Looking at the handsome **Alexandrinsky Theatre** (known as the Pushkin Theatre in Soviet times), it comes as no surprise to find that theatre ran in Carlo Rossi's blood. His mother was a ballerina, and the building resembles a three-dimensional stage design, a backdrop for the drama of autocratic imperial life. Built in 1828–32 and named after Nicholas I's wife Alexandra Fyodorovna, it is adorned with straightforward dramatic metaphors—the chariot of Apollo on the roof and statues of the muses Terpsichore (lyric poetry and dancing) and Melpomene (tragedy) on either side of the main façade. These external decorative touches, which run right round the building enlivening the porticoed façades, were again executed by Pimenov and Demut-Malinovsky with the help of Triscornia.

*In the far left-hand corner of the square, the **Museum of Theatre and Musical Arts**, Ploshchad Ostrovskovo 6 (© 311 2195; open daily 11–6, Wed 1–7pm, closed Tues) overlooks the Alexandrinsky.*

Its four rooms are plastered with the history of the dramatic arts in Russia, in a floor-to-ceiling display of photographs and theatrical posters. The origins of Russian theatre—in churches, serf theatres and the early imperial theatres—pave the way for turn-of-the-century developments, including Mayakovsky's avant-garde approach in St Petersburg and the establishment of the Moscow Arts Theatre (**MXAT**) by Stanislavsky and Nemirovich-Danchenko. Revolution breaks out in Room 3, with a riot of Constructivist designs and experimental photographs of leading activists such as Meyerhold, photographed by Rodchenko. While the world-renowned bass singer Fyodor Chaliapin's St Petersburg flat is being restored, the last room provides a home for some of the maestro's effects. The gramophone in the golden cabinet was a gift from his Anglo-American recording company.

The street leading away from the back of the Alexandrinsky Theatre has been renamed in honour of the creator of its symmetry, Ul. Zodchevo (master builder) Rossi. Looking back from the far end, you can appreciate its perfect proportions. The buildings are exactly the same height as the width of the street, while the street is exactly ten times as long. However tired your legs, spare a thought for the denizens of the **Vaganova Ballet School**, hidden behind the blank windows of the left-hand building as you walk down. Their eyes are on the heights attained by previous pupils of their *alma mater*, Pavlova, Nijinsky, Nureyev, Baryshnikov and Makarova. Like them, they may end up working in the West, though they will be choosing New York or London for economic reasons without having to seek political asylum.

Rossi's work continues in the crescent of creamy yellow buildings at the far end of the street. Formally Ploshchad Lomonosova, with a bust of the scientist looking towards the decorative Lomonosov Bridge over the Fontanka, it is affectionately known as the *vatrushka*, after the much-loved round cheese pie of the same name.

Turn right, walk through the arch and down Ul. Lomonosova. You will pass the restaurant Graf Suvorov before you hit Sadovaya Ul.

Between Nevsky Prospekt and Sennaya Ploshchad on Sadovaya was once the hub of commercial St Petersburg, boasting three major department stores excluding the four market buildings on the square itself. Today trading continues, but it's a far cry from its heyday of precious furs and jewellers' arcades.

*Turn left briefly on Sadovaya, opposite the grand neoclassical crescent of what was once the **Imperial Bank**, to dive into **Apraksin Dvor** (formerly Apraksin Market) and enter its poverty-driven flea market, Veschovy Rynok. Turn on your heels to continue the walk north along Sadovaya Ul..*

Just beyond Ul. Lomonosova on the right rises the former **Vorontsov Palace**, which is sadly inaccessible. Built by Rastrelli in 1749–57, its charming, light three-storey central corpus is flanked by two-storey wings, all in pale yellow and white. Iron railings separate the palace's front garden from the pavement. It was chosen by Paul I as the headquarters for the Knights of Malta, gaining a delightful chapel by Quarenghi in the process. Chased from their island habitat by Napoleon, the Catholic order found an unlikely ally in the Orthodox emperor. Paul became Grand Master of the Order in 1798, though his election was not legal. Russia's involvement finished with his assassination, suggesting that the snub-nosed madman was driven more by his love of dressing up than by a desire to provide Russia with a naval toehold in the Mediterranean. From 1810 the building sheltered the Corps of Pages, educating the sons of army officers. It has remained a military school, the Suvorovsky Academy, to this day, with distinctive black and red uniforms.

On the other side of the street running all the way to Nevsky Prospekt is the arcade of **Gostiny Dvor**, St Petersburg's main bazaar since it was erected in 1761–85 by Vallin de la Mothe, and now a department store. Dive into one of the doors and follow its corridors for as long as you can, keeping an eye out for occasional gems: stationery, scarves, fur hats and children's toys.

Far more absorbing, even if you don't understand a word, is the street theatre that takes place in front of the building on Nevsky Prospekt. Here, little knots of citizens practise their right to free speech by haranguing one another. Using humour to win over your audience has yet to take off. Arguments are fast and furious, often involving racist attitudes you would be arrested for airing in London or New York.

Before disappearing into ⓂNevsky Prospekt, use the underpass to visit the heavenly blue and white Armenian Church, recently reopened.

Set back from the street, the church was built in 1771–80 and is an excellent example of its architect Yuri Velten's light, decorative neoclassical style. Its pillared interior is in serious need of repair but with their motherland bankrupt it is hardly a priority for the city's Armenian population. Light a candle for their sake.

Ⓜ *Gostiny Dvor and* Ⓜ *Nevsky Prospekt are both at hand.*

V: Tauride Palace and Smolny Region

Start: Ⓜ *Chernyshevskaya*
Walking Time: *2 hours*

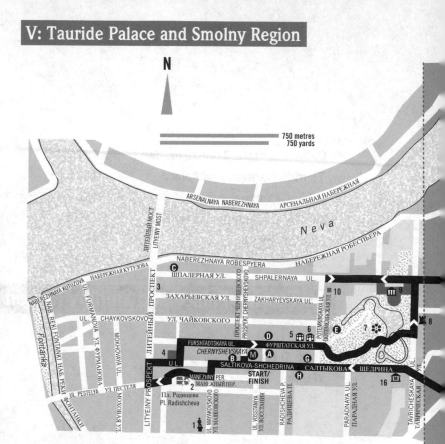

N

750 metres
750 yards

Sites

1   Bust of Mayakovsky
    Byust Mayakovskovo
    Бюст Маяковского

2   Cathedral of the Transfiguration
    Preobrazhensky sobor
    Преображенский собор

3   Bolshoi Dom
    Большой дом

4   Former Church of St Anna
    Tserkov sv. Anny
    Церковь св. Анны

5   Ignatieff House
    Ignatievskaya usadba
    Игнатиевская усадьба

6   Spiridonov House
    Spiridonovskaya usadba
    Спиридоновская усадьба

7   Tauride Gardens
    Tavrichesky sad
    Таврический сад

8   Ivanov Tower
    Ivanovskaya bashnya
    Ивановская башня

9   Tauride Palace
    Tavrichesky dvorets
    Таврический дворец

10 Horticultural Exhibition Hall
    Vystavochny zal 'Tsvety'
    Выставочный зал 'Цветы'

11 Kikin Chambers
    Kikiny palaty
    Кикины палаты

12 Smolny Convent and Cathedral
    Smolny monastir i sobor
    Смольный монастырь и собор

13 Smolny Institute
Smolny institut
Смольный институт

14 Statue of Lenin
Pamyatnik V. I. Lenina
Памятник В. И. Ленина

15 Square of the Proletarian Dictatorship
Ploshchad proletarskoy diktatury
Пл. пролетарской диктатуры

16 Suvorov Museum
Muzei A. V. Suvorova
Музей А. В. Суворова

Restaurants and Cafés

A Three Bears
   Tri Medvedi
   Три Медведы

B Bakery
   Bulochnaya
   Булочная

C Café Rioni
   Кафе Риони

D Café Sunduk
   Кафе Сундук

E Tauride Park Café
   Café v. Tavricheskom sadu
   Кафе в. Таврическом саду

F Smolnensky Hotel/Restaurant
   Gostinitsa Smolenskaya/Restoran
   Гостиница Смоленская/Ресторан

G Café-bar
   Кафе/бар

H Café Bistro No.1
   Кафе/бистро 1

This spacious corner of St Petersburg, beyond the concentric canals that hem in the centre, remained a region of aristocratic country estates right up until the mid-19th century. Most of it is well over four metres above sea level, saving it from the unhealthy marshy miasma and the floods which have left such a psychological scar on the rest of the city. In the last 150 years these estates have been built over to create a series of stately streets. The houses themselves now shelter consulates or public services such as the register offices for marriages and births. In between, examples of much later architecture, apartment blocks in the self-important eclectic and *Style Moderne* styles, make many of the streets into an illustrated textbook of Petersburgian architecture.

On the far side of the Tauride Gardens, much to the region's misfortune, Lenin decided to turn the Smolny Institute, then Russia's foremost school for the daughters of the nobility, into the Bolshevik Party headquarters in 1917. With such revolutionary credentials the area was doomed to a busy life as a communist heartland. Older, characterful buildings were flattened to create the Square of the Proletarian Dictatorship, a construction as clumsy and ugly as its name. Somehow Rastrelli's neighbouring masterpiece, the Smolny Cathedral, manages to ignore the concrete and tarmac hell with the aloof superiority of a proud 18th-century courtier. Together, the square and cathedral are an eloquent statement of the extreme nature of Russia, her people and their history.

As you weave your way between these two worlds, a varied crowd will accompany you. Furshtadtskaya Ul. has the self-confident air of private business and foreign embassies, the gardens are the province of local children, while poor Smolny is still overrun by state employees. Avoid this itinerary on Thursdays, when the Smolny Cathedral is closed. As it is the only building you will be spending any time in apart from restaurants, a windy wet day would be miserable.

---

lunch/cafés

This area of town is developing rapidly, with cafés appearing all down Saltikov-Schedrin street and Suvorovsky Prospekt. If it is warm, you could also bring a picnic to eat in the Tauride Park.

A **Three Bears**, Furshtadtskaya Ul. 35, © 272 3533, *open 11–12pm*. Look for the gaily painted street-level windows. This bright basement cooperative resounds bearably to the beat of MTV and serves spicy food from the middle eastern republics, tea and alcohol. Their soups are original hot creations, though sometimes a little greasy, and the *shashliks* are excellent. Around $5 a meal.

B Opposite the Chernyshevskaya metro station is one of the best **bakeries** in St Petersburg for pastries, pies, cakes and coffee.

C **Café Rioni**, Shpalernaya Ul. 24, ✆ 273 3261; *open weekdays 11am–11pm, Sat, Sun 1–11pm.* Family-run restaurant serving the best Georgian food in the city.

D **Café Sunduk**, Furshtadtskaya Ul. 42, ✆ 272 3100; *open daily 10am–11pm.* An atmospheric little bar with tables outside, serving food and freshly squeezed juices.

E **Tauride Park Café**, in a garden rotunda, past the statue of Lenin in the park itself. Sitting pretty on top of a small rise, this café only operates in summer and mostly just sells beer and crisps.

F **Smolnensky Hotel**, Tverskaya Ul. 22, ✆ 276 6217; *open 8am–10pm.* The Soviet-style décor of this well-located hotel directly opposite the Smolny complex will be familiar to fans of Cold War spy movies, but its clean restaurant offers a typical Russian menu.

G **Café/Bar**, Saltikova-Shchedrina 36, ✆ 272 0935; *open 12 noon–11pm.* For speedy service and a traditional Russian menu, try this courtyard bar with a choice of indoor or garden tables.

H **Café Bistro No.1**, Kirochnaya Ul. 29 (on the corner with Saltykova-Shchedrina), ✆ 275 0218. Good for a quick bite: soups, sandwiches, hot dishes, cakes and beer in a clean, modern café.

Turn left on Prospekt Chernyshevskovo outside the metro and right at the T-junction with Ul. Saltikova-Shchedrina, named after the 19th-century satirical journalist.

In the 1860s and '70s Mikhail Saltikov-Shchedrin collaborated with the poet Nekrasov in publishing an important radical literary periodical, *Notes from the Fatherland*, from a flat on Lityeiny Prospekt. It was between its covers that both Dostoyevsky and Tolstoy first came to the attention of the wider public. His own literary fame rests on one masterpiece, *The Golovlevs*, which depicts a family from the rural gentry falling apart after the emancipation of the serfs in 1861, hailed by the Soviets as a truthful exposé of the rotten core of the upper classes.

Crossing the road, take the first left on to Ul. Mayakovskovo, named after another writer, this time the poet Vladimir Mayakovsky.

Assured of his reputation by Stalin's posthumous praise of him as 'the greatest Soviet poet', Mayakovsky had welcomed the Revolution and devoted himself to writing poetry appropriate to the new world it had created. It was partly because of events that took place on this street that he committed suicide in 1930. For seventeen years he was in love with the married Lily Brik, and even lived here, at No. 52, *à trois* with her and her husband Osip. The social-realist portrait bust of him further down the street conveys his strength and commitment but not his idiosyncrasy, which towards the end of his life was attacked by the conformist writers under Stalin.

*If you go to look at it, you will have to return to turn down Manezhny Pereulok and reach the back of the **Cathedral of the Transfiguration** (Преображенский Собор—Preobrazhensky Sobor).*

This delightful Empire-style cathedral is surrounded by a small garden and handsome chain fence; the gate is opposite the lane. The cathedral was built in 1827–29, and the fence is suspended from Turkish cannons captured in the Russo-Turkish war of 1828. Each cannon is decorated at the top with a tugra, a piece of heraldic calligraphy created in the Topkapi Palace in Istanbul to be the signature of each new sultan. Presumably cannons were thought suitable for inclusion since this building, by the Moscow-trained V. P. Stasov, replaced St Petersburg's foremost military church, which had burned down in 1825. It was here in 1741 that the future Empress Elizabeth rallied the guards to support her *coup d'état* against the infant Ivan VI, and in memory of their support she built a wooden church on the spot, naming it after the Transfiguration (Preobrazhensky) Regiment. Until the Revolution the interior of the church dripped with guards' memorabilia: captured standards, keys of fortresses, the uniforms of several tsars and even the sword worn by Tsar Alexander II at his assassination. The bronze and crystal chandeliers were made specially for the building, echoing the religious element in the external decorative reliefs: Moses' tablets, along with angels and crosses. The dramatic iconostasis was built to a design by Stasov himself, its royal gates, enclosed in a classical apse, surmounted by a brilliant gilded sunburst. There are a number of fine icons in the church; appropriately perhaps the best hangs off a side column to the right, showing the Transfiguration of Christ. It tells of the moment on Mount Hermon when Peter, James and John witnessed the transfiguration of Jesus, and saw the prophets Elijah and Moses appear to talk to him. Jesus is portrayed on the mountaintop abounding in glory while the disciples cower in terror at its foot.

> *Leave the cathedral through its main door and portico, giving what you can to the beggars who normally lie in wait here, and walk straight on to busy Lityeiny (Smelting) Prospekt.*

This was one of the first streets in the city, named after the armaments foundry built in 1711 on the river, and connecting it with Nevsky Prospekt. This century 'on Lityeiny' has come to mean something more sinister, as the KGB headquarters and prison are located in **Bolshoi Dom**, opposite the former foundry.

> *Turning right and right again back on to Ul. Saltikova-Shchedrina, the first building to command attention is the turquoise and white former Lutheran **Church of St Anna**, some 100 metres up on the left.*

Unfortunately there is nothing to be seen in the interior as in 1939 the church was converted into a cinema, the Spartak, which still shows high-quality old European films and often hosts film festivals. It was built in 1775–9 by Yuri Velten, the man responsible for girding the Neva with granite banks; appropriately for the designer of a Lutheran church, Velten trained in Germany. If you cut through beside the church you will come to its elegant eastern end, where the internal apse is mirrored externally by a graceful semi-circular Ionic portico topped by a cupola.

You are now on Furshtadtskaya Ul., which is rapidly regaining its feel as one of St Petersburg's smartest streets, with a boulevard atmosphere and a smattering of embassies.

Furshtadtskaya Ul. was already a fashionable street by the time the *duma* (parliament) began to sit in the nearby Tauride Palace in 1905; but, finding itself within the metaphorical sound of the division bell, it soon gained several parliamentary residents. Turning right, one walks through a living manual of St Petersburg architecture, containing everything from low, crumbling Petrine houses (No.34) to disintegrating concrete Constructivist flat blocks (No.26). In between there are contrasting examples of northern *Style Moderne* in the functional pale brick building at No.24, which borrows and modernizes various 'Empire' motifs, and the aquamarine and white building at No.28, which is much more flamboyant. But the majority of the buildings date from the second half of the 19th century, when eclecticism in architecture saw a neo-Russian 'medieval' construction rise side by side with a piece of pseudo-classicism. Two of the finest examples lie at the end of the street, at Nos.52 and 58: these were the town houses of the aristocratic Ignatieff and Spiridonov families, respectively. Both were built in the late 1890s and now serve to record important rites of passage: the first as a Palace of Weddings and the second as the local registry for births. In his admirable reconstruction of his family saga, *The Russian Album*, Michael Ignatieff enumerates the household as it was on the night in February 1917 when the revolutionary mob marched past on their way to the *duma*. Aside from the family, there were 21 servants living in the house, ranging from young messenger boys to an English governess and a French tutor. Two years later the family, accompanied only by the English governess, were lucky to find passage on a boat across the Black Sea to Istanbul, where they lived in two rooms of a cheap boarding house. The ghosts of the revolutionary upheaval seem particularly vivid on Furshtadtskaya Ul.

Tauride Gardens and Palace

*An entrance to the **Tauride Gardens** (Tavrichesky Sad), designated a children's park, opens opposite the end of the street. Threaded with would-be streams and lakes and landscaped with small hills, in winter it is criss-crossed by the swish of diminutive skaters, skiers and tobogganists. While exploring, bear in mind that you should be heading for a gate straight across the park, directly opposite where you came in.*

This park was once the private garden of Catherine the Great's influential lover, the one-eyed Grigory Potemkin (pronounced Potyomkin), for whom she had the gardens and neighbouring Tauride Palace (Tavrichesky Dvorets) built in 1783–9. Following Crimean victories against the Turks, she crowned her gift of thanks by making him Prince of Tauris (a contemporary name for the Crimea) in 1787, but it was only after his death in 1791 that she named the palace and gardens after him.

This park was laid out by an Englishman called Gould in the informal style of landscaping preferred by Catherine. As you stride past one of the last statues of Lenin in the city at the entrance, on the left is the only original garden pavilion remaining, now a small café. Reading of the park's well-tended gazebos, islands and grottos of yesteryear, it is tempting to echo Catherine's words as she walked mournfully through the gardens less than a year after Potemkin's death. 'Everything here used to be charming,' she murmured wistfully, 'but now everything is not right.' Despite the modern concrete open-air theatre and caged sports pitches, the park is still undulating and sylvan. Near the centre, the Monument to the Young Defenders of Leningrad during the 1941–4 siege faces the back of the palace across a lake, its three conspirators emerging stealthily out of a camouflage of stone. A poignant story is told of the adolescent girls who volunteered to look for mines, barefoot, after the German retreat. Suzanne Massie in her book on Pavlovsk tells how 'in the morning the girls would go out to work singing songs, and in the evening would return in silent formation, carrying a wounded or dead friend on a field stretcher.' All occupied areas round the city were scattered with mined toys—dolls, rabbits, elephants and cars—designed to continue the German reign of terror over the children of the city well after the Germans themselves had gone.

From this angle, the most prominent feature of the palace is the roof of its conservatory. These popular features of Russian houses were known as **Winter Gardens**. Now distinctly dishevelled, this was one of the most splendid ever conceived: the 18th-century French traveller C. P. Masson describes how 'the delicious temperature, the scented plants and the voluptuous silence of this magic spot throw the soul into gentle dreams and carry away one's imagination to the woods of Italy. The enchanted illusion is only destroyed by the view out of the windows on to icicles and frosts.' In the middle of the 19th century it was used as the imperial kitchen garden, where one visitor noted 15,000 pots of strawberry plants. After radical reconstruction, it was here that the *duma* held their parliamentary sessions from 1906 to 1917. This large auditorium went on to be used by the Petrograd soviet and for congresses of both the soviets and the Communist party, before becoming an élite Higher Party School. It is now used as offices and for meetings between the representatives of the different nations of the CIS, and is, sadly, closed to tourists.

> Leaving the park by the Tavricheskaya Ul. exit, turn left. There will doubtless be a queue on the other side of the road, at the doors of Karavanaya, a popular Scottish bakery that also serves milkshakes.

On the top floor of the round tower on the corner with Tverskaya Ul., the uncrowned king of the pre-Revolutionary St Petersburg's literary scene, the Symbolist poet Vyacheslav Ivanov presided over his Wednesday salon, known as **The Tower** (*Bashnya*), which was renowned for its intellectual punch-throwing. The battle of the time was between the Symbolists, who had rather run out of steam, and the younger generation of poets, the Acmeists, among them Nikolai Gumilev, Anna Akhmatova and Osip Mandelstam. Akhmatova remembered being taken there at the age of 21 and reciting a recent poem to the 'Tauride Sage', who responded 'with indifference and irony: "What pure Romanticism."'

Continue to the end of the park and turn left on Ul. Shpalernaya to come to the front of the **Tauride Palace**.

On the left, opposite a 19th-century brick water tower, are the severe neoclassical portico, sweeping drive and single-storey wings of the main façade. The architect chosen by Catherine in 1783 to laud her conquering hero was Ivan Starov, one of Russia's first home-grown architects. Starov had followed his studies in Moscow by travelling to France and Italy. A passionate disciple of the neoclassicist Palladio, he was the obvious choice for a building which Catherine wanted to be inspired by the Pantheon in Rome. This muse explains the flattened dome atop a circular hall. On the other hand the inspiration for the colour scheme, a hopeful spring-like yellow, green and white, could only be the long grey Russian winter.

Potemkin was a bold strategist, shrewd advisor and passionate lover, Catherine's 'greatest, most bizarre and most entertaining of eccentrics'. The palace's finest moment, a year or so after its completion, was the great party Potemkin threw for his former lover, now respected friend, in April 1791. Preparations took months, and the seven-hour extravaganza was said to have cost 150,000 roubles. It began with Catherine's arrival, greeted by a fanfare from 300 musicians, and continued with ballets, a comedy, a costume ball and more music. The highlight was a sit-down dinner for a select 600, served on gold and silver platters, with the rest of the guests eating standing up. In the meantime the gardens and rooms were ablaze with light and covered with sparkling reflective stones, mirrors, crystal pyramids and globes. When the empress eventually left for bed, past midnight, Potemkin, according to Masson, 'threw himself at her feet, took her hand and burst into tears.' Within six months Potemkin was dead, and Catherine honoured his memory by living in the palace during the spring and autumn. After her death her son Paul, who hated his mother and desecrated all her favourite places, gave the palace over to a regiment of the horse guards, who used the halls as stables.

Beyond the palace, on the corner with the street named after Grigory Potemkin (Ul. Potyomkinskaya), there is a promising-looking garden centre and **horticultural exhibition hall**, *supposedly open every day except Sunday and Monday. Further on, the road leads past the Tsarist Detention Centre at No. 25 Shpalernaya Ul. and back to the KGB, or rather the Russian Security Ministry as it is now known, on Lityeiny.*

The walk continues in the opposite direction, and is spectacularly punctuated by Rastrelli's greatest surviving masterpiece, the **Smolny Cathedral** *(Смольный Собор—Smolny Sobor), rising beatifically straight ahead.*

Before getting to the cathedral, you will pass a statue of 'Iron' Felix Dzerzhinsky (*see* p.75), first head of the Bolshevik secret police, the Cheka, which means linchpin. Beyond, your attention will be drawn to the highly decorative **Kikin Chambers** (Kikiny Palaty) on the left. One of the city's earliest surviving structures, it was built in 1714 for Peter the Great's naval advisor, A. V. Kikin, one of the bright young men whom he had sent to Europe to study; in this case the student learned ship-building in Holland. Granted a piece of what was then open countryside, Kikin planned this building in the Petrine Baroque style favoured by his master, but with grandiose embellishments such as the double staircase entrance. It was perhaps just such tactless foolishness that led to him being dismissed from the Admiralty while the house was still being built, and eventually to his execution in 1718 after he saw some advantage in championing the cause of Peter's ill-fated son and heir, Alexei. From 1718 to 1727 the palace housed Peter's collection of nature's curiosities, his Kunstkamera, and his scientific library, Russia's first museum. Such was Peter's enthusiasm for education that he encouraged visitors with the enlightened bribe of a pie and a shot of vodka before they left. After the collections were moved to their present locations on Vasilievsky Island, the building became a barracks and hospital to a regiment of the horse guards. It was greatly added to, and it is largely due to heavy damage during the Second World War that the original house was rediscovered and restored to its current striped originality in the 1950s. The chambers are used by a local children's music school and are out of bounds to tourists.

> *For those interested in shipbuilding or naval history, ten minutes north of Smolny is the reconstruction of Peter the Great's flagship,* Shtandart. *The project is run by Vladimir Martous, who speaks English and who will enthusiastically show visitors around the handmade boat, especially if you call beforehand on © 230 3736 (Tues–Sat 9–4.30).*

Smolny Cathedral and Smolny Institute

The Smolny ensemble ahead grew out of the 'petticoat period', or era of empresses, when out of an unprecedented and unrepeated period of 71 years (1725–96) Russia was ruled by women for all but five. Successive empresses added to this female enclave, which began with a convent for female orphans and grew to include a school for the daughters of the nobility and a home for widows. This feminine tradition was sharply disrupted in 1917 when the Petrograd Soviet requisitioned the Smolny Institute and, dominated by the Bolsheviks, went on to direct the October Revolution from here. Doubtless no one at the time worried about the symbolism of such a move, but with the benefit of hindsight it seems the early Communists subconsciously began as they intended to continue. For all the talk of equality, the well-being, both physical and mental, of women has for 70 years been one of the most forgotten corners of the socialist utopia.

Empress Elizabeth first commissioned a nunnery for poor orphans here, at what had been the naval tar yard (Smolny Dvor), which served Peter's nascent fleet. Bartolomeo Francesco Rastrelli began the **cathedral** (*open 11–6, 11–5 Wed and concert days; closed Thurs; adm exp*) and encircling convent buildings in 1744. Rarely do patron and artist appear so well suited, a fact Elizabeth had already acknowledged by making him chief architect in 1736. Like Rastrelli's cathedral building, Elizabeth was a mixture of worldliness and piety. She loved to adorn herself with exquisite ornaments (she was said to have had 15,000 gowns), adding a judicious smattering of jewellery, and to flirt and chatter in a superficial manner, yet she was also one of Russia's most pious monarchs. It is even said that she thought of retiring here in penitence at the end of her life. For all its decoration, pilasters, sunbursts, architraves and capitals, the building, with its five cupolas crowned by golden crosses reaching into the sky, is a brilliant homage to the Creator. Its masterstroke is the use of light grey leaded roofs, which allow the cupolas and dome to float at one with the predominantly overcast St Petersburg sky.

The stern interior shows the vigorous, no-nonsense body on to which the building's Baroque ornament was once grafted. It was only completed to Rastrelli's plans by Stasov in 1835, but seventy years of Soviet rule have robbed it of all decoration, save the contrasting grey marble floor and yellow marble steps leading up to the altars. Everything else is long since gone, and the cathedral is used as both a choral concert hall and a space for exhibitions about the city. Included in the price of the ticket is a fascinating climb into the upper ducts and arteries of the building for a magnificent view of the city and river.

The original **convent buildings**, which Catherine partly used when she set up her Institute for the Education of Well-born Young Ladies in 1764, form a square around the cathedral, leaving a peaceful processional way in between. At each corner tall thin domes rise to ornate cupolas. The buildings were used as Party offices until the downfall of the Communists in 1991, and now house, one suspects, the same former party members in disguise as impartial civil servants.

> *Walking away from the cathedral entrance, across the square on which Rastrelli planned to build the highest tiered belltower in Russia, you pass other buildings in Rastrelli's style dating from the 1860s. Turn left and hug the convent walls on Quarenghi Lane, named after the Italian architect of the **Smolny Institute**, whose yellow classical façade appears ahead (open Mon–Sat 10–5 for prearranged excursions by English-speaking guide, © 276 1321/1461; Fridays for unguided individuals 3–5pm).*

Whether, as one of its teachers remarked early in his career, its 'only concern is dancing, singing and curtseying' or, as he eulogized with hindsight, it transformed the girls 'from a piece of sweetmeat or pie filled with physical delights, into thinking, noble beings', Catherine's school was a great success. In the early 19th century it was enlarged under her grandson and new buildings, commissioned from Quarenghi, were built in 1806–8. Born in Italy in 1743, he had been at the forefront of the neoclassical movement under Catherine. His long porticoed building is prefaced by one of the earliest and most human statues of **Lenin**, sculpted by V. V. Kozlov and erected in 1927. It commemorates the six months during which Lenin headed the government here before moving the capital back to Moscow in 1918. More dramatically, it was here that Sergei Kirov, head of the Leningrad Communist Party, was assassinated on the orders of Stalin in December 1934, giving the paranoid Georgian an excuse for his purge of the Party, which resulted in an unbelievable 1.5 million deaths. The guided tour shows you Lenin's office and bedroom, and Quarenghi's huge White Hall, originally the noble girls' ballroom and graduation hall, which later became known as the Assembly Hall for the Soviets.

> *Back on the main walk, a processional avenue runs from the Smolny Institute, between busts of Marx and Engels, to a pair of 20th-century classical gatehouses inscribed with an exhortation to the workers of the world to unite, and an announcement of the Soviet of Proletarian Dictatorship. Ahead lies the massive expanse of the **Square of the Proletarian Dictatorship**.*

Almost all the buildings in sight were used by the Party. A graphic illustration of the self-importance of Soviet bureaucracy is given by the building at the end of the square on the left; its hideous grandiosity housed nothing more than the executive committee of the local district deputies.

> *Taking your life in your hands, cross the tarmac on to Suvorovsky Prospekt and take the third right down Ul. Saltikova-Shchedrina.*

Arriving at the corner of the Tauride Park, the splendid fortified pseudo-Russian castle of a building on the left, opened in 1904 by Nicholas II, houses the **Suvorov Museum** (*open Thurs, Fri, Sun, Mon 10–6, Sat 10–7; closed Tues, Wed, first Mon of month*). After ten years of renovation, the museum has reopened to commemorate the life and times of the much admired Generalissimo Count A. V. Suvorov, who spanned the 18th and 19th centuries and was one of Russia's greatest military figures. Under Catherine the Great he campaigned successfully against the Turks; under her son Paul I he defeated the French. The external mosaics represent, on the right, Suvorov's recall from retirement in Konchanskoye by Paul I, and on the left his crossing of the Alps on the Italian campaign.

> *To regain Ⓜ Chernyshevsky, follow Ul. Saltikova-Shchedrina along the edge of the park. Third right after the park is Chernyshevsky Prospekt, and the station is down it on the right.*

VI: Vasilievsky Island

Start: Ⓜ *Vasileostrovskaya*
Walking Time: *2½ hours*

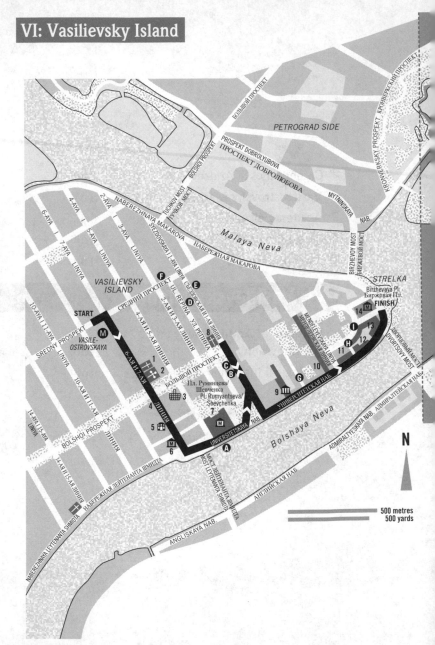

VI: Vasilievsky Island

PETROGRAD SIDE

PROSPEKT DOBROLYUBOVA
ПРОСПЕКТ ДОБРОЛЮБОВА

БОЛЬШОЙ ПРОСПЕКТ

MYTNINSKAYA

КРОНВЕРКСКИЙ ПРОСПЕКТ
KRONVERKSKY PROSPEKT

NAB.

Malaya Neva

НАБЕРЕЖНАЯ МАКАРОВА
NABEREZHNAYA MAKAROVA

ТУЧКОВ МОСТ
TUCHKOV MOST

СРЕДНЯЯ 1-АЯ ЛИНИЯ
SREDNYAYA 1-AYA LINIYA

6-AYA
4-AYA
2-AYA
5-AYA LINIYA
3-AYA LINIYA
7-AYA LINIYA

VASILIEVSKY
ISLAND

СРЕДНИЙ ПРОСПЕКТ
UL. REPINA УЛ. РЕПИНА
2-AЯ И 3-АЯ ЛИНИЯ
4-АЯ И 5-АЯ ЛИНИЯ

F **E** **D**

BIRZHEVOY MOST
БИРЖЕВОЙ МОСТ

STRELKA

Birzhevaya Pl.
Биржевая Пл.
FINISH

14

START

VASILE-
OSTROVSKAYA **M**

SREDNY PROSPEKT
СРЕДНИЙ ПРОСПЕКТ

10-AYA 11-AYA LINIYA

8

6-АЯ И 7-АЯ
ЛИНИЯ

1 ✝

2

БОЛЬШОЙ ПРОСПЕКТ

Пл. Румянцева/
Шевченко
Pl. Rumyantseva/
Shevchenko

C
B

МЕНДЕЛЕЕВСКАЯ ЛИНИЯ
MENDELEYEVSKAYA LINIYA

I **13**

H **12**
11

10

G

ДВОРЦОВЫЙ МОСТ
DVORTSOVY MOST

3

7

4

M

9 III

10-АЯ И 11-АЯ
ЛИНИЯ

BOLSHOI PROSPEKT
БОЛЬШОЙ ПРОСПЕКТ

14-AYA 15-AYA
LINIYA

5

6

M

A

УНИВЕРСИТЕТСКАЯ НАБ.
UNIVERSITETSKAYA NAB.

УНИВЕРСИТЕТСКАЯ НАБ.
UNIVERSITETSKAYA NAB.

Bolshaya Neva

АДМИРАЛТЕЙСКАЯ НАБ.
ADMIRALTEYSKAYA NAB.

N

12-АЯ И 13-АЯ ЛИНИЯ

НАБЕРЕЖНАЯ ЛЕЙТЕНАНТА ШМИДТА
NABEREZHNAYA LEYTENANTA SHMIDTA

МОСТ ЛЕЙТЕНАНТА ШМИДТА
MOST LEYTENANTA SHMIDTA

АНГЛИЙСКАЯ НАБ.

ANGLISKAYA NAB.

500 metres
500 yards

Sites

1 Church of the Three Saints
Tserkov tryokh svyatiteley
Церковь трёх святителей

2 Cathedral of St Andrew
Andreyevsky sobor
Андреевский собор

3 Vasileostrovsky Market
Vasileostrovsky Rynok
Василеостровский Рынок

4 Pharmacy
Apteka
Аптека

5 Trezzini House
Dom postroyen Trezzini
Дом построен Трезини

6 Pavlov's Flat in Academicians' House
Dom Akademikov
Дом Академиков

7 Academy of Arts
Akademiya khudozhestv
Академия художеств

8 Church of St Catherine
Tserkov sv. Yekateriny
Церковь св. Екатерины

9 Menshikov Palace
Menshikovsky dvorets
Меншиковский дворец

10 Twelve Colleges
Zdaniye Dvenadtsati kollegii
Здание двенадцати коллегии

11 Academy of Science
Akademiya nauk
Академия наук

12 Kunstkamera/
Museum of Anthropology and Ethnology
Kunstkamera/
Muzei antropologii i etnografii
Кунсткамера/
Музей антропологии и этнографии

13 Museum of Zoology
Zoologichesky muzei
Зоологический музей

14 Naval Museum/Stock Exchange
Voenno-Morskoi Muzei/Birzha
Военно-Морской Музей/Биржа

Restaurants and Cafés

A New Island Ship Restaurant

B Sirin-Bar
Сирин-Бар

C The Golden Leaf
Tinyen
Тиньен

D Inkol
Инкол

E Kalinka
Калинка

F The Great Wall

G Café Arka
Кафе Арка

H The Old Customs House
Staraya Tamozhnya
Старая Таможня

I Academia
Академиа

Wedged into the mouth of the River Neva, Vasilievsky (St Basil's) Island is both integral to St Petersburg's central riverfront façade and a quiet residential backwater, far from the hurly-burly of downtown Nevsky Prospekt. The river divides as it hits the island's picturesque pointed tip, the Strelka, flowing as the Bolshaya (Large) and Malaya (Small) Neva round the ever-widening landmass. At its far end the island buffers the Gulf of Finland with a long, low shoreline.

The far reaches of the island, subsumed by the port of Gavan, are of little interest to visitors, even those billeted there in the massive Pribaltiskaya Hotel. This walk concentrates on the historical sector of the island, close to the centre. Peter the Great originally envisaged the area as the centre of his new city, but the disadvantages of siting a capital on an island in the middle of a powerful river, at times alive with the groans of breaking ice, were made manifest when the tsar's own physician drowned. The scheme was dropped, and the first bridge over the river was only erected after the tsar's death. Even then it had to be taken down each autumn until after the thaw in the following spring. Instead of becoming the centre of the capital, in the lifetime of Peter the Great Vasilievsky Island began to take on its present-day character as an area of learning, St Petersburg's Bloomsbury. The country's first permanent museum was sited here in 1718, doubling as an observatory. In the early 19th century the Twelve College buildings designed to house Peter's civil service were given to the fledgling St Petersburg University. Today, the joy of the area is its clutch of architectural survivors from the 18th century, including the highlight of the walk, the recently restored palace of the first governor of the city, Prince Menshikov.

Russia's industrial revolution in the late 19th century made itself strongly felt on the island. A number of large factories were built on its far reaches, with nearby accommodation to house the workforce. By the early 20th century, reactionary government ministers could hardly bear to think about the island, with its explosive mix of radical students and discontented workers. With better shopping at this end of the island, today workers and students still mingle in the shadows of its historic buildings, much as they have for 300 years.

To make the most of this walk, plan to do it on Tuesday to Thursday or Sunday. Since tours at the Menshikov Palace are conducted on the half-hour in Russian, it's worth getting someone to ring © 323 1112 to see if they can give you an English-speaking guide at a

At the beginning of this walk there is a McDonald's, on the corner opposite the metro station.

(A) New Island Ship Restaurant, moored near Most Leytenanta Shmidta, ℗ 963 6765. A 1hr 15min river cruise on a floodlit steamboat-style ship, with food and drink. Leaves at 2, 4, 6, 8 and 11pm; the 8pm dinner cruise is longer.

(B) Sirin-Bar, 1-aya Liniya 16, ℗ 323 7282; *open 11am–11pm*, is a stygian basement bar and restaurant, enlivened by a wide choice of drink and a lengthy well-cooked Russian menu. Further along 1-aya Liniya there are four or five different cafés and snack bars, the nicest of which is the cosy non-smoking **Inkol (D)** at No.32.

(C) The **Golden Leaf**, Syezdovskaya 1-aya Liniya 18; *open 1–11pm (kitchen closes 9.30)*. North Chinese food; beware the Chinese vodka with marinated lizards...

(E) Kalinka, Syezdovskaya 9-aya Liniya, ℗ 323 3718; *open 12 noon–11pm, no credit cards*. A fairly expensive, good three-star Russian/ Georgian restaurant which can be over-warm in summer but is a warm and atmospheric retreat in winter. You will be met by a wolf at the door and a bear at the bar (stuffed, of course), and at 8pm nightly there are Russian folk songs and ballads.

(F) The Great Wall, Sredny Prospekt 11, ℗ 323 2638. Reliable Chinese restaurant.

(G) Café Arka, between the university buildings; *open 11am–10pm*. Cheap café-bar with outside tables in the student district.

(H) The Old Customs House (Staraya Tamozhnya), Tamozhenny Per 1, ℗ 327 8980; *open 1pm–3am, credit cards accepted*. For a real splash, this five-star restaurant serves European cuisine in a high-class setting—make sure you look the part.

(I) Academia, 1st Birzhevoy Proezd, ℗ 327 8949; *open 12 noon–5am, with disco 9pm–12.30am; credit cards accepted*. Huge trendy delicious pizza restaurant, some tables outside.

particular time. If you do this, start the walk about ¾ hour before your allotted time to tour round the palace. Of minor interest is the memorial museum to physiologist Ivan Pavlov, which is closed Thurs, Sat and Sun. If you are intent on including it in your itinerary, ring in the morning on ℗ 323 7234 to make an appointment.

Leaving (M) Vasileostrovskaya, turn right and first right down the street known as 6-aya and 7-aya Liniya (6th and 7th Line).

Whoever came up with the bright idea of giving most of the north–south streets on the island two names, one for each side of the road, should be awarded a medal for lateral thinking, even if it does make things rather confusing at first. As a rule of thumb, remember that the even-numbered 'lines' refer to the east side of the streets. True to the name, the street pattern is very linear, like a mini Manhattan, a grid that dates back to Peter's original plans for the city centre. Inspired by the tsar's admiration for Amsterdam, his French architect Jean-Baptiste Leblond came up with a scheme to chequer the island with a mass of parallel and intersecting canals. When Peter came to inspect the work in 1718 he found that they had been dug too narrow for two vessels to pass and, fuming, ordered them to be filled in.

These streets are still peppered with two-storey 18th-century façades, although most of the buildings are in the eclectic 19th-century style, with a smattering of *Style Moderne* apartment blocks thrown in. As you walk down the street, look out for the shop at 7-aya Liniya 40, on the right-hand side of the road. Beneath the 'Грамиластинки' sign, you can buy cheap records and CDs.

As the street nears the intersection with Bolshoi Prospekt you find the **Church of the Three Saints**. It is the oldest surviving church on the island, so run down that it is hard even to recognize its original function. It was built in 1740–60 by Domenico Trezzini, the (by then) elderly Italian architect whom Peter had recruited from the Dutch court to oversee the construction of his capital.

Cathedral of St Andrew

The pink and white **Cathedral of St Andrew** next door, on the corner of Bolshoi Prospekt, is in much better shape. Beneath its cupolas lies one of the best kept aesthetic secrets in the city, its unrestored mid-18th-century iconostasis. You can usually get in through the door on Bolshoi Prospekt.

The cathedral was built in 1764–80 by a little-known architect, A. F. Vist, on the site of an earlier wooden church that had burned down. Its more recent history is typical of religious buildings throughout the country. Until 1937 it remained open, serving the increasingly embattled spiritual needs of the local community until the height of Stalin's terror, when its priests were taken out and shot by the NKVD, forerunners of the KGB. For the rest of the Soviet period it was given over to the Museum of Ethnography of the Peoples of the USSR, who used it to store skulls and bones. Services are now held in its partially repaired blue and white interior, beneath a dome upheld at its four squinches (arches across the interior corners) by the Apostles Matthew, Mark, Luke and John. You can identify them by their attributes: an angel for Matthew, a lion for Mark, an ox for Luke and an eagle for John.

The glory of the church is its iconostasis, which is one of the few 18th-century gems in and around the city that has not been over-restored. The spirit of this staggeringly beautiful, delicate Baroque masterpiece simply soars, entirely unnoticed by tourists. The fine wooden tracery of the doors is surmounted by a filigree sunburst, and the icons, though of differing ages, nestle happily amongst the gilding, mottled with the patina of age.

It was at a ceremony in the earlier church here that Mikhail Lomonosov (1711–65) was installed as professor of chemistry in the nearby Academy of Sciences in 1745. Lomonosov personified the spirit of 18th-century Russia, particularly the intellectual daring embodied by the early buildings on Vasilievsky Island itself. Born the son of a fisherman on the north coast of Russia near Archangel, the teenage Lomonosov is said to have walked barefoot to Moscow in search of an education. He was an astounding polymath: after studying philosophy in Germany he turned to science, returned to Russia, ran the country's first chemistry laboratory, wrote works on Russian history, systematized the Russian language and its grammar, set up factories for the production of ceramics and mosaic *tesserae*, and in 1755 founded Moscow University. Lomonosov's rise from peasant to imperial advisor signalled the arrival of the enlightenment on Russian shores and the introduction of rational science to its superstitious, religious and intellectually backward people.

Within a few hundred feet of this intersection lie a number of other 18th-century buildings.

The most prominent is the low arcaded yellow and white building on the opposite side of Bolshoi Prospekt, which was built as trading rows for the island's merchants. Traders still occupy the **market**, as well as the less pleasing 1950s building next door. Outside, citizens sell anything they can get their hands on. Inside is strictly the preserve of food sellers. Depending on the season you might want to buy fruit, vegetables, pickled cucumbers and garlic, cured meats or cheese for your picnic. There is also a café serving soup and sandwiches near the meat counters.

Once you have done your shopping, continue down 6-aya and 7-aya Liniya towards the River Neva.

The mid-19th-century **pharmacy** at 16 7-aya Liniya has been partly turned into a museum, its floor-to-ceiling Empire cabinets used to house old bottles, pharmaceutical instruments, Chinese pots and pestles and mortars (*open 8am–8pm weekdays, Sat 10–5; closed Sun*). It was established by the city's leading pharmacist, Alexander Vasilievich Pel (1850–1908). One of the oldest houses in the city is the pink and white two-storey **house** at 12 7-aya Liniya, built by Trezzini in 1720–26. As first director of building in the city, he designed three basic house plans which the population, conscripted from their cosy wooden Moscow homes, were obliged to follow when building their new residences: Peter the Great was taking no chances with his European capital. This now undistinguished building followed the scheme for the so-called 'House for the Distinguished', and long functioned as an outbuilding of the Alexander Nevsky Lavra at the far end of Nevsky Prospekt.

On the building at the corner of 7-aya Liniya and Naberezhnaya Leytenanta Shmidta, 26 memorial plaques commemorate the distinguished scientists who have lived here, in **Academicians' House** (*open Mon–Wed and Fri, 11–5*), since the foundation of the nearby Academy of Sciences in the 18th century. The apartment of the most famous, Ivan Pavlov (1849–1936), whose work on conditioned reflexes netted him a Nobel Prize in 1904, has been turned into a memorial museum. Son of a country priest, Pavlov began his education in a seminary but went on to university and was made head of the Institute of Experimental

Medicine in St Petersburg. In his most famous experiments, which gave us the term 'Pavlovian reaction', his dogs became accustomed to being fed after hearing a particular bell. Pavlov went on to ring the bell without providing food, and observed that the dogs salivated nonetheless.

The embankment is named after Lieutenant Pyotr Schmidt, one of the leaders of the 1905 naval mutiny that pressurized Nicholas II into agreeing to the election of the Russian parliament, the duma. *If you look right you will see the five green domes of the late 19th-century* **Church of the Nativity,** *built with mock Byzantine grandeur, silhouetted against a background of belching factory chimneys.*

These are the only hint you get on this walk of Vasilievsky Island's other face. The industrial suburb, so close to the centre of the city, gave the island an ominous reputation during the unsettled years before the Revolution. It is no coincidence that in Andrei Bely's novel *Petersburg,* set in 1905, the first revolutionary we meet lives on the island. The population is described as 'industrial and coarse', a 'many-thousand human swarm which shuffled in the morning to the many-chimneyed factories'. Into the mouths of the bourgeoisie, living on the other side of the river, Bely inserts the entreaty: 'Don't let the crowd of shadows in from the islands! Black and damp bridges are already thrown across the waters... If only they could be dismantled...'

Turn left towards 4-aya and 5-aya Liniya.

Here, on 9 January 1905 (later known as Bloody Sunday) a 6,000-strong 'crowd of shadows' was halted abruptly by a hail of gunfire and charging soldiers as they marched peacefully to petition the tsar. The bridge opposite, Most Leytenanta Shmidta, was the first permanent link with the mainland, completed in 1850. Just beyond, a pair of sphinxes punctuate the granite embankment. Excavated in Thebes, the sphinxes are the oldest architectural features in the city, dating from the 14th century BC. Their inscription celebrates Pharaoh Amunhotep III, 'ruler of Thebes, builder of monuments rising to the sky like four pillars holding up the vault of the heavens.' They were moved here in 1832 to glorify the river approach to the **Academy of Arts**, Universitetskaya Nab. 17, ✆ 323 6496 (*open Wed–Sun 11–6*).

The Academy itself had been built in 1763–88, designed by Vallin de la Mothe and overseen by Alexander Kornilov. Its cream and peach façade marks the very beginning of the classical revival under Catherine the Great; the only decoration is a minimal frieze showing the tools of the three major arts—sculpture, architecture and painting. Inside the building there is a museum of the academy but, with no-one around to tell you where to go, you feel rather like a trespasser if you try to find it. Don't be put off. Having admired the circular courtyard at the centre of this massive square building and the sculpture on the ground floor, walk up the magnificent pillared staircase. Wander through the round red senate room and turn left to see paintings by past and present pupils of the Academy. Further on you will come to the copies of Renaissance paintings, which the pupils copied in turn to learn their skills. On the top floor you should find architectural models of many of St Petersburg's most notable buildings. Although the great mid-19th-century revival of Russian art initiated by the group of painters known as the Wanderers took the form of a rebellion against the classical focus of the Academy, many of its practitioners were nevertheless trained here. Among them were the painters Karl Bryullov and Ilya Repin, Andrei Voronikhin (serf-architect of the Stroganov family), and the 19th-century sculptor Pyotr Klodt, who was responsible for almost all the equestrian statues in the city.

> *For the rest of this walk we will carry on along the Universitetskaya Naberezhnaya, looking across to monumental St Petersburg on the far side of the lugubrious Neva.*

The wooded square beside the Academy of Arts is the best place for picnics. It is known, incongruously, as both **Rumyantsev** and **Shevchenko Ploshchad**, after a Russian general and a Ukrainian poet respectively. Both of them studied in neighbouring institutes. In the 18th century Rumyantsev, who was to lead numerous successful battles against the Turks under Catherine the Great, was educated at the Military Cadet School housed in Menshikov Palace beyond, while Shevchenko studied at the Academy of Arts in the middle of the 19th century. The granite obelisk at the centre of the garden, between two broken fountains, is inscribed 'to the victories of Rumyantsev', and topped by a golden eagle. It was moved here in 1818 from the Field of Mars. A new bust of Ilya Repin faces the embankment.

> *Those seriously interested in church architecture (or hungry) at this point could walk diagonally through the park and up 1-aya Liniya back to Bolshoi Prospekt. On the corner of Bolshoi Prospekt and 1-aya Liniya is a sign marking the high water line of the disastrous 1824 flood (see p.80).*

The classical green and white **church of St Catherine** at the beginning of the avenue was designed by Yuri Velten, a native of St Petersburg and the first director of the Academy of Arts. The interior is occupied by the Gramzapis recording studio, but the church also holds choral and organ concerts on Sundays at 3pm. St Catherine's was a Lutheran church, serving the city's foreign community, many of whom lived on the island in the early days. As well as architects, they included mercenaries employed in the army and navy, portrait painters and doctors. Indeed, it became a habit for the Russian imperial family to employ a Scottish physician. Catherine the Great's regular physician was Dr John Rogerson, whom she grew to distrust. 'It seems to me that who ever falls into Rogerson's hands is already a dead man' she inveighed in 1783. At the height of a smallpox epidemic in 1768, Catherine the Great sent to London for Dr Thomas Dimsdale, whose 1767 treatise on inoculation had been a runaway success. The treatment was then at the forefront of medicine, and most people considered it too risky. Catherine was determined to be inoculated herself, however, and, when she survived, her son Paul, and later her grandchildren, were also inoculated.

Alternatively, skip the church and carry on along the embankment, across 1-aya and Syezdovskaya Liniya to the **Menshikov Palace.**

Menshikov Palace

Дворец Меншикова—*Dvoryets Menshikova; Universitetskaya Nab. 15. Open Tues–Sun 10.30–5, last entry 4.20; closed Mon; call© 323 1112 to organize an English-speaking tour in advance. Entrance is through a door in the basement of the first wing. Mind your heads in the cloakrooms.*

The first thing you see is the end wing, a later addition to the yellow stucco palace. Beyond it stands Menshikov's original palace, with its porticoed porch flanked by two gabled projecting bays. Restored since 1967 almost to its original look, the palace was the earliest stone structure on Vasilievsky Island and, topped with statues and coronets, the most extravagant building in the city. Started in 1710 by an Italian architect and finished in 1716 by a German, it was built for Prince Alexander Menshikov. This legendary figure rose from humble beginnings as the son of an ordinary soldier to become Peter the Great's prime minister, military commander, pimp, rumoured lover and governor of St Petersburg. At the time, the rest of the island was a building site, a chequerboard of canal trenches and boggy streets on which people were still devoured by wolves in broad daylight. The tsar was away when it was completed; his reaction on his return is subject to much speculation. Was he angered by his favourite's scene-stealing grandeur, or had he expressly told Menshikov to build a palace in which the tsar could also work and entertain? Certainly, Menshikov's countryside extravaganza, the palace at Oranienbaum, provoked Peter to build himself a great palace at Peterhof in friendly rivalry.

Menshikov, vain and addicted to corruption on a huge scale, was not destined to outlive his master long. He oversaw the accession of Peter's wife and his own former mistress, Catherine I, to the throne in 1725, and acted as her principal advisor. Unfortunately for Menshikov, she died after a reign of little more than two years. Her successor Peter II (Peter the Great's 12-year-old grandson by his first wife) was less fond of grandfather's old crony, and packed him off to Siberia. Within two years Menshikov was dead. His palace was taken over by the state and in 1732 became the school for military cadets, which Rumyantsev attended. It was at this time that the wings were added to the building to house the hundreds of potential officers. Most of the boys were of noble birth. They entered the school at the age of five, when their parents signed away their rights to see them for 15 years, except at public functions.

The collection of interiors, costumes, furniture, prints and portraits within the palace goes under the title **Russian Culture 1700–30**, and memorably includes a beautifully shaped Italianate staircase and a suite of rooms decked out in blue and white Dutch tiles. You start in the kitchen, lined with huge wooden vessels. In the main reception room, Italian tapestries and sculptures compete with massive German cupboards. The room opens into the hall, from which one of the oldest wooden staircases in the city rises in two branches to meet in a single flight and double back on to the next floor. Its wrought-iron balustrade is of the utmost delicacy, entwining the initials PP (Petrus Primus) and AM (Alexander Menshikov), in Latin rather than Cyrillic script.

The first floor rooms begin with the vestibule and study in which the virtually illiterate Menshikov and his secretary would oversee the affairs of state. The German desk contains many a secret drawer beneath its busts of Roman emperors. Next comes a series of outrageously tiled bedrooms, originally revetted entirely with 18th-century Delft tiles. The Russian appetite for Dutch tiles was enormous, and when the bills became too dizzy Menshikov simply imported two masters from Delft. The products of the Russian kilns they set up are charmingly naïve; those over the far door in the third room are decorated with fine line-drawings of household implements, isolated pieces of architecture and cherubs. Menshikov's walnut office is a jewel of inlaid woodwork, highlighted by gilded Corinthian capitals. With the help of a secretary the Prince oversaw much government paperwork, though he never learned to write more than his signature. Finally we come to the Great Hall, decorated later in the early classical style. The 18th-century clock and organ at the far end were designed as a single piece of furniture; the organ is still used for concerts, but the clock has long since ceased to function. The tour reaches its conclusion through the four recently restored rooms belonging to Menshikov's wife Daria, and a room displaying 18th-century Chinese wall-hangings which were given to Peter. In the final room you can recognize the portrait of Peter's father Tsar Alexei, wearing what looks like a dunce's cap.

> Leaving the palace, turn left on the embankment, passing the disintegrating building of the military cadets' former riding school (No.13) which is occupied by the army to this day. Next comes the university's Faculty of Languages, housed in a green and white 18th-century building, and beyond it the more intimate proportions of the Rector's Wing (No.9).

A plaque on the wall states that the Symbolist poet Alexander Blok was born here in 1880. His grandfather, a botanist, was rector of the university at the time. The heart of the university beats in the extraordinary, long, early Baroque terrace which runs at right angles to the embankment from here. To get a good look at it you will need to walk all the way round. The interior is a warren of subdivided spaces.

Started during the reign of Peter the Great to house part of his revamped civil service, the building was intended by the tsar to line the embankment, but while he was away Prince Menshikov changed the brief so that it would not dwarf the façade of his own nearby palace. Perhaps because of this, work on the **Twelve Colleges**, as it became known, progressed slowly, and the terrace was only completed in 1742. In 1819 it was given over to the new University of St Petersburg.

The street in front of the terrace is named after one of the university's most distinguished alumni, Dmitri Mendeleyev (1834–1907). He formulated the Periodic Table, known to pupils of chemistry throughout the world, and in so doing was able to predict the existence of a number of elements which were only subsequently discovered. One of them, element 101, is known as mendelevium. His office and library from the time he was professor of chemistry at the university can be viewed here (*open 10–5 weekdays, Sat by arrangement, ✆ 328 9744*), and above it is the **university museum** (*open weekdays 11–5, tours by arrangement ✆ 328 9683, open to individuals on Weds*).

Another student who had an even greater impact on the world was Vladimir Ilyich Lenin, who graduated with honours from the Faculty of Law in 1891. Lenin was only one of a string of revolutionaries to be educated here. Almost from the beginning of the university's existence, the authorities were terrified by the beast they had created, closing it down regularly to quell surges of political radicalism. On the day of Pushkin's funeral in January 1837, orders were received that all professors and students must be present at lectures. The authorities feared that the students 'might band together and carry Pushkin's coffin—they could "go too far"' (Alexander Nikitenko, *The Diary of a Russian Censor*). The regime was right to fear the university, but only for as long as tsarism refused to reform itself. Had the Romanovs agreed to reign as constitutional monarchs earlier, it is likely that the sons of the enlightenment at the university would have been their staunchest supporters. As it was, these educated and talented free-thinkers, their career paths dictated by an outdated hierarchical structure, became their implacable foes.

> Back on the embankment, we quickly bypass the **Academy of Science**, built in 1783–9 by Catherine the Great's favourite classical architect Quarenghi, to house the institution set up by Peter the Great in 1724. Initially the Academy was staffed by 17 German scientists, but soon home-grown scientists of the calibre of Mikhail Lomonósov began to take their seats here. Since 1934 the headquarters of the Academy has been in Moscow, and this building has become the St Petersburg branch.

Museum of Anthropology and Ethnography

> Музей Антропологии и Этнографии—*Muzei Antropologii i Etnografii*; ✆ 328 1412; *open 11–4.30; closed Mon and last Tues; entrance in the alleyway before the building.*

The large green and white building was the city's first purpose-built museum. Don't confuse this place with the Museum of the Ethnography of the Peoples of the

USSR (*see* p.211); it was designed to showcase the pickled human and animal freaks that Peter the Great had begun to collect in 1714. Peter decided to house his grotesque collection on this spot when he noticed a curious pine tree, one branch of which had grown back into the main trunk, standing here. The building was begun in 1718 and was always erroneously known as the **Kunstkamera** (German for 'art chamber') after the museum in Dresden which Peter had so admired. As well as the pickled wonders, it sheltered a library, an anatomy theatre and an observatory in the tower. Peter encouraged his subjects to preserve any curiosities they came across in vodka and bring them in, and encouraged visitors with a free shot of the spirit and a pie.

The large collection of artefacts from all over the world now housed in the building is a paean to man's practicality and his ceaseless spiritual quest. There is little here that is not directly useful, either physically or as a tool for communicating with God. The ingenuity with which man has used the materials available to him, the care that he has lavished on the aesthetics of everyday objects and the imagination he has shown in his different approaches to the divine are heart-warming.

The first rooms you enter contain exhibits from the continent of North America, beginning with the Inuit tribes of the northern reaches and travelling southwards towards the Pueblo Indians of New Mexico. Waterproofs made of fish skins, shamanistic masks and an elk-skin quiver vivid with red-painted hunting scenes give way to birch-bark canoes, dioramas showing scenes from Indian religious rituals and magnificent woven baskets, which held water when saturated and could be heated by dropping in stones from the fire.

Beyond the Japanese collection to the left, the central rotunda was once the forum for anatomical dissections, which visitors and students watched through the gaps in the ceiling now occupied by gesticulating dummies dressed in native garb. Today it houses Peter's Kunstkamera, in all its grisly B-movie sci-fi glory. The curiosities are none the better for the 275 years that have elapsed since he bought the bulk of them, and there is little pleasure in ogling the pickled two-headed calf and human Siamese twins. They should revive the practice of giving out a shot of vodka here, to stiffen the resolve before taking a look. Less sickening are Peter's personal surgical instruments in the cabinet. Beside them lie teeth that the tsar himself extracted. He is said to have greatly enjoyed playing dentist; from the look of the teeth, when the urge took him he extracted them, whether healthy or unhealthy.

The African room comes next, with an exquisite Azandi harp and bronze cast objects from Benin. The pride of the collection, a magnificent cast head, was stolen in 1993. The exhibition continues upstairs with a room devoted to Australia and Oceania, in which you can see the mummified head of a Tahitian chieftain, complete with traditional tattoos, bought by James Cook shortly before his death in Hawaii. His sailors presented it to the governor of the far eastern Russian province of

Kamchatka in recognition of his hospitality. In the centre of the room are the cloak and helmet of a Hawaiian king, made from luminous feathers. The rooms beyond cover Indonesia, India, China, Tibet and Mongolia, and there is a memorial museum to Mikhail Lomonosov, the talented poet, scientist and linguist who worked here from 1741 until his death in 1765. With the help of the telescope in the tower above the museum, he and other astrologers created an early planetarium, known as the Great Academic Globe (*under repair until 2003*). Spectators got into the globe which revolved around them, with models of the planets giving an inaccurate, but at the time thrilling, impression of the movement of the heavens.

Retracing your steps to the entrance of the museum, turn left on the embankment to reach the last museum on this extensive trail.

Zoological Institute

Зоологический музей—*Zoologichesky muzei; © 328 0112, open 11am–5pm; closed Fri. It can be unbearably crowded during the school holidays. You will know if you have hit it at the wrong time, not necessarily by the crowds outside, but by the fact that you simply can't buy a ticket; they will all have been pre-booked.*

Inside you will be faced with one of the largest collections of stuffed animals in the world, often placed together in dioramas recreating their natural habitats. The mammoths unearthed from the permafrost in Siberia in the course of this century are the most unusual sight, though there is plenty to keep you gasping—blue whales, polar bears and tray upon tray of insects as well as a live insect zoo. A number of the animals once belonged to Peter the Great, including the horse he rode at the battle of Poltava.

Leaving the museum, a left turn takes you on to the tip of the island (the strelka*) with its majestic view of St Petersburg's main waterfront.*

Directly ahead the golden spire of the SS Peter and Paul Cathedral, burial place of the Romanovs, pierces the sky from within the sombre confines of the Peter and Paul Fortress. On the right bank of the river, Palace Embankment unfurls in an endless succession of extravagant façades. Starting with the countless columns of the Winter Palace, it extends through Renaissance and Classical exteriors to the smooth veneer of the Marble Palace.

The walk is at an end, and you are unfortunately miles from a metro station. Either flag down a taxi or catch a bus or trolleybus from the stop in front of the former stock exchange (Birzha), which looks on to the strelka *through the brick-red rostral columns. Bus no.44 and trolleybus nos.1, 7 and 10 will all take you over Dvortsovy Most to* ⓜ *Nevsky Prospekt. Otherwise, you could pick up Walk I in the middle by turning to p.76, and actually visit the stock exchange and naval museum.*

Walk VII: The Hermitage

Start: *Ticket Hall, Hermitage Museum*
Walking Time: *3 hours for each walk*

There could hardly be a less appropriate name for this priceless labyrinth of a museum with its superlative collection of works of art housed in a series of Baroque and classical palaces once inhabited by the tsars. No self-respecting hermit would go near a place that attracts three million visitors a year. To Catherine the Great in the 1760s, though, it seemed entirely appropriate to call the small building that she had commissioned to adjoin the Winter Palace her 'hermitage'. This was the place where she retreated from the affairs of state to admire her latest artistic acquisitions in selected company.

Since the Revolution, when the royal collection was augmented by the confiscation of private art treasures, the whole ensemble of buildings has been open to the public. It is said that to spend one minute looking at every piece, displayed in over 10 kilometres of halls and corridors, you would need to put aside six days a week in the museum for nine years. The visitor with just a day or less must therefore approach the place with surgical precision. Simply to cover the highlights of the museum—the state rooms and masterpieces by Rembrandt, Leonardo, Picasso and Matisse—will take a good day. At some point a trip should also be made to the small Special Collection, where the opulent but contrived baubles of the Romanovs vie with the raw energy of the golden belts, scabbards and amulets worn by Scythian princes some 2,000 years earlier. With less than a day to spare, you will have to choose between the two suggested itineraries, each of which is enough to fill three hours with spectacular images and impressions. Those who have a particular interest should refer to the gazetteer, under What is Where in the Hermitage (*see* p.192).

Dvortsovaya Naberezhnaya 36, © 110 9625. Open 10.30–5, until 4 on Sundays; closed Mon.

lunch/cafés

Hermitage Buffet, Room 77, first room on the right in a dark corridor at the bottom of Jordan Staircase, serves sandwiches, hamburgers, soft drinks, tea and coffee to a long queue.

Café House of Scholars, Dvortsovaya Naberezhnaya 26, is the closest café to the Hermitage, and serves tea, coffee, alcohol and simple snacks in its cosy interior overlooking the Neva.

City Bar Kapella, 2nd floor, Moiki 20, © 314 1037; *open 11am–midnight*. A fun, popular hang-out with a mixed crowd of students and musicians. An amusing American cook prepares good salads and other European dishes. Some outside tables for a sunny day.

Le Chandeleur, Bolshaya Konyushennaya Ul. 1, © 314 8380; *open 11am–midnight*. French crêperie.

Practical Hints

Great efforts are being made to bring the Hermitage displays up to the standard of other great museums of the world in time for the tricentenary of the city in 2003, but there is a serious lack of cash for the job. Tourist tickets, you will have noticed, are twenty or more times the cost of a ticket for a Russian visitor, but this is how the museum earns money to subsidise access to culture for local art-lovers, whose salaries are too low to pay Western prices.

Tickets are valid for all but the Special Collection and occasional visiting exhibitions. Tickets for the Special Collection are available from the central glass section, where the times of the next available tours are clearly displayed.

Many less popular rooms are sometimes closed to visitors, and you can never tell when others will be temporarily out of bounds for restoration or through lack of staff. These closures could disrupt the itineraries below, in which case you will have to use the maps to negotiate your way to the next open area.

Occasionally you will come across signposts in Russian and English pointing to different collections. Treat them with caution, as they frequently point in the wrong direction. The artworks themselves are labelled in Russian, with only the name of the artist appearing in Latin script. There are plans to change this.

History of the Buildings and Collections

It was Peter the Great, with his bizarre purchase of 2,000 embalmed 'curiosities' from Frederick Ruysch, who first introduced the concept of a museum to Russia. He also bought a number of Dutch pictures. Most were seascapes, as befitted his obsession with boat-building, but among them were important works by Rembrandt, Van Dyck and Rubens. Peter also encouraged the preservation of the Scythian gold being uncovered at that time from burial mounds.

In the 1760s, Catherine the Great began to buy up collections of European art wholesale. She instructed Vallin de la Mothe, then head of the Academy of Arts, to design an annexe to the palace in which to house them. The result was the classical Hermitage. Here, in candle-lit privacy, she would gloat over newly arrived crates of canvases and books. 'Only the mice and I can admire all this,' she wrote possessively on the arrival of the Walpole collection, which she bought from England in 1779. To Catherine, the acquisition of these artefacts from western Europe seems to have symbolized her bringing civilization to Russia. In buying a great collection from Prussia, England or France and, if possible, provoking furore at its leaving the country, she proved the Russian monarchy more 'enlightened' than the local competition; and herself more deserving of the admiration of such great thinkers of the time as Voltaire and Diderot. Not that this vanity meant Catherine could not appreciate art for its own sake: one of the most important documents concerning the collection today is her own eight-volume catalogue.

Within five years, it was clear the collection would soon outgrow the Small Hermitage, as it is known today. Catherine commissioned Yuri Velten to extend it with the Large Hermitage, which marches on along the Neva embankment. In the late 1770s artists in Rome began the task of copying Raphael's Loggia at the Vatican on to canvas, so it could be perfectly reproduced by the Italian architect Quarenghi down the side of the Large Hermitage, overlooking the Winter Canal and Quarenghi's Imperial Theatre. Catherine's grandson, Alexander I, continued to fill the walls and halls of this and other royal palaces. His largest contribution was the purchase of the collection of Josephine, wife of his vanquished enemy Napoleon.

A devastating fire in the Winter Palace in December 1837 burned for an entire day, filling the sky with flames. Thanks to the selfless behaviour of firemen and soldiers, some of whom died, it did not spread to the Hermitage. Within two years all the state rooms had been rebuilt and Nicholas I and his family were again in residence. It was during his otherwise unenlightened reign that the royal collection took the step of opening its doors to the public. Behind the Large Hermitage, building work began in 1840 on the New Hermitage. The architect was the German Leo von Klenze, already known for his museums in Munich.

With the Revolution the trickle turned into a flood. Aristocrats and other collectors fled from Russia, and the state lost little time in nationalizing the collections left behind. Over the next 30 years paintings, sculpture, furniture and *objets* were gradually shared out between the major state museums. Among the most important gains of the Hermitage was the collection of modern European painting shared with the Pushkin Gallery in Moscow, the majority of it collected by just two men, Ivan Morozov and Sergei Shchukin. Morozov reflected philosophically in exile that he had always intended to give the collection to the state, but Shchukin's heir in France has recently been making different noises. Emboldened by the collapse of the Soviet Union and its legal system, she claimed that the works had been stolen and that she intended to fight a legal battle to get them back. When the recent Matisse exhibition arrived in Paris, it did so without a number of the works from Russian museums which had been shown in New York. The Russians feared that the French courts would side with her and impound the canvases.

This is a very different attitude from that of the state in the 1920s and '30s, which regularly sold off major works of art for hard currency. The two biggest buyers were Calouste Gulbenkian, an oil magnate who helped open the world market to Soviet oil, and the American Secretary to the Treasury Andrew Mellon, who offered loans to the Soviet Union on terms which included the purchase of important works of art. The Hermitage claims to have lost 52 major works through such sales, which were conducted in complete secrecy by an arm of government called the Antiquariat. More revealing still is an episode that took place in the seventies, in which several pieces of a unique imperial dinner service were broken when the then mayor of St Petersburg, the aptly named Grigory Romanov, borrowed it for his daughter's wedding banquet.

After the declaration of war in 1941 and before the German blockade of the city, three trainloads of the most valuable works were shipped to Yekaterinburg (then Sverdlovsk) in the Ural Mountains. Everything else was moved into the basement and ground floor, where thousands of statues and pieces of porcelain were buried in piles of sand. The staff continued their academic studies while living for stretches in the museum, doing their best to protect it from bombardment. If stories are to be believed, one group of soldiers drafted in to clear up glass were treated to a tour of the gallery's empty picture frames, the guide conjuring the pictures before their eyes by the sheer power of description. When the consignment returned in the autumn of 1945, only one picture, a Van Dyck, was missing.

It has recently transpired that the Hermitage cellars do contain, as has long been thought, a hoard of important Impressionist and Post-Impressionist paintings looted from Germany by Soviet soldiers in 1945. The collection is now on permanent display under the name 'Hidden Treasures'. The Russians claim that the loot is nothing compared with the damage wrought by invading German soldiers on their own cultural heritage, and that they should not therefore be returned to their former owners. Not surprisingly, the Germans think otherwise.

Special Collection (Osobaya Kladovaya—Особая Кладовая)

Following your guide to this guarded strongroom at the heart of the Large Hermitage, you will find yourself surrounded by glistering precious treasure. The exhibits divide roughly in two: firstly the best collection of Scythian, Greek and early Siberian gold anywhere in the world, mostly worked between the 7th and 2nd centuries BC, and secondly jewels and precious stones that belonged to the tsars, dating from the 16th to 19th centuries.

The Scythians were a group of tribes, united by their Farsi-related language, who lived in the European southern steppe and North Caucasus. They have gone down in history as some of the finest early metalworkers. As well as intricate filigree jewellery and amulets, you will see larger golden beasts used to decorate shields, and a comb, surmounted by a fight scene. The motif of an animal, often a horse or stag, preyed upon by a magnificent lion or griffon was widespread from Greece to Persia, particularly on golden ornaments. The golden predator symbolizes the sun, a deity to these tribes, accepting an animal sacrifice. Looking at these treasures, the genesis of the myth of Jason and the Argonauts comes to mind, for it was on this Black Sea coast, so abundant with gold, that he found the Golden Fleece. Most of these objects were found in the burial mounds of princely warriors in the 19th century, though some were uncovered as early as the reign of Peter the Great, who gave rewards for their preservation to stop the common practice of melting them down.

When Rastrelli got the commission to design the Winter Palace for the good-looking, quixotic Empress Elizabeth in the mid-18th century, the brief would have thrown most architects. The principal residence of the royal family, it needed to include living accommodation for over 1,000 court officials as well as the servants required to run it. In addition, Elizabeth needed magnificent rooms in which to preside over investitures, balconies from which to watch parading troops and a grand staircase down which to pass for the ceremony of the Blessing of the Waters. More personally, she required ballrooms in which to indulge her passion for dancing, an enormous boudoir for her 15,000 dresses and a church to which she could retire when her passionately religious side was in the ascendancy.

All this Rastrelli satisfied in a simple but highly decorative scheme. The ground floor was taken up with palace administration, storerooms and servants' quarters, but once you had taken the grand staircase to the first floor you found yourself at every turn in an enfilade of imposing state rooms, interrupted at the corners of the palace by marginally more intimate royal suites. On the second floor were bedrooms and living quarters of the courtiers. Today some of the highlights of the museum, including sculpture by Rodin and paintings by Van Gogh, Gauguin, Matisse and Picasso, are housed here beneath the eaves. To get to them, this walk takes a sweep through the State Rooms, where round-faced *babushki* in scarves have replaced the giant Ethiopian royal guard, and flocks of schoolchildren the knots of well-dressed ambassadors.

> *From the ticket hall enter the long white vaulted room, the main entrance to the museum known as the **Rastrelli Gallery**. Its left-hand side is lined with sales desks offering a disparate selection of souvenirs and art books, but sadly only a few postcards of the museum's collection. Straight ahead the red carpet beckons.*

It leads up the white marble steps of the **Jordan Staircase**, dividing in two before meeting up again between the sets of double marble pillars that line the balcony. The ornate Baroque stairwell, a confection of white and gold, gives the visitor her first sense of the airy scale on which the palace was conceived. Unlike many of the other state rooms, this is one of Rastrelli's original designs, considered so vital an introduction to the palace that it was faithfully recreated after the 1837 fire, when many of the other rooms were rebuilt in the more classical style of the period.

The stairs owe their name to the arcane ceremony of the Blessing of the Waters, performed by the Russian tsars on 6 January since way before the capital was moved to St Petersburg. To commemorate the baptism of Jesus in the River Jordan, the entire court and leading churchmen descended the stairs and, bare-headed in the sub-zero temperatures, walked out on to the icy Neva where a hole was cut

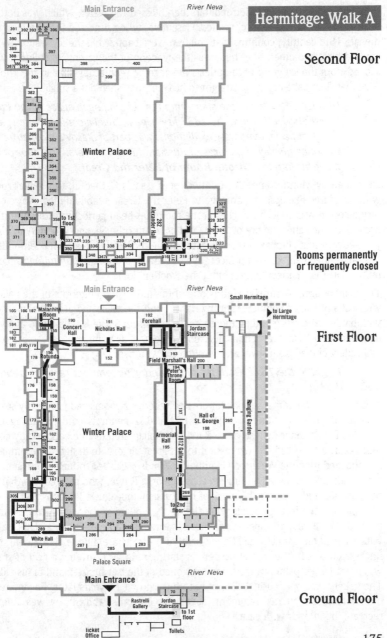

Second Floor

Main Entrance

River Neva

Winter Palace

391 392 393 396
390
389
388
387 386 385 384
397
383
382
381a
367 351a
366 352
365
364 353
363 354
362 355
361 356
360 357
370 369 368 358 to 1st floor
371 375 376
333 334 335 337 339 341 342
350 336 338 340 334
349 348 347 345 346 343

Alexander Hall
282
315 314 312 332 331 330 323
316 317 318 319 320 321 322
327 326
328 325
329 324

Rooms permanently or frequently closed

First Floor

Main Entrance

River Neva

Small Hermitage

to Large Hermitage

105 106 187 189 Malachite Room
184
183
182
181 180 179 188 185
190 Concert Hall
191 Nicholas Hall
192 Forehall
Jordan Staircase
153
156 Rotunda
178
177 157
176 158
174 159
173 160
172 161 Dark Corridor
171 162
170 163
169 164
168 165
166
167
152
151
193 Field Marshall's Hall 200
194 Peter's Throne Room
197
260
Hall of St. George 198
Armorial Hall 195
1812 Gallery
Hanging Garden

Winter Palace

300
305 301
306 307 302
304 308 299
298 297 296 295 294 293 281 290
289 288 292
White Hall
287 286 285 284 283
196 270
269
to 2nd floor

Palace Square

Ground Floor

Main Entrance

River Neva

Rastrelli Gallery
Jordan Staircase
to 1st floor
70 71 72

Ticket Office
Toilets

175

through the ice. Tsar and Metropolitan then blessed the water, which was bottled for use as baptism water in churches. Casanova, who witnessed the ceremony in the late 18th century, confirms that children were baptized in the icy waters. What amazed him, and others after him, was the reaction of the parents of children who slipped from the icy grasp of the priests never to be seen again: sure in the knowledge that their babe had gone straight to heaven, they shed not a single tear.

> Turn left at the top of the stairs, into the echoing open space of the **Field Marshals' Hall** where the 1837 fire began. This balconied white space, used for special temporary exhibitions, was part of Stasov's reconstruction and once displayed pictures of Russian military leaders. The door opposite leads into the **Throne Room of Peter the Great**.

Decorated by Montferrand, the architect of St Isaac's Cathedral, this velvet room with its church-like apse is a homage to Peter the Great, who had died over a century before it was conceived. The throne room has been perfectly restored on two occasions, once after the fire of 1837, and once after the Second World War. Here you get your first glimpse of the intricate parquet flooring that is such a leitmotif of this, and indeed all, Russian palaces; even in the most humble *kommunalka* (communal flat) the smartest thing is often the wooden floor.

The neighbouring **Armorial Hall** is one of the most gaudy interiors in the palace, with pairs of golden columns running right round the walls and groups of warriors with battle standards guarding the doors. It dates from Stasov's rebuilding, and was intended for balls and receptions. Its cabinets contain all manner of valuable objects exquisitely crafted from silver and semi-precious stones.

> To get to the **1812 Gallery** (partly under restoration) take the door on the left.

This red room, an immense corridor created where six rooms had previously stood, is covered floor to ceiling in portraits of the 332 generals who fought against Napoleon. Alexander I chose Carlo Rossi, the Italian architect he consistently commissioned to give aesthetic expression to his great victory, to design the room, and he modelled it on the Waterloo Chamber at Windsor Castle. To further the similarities, Alexander imported an English artist, George Dawe, who painted over half of the portraits and oversaw the work of his Russian colleagues, Poliakov and Golik, who painted the rest. Generals who died in the course of the victory were either painted from earlier portraits and miniatures, or were represented by a blank frame with their name beneath it. The majority of portraits are all one size, giving the impression of a host of romantic heroes staring in at you through a grid of small windows. Larger paintings were commissioned of the tsar himself, and of his allies. The gallery was opened in 1826, only to burn down 11 years later. Fortunately, members of the guards' regiments saved the portraits, and Stasov was able to recreate the interior with ease.

*Directly opposite the entrance into the 1812 Gallery is an impressive gilded door leading into the Great Throne Room or **Hall of St George**.*

The hall is used to house major travelling exhibitions like the recent hoard of Fabergé objects that did the rounds of the world's major cities. Notice that the inlaid floor is an exact mirror of the patterned ceiling above. Under the Soviet regime the throne was replaced by a giant semi-precious mosaic map of the USSR. Above it is an Italian bas-relief of St George, carved from the same Carrara marble used to decorate the rest of the room. From 1795, when the window-lined room was added on to the palace, the tsars held their most solemn receptions and delivered important speeches here.

Return to the 1812 Gallery and leave by the door at the far end from the equestrian painting of Alexander I. Left off the first of two badly lit rooms of European porcelain is the towering Rastrelli chapel, flooded with light and magnificent porcelain. Retracing your steps into the gloom you will find a staircase on the left, which takes you up to the department of **Modern European Painting***.*

A tendency to rehang the exhibition here makes it difficult to take you through the stunning collection room by room. Highlights include rooms of Impressionists, the group of French painters who first ventured out of the studio to paint what they saw *en plein air*. Without the new widespread availability of tubes of oils, which freed them from mixing their own paints in the studio, the experiment would have been impossible. Startling too are the Post-Impressionists, particularly a number of **Cézanne** (1839–1906) landscapes and still lifes, a clutch of vivid, little-known **Van Goghs** (1853–90), and the large collection of Tahitian paintings by **Gauguin** (1848–1903); you can see the primitive canvas he used for his work, resembling nothing so much as potato sacks. Most famous of all are the museum's extensive collections of works by **Matisse** (1869–1954) and **Picasso** (1881–1973).

For all these paintings, and for the explosion of creativity they engendered here in the early 20th century, Russia is indebted to Sergei Shchukin and Ivan (and to a lesser extent his brother Mikhail) Morozov. Of the two men, Shchukin was the more gifted and prolific collector. As the years went by he became increasingly sure of his own eye, and by 1917 had collected some 200 major canvases. It all began in 1897, when he fell in love with a Monet in Paris and bought it on the spot: it was the first Impressionist painting to come to Russia. For the next seven years he collected Impressionists, mostly Monet and, to a lesser extent, Sisley and Pissarro. The discovery of Gauguin, from whom he bought 16 Tahitian canvases to hang in his dining room, inaugurated Shchukin's Post-Impressionist phase. Sure of his own taste, he bought two oils from the young Henri Matisse's studio before the painter had been fully recognized even in Paris. The two became friends, and Matisse eventually came to Russia, where he was fascinated by early icons. In 1909, Shchukin commissioned Matisse to make three paintings for his stairwell. Only two—*Dance* and *Music*—were painted, but they are among Matisse's greatest works. You will find them here if they are not out on loan. It must have been startling to come across them in the stucco and parquet interior of a Moscow palace.

Shchukin's last love was Picasso. Of the 51 canvases he bought between 1909 and 1914, the majority are held by the Hermitage. As well as Shchukin's own favourite Cubist period, there are also paintings from Picasso's earlier blue and pink periods.

Morozov was less sure of himself than Shchukin, and his collection was also more colour-led. It was said that he looked at a wall like a tapestry, and would leave spaces blank until he found something of exactly the right shade to fill it. The difference between Shchukin's and Morozov's style as collectors is illustrated by the following story, related by the French painter Maurice Denis. 'When Morozov visited Ambroise Vollard [the famous Paris dealer], he would say: 'I want to see a very fine Cézanne.' Whereas Shchukin would ask to see all the Cézannes and make his own choice.' Though Morozov also counted 11 Matisses and three Picassos among his collection, it was particularly rich in Cézanne and the Impressionists.

During the modern European painting exhibition you will find yourself on a balcony overlooking the delicate decoration of the **Alexander Hall**, *commemorating the victory over Napoleon. The stucco bas-reliefs include scenes from the war, and a portrayal of Alexander I on the far wall. The hall is used for temporary exhibitions from the museum's vast stocks.*

After the works by Picasso and Matisse come a series of rooms devoted to painters associated with the movement known as Fauvism. Most typical of the group's simplification of composition, often reduced to a series of blocks of colour, are the canvases by **Derain** (1880–1954). The last room, Room 333 at the top of the stairs (*closed at time of writing*), is hung with canvases by **Kandinsky** (1866–1944), a Russian who spent most of his life in Germany. His concern was with the hidden essence of life, which he sought to express by capturing aspects of it—light, laughter, emotion and music—in his will-o'-the-wisp compositions.

Taking the stairs down, you will find yourself with a shock back in the mannered world of late 18th-century France (Room 288), as portrayed by **Jean Honoré Fragonard** *(1732–1806).*

This suite of rooms, looking out on to Palace Square, was known as the First Guest Suite when this was a royal palace. Beneath its painted vaulted ceilings and decorative chandeliers stayed the most important guests of state.

Turn right into the **White Hall** *(Room 289), decorated after the fire using Roman baths as a model. You are now in the west wing of the Winter Palace, whose smaller rooms betray its use as the living quarters of the last two tsars and their families. The southwest corner suite leading off the hall was lived in by Maria Alexandrovna, the wife of Alexander II, and is usually open. (If it isn't, skip to the next set of italics).*

Though the rooms are relatively small, their décor is overpowering: a surfeit of gold and silk brocade wallpaper that sums up the decorative tastes of mid-19th-century Europe. The first room, with its exhibitions of seals, cameos, brooches and semi-precious gemstones, is the most vulgar in the palace and is known, for obvious reasons, as the **Gold Drawing Room**. This is followed by the **Raspberry Drawing Room**, the **Boudoir** and, thankfully, by the sombre **Blue Bedroom**, with its cabinet of fine glassware. The suite disgorges into Room 167, where a heavy Russian carnival sledge, modelled on an enormous clam shell, gives a hint of the gaiety of the afternoon promenades that took place during the week before Lent. This was known as *maslenitsa* or Butter Week; in preparation for the fast, the entire population set about feeding themselves to the limits of their purse with a surfeit of buttery pancakes. In the afternoons they would squeeze themselves into a favourite sleigh for a breath of fresh air and to see and be seen on Nevsky Prospekt.

*If the suite is out of bounds you can reach the sleigh by returning to the staircase you recently came down, and walking through Room 302. The only room of **English Art** normally open, this is an embarrassment to any sentient English person. The nation's heritage is represented by one measly sub-Arts and Crafts chair, while canvases by Reynolds (1723–92) and Gainsborough (1727–88), and an Imperial Wedgwood service, are hidden away behind closed doors. Having said that, when the Hermitage opened to the public in 1852, it was the only European museum outside England with an English collection at all.*

The **Dark Corridor** (Room 303) which stretches beyond is hung on either wall with large French and Flemish tapestries. Behind them run more rooms lived in by Alexander II and Maria, with their displays of Russian 18th- and 19th-century applied art and paintings. The corridor opens out into the top-lit **Rotunda**, a balconied splendour whose parquet floor reflects its coffered ceiling. It was once hung with portraits of Russian rulers, but is now devoted exclusively to Peter the Great. The bronze bust of the tsar was sculpted by Carlo Bartolomeo Rastrelli, the father of the architect of the Winter Palace.

The rooms beyond were occupied by the last royal family, that of Nicholas and Alexandra, on their infrequent visits to the city from Tsarskoye Selo. They had all, including the Rotunda, been redecorated after the 1837 fire by the architect A. P. Bryullov, who was Stasov's assistant yet arguably more talented than his master. The **Moorish Dining Room** probably owes its inaccurate name to the tsar's personal bodyguard of giant Ethiopians who protected the entrance to the royal suite.

*Straight ahead lies the entrance to Bryullov's masterpiece of a royal drawing room, the **Malachite Room**, decked out in what must be the grandest of all materials.*

Nothing prepares you for the luscious sheen of the grainy, bright green malachite of these pillars, pilasters, vases and objects, set off by gold doors and the low golden vaults of the ceiling. Seams of malachite, a derivative of copper, were found in the Ural mountains in the 18th century by the Demidov family, who were granted land there by the tsars. They pioneered the working of it, which entailed cutting it into thin slivers and mounting it on a special clay in such a way as to create agreeable patterns. Veins of a milkier-coloured malachite have been discovered in Madagascar, but only those in the Urals had this deep imperial hue. For a few months before the 1917 Revolution, the Malachite Room made a dignified backdrop for Kerensky's increasingly powerless cabinet meetings. When the Bolsheviks began shooting at the Winter Palace from the Peter and Paul Fortress across the river on the night of 25–26 October, the politicians retreated into the **Small White Dining Room** next door. Kerensky had already escaped, but the rest of the cabinet were captured here in the early hours of the morning. This insubstantial room, a cosy, private royal dining room hung with Russian tapestries representing Asia, Africa and America, was elevated by the Soviet propaganda machine into the site of the last stand of the reactionaries. The clock on the mantelpiece shows the time of their arrest, 2.10am.

A door leads from the Moorish Dining Room into a long corridor (Room 151–3) devoted to early Russian culture.

Chronologically you are walking the wrong way down the corridor, so that the first cabinets you come to are filled with 17th- and early 18th-century telescopes and other scientific instruments, which belonged to Peter the Great. Beyond them and in Room 152, which was once an interior winter garden, are religious and other artefacts from the 15th–17th centuries. Alongside icons, painted altar doors and manuscripts are palace windows of mica, portable lanterns, drinking vessels and a 17th-century map of Siberia, painted in the Oriental manner with south at the top and the rest of the compass points mapped accordingly.

Three doors in the left wall of the corridor lead into the three big halls that made up the second suite of State Rooms on the first floor of the palace.

The first, the **Concert Hall** (Room 190), houses an exhibition of Russian silver dominated by the silver sarcophagus of Alexander Nevsky, crafted in the St Petersburg Mint in the mid-18th century, and brought here from the Alexander Nevsky Monastery by the Bolsheviks. As well as concerts, this was also the venue for small imperial balls.

The **Nicholas Hall** next door was used when the guest list numbered up to 5,000, most of whom could dance between its towering Corinthian columns at any one time. In those days a portrait of Tsar Nicholas I, placed there by his son Alexander II, made sense of the hall's name. This and the adjacent **Fore Hall** are now used to house temporary exhibitions. At the centre of the Fore Hall is the malachite pavilion from which champagne was served to refresh the dancers.

At the far end of this room, grand double doors open out on to the Jordan Staircase where this walk began. Anyone with the energy or determination to go straight on to Walk B will be able to pick it up at the bottom of the stairs.

Walk B: Highlights of the Museum Collection

Ask a series of art historians what they would look at if they could only see one piece of West European art in the Hermitage, and the same names would come up again and again: Matisse, Picasso, Rembrandt, Leonardo, Caravaggio, Giorgione, Poussin, El Greco and Van Dyck. We came across the first two artists in the Winter Palace on the last walk, but the rest are hung in the various Hermitages attached to the palace. The aim of this walk is to seek them out while negotiating the labyrinth of halls, corridors and stairways on two floors and in three different buildings. On the way we will also pass through collections of ancient Egyptian, Italian and Greek art and a number of sumptuous interiors.

Rooms containing the supreme masterpieces of the collection are normally kept open all the time, but in the Hermitage there are no hard and fast rules. If you do get turned back, or if rooms that are normally shut open before you, use the map to negotiate yourself back onto the route of the walk. Good luck!

*Walk through the low vaulted hallway known as the **Rastrelli Gallery** beside the ticket hall, and turn right at the bottom of the stately Jordan Staircase. Halfway along this dismal corridor, constantly lined with packing cases, a left turn takes you into Room 100, the only room in the museum still exhibiting ancient Egyptian artefacts.*

Covering over 2,000 years of **Ancient Egyptian** history, this dusty forgotten corner of the museum is dominated by the massive basalt sarcophagi in the middle of the room. All Egyptian collections revolve around artefacts associated with death and burial, since most of the objects to survive into the 20th century were excavated from tombs. In the third cabinet on the left you can see a series of crude wooden painted statuettes from the Middle Kingdom (2100–1788 BC), the greatest period of ancient Egyptian culture. Known as *ushabti*, they depict servants going about their daily tasks: the group on the plank are making beer and behind them is a cook, with a goose propped up against his legs. For a rich person to be buried without such maquettes was to risk having no one to perform these tasks for him in the afterlife. The tombs were kitted out with everything considered vital to everyday life, including luxuries such as jewellery. The nearby alabaster pot was probably a canopic jar, used for storing the pickled organs of the deceased.

In the far right-hand corner of the room is the mummified body of a man called Padiist, who lived over a thousand years before Christ. Herodotus, in his *Histories*, gives a graphic description of the process of mummification: 'As much as possible of the brain is extracted through the nostrils with an iron hook, and what the hook cannot reach is rinsed out with drugs; next the flank is laid open with a flint knife and the whole contents of the abdomen removed; the cavity is then thoroughly cleansed and washed out, first with palm wine and again with an infusion of pounded spices.' Before being wrapped in strips of gummed linen, the body was soaked for several months in natrum. Once all this was done, the body was usually placed in three wooden cases, an inner, a middle and an outer, such as you can see here. Only then was the deceased entombed in the carved stone sarcophagus. As you can imagine, this was an expensive process which only the rich could afford.

The steps out of the room lead into a corridor which runs beneath Catherine the Great's first, **Small Hermitage**. *Its walls are lined with 2nd- and 3rd-century AD marble reliefs from Roman sarcophagi. The first on the left depicts scenes from the Greek tragedy* Hippolytus, *the second stories from the Trojan war, while the third illustrates the ritual of a Roman wedding.*

At the bottom of the stairs beyond are the grandiose interiors of von Klenze's **New Hermitage**, *the building Nicholas I commissioned as a public museum. The highlights of the collection of* **Greek and Roman sculpture** *and pottery can be perused on a brief diversion to the right, but if you aren't interested in them skip to the next but one set of italics.*

Room 107 was specially designed to house monumental classical sculpture, in this case Roman pieces from the 1st–4th centuries AD. The most impressive is the huge cult statue of Jupiter, found at the country villa of the Emperor Domitian. His clothing, now plaster, would originally have been made of gilded wood, and gold would also have covered his hair and beard. The classical world was much more colourful than we imagine from the bleached statues that have survived. Their bright covering of paint, and that on the interior of classical temples and houses, perished long before most of them were unearthed. At the far end of the room, a gallery of portrait busts contains a number of Roman examples from the 2nd and 3rd centuries AD, with their vivid expressions of melancholia, dignity or disdain.

The next room, 108, was designed by von Klenze to resemble the courtyard of a classical villa, though with St Petersburg's foul climate he never contemplated leaving it open to the heavens or installing a central pool and fountain. It houses Roman copies of Greek sculptures, many of them featuring children. Room 109 features the first classical statue ever to be imported into Russia. Known as the Tauride Venus, after the years she spent in the nearby Tauride Palace, she is a very fine 1st- or 2nd-century AD Roman copy of a 3rd-century BC Greek original, and was

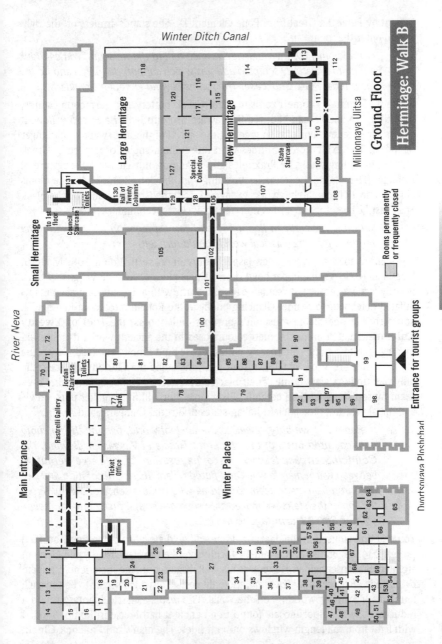

bought by Peter the Great from Pope Clement IX. She stands armless on the right as you enter the room.

*From Room 110, the original entrance hall to the museum, you can look out on to the sturdy sculpted atlantes which support the porch and up the magisterial **State Staircase**. The rooms beyond are open irregularly.*

Room 111 contains some exquisite early Greek pottery and terracotta figures, including the double-handled, red-figureware urn entitled *The First Swallow*. It shows three generations of men greeting the arrival of the first swallow, harbinger of spring. The exhibition continues with fine Roman copies of important Greek statues, including works by Praxiteles and a famous, muscle-bound sculpture of Herakles (Hercules to the Romans) wrestling with the lion (Room 114). The rooms (115–7 and 121) containing works excavated from the Greek colonies on the Black Sea coast (7th century BC–3rd century AD) have long been under wraps.

Return to the stairs in Room 106 and carry straight on. Those who never ventured into the classical world should turn left.

You cannot miss the vast green jasper **Kolyvan Vase** in Room 108. Made in Siberia in 1829–43, the upper bowl from a single piece of stone, it weighs 19 tons. Nearby is a 1st-century AD Roman decorative urn with a lid, whose grace puts its inflated neighbour to shame. Glancing briefly at the Roman mosaics in Room 129, you arrive in one of the museum's purpose-built rooms, the **Hall of Twenty Columns**. Painted in the flat matt colours used in the ancient world, it is forested by grey granite columns alternating with purpose-built Empire cabinets. Down the left-hand side are a row of tall Etruscan urns, including the **Queen of Vases**, the only one under a glass dome. Their black surfaces are so smooth and shiny they seem more like metal than ceramic. Elsewhere you will find smaller pots, bowls and metalware from the ancient Italian states of Etruria, Campania and Apulia.

*In Room 131 we bid farewell to the ancient world, passing the splendid multicoloured busts of the emperors Titus and Vespasian. Beyond, the **Council Staircase** leads up on to the first floor of the Large Hermitage between warm marble walls and fluted pillars. Its rich decoration and delicate iron balustrade seem to lend all who use it a sense of dignity. From the top of the stairs we make three separate forays, firstly into the neighbouring **Small Hermitage** to the left.*

You will find yourself in the dazzling white and gold elegance of the **Pavilion Hall** (Room 204) decorated in the mid-19th century, like the staircase, by the German architect Stakenschneider. He took as his well-disguised theme the orientalist poem by Pushkin, *Bakhchisaray Fountain*, the only vestige of which seems to be the shell fountains, no longer working, on the walls. The rest is a classical fantasy round a reduced copy of a floor mosaic found in an ancient bathhouse in Rome, flooded with light from full-length windows on both sides. The man-sized **Peacock Clock**, which has recently been reinstalled after restoration, was given to Catherine the Great by her one-time lover Grigory Potemkin (*see* pp.149, 151 (**Walk V**)).

The most unusual feature of Catherine's Hermitage is its so-called **Hanging Garden**, a first-floor courtyard off the Pavilion Hall, decorated with statues and fountains. Now forlorn and neglected, it is not hard to imagine a time when the empress might have sat there with Diderot, discussing the formation of St Petersburg's University, or with Prince Dmitry Golitsyn, a diplomat and Catherine's principal art buyer, working out what works they should pursue next for the collection. From time to time she would invite groups of close friends to a party here, often after a performance in the Hermitage Theatre, who would have been aware of the Rules of Conduct the empress had compiled, which included:

Rule 1   *Guests should leave every kind of rank at the door,*
            likewise hats, and above all, swords.

Rule 9   *Guests shall eat with pleasure, but drink in moderation,*
            so that each can leave the room unassisted.

Beyond the Pavilion Hall, Room 259 exhibits examples of West European applied art, including fine 12th- and 13th-century **enamel reliquaries** from Limoges and an early piece of Andalucian lustreware, the 14th-century **Fortuny Vase**. Rooms 143–6 run back through Spanish 17th- and 16th-century art, housing a temporary exhibition while the customary Spanish rooms are renovated. One of the earliest paintings is the entrancing double portrait of *The Apostles Peter and Paul*, painted by **El Greco** (1541–1614). It feels as if El Greco knew both of them well. On the right is the bald, convinced convert Paul, both hands asserting his belief in the Holy Bible. Peter, with his contemplative look, clutching the keys of the church, represents its stable foundation.

> *Return to the top of the Council Staircase and continue straight on into*
> *the large collection of Italian painting which begins in Room 207. These*
> *elaborate interiors, a bizarre contrast to the relative simplicity of the paint-*
> *ings, are also the work of Stakenschneider.*

The Italian collection is strong in works from the height of the Renaissance in the late 15th and early 16th centuries. Walking through the rooms of earlier paintings and sculpture, you will be able to follow the development of the characteristic features of the Renaissance. With the general surge of belief in the rationality and abilities of mankind came an unprecedented flood of developments in the artistic sphere: the appearance of a sense of perspective and three-dimensionality, an understanding of the true proportions of the human body, as well as the introduction of a secular reality into the religious subject matter. Viewing these paintings in Russia makes the changes particularly poignant, for this is the point at which west European art diverged from the medieval Orthodox traditions that govern religious painting here to this day.

The first room contains a fine example from early 14th-century Siena against which to measure the changes. **Simone Martini's** *Madonna of the Annunciation*, in which the Virgin is depicted alone, listening to the Angel Gabriel's news, shows an elongated figure, swathed in her traditional deep blue cloak over a red dress, silhouetted against the gold background that symbolizes the heavenly sphere. Two rooms later, a fresco by **Fra Angelico** (1387–1455), depicting the *Madonna and Child with St Dominic and St Thomas Aquinas* and painted almost exactly 100 years later, has dispensed with the symbolic golden background and replaced it with the blue sky that all four figures would have recognized from their earthly life. St Dominic, the founder of the Dominican order, is depicted holding the lily of purity, while his fellow Dominican St Thomas is distinguished by the shining star on his chest, an echo of the star that his mother is said to have seen shortly before his birth. Shading on their faces shows a deepening of the painter's sense of dimensionality. Room 213, which also contains two late paintings by **Botticelli** (1445–1510) of *St Dominic* and *St Jerome*, is dominated by **Filippino Lippi's** delicate *Adoration of the Infant Christ*, with its overt division of the canvas between the worldly and heavenly realms. Painted in the 1480s, its landscape background shows a well-developed sense of perspective, while the Virgin's page introduces an earthly relationship into an otherwise holy scene.

Two exquisite Virgins by **Leonardo da Vinci** (1452–1519) occupy pride of place by the windows in Room 214. Although both are masterpieces of the Renaissance, they are very different from one another. The earlier *Benois Madonna* ('The Madonna with a Flower') was painted in 1478 and bought by Nicholas II from the Benois family in 1914. The Benois, an artistic Russian dynasty, claimed to have acquired it in the early 19th century in Astrakhan from a travelling Italian musician. The Madonna, a young girl intrigued by her child's interest in the flower, is definitively worldly, dressed as she is in the clothes of a smart 15th-century Florentine woman, her hair braided in the fashion of the day. The intriguing window with its view of the sky seems almost like a cerebral joke. By contrast the later *Litta Madonna* is once again dressed in her traditional red and blue robes and looks down at her child with an iconic serenity. And yet she and Jesus, with his fine red curls, are also fully human. While drinking from his mother's breast, the child turns his steady, all-knowing gaze on the spectator, and out of the rationally symmetrical windows you can see the earthly landscape in which Leonardo has chosen to set them.

If open, you should try to visit both Room 227 and 229 round the corner. The former houses Quarenghi's copy of Raphael's Vatican Loggia in Rome, for which a team of artists copied the original frescoes on to canvas. In the latter hang two consummate paintings by **Raphael** (1483–1520), the *Madonna Conestabile*, a study in innocence painted when he was only 17, and the *Holy Family*, a much more mature

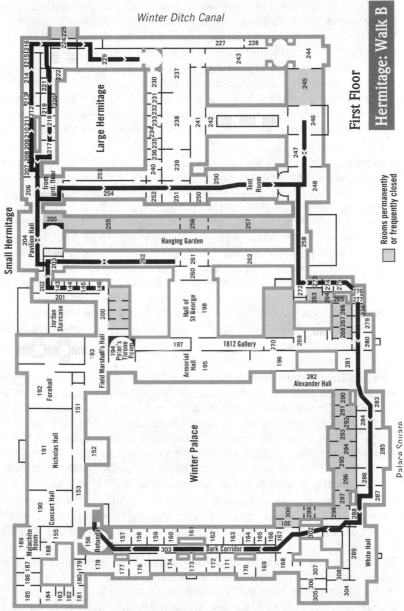

Winter Ditch Canal

Hermitage: Walk B

First Floor

□ Rooms permanently or frequently closed

River Neva

Large Hermitage

Small Hermitage

Pavilion Hall

Hanging Garden

Tent Room

Jordan Staircase

Field Marshall's Hall

Peter's Throne Room

Hall of St George

1812 Gallery

Armorial Hall

Alexander Hall

Forehall

Winter Palace

Nicholas Hall

Concert Hall

Malachite Room

Rotunda

Dark Corridor

White Hall

Palace Square

work painted a mere five years later. Room 230 contains Russia's only **Michelangelo** (1475–1564), an unfinished sculpture of a *Crouching Boy*, destined for a Medici tomb. Unleashed from the stone in the 1530s, the youth continues to exude an extraordinary inner strength and restlessness.

> *The Italian rooms beyond are open, and in them you can see works by Tintoretto, Veronese, Caravaggio and Magnasco, which lead on to Spanish art. Then retrace your steps and return to the Council Staircase via the suite of rooms containing paintings by the Venetian rather than Florentine Renaissance school. In Room 216 take the first turning left into Room 222.*

A recent tendency to move things around makes it difficult to say precisely where you will find the museum's valuable hoard of canvases by **Titian** (*c.*1487–1576), last seen in Rooms 221 and 219. The masterful *Danaë* shows the ecstatic Princess Danaë being visited by Zeus disguised as a shower of golden rain. (It is interesting to compare this with Rembrandt's *Danaë*, now restored in Room 253 after having had acid thrown at it in the 1970s.) Both *The Repentant Magdalene* and *St Sebastian* are later works. They show a consummate painter who not only valued mankind highly enough to take its depiction absolutely seriously, but also understood the innate drama of its existence. Two other famous canvases that used to hang in the collection, Giorgione's *Judith* and Caravaggio's *The Lute Player*, have been under restoration, but apparently the **Caravaggio** (1573–1610) is on view once more.

> *Returning to the Council Staircase, we leave it for the last time, and enter the Hermitage's huge collection of Dutch and Flemish painting, beginning at the end, with Rembrandt (Room 254).*

Except in Holland itself, there is no greater collection of works by **Rembrandt Harmensz van Rijn**, the greatest painter of his age, who was born in Leiden in 1606. Dutch 'Friends of the Hermitage' have recently paid for blinds and subdued lighting in the room, making this the best collection of his work in the world. This is especially crucial since Rembrandt relied so much on the contrast of light and shadow for his effect, building up the emotional intensity and depth of the picture with indistinct figures in the background. The pictures down the left wall were all once attributed to Rembrandt, but are now recognized to be by his pupils.

Many of the larger canvases belong to the most successful period of Rembrandt's career, the 1630s, which coincided with his first marriage, to Saskia van Ulenburgh, whose likeness you can see disguised as *Flora*, the goddess of spring and flowers. Light is everywhere important, but nowhere more so than in Rembrandt's restored painting of *Danaë*, where Zeus is represented not as a shower of gold but as light itself, flooding in and saturating his welcoming beloved. In the *Descent from the Cross* it provides the focus for an event of tangible tragedy. As the years went by Rembrandt's palette became warmer, disregarding the greens and blues of the earlier years in favour of oranges, reds and golds. In the small depiction of *David's Farewell to Jonathan*, light falls upon the parting friends, illuminating David's hair and back as he collapses weeping against his friend, and Jonathan's tragic look of resignation. Jonathan's face bears an uncanny resemblance to the artist himself, and the painting may have been an exercise in mourning for Rembrandt, whose wife died at around this time.

Of similar tenderness is his slightly later *Holy Family*, but it is in *The Return of the Prodigal Son* that we see all the artist's talents combined. The brightest part of the canvas is occupied by the abjectly repentant son, on his knees before his father, eyes closed and head leaning into the old man's body. Gently reacquainting himself with his son, the blind old man bends over to put his inquisitive hands on his shoulders, caressing the torn and filthy garments with the lightest of touches. Only after the intensity of this image has been absorbed do you see the host of spectators in the background, getting gradually more shadowy until the ghostly female figure in the top left corner. A clutch of magnificent portraits hangs on the end wall. The *Portrait of an Old Man in Red* seems to sum up Rembrandt's empathetic genius cradled in his profound use of colour.

> *Take the opportunity afforded in the next three rooms of Dutch art to rest on one of the few sofas proffered to the public in the whole museum. Their age and beauty rather makes up for the lack elsewhere.*

Room 249, a huge space with a painted coffered ceiling, is known as the Tent Room and is one of the original interiors created by von Klenze in the mid-19th century. Amongst its many late 16th- and 17th-century Dutch pictures are romantic landscapes by **Jan van Goyen** (1596–1656) and **Jacob van Ruisdael** (1628–82)—one of the greatest of the the Dutch landscape painters—and portraits by **Frans Hals** (1580–1666). They hang among a myriad of the genre paintings which reached an apogee in this golden era of Dutch creativity. In many, the exact reproduction of the subjects' clothes, their interiors and furniture seem more important than the people themselves. Vegetarians will be particularly amused by Paulus Potter's fantasy inspired by the story of St Hubert, who was converted to Christianity while out hunting when a white stag appeared before him, a shining cross between its antlers.

> *Turn left in grandly decorated Room 248.*

Room 247 is hung with a works by the Flemish painter **Peter Paul Rubens** (1577–1640), among them a copy of his acknowledged masterpiece *Descent from the Cross*, the original of which is in Antwerp Cathedral. The effect here, which emphasises the immutable deadness of Christ's physical body, is produced by the contrast between his pale body and the brightness of the clothes around him. The contrast is particularly poignant where his hand rests in Mary Magdalene's lively pink one.

Rubens is best remembered for his lively canvases saturated with people and movement, well represented here by the picture of *Perseus and Andromeda*. Having rescued Andromeda from the monster that lies at the bottom of the picture, Perseus is crowned by Glory with a laurel wreath. The question the picture seems to be asking is how long it will take him to fall, senseless, for the glowing, rounded form of coy Andromeda. The limpid *Portrait of a Lady in Waiting* strikes a very different note, her face and hair a soft mass of gentle brush-strokes.

Next, Room 246 is the unchallenged territory of **Anthony Van Dyck** (1599–1641), who had been one of Rubens' assistants, and had actually worked on *Feast at the House of Simon the Pharisee* next door. To get to grips with the man himself, seek out his *Self-Portrait*, painted when he was in his early twenties. Still showing signs of puppy fat, his expression betrays a lack of confidence which is completely absent in his depiction of his long, highly prized and competent hands. Van Dyck is perhaps best known for the grand portraits he executed as court painter to Charles I of England from 1632 until his death. Aristocratic though most of his subjects are, they have not escaped Van Dyck's probing insight. Thomas Wharton, Inigo Jones and even the king and queen appear to have been caught with the effect of their own musings written on their faces.

> *Since the rooms beyond are not usually open, retrace your steps and continue straight through Room 248, passing through more Dutch 16th-century land- and seascapes which line the Room 258. You are now in the Winter Palace, at the start of the museum's hoard of French 16th–19th-century painting, furniture and sculpture.*

By comparison with much of the Italian and Dutch work we have already seen, the French collection may well seem frothy and insubstantial. Its size is due to the close relationship that existed in the 18th century between the rulers of Russia and architects, sculptors, painters and men of letters from the Bourbon kingdom, many of whom were recruited to work here. Early Limoges enamel objects and paintings give way, in Room 278, to work by the Le Nain brothers whose 17th-century genre scenes seem flat by comparison with their Dutch contemporaries.

Room 279 is dominated by the extraordinary talent of **Nicholas Poussin** (1594–1665), the best known of all French 17th-century painters. Whether you like his work or not (some people decry its lack of psychological depth and humour) you have to admit that these strictly classical canvases, painted with the lustrous palette of the Venetian Renaissance, are the product of a very idiosyncratic vision. It doesn't seem surprising that Poussin's talents were more appreciated in Rome, where he lived for most of his life from 1632, than in Paris. As well as focusing attention back on the lessons of classical artists, Poussin is credited with inventing the genre of the history picture, which was to become so popular in the late 18th and 19th centuries. The next room (280) belongs to his contemporary **Claude Lorrain** (1600–82), whose landscapes, with their romantic classical scenery and obvious fascination with light, became models for Watteau and Turner.

*The **Alexander Hall**, redecorated after the 1827 fire in celebration of the victory over Napoleon, houses temporary exhibitions from the museum's stores, often on light-hearted themes.*

Room 284 beyond the hall is devoted to **Antoine Watteau** (1684–1721) best known for his *fêtes galantes*, conversation pieces that place well-dressed sophisticates in idyllic rural settings, as in *An Embarrassing Proposal*. Though Watteau succeeds in his intention of abandoning the exaggerated gestures and self-conscious poses of his contemporary painters, the combination of subjects is in itself so contrived that it rather cancels out the desired sense of naturalism. However an aura of charm clings to everything he paints, even the earlier painting, sketched in oil, *Actors from the Commedia dell'Arte*, which places five characterful, contrasting heads in close proximity.

The next few rooms are peppered with sculpture between the canvases. Notice the works by **Falconet** (1716–91) in Room 285. It was he who created that symbol of St Petersburg, the huge Bronze Horseman on the banks of the Neva. The seated statue of Voltaire in Room 287 was sculpted by **Jean-Antoine Houdon** (1741–1828) and shows the man months before death, sans teeth perhaps, but still possessed of a lively mind behind amused eyes.

Moving on to the full bloom of the 18th century with which this walk ends, Room 288 proffers a number of tableaux by **Jean-Honoré Fragonard** (1732–1806) and the didactic moralizing canvases of **Jean-Baptiste Greuze** (1725–1805). If you have already taken Walk A you will recognize the White Hall (Room 289) with its decorative, classical landscapes by **Hubert Robert** (1733–1808).

By now you will probably be reeling with the accumulated impressions of over 600 years of European painting, not to mention classical statuary. Your escape from the museum lies a few hundred yards away. Return to Room 288, and turn left into the Dark Corridor (Room 303). Leaving the Rotunda by the right hand door, take the stairs to the ground floor. Turn right at the bottom and right again to the Ticket Hall where you began.

What is Where in the Hermitage

Primitive and Early Art and Culture of the Peoples on the territory of the former Soviet Union, Winter Palace Ground Floor, Rooms 11–69. Includes some spectacular finds, including a piece of tattooed human skin, early felt saddles, copies of Scythian artefacts and the world's oldest carpet, known as the Pazaryk Carpet, in Room 34. The most valuable original gold objects can be seen in the Special Collection.

Ancient Egyptian Art, Winter Palace Ground Floor, Room 100 (*see* p.181–2).

Special Collection, Large Hermitage Ground Floor (*see* p.173).

Ancient Greece, Large Hermitage Ground Floor, Rooms 111–114 (*see* Greek Department, p.184).

Art from Ancient Black Sea Cities, Large Hermitage Ground Floor, Rooms 115–7, 121. Rarely open.

Ancient Italian and Roman Art, Large Hermitage Ground Floor, Rooms 106–109, 127–131 (*see* pp.182–4).

Department of Russian Culture, Winter Palace First Floor, Rooms 147–187. Only Rooms 151–6 and 167–8 are regularly open.

Department of Italian Art, Large Hermitage First Floor, Rooms 207–224, 229–238, 241 (*see* p.185–8).

Spanish Art, Winter Palace First Floor, Rooms 143–6. Moved from Rooms 239–40 which are currently being restored.

Flemish and Dutch Painting, Large Hermitage First Floor, Rooms 245–252, 254, 258, 260–262 (*see* pp.188–90).

German Art, Winter Palace First Floor, Rooms 263–8. Currently rarely open.

French Art, Winter Palace First Floor, Rooms 272–281, 283–297. The last seven rooms have not been open for ages (*see* pp.190–91).

English Art, Winter Palace First Floor, Rooms 298–302. Largely closed (*see* p.179).

West European 19th–20th Century Art, Winter Palace Second Floor, Rooms 314–325, 328–350 (*see* pp.177–8).

Oriental, Byzantine and Near and Middle Eastern Departments, Winter Palace Second Floor. Rooms 351–371 cover China, Indonesia, Mongolia and India; Rooms 381–2 concentrate on Byzantium, with some fine icons and ivory carving; and Rooms 383–397 contain ceramics and metalware from Iran, Iraq, Syria, Egypt and Turkey. The only rooms that tend to be open are the Byzantine ones.

Numismatics, Winter Palace Second Floor, Rooms 398–400.

Of Boats and Buddhists

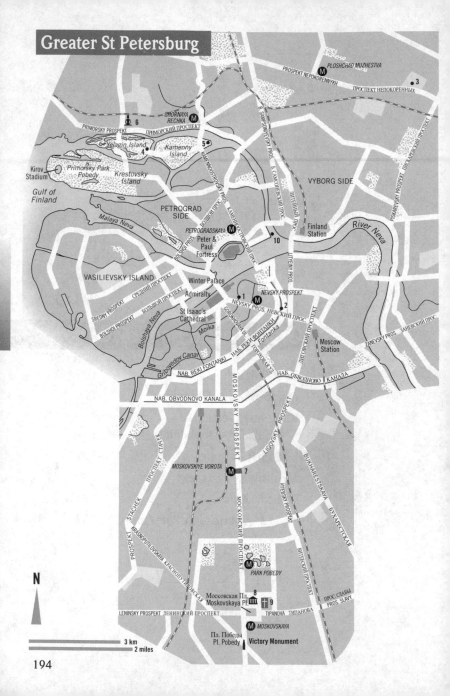

Greater St Petersburg

Gulf of Finland

Kirov Stadium

Primorsky Park Pobedy

Krestovsky Island

Kamenny Island

Yelagin Island

VASILIEVSKY ISLAND

PETROGRAD SIDE

VYBORG SIDE

River Neva

Finland Station

Moscow Station

Winter Palace

Peter & Paul Fortress

Admiralty

St Isaac's Cathedral

PLOSHCHAD MUZHESTVA

CHORNAYA RECHKA

PETROGRADSKAYA

Malaya Neva

Bolshaya Neva

Moika

Fontanka

Griboyedov Canal

MOSKOVSKIYE VOROTA

PARK POBEDY

Московская Пл.
Moskovskaya Pl.

MOSKOVSKAYA

Пл. Победы
Pl. Pobedy

Victory Monument

PROSPEKT NEPOKORENNYKH
ПРОСПЕКТ НЕПОКОРЕННЫХ

PRIMORSKY PROSPEKT
ПРИМОРСКИЙ ПРОСПЕКТ

B. SAMPSONIEVSKY PROS.

Б. САМСОНИЕВСКИЙ ПРОС.

КАМЕННООСТРОВСКИЙ ПРОС.

КАМЕННООСТРОВСКИЙ ПРОС.

БОЛЬШОЙ ПРОС.

ЛИТЕЙНЫЙ ПРОС.

NEVSKY PROSPEKT
NEVSKY PROS. НЕВСКИЙ ПРОС.

ЛИГОВСКИЙ ПРОСПЕКТ

ГОРОХОВАЯ УЛ.

БОГОВАЯ УЛ.

НАБ. РЕКИ ФОНТАНКИ

НАБ. РЕКИ ФОНТАНКИ

ЗАНЕВСКИЙ ПРОС.

ZANEVSKY PROS.

ПИСКАРЕВСКИЙ ПРОСПЕКТ

ПИСКАРЕВСКИЙ ПРОСПЕКТ

NAB. OBVODNOVO KANALA

НАБ. ОБВОДНОВО КАНАЛА

NAB. OBVODNOVO KANALA

MOSKOVSKY PROSPEKT

МОСКОВСКИЙ ПРОСПЕКТ

PROSPEKT STACHEK

КРАСНОПУТИЛОВСКАЯ КРАСНОПУТИЛОВСКАЯ

LENINSKY PROSPEKT ЛЕНИНСКИЙ ПРОСПЕКТ

LIGOVSKY PROSPEKT

BUKHARESTSKAYA БУХАРЕСТСКАЯ

ВИТЕБСКИЙ ПРОС. ПРОСПЕКТ

ПРОС. СЛАВЫ
PROS. SLAVY

ТИПАНОВА ТИПАНОВА

N

3 km
2 miles

194

Owing to the youth of the city, and the fact that it was built on marshland that had only ever been seasonally inhabited by fishermen, there are no medieval treasures hidden amongst the towering housing developments which now surround St Petersburg. In this sense, if the weather were more reliable, St Petersburg would be the perfect tourist city, with almost everything of interest within walking distance of the centre.

A number of the things covered in this chapter are central (boat rides, the *Aurora* and most of *Style Moderne*) but didn't, for one reason or another, fit into any of the walks. Otherwise it covers places for walks and picnics, and sites from the sublime (the Buddhist Temple), to the faintly ridiculous (the Lenin statue on Moskovsky Prospekt). Lovers of architecture should be sure to make a pilgrimage to the Chesme Church on Moskovsky Prospekt—it is a gem of a building, like something out of a fairytale.

Boat Rides

If the sun is shining on your first day in the city, you are in for the best possible introduction. Go to Politseisky Bridge over the River Moika on Nevsky Prospekt, and you will find the owners of small motorboats waiting to take you on a one-hour cruise along the waterways of the city. They should not charge more than US$10 per person. Most of them speak a modicum of English, just enough to recite a litany of names as you pass Baroque palaces, churches and 18th-century naval yards. If you have a Russian speaker with you, one of the most knowledgeable captains is Grigory Sergeievich Philipov (℗ 164 1623), a wizened old gnome with a poetic streak who does the evening shifts.

It is hard to imagine anyone who doesn't find this trip the best way to spend ten dollars in the city. If you just don't think your purse can stretch to it, from June to September you can pick up one of the tourist motor launches which leave regularly from the pier below the Anichkov Bridge over the Fontanka River on Nevsky Prospekt. This option has one advantage (it costs just over US$1) and two big disadvantages: you cannot sit outside, and once inside you are never spared a monotonous, recorded Russian commentary. Check your purse again.

One other boating option is one of the double-decker cruise ships that leave from the pier in front of the Hermitage Museum on the River Neva. They make a rather desultory circuit down to the Smolny Cathedral and back, but if the weather is right it can be the perfect antidote to hours looking at paintings.

Piskarovskoye Memorial Cemetery

Пискаровское мемориальное кладбище

Getting There

Ⓜ Ploshchad Muzhestva and bus 123 up Prospekt Nepokorennykh. *Open daily, 9–5.*

Thankfully nothing can conjure up the horror of Leningrad's blockade to those who didn't experience it, but this cemetery, where over two-thirds of its victims lie buried, is as good a place as any to contemplate it. As with many war cemeteries, it has an eerie, innocent tranquillity about it. The two pavilions which flank the entrance to the cemetery house exhibits giving something of the history of the blockade, which began when German troops encircled the city in early September 1941, intending 'to wipe the city of Petersburg off the face of the earth…it is proposed to tighten up the blockade of the city and level it to the ground by shelling and continuous bombing from the air.' The population of Leningrad at this time, in the absence of soldiers and the tens of thousands imprisoned in the gulag, was some 2½ million. The city was totally unprepared for a siege, and as early as 21 November 1941 all electricity was cut off, leaving the citizens to face winter heated only by what could be scavenged. The lack of antique furniture in many homes today owes more to the blockade than to anything else. On 6 December the water supply was cut. Subsisting on a daily bread ration that dipped as low as 125 grammes per person, each household had to carry buckets of water back from holes made in the ice on the canals and rivers.

Later that month all public transport in the city stopped, many people began living at their place of work and it became increasingly difficult to bury the dead individually. To get them to the chosen plot was the first problem, let alone finding someone with the strength to dig a grave in the frozen ground. An elderly friend who worked in a bakery at the time remembers feeling tremendous compassion for the 'intellectuals' who stood emaciated in the day-long queues. Their coats were good quality but it had been obvious from the start that they would be early victims, lacking the physical strength of their worker comrades. It was they who made up a disproportionate part of the heaps of corpses which began to be dragged on sledges to collection points, whence they were spirited to the then village of Piskarov. On 20 February 1942 the cemetery records show that 10,043 bodies were delivered for burial in the vast gelignited pits. The left-hand pavilion contains an exhibition about the 'Road of Life'. This winter-only route allowed supplies to be brought into the city across the ice of Lake Ladoga, but in nothing like the quantity needed to stop wholescale starvation. Another old lady told me how her boss, a doctor, had been killed and eaten by the friendly neighbouring family in her communal flat; she called it 'the psychosis of hunger'.

Beyond the pavilions the cemetery stretches out, a vast expanse of green or white, depending on the season. Beneath flat-topped mounds the size of cricket pitches lie 490,000 Leningraders, identified only by a granite slab engraved with the year of their death, a star if they were soldiers who died on the surrounding fronts, or an oak leaf and hammer and sickle if they were civilians. At the far end of the cemetery, a towering bronze statue of Mother Russia proffers a wreath. On the sculpted memorial wall the heroic tragedy is depicted in classic realism, illuminated by the poetry of one of its survivors, Olga Bergholts:

> *We cannot remember all their noble names here,*
> *so many lie beneath the eternal granite,*
> *But of those honoured by this stone,*
> *Let no one forget*
> *Let nothing be forgotten.*

Kamenny, Yelagin and Krestovsky Islands

остров Каменний, остров Елагин, остров Крестовский

North of the Petrograd Side, three small islands are separated one from another by tributaries of the Neva, the Small, Large and Middling Nevka rivers. Thought of as oases of calm since the foundation of the city, they are still largely green spaces, good for walks and picnics. Each has its own slightly different character.

Getting There

Kamenny Island straddles Kamennoostrovsky Prospekt ten minutes' walk south of Ⓜ Chornaya Rechka. From the small roundabout just off the Prospekt you can catch the infrequent services of bus 134, which wiggles round the island and over on to **Krestovsky Island**. There are two useful footbridges on to **Yelagin Island**. One is a short walk across Kamenny Island, the other, by the Buddhist Temple (*see* below) can be reached by buses 411 or 416 along Primorsky Prospekt from Ⓜ Chornaya Rechka, getting off at the stop called Lipova Alleya.

Kamenny Island (Stone Island) passed through the hands of a variety of courtiers in the 18th century before being bought by Catherine the Great in 1765 for her son Paul. In 1776 she commissioned a palace for him on its eastern tip, **Kamennoostrovsky Palace**, one of the first strictly classical buildings in the city.

Though it still stands, everything but its small Gothic chapel is out of bounds to the public, given over as a hospital for veterans. After Paul's death the island was taken over by his son Alexander I. It was here that he met with Field Marshal Kutuzov in August 1812, to plan the strategy that sent Napoleon packing later that winter.

The accessible end of the island, to the west of Kamennoostrovsky Prospekt, was colonized by the summer dachas of select aristocratic families from the early 19th century. One, the **Dolgoruky Mansion**, survives on the southern embankment, a couple of hundred metres from the prospekt. By the end of the century it was becoming positively suburban, and with the advent of the Soviet Union its KGB aristocrats took over. Today the mafia rules the roost, swooshing through guarded gates in smoked glass limos. Those with a taste for architectural whimsy will enjoy the combined impression these individual houses make, peeping from behind their secure walls—some traditionally wooden, some ostentatiously '*moderne*', others nothing less than eclectically fairytale. At the far end of the island are two sites to enjoy: **Peter's Oak**, supposedly planted by the tsar in 1718, and the slightly later, classical wooden **theatre** by the bridge over to Yelagin Island, once a summer theatre but now sadly in such a bad state of repair that it is rarely used.

Yelagin Island is a traffic-free haven of boating ponds and leafy avenues, which fills up on summer weekends, particularly during the 'White Nights' in June. On its eastern tip is a palace, this time open to the public, commissioned by Alexander I for his mother (built in 1818–22) on the site of an earlier palace belonging to one of Catherine the Great's courtiers. **Yelagin Palace** (*open 10–6; closed Mon and Tues*) was the first major commission for Carlo Rossi, who so impressed the tsar that he left more buildings in St Petersburg than any other architect of the reign. Such was his favoured status that the rumour that he was actually Alexander's half-brother, son of Paul I and an Italian ballerina mother, has never died away.

The classical palace is indeed a success, if not in perfect condition. Only a selection of the ground-floor rooms are open but these include the Oval Hall, which looks out through its bay windows on to long flights of steps leading down to the water. The room itself is surrounded by columns, interspersed with statues. The connected rooms vary in their decoration—some with painted *trompe l'œil* in shades of grey (*grisaille*) to look like relief sculpture, others in colour against white stucco walls. None of the original furniture, all Russian, with which the empress furnished her new palace survived the Revolution, though the parquet floors and mahogany doors with gilded fittings have been restored. On the second floor, the curators have tried to create a museum for children with porcelain figures from Russian fairytales and beanbags for children to sit on while listening to a narrator. The outbuildings of the palace, flanking the grand drive, consist of kitchen, stables and orangery, the former designed with the help of Signor Belardelli, the court confectioner and official taster at the time.

If you have the stamina for the walk, it has long been a tradition to watch the sun set over the Gulf of Finland from the far point of Yelagin Island, where, as a certain Professor Smythe put it in 1860, you can enjoy 'on foot the pure, balmy air and the exquisite western scenery'.

Krestovsky Island, the largest of the three, is also the least pleasant, given over to sporting pursuits with its swimming pools, tennis courts, yacht clubs and indoor and outdoor stadia with go-karting (*see* **Sports**, pp.26–7). The vast Kirov Stadium that crowns its western tip was hollowed out of a hill built of mud pumped out of the gulf, while the Seaside Victory Park (Primorsky Park Pobedy) which leads to it was planted by survivors of the blockade in memory of the dead and in celebration of the end of the Second World War in 1945.

Buddhist Temple

Буддийский храм (Buddiysky khram)

Getting There

The temple is at Primorsky Prospekt 91. Ⓜ Chornaya Rechka, then bus 411 or 416 along Primorsky Prospekt to Lipova Alleya stop.

While St Petersburg and its architecture have so often looked to the west and aped its styles, it is refreshing to find a building that tells of the other, Asiatic face of Russian history. The Buddhist temple was designed in a unique fusion of Tibetan Buddhist and northern Art Nouveau styles, and built between 1909 and 1915. Pyotr Badmayev, the tsar's Buddhist physician, took the initiative, collecting money from the open-minded members of turn-of-the-century St Petersburg society, such as Nikolai Roerich who went on to champion the mystical supremacy of the Himalaya, and from the Dalai Lama himself. It is a tapering stone building, hidden from the hurtling traffic behind a secretive fence. Behind its red entrance portico lies a working monastery, revived in 1990 and run by monks from Buryatia, the small Buddhist Republic centred on Lake Baikal. In the red and yellow prayer hall monks sit cross-legged, reciting from their long thin texts, lighting incense and clanging cymbals as required. It feels like a different world.

Moskovsky Prospekt

Московский Проспект

Moskovsky Prospekt, the main radial road out of St Petersburg to the airport and beyond it to Moscow, runs 9km from its start at Sennaya Ploshchad to the Victory Memorial at Ploshchad Pobedy. The buildings on either side of its motorway include educational institutions dating from tsarist times, Stalinist apartment blocks and sprawling heavy-industrial factories—this is not a place for walking.

Luckily a metro line runs the length of the *prospekt*, while above ground you can use bus 50, or trams 29 and 35 between Ⓜ Frunzenskaya and Ⓜ Moskovskaya. For a full tour of the highlights of this section of town, you should poke your nose out of Ⓜ Moskovskiye Vorota to see the Triumphal Arch, and then walk between Ⓜ Park Pobedy and Ⓜ Moskovskaya.

The **Triumphal Arch** was erected in 1838, not, as you might expect, as a posthumous tribute to Tsar Alexander I's defeat of Napoleon in 1814, but rather to celebrate the lesser military achievements of the then Tsar Nicholas I. It owes its unearthly green hue to the fact that it is made of metal, and was the largest cast-iron structure in the world when it was put up. Loosely modelled on the Brandenburg Gate in Berlin, it was taken down on Stalin's orders in 1936, only to come in handy as barricading during the siege of Leningrad. In 1960 it was re-erected.

Beyond the gate lies a no man's land of industrial depression. The factories here were among the most important in the city, and during the siege their workforce, like that of the Kirov Factory, heroically continued to manufacture arms and tanks, despite daily rations of only 250 grammes of bread. The end of the Cold War has forced many factories to adapt their production lines to produce consumer electronics and machinery; they are now working well below capacity, and some are even closed for months at a time. Take the metro through Electrosila station, named after one of the largest factories, emerge at Ⓜ Park Pobedy. Turn left out of the station, walk for about seven minutes down Moskovsky Prospekt and you will come to Ul. Gastello, also on the left. You can't miss the conspicuous Zenit cinema that sits in the middle of its avenue.

Down Ul. Gastello, beyond the cinema on the right, is an unmistakably dignified building, much altered and now a hospital for Air Force veterans. It is the **Chesme Palace**, originally built by Velten in the 1770s for Catherine the Great as a rest stop on the road to her palace at Tsarskoye Selo. It was named after the first great naval victory in Russian history, when Russia defeated the Turks at Chesme in the Aegean in 1770. The palace, a hospital since the mid-19th century, is associated more with dead royalty than with live, for it was here that the bodies of both Alexander I and his wife spent their first night back in the capital on their way for burial in the Peter and Paul Fortress. It was also in this triangular palace, which still retains its fine stone-carved Gothic windows and small towers, that Rasputin's body lay waiting after his murder in 1916.

Turn right at the end of this building and you can't miss the flight of fantasy that is the **Chesme Church** (*open only for church services*), which brings a whole new meaning to the expression Perpendicular Gothic. Built in 1777–80 by Velten, it looks like a cross between a traditional Russian woman's headdress, a *kokoshnik*, a terracotta and white iced cake, and a toy fort. Mesmeric stripes of white piping lead up to the five-domed roof which crowns this most unusual of buildings.

Returning to Moskovsky Prospekt and walking on towards Ⓜ Moskovskaya, you come to **Moskovskaya Ploshchad**, a monumental square which lay at the centre of Stalin's 1930s plan to relocate the centre of St Petersburg away from its aristocratic past and into the heart of its proletarian future. Its centrepiece, the **House of Soviets**, rears its inhuman façade behind a huge **statue of Lenin**. All round the square are apartment blocks built on an equivalent scale, though after the expense of the war Stalin's plan was considerably scaled down and, on completion of this square, abandoned.

Beyond the square and metro station, it is a few minutes' walk to Ploshchad Pobedy and the **Victory Monument**, which stands in front of the Pulkovskaya Hotel. Occupying the centre of an enormous roundabout, Mikhail Anikushin's Monument to the Defenders of Leningrad, as it is also known, was erected in 1975 on the site of one of the siege barricades. At the bottom of its red granite obelisk, dated '1941–45', are groups of heroic black figures defending the city. The monument is best seen from a distance, but there is also a memorial hall sunk in the ground beneath it (℗ 293 6563, open 10am–6pm, closed Wed and last Tues).

Cruiser *Aurora*

Крейсер Аврора

> *Petrogradskaya Naberezhnaya 4; ℗ 230 8440,* Ⓜ *Gorkovskaya. Open 10.30am–4pm; closed Tues and Fri.*

Moored on the Petrogradskaya Nab. opposite the St Petersburg Hotel, this pristine battleship must rank among the world's great touristic anti-climaxes. A victim of the bogus 'crucial event' theory of history, it is billed as the ship that launched the Revolution, though its sterile, well-swabbed deck and exhibition do little to conjure up the events of that night in October 1917. The cruiser was not even moored here, but way downstream by Lieutenant Shmidt Bridge on Anglisky Embankment, when it fired the blank shot at the Winter Palace which signalled the final assault on the members of Kerensky's provisional government who were still inside.

Originally built in 1903, the *Aurora* was a lucky escapee from the naval disaster at Tsushima Bay during the Russo-Japanese War. Militarily obsolete, she was in St Petersburg for a refit in 1917 when the Bolsheviks managed to win over her crew. During the Second World War she was sunk, for her own safety, near Kronstadt in the Gulf of Finland, only to be raised afterwards and turned into a museum in the 1950s. The exhibition includes photographs and biographies of the 'heroic' 1917 crew, as well as later Soviet naval good guys, and tokens of fraternal fellowship from friendly naval institutions worldwide.

Fans of Art Nouveau architecture will need little prompting to notice the contribution made by the genre, known in Russia as *Style Moderne*, to the city. Most of the Art Nouveau buildings are concentrated on the Petrograd Side; the development of this quarter was heralded by the building of the new **Trinity Bridge**, 1897–1903, which connected with downtown St Petersburg. The bridge itself was built by a French company with strong *nouveau* influences. By the Revolution, the population of the island had more than trebled, and many of the apartment blocks built to house the explosion, still standing, are detailed from the pattern book of *Style Moderne*. Among the most remarkable and easily accessible are the **Lidval Building** and **Mathilda Kshessinskaya's house**, both a stone's throw from Ⓜ Gorkovskaya. The former (Kamennoostrovsky Prospekt 1–3) is an apartment block named after St Petersburg's most famous architect of the *moderne*, Fyodor Lidval, and was built in 1902. Its detailing is not immediately apparent, but gradually fishes and owls, spiders and webs appear out of the stone. Though most of the stained-glass staircase windows within have been destroyed in the course of this tumultuous century, a few still hang precariously in their frames. Mathilda Kshessinskaya was one of the most famous ballerinas of the turn of the century, and had also been the lover of the last tsar, Nicholas II, when he was still heir to the throne. Her mansion (Ul. Kuybysheva 4, ✆ 233 7052; *open 10–5; closed Thurs*), built in 1904–6, combines the plasticity and variety of materials which were such a hallmark of the style. Today it houses the Museum of Russian Political History (*see* p.83), and the only stained glass is of a distinctly socialist hue.

South of the Neva there are also a number of buildings of note. Look out for the **Singer building**, which now houses the city's main bookstore, on Nevsky Prospekt opposite the Kazan Cathedral (*see* p.118), and **Yeliseyev's Grocery Store** at Nevsky Prospekt 58 (*see* p.139). The so-called **Tolstoy Apartment House** stretches between Ul. Rubinshteyna and the Fontanka River, the **German Embassy** is on Isaakiyevskaya Ploshchad and the **Astoria Hotel** opposite it. The iron **railings of the Mikhailovsky Gardens**, next to the Cathedral of the Saviour on the Blood, and those round the cathedral itself, are the height of *nouveauté*, as is the **Vitebsk Railway Station** (Ⓜ Pushkinskaya), with curvaceous porches, tiled interiors and a glorious Royal Waiting Room on the first floor to the right.

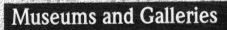
Museums and Galleries

For its size, St Petersburg is studded with museums, a measure of a city that once played a greater role in the history of its country than it does now. As well as a gazetteer of places visited in the course of the walks, this listing contains a fuller description of the handful of places that could not be worked into any of them. Many of these are the former flats of figures from the cultural world—poets, journalists and composers—where a combination of personal effects and furniture blend with more objective information about the character's creative life. Depending on how interested you are in the person in question, some museums are more successful than others at evoking the era and personality of their owners. Of the other museums mentioned only here, the Alexander Nevsky Lavra allows a gentle half-hour stroll through its monument-strewn cemeteries and Baroque courtyard, while the gentle quirks of the Museum of the Arctic and the Antarctic in the Church of St Nicholas are quite unique. The Museum of the Ethnography of the Peoples of the USSR is a rambling treat for fans of costume and lifestyle, each ethnic display competing for your attention with its jewellery, stuffed animals, dioramas and model housing from tents to wooden huts. Furniture and applied arts buffs would certainly regret missing the ill-lit chasms of the Stieglitz Museum of Applied Art.

House Museums

Yusupov Palace, Naberezhnaya Reki Moiki 94, Ⓜ Nevsky Prospekt. 18th-century palace where Rasputin was assassinated. There is a cassette player guide, or come with your own translator. Concerts are held Oct–May. *By appointment for groups noon–3pm daily (ring in advance on Ⓒ 314 8893); individuals can just turn up or join the guided tours at 12, 1, 2 and 3, plus also 11 in summer. See* p.111.

Summer Palace, Summer Gardens, Ⓒ 314 0456, Ⓜ Nevsky Prospekt. Peter the Great's small summer residence. *Open 11–6; closed Tues and last Mon of the month, and from 11 Nov–30 April* (*see* p.85).

Peter the Great's Cabin, Petrovskaya Naberezhnaya 6, Ⓒ 232 4576, Ⓜ Gorkovskaya. The oldest surviving structure in the city. *Open 10–5.30; closed Tues* (*see* p.83).

Pushkin's Flat Museum, Nab. Reki Moiki 12, Ⓒ 314 0006, Ⓜ Nevsky Prospekt. Shrine to Pushkin. *Open 11–5; closed Tues and last Fri* (*see* p.100).

Dostoyevsky Memorial Flat, Kuznyechny Pereulok 5/2, Ⓒ 311 4031 to arrange a tour in advance. *Open 11am–5.30pm; closed Mon and last Wed.*

Set up in 1971, to mark the 150th anniversary of his birth, this is not the flat as Dostoyevsky left it but a painstaking re-creation of what it would have been like, using photographs and reminiscences, spiced up by the odd personal family possession. As you walk through the flat door bearing Dostoyevsky's name plaque, you enter a surreal vacuum in which two umbrellas stand to attention near the writer's top hat, lovingly preserved beneath a glass bell.

Dostoyevsky lived in this building twice. His first stay was at the beginning of his career in 1846, when he wrote *The Double*; then, over 30 years later, he escaped from the flat in which his son Alexei had died of epileptic convulsions, and returned to live here with his family from October 1878 to his death in January 1881. In the meantime, Dostoyevsky's life had gone full circle. Arrested and almost executed in 1848 for revolutionary activities, he was sentenced to four years in Siberia, married disastrously, returned to the capital and found himself perennially in debt. In 1866 he neatly used the cause of his misfortune to pull himself out of it, finding himself a more loving wife into the bargain. Faced with the penalty of losing the royalties from his previous books for nine years if he didn't produce a novel in 27 days, Dostoyevsky hired Anna Grigoryevna as a secretary. By day, she took down *The Gambler* as dictation, by night she typed it out, and in 26 days Dostoyevsky was able to deliver the book to his exploitative loan shark.

Anna and Dostoyevsky were married, but financial crises dogged the couple for years. By the time they moved here, however, Dostoyevsky had finally earned security and fame with his monthly serial *The Diary of a Writer*, to which people across the nation subscribed. He was an habitué of the smartest Petersburg literary salons, where he exerted a mesmeric charm on young women. Anna left the socializing to her husband and continued to work as his secretary, looked after their surviving children, and organized every detail of her husband's life. As well as *The Diary*, Dostoyevsky wrote his final masterwork, *The Brothers Karamazov*, while living in this flat, but died before embarking on the envisaged sequel. The clock in his study still registers the day, date and exact time of his death.

If you become intrigued by Dostoyevsky's Petersburg, downstairs you can find out about walking tours around the locations used in *Crime and Punishment*, his quintessential Petersburg novel, and at midday on Sundays you can watch various films of Dostoyevsky's novels. Also sheltering in the building are a number of art galleries, the most interesting being the Petersburg Gallery of Naïve Art.

Rimsky-Korsakov's Flat, Zagorodny Prospekt 28, flat 39, Ⓜ Vladimirskaya.
Open 10–6; closed Mon, Tues and last Fri of month (call Larissa Ivanovna on Ⓒ 113 3208 for a guided tour in English or just turn up and hope). Concerts on Wed, Sat, Sun.

The composer's flat, in the central block in the courtyard, is not well signposted. It is on the first stairwell/entrance on the left-hand side of the building. Nikolai

Rimsky-Korsakov (1844–1908) lived here until his death; before his wife moved out in 1918, she made a detailed plan of their interior. Thanks to the determination of Rimsky-Korsakov's children, who kept all the furniture and objects you see here throughout the turbulent 1920s–60s, this museum was set up in 1971. Four of the rooms are just as they were when Rimsky-Korsakov lived here, right down to the wallpaper commissioned by the only son still alive when the museum opened.

The story of the composer's beginnings are highly theatrical. Rimsky-Korsakov's mother, the daughter of one of the frequent liaisons between an aristocrat and a serf, was very religious. She had her first child when she was 20, but in her early 40s, when her husband was 60, an angel came to her in a dream, carrying a candle from the heavens. She interpreted this as a sign that she had been chosen to provide a body for the flickering new soul, and Nikolai was born some months later. As her son's talents blossomed she needed no persuading that she had been right.

Over the sofa in the study where the composer worked until noon every morning, you will find an address painted by Vrubel, in the neo-Russian style, celebrating his 35th birthday. There is also a copy of the oil portrait Serov painted of him. On the first and third Wednesdays of the month, the drawing room would be filled with friends and admirers for the Korsakovs' regular *soirée*. It was here that the world-famous bass Fyodor Chaliapin sang both parts of the opera *Mozart and Salieri* from beginning to end, and here too that another Rimsky-Korsakov work, *The Snow Maiden*, was performed for the first time before an audience of a hundred.

Rimsky-Korsakov was part of the first great generation of Russian composers, and played an important role in establishing the nation's international musical reputation. He and his contemporaries Mussorgsky, Cui, Borodin and Balakirev, all based in St Petersburg, became known as 'The Mighty Handful' and later 'The Five'. His first symphony, indeed the first full symphony by a Russian composer, was performed when he was only 21. A prolific composer, particularly of operas, Rimsky-Korsakov was also professor of composition at the St Petersburg Conservatory and the main editor of a new publishing venture set up systematically to publish Russian music. It was in this role that he issued his own radical posthumous redraft of Mussorgsky's opera *Boris Godunov*, which has now been abandoned in favour of the original by most of the world's great opera houses.

Anna Akhmatova's Flat Museum, Nab. Reki Fontanki, 34 ✆ 272 2211 (back of wing of Sheremetiev Palace), Ⓜ Mayakovskaya. Quiet homage to the great voice of anti-Stalinism. *Open 11–5; closed Mon and last Wed (see p.136).*

Blok's Flat Museum, Ul. Dekabristov 57, ✆ 113 8633, Ⓜ Sennaya Ploshchad/ Sadovaya and a long walk. *Open 11–5; closed Wed and last Tues of the month.*

There are two flats in this building dedicated to the memory of the Symbolist poet Alexander Blok (1880–1921). That of his mother, on the first floor, contains a chronicle of his life and career through photographs, manuscripts and objects. Blok's own flat on the third floor, where he lived with his wife Liuba Mendeleeva, daughter of the creator of the Periodic Table, has been recreated, and also contains an exhibition based on his most famous poem, *The Twelve*.

Blok was born and raised in a hothouse of intellect. His father was a professor of law, his mother, with whom he stayed after the breakdown of his parents' marriage, was the well-educated daughter of a distinguished botanist, the Rector of St Petersburg University. The first room in the museum recalls these years: his early writings and drawings on his own childhood table, pictures of his family and of Liuba, his future wife, playing Ophelia opposite Blok's Hamlet at his grandparents' dacha. Even on holiday he was surrounded by St Petersburg's intellectual élite and their children.

After the 1905 revolution, Blok became preoccupied with his motherland and the theme of revolution, falling in with such distinguished Symbolists as the theoretician Vyachislav Ivanov and the journalist and poet Solovyev. His poems were first published in the Symbolist magazine, *Griffon* (Room 2). By 1910, however, Blok was beginning to turn his back on the sterile intellectualism of the Symbolists, seeking to throw his lot in with the Bolsheviks who he felt better represented the Russian people and their future (Room 3). Unfortunately they never really took to him. His combination of eastern Orthodox spirituality and modernism was hardly proletarian fodder. Even his masterpiece *The Twelve*, written at the height of the Civil War in 1918, resonating with his unerring use of rhythm and sound, went without acclaim from the party. It follows a motley band of twelve Red Army soldiers looting and killing their way through a fierce blizzard, with a Christ figure at their head—hardly the orthodoxy the Bolsheviks were seeking to spread. Though applauded by his fellow writers, some of whose pictures (Akhmatova, Yesenin, Mayakovsky and Bely) hang in the dining room, Blok wrote that 'Dirty rotten Mother Russia has devoured me as a sow gobbles up her sucking pig.' Within three years he was dead, his depression exacerbated by the starvation and cold of the Civil War years. The last room in the first floor flat bears the poet's death mask and details of his death and funeral.

Suvorov Museum, Ul. Saltikova-Shchedrina at the corner of the Tauride Park. On Catherine the Great's general A. V. Suvorov. *Open Thurs, Fri, Sun, Mon 10–6, Sat 10–7; closed Tues, Wed, first Mon of month (see p.154).*

Nekrasov's Flat Museum, Lityeiny Prospekt 36, ☏ 272 0165, Ⓜ Mayakovskaya. *Open 11–5; closed Tues and last Fri of month.*

Nikolai Nekrasov (1821–77) was a poet and journalist, who, with his next-door neighbour Ivan Panaev, edited the leading literary magazine *Sovremennik (The Contemporary)* from this flat between 1846–66. Started by the illustrious Pushkin, the magazine had lost its shine, but under Nekrasov's editorship it rose again to publish new works by Turgenev and Tolstoy. Gradually monopolized by its radical young sub-editor Chernyshevsky and his generation, it was closed down by the government for its political tone in 1866. Literary magazines, known in Russia as 'fat magazines', were a vital part of the publishing process, and most of the great works of Russian literature were first published in them, only later achieving book form. To this day much important new writing is published in the 'fat magazines', led by *Novy Mir* (*New World*), which was the first Russian publisher of Solzhenitsyn's *The Gulag Archipelago* in 1989.

Nekrasov, whose poetry mostly concerned itself with the life and hardships of the peasantry, was mad about nature and the countryside. Even in these patrician rooms he kept as many as three dogs at a time, and when his wife accidentally killed one of them while out hunting he wouldn't speak to her, and developed a high temperature. The shade on the overhead light in his study continues the hunting theme. He also kept countless songbirds, which were allowed to fly freely around the rooms. It was Alexandre Dumas who remarked that it was because the Russian winter was so long that the Russians so often brought birds indoors to sing. Panaev's flat next door has a convenient connecting door. Not only did the two men co-edit a magazine, they also shared a love of Panaev's wife Avdotya, a writer with whom the men campaigned for women's rights.

Historical Museums

History of Leningrad Museum, Naberezhnaya Angliskaya 44, ☎ 311 7544, Ⓜ Sennaya Ploshchad/Sadovaya. *Open Tues 11–4, otherwise 11–5; closed Wed and last Thurs of month.*

This large and very neglected museum is housed in the 19th-century Rumiantsev palace on what used to be called the English Embankment, the dock where all the English traders and merchants used to moor their ships. Her Majesty the Queen docked her yacht Britannia there in 1994. Walking through the rooms on the museum's first floor, which run through the history of the city from the Revolution to the Second World War, is akin to walking through a ghostly memory. Few of the lights work and museum staff are notable by their absence, while out from the walls stare the faces of Lenin, haranguing the crowd from his armoured car in April 1917, and a thousand other Soviet heroes, demonstrating, fighting, working, educating and relaxing.

The floor above is devoted to the heroic role played by the citizens during the Siege of Leningrad in the Great Patriotic War (as the Second World War is still known in Russia). Setting the scene are photographs of women being hanged and men shot under the banner 'This is Fascism'. There are pictures of children doing their lessons and eating in bomb shelters, and of women planting cabbages beneath the dome of St Isaac's Cathedral. In one display cabinet is a tiny square of bread, a day's ration at the worst moment of the siege. Its ingredients include defective rye flour, wallpaper dust, cellulose and bran. Nearby, a photograph of 11-year-old Tanya Savicheva and copies of her diary tell one of countless tragic stories. Tanya watched the deaths of her sister, grandmother, brother, uncles and mother, and the last page reads: 'The Savichevs have died. They have all died. Only Tanya remains.' Shortly after her own evacuation, Tanya also died.

Museum of Russian Political History, Kshessinskaya Mansion, Ul. Kuybysheva 4, ✆ 233 7052, Ⓜ Gorkovskaya. *Open 10–5; closed Thurs (see p.83).*

Peter and Paul Fortress, including the **Museum of the History of St Petersburg**, ✆ 238 4540, Ⓜ Gorkovskaya. Includes the burial vaults of the tsars in its cathedral, and a gruesome prison museum. *Open 11–5, Tues until 4; last tickets one hour before; closed Wed and last Tues of month (see p.77).*

Cruiser Aurora, Petrogradskaya Naberezhnaya, ✆ 230 8440, Ⓜ Gorkovskaya. *Open 10.30–4; closed Tues and Fri (see p.201).*

Monasteries and Churches

Alexander Nevsky Monastery, Ploshchad Alexandra Nevskovo, ✆ 274 2635, Ⓜ Ploshchad Alexandra Nevskovo. Also known as the **Museum of Urban Sculpture**. *Cemeteries open 10am–7pm (til 4pm in winter); closed Thurs. Services in the cathedral at 7am, 10am and 6pm: closed 2–5pm for cleaning.*

Like most of Russia's religious buildings today, the Alexander Nevsky Monastery is in a state of flux. The Museum of Urban Sculpture which the Soviets housed in the Church of the Annunciation is closed while the church is being restored, and monks are creeping back into the Baroque courtyard. Visitors can expect a star-studded game of hunt the gravestone in two bristling cemeteries and a peaceful walk before entering the often hectic nave of the Cathedral of the Trinity, a neo-classical intruder in an otherwise Baroque ensemble.

The monastery, which became one of Russia's four great seminaries, was founded by Peter the Great in 1710 on the spot where he liked to imagine Grand-Prince Alexander of Novgorod, later St Alexander Nevsky (*i.e.* of the River Neva) had defeated the Swedes in 1240. He knew quite well that the battle had actually taken place 20km upriver, but in his determination to legitimize his marsh-encircled city, he had the saint's bones brought here from Vladimir in 1724.

A neoclassical arch leads south off Ploshchad Alexandra Nevskovo into the monastery grounds. Buy tickets at the booth for the two 'museum' graveyards, which lie on either side of the path ahead. The Lazarus Cemetery on the left is the oldest extant place of burial in the city, begun when Peter I's favourite sister

Natalya Alexeyevna was buried here in 1716. From then on it was the chosen resting place of imperial favourites, princesses, generals, government ministers and a host of discerning architects. Pushkin's wife is buried against the wall closest to Ploshchad Alexandra Nevskovo, just in front of the tall, black pillared monument with a cross on top. A gilded marble headstone, inscribed in Latin, marks the spot where the great 18th-century Renaissance man Mikhail Lomonosov lies over on the far side. In between, the jumble of funerary sculpture includes delightful 18th-century neoclassicism, marking the graves of Starov, who built the monastery's cathedral (*see* below); Voronikhin, the architect of the Kazan Cathedral; and Giacomo Quarenghi and Carlo Rossi. In the Tikhvin cemetery on the right, known as the Cemetery of the Masters of Art, the important graves are signalled by bilingual Russian/English bronze markers. In Composers' Row, against the wall nearest Ploshchad Alexandra Nevskovo, a barrage of unusual gravestones commemorate Rimsky-Korsakov, Tchaikovsky and Mussorgsky. Look out also for Dostoyevsky.

Beyond the bridge over the small Chornaya Stream, with its peaceful leafy views, lies the central monastery courtyard, a large, forested square. Immediately on the left is the earliest remaining Church of the Annunciation, designed in 1717–22 by Domenico Trezzini, a light, playful Baroque structure with a forest of pilasters and a high delicate dome from which a golden cupola emerges. After the royal mausoleum in the Peter and Paul Fortress it was the smartest place in the city to be buried, an honour lavished on Catherine the Great's inspired general, Suvorov, and on her son Paul's tutor, Nikolai Panin. It was turned into a Museum of Urban Sculpture by the Soviets, sheltering some of the most important funerary monuments in the city beside images of Lenin and Dzerzhinsky. Now it is closed while the church is repaired and state and church deliberate over its future.

The main monastery courtyard is surrounded by a series of deep red Baroque buildings, characterized by vast windows divided only by pilasters and surmounted at each corner by a cupola and cross. Built in 1756–71, these buildings include the residence of the Metropolitan of St Petersburg, the city's senior man of the cloth, directly opposite the cathedral. Littered amongst the mature trees in the courtyard are the graves of heroes of the Civil War and the Second World War, their atheist graves a provocation on such prominent holy turf. Dominating the whole ensemble is the neoclassical Cathedral of the Trinity, built for Catherine the Great by Ivan Starov in 1776–90. No church in either Moscow or St Petersburg is quite so foreign to the Russian tradition. Inside, a broad nave flanked by Corinthian pillars leads to the classical iconostasis. As is customary, the gilded wrought-iron gates, with a delicate tracery of floral bracts and swags, enclose six images, two depicting the Annunciation (the Angel Gabriel in one, the Virgin in the other) and four of the apostles. Yet these are not icons but pictures in the western European, post-Renaissance tradition, and many of those in the rest of the iconostasis and hung in frames on the walls are copies of paintings by Dutch and Italian masters, Raphael Mengs, Rubens, Van Dyck and Perugino amongst them. Even some of the decorative marble was imported from Italy. Very fine *trompe l'œil* architectural details adorn the ceilings and upper walls.

To the right of the iconostasis, beneath a magnificent gilded Baroque baldacchino hung with coloured oil lamps, lie the remains of St Alexander Nevsky. Though his current silver sarcophagus seems splendid enough, the original Baroque edifice, now in the Hermitage, was even better. The Empress Elizabeth donated 3250lbs of silver for its adornment. Behind hangs a romantic painting of the saint in prayer, his rowdy jostling troops relegated to the background.

Behind the cathedral stretches the extensive Nicholas Cemetery, where church-men and laymen lie peacefully side by side.

Chesme Church, Ul. Gastello, Ⓜ Park Pobedy. This Gothic jewel is a must for architecture buffs. *Open 10–5; closed Mon and Tues* (*see* p.200).

Church of the Saviour on the Blood, Naberezhnaya Kanala Griboyedova, Ⓒ 315 1636, Ⓜ Nevsky Prospekt. Fabulous *style moderne* mosaics recently restored *Open daily 11–6* (*see* p.100).

St Isaac's Cathedral, Isaakievskaya Ploshchad, Ⓒ 315 9732, Ⓜ Nevsky Prospekt. A great view of the city from the dome balcony. *Open 11–6; closed Wed* (*see* p.114).

Kazan Cathedral, Nevsky Prospekt, Ⓒ 311 0495, Ⓜ Nevsky Prospekt. A glittering selection of church vestments, silver and icons. *Open 11–5 weekends 12.30–5; closed Wed* (*see* p.117).

Special Interest Museums

Museum of the Ethnography of the Peoples of the USSR, Inzhenernaya Ul. 4/1, Ⓒ 210 4320, Ⓜ Gostiny Dvor. *Open 10–5; closed Mon and last Fri of month.*

Originally part of the Russian Museum, this collection of ethnographic material, housed in its purpose-built neoclassical wing (1903–10), became a separate museum in 1934. It was heavily bombed during the war, and much of its collection was destroyed, only the very best having been evacuated. The collection swelled again in 1948, however, when the ethnographic collection in Moscow was sent here. Since then it has been the home of Soviet and now Russian ethnography, with a rich store of manuscripts (some on birch bark, others in hieroglyphs) and texts in its library and research facilities. A major contribution to the museum's Siberian collections, and to the study of Siberian tribes in general, was made by the so-called 'scholar-exiles', intellectuals exiled by the tsarist regime to darkest Siberia. During the Soviet era, things were put on a more 'scientific' basis, with expeditions going out to the four corners of the empire, charged with studying, recording and plundering the applied and folk arts of the peoples.

The museum is currently beset by the usual problems, economic and political, starting with its name and scope. Exhibits in the vast hall at its centre reek of a time when one of the avowed policies was to 'reveal those processes in the lives of the peoples of the USSR that had been taking place during the formation of a new historical entity, the Soviet people.' Other rooms, organized geographically, have been closed down for a rethink; still others are suffering a lack of attention. Nevertheless its endless cabinets, photographs, models and maps reveal a wealth of material about a group of peoples who range from nomadic reindeer farmers to desert dwellers. Besides a formidable collection of costumes, you will also find methods of transport (boats, skis and sleighs), tools for weaving and hunting, fishing and harvesting, models of the interiors of Central Asian *yurts* and Eskimo igloos, ceramics, embroideries and metalware.

Throughout the museum, but particularly in the Siberian section, are fascinating exhibits attesting to the folk beliefs still widespread among these peasant peoples at the time of the Revolution, and probably today. Look out for ritual wooden dolls from Russia, masks from the Caucasus, Siberian shamans' robes and headdresses aclutter with amulets, feathers, teeth and antlers, and complex Ukrainian corn dollies. Shamanism is now so in vogue that, at the opening of one gallery, a Yakutian woman shaman completely stole the show, going into a bellowing trance after several neat shots of vodka.

Kunstkamera/Museum of Anthropology and Ethnography, Universitetskaya Nab. 3, ✆ 328 1412, Ⓜ Vasileostrovskaya. Medical curios and Benin bronzes. *Open 11–4.30; closed Mon and last Tues (see p.166).*

Naval Museum, Former Stock Exchange, Birzhevaya Ploshchad 4, Vasilievsky Island, ✆ 328 2502 for a tour, Ⓜ Vasileostrovskaya. Model boats and more technical exhibits. *Open 10.30–4.45; closed Mon and Tues (see p.76).*

Museum of the Arctic and Antarctic, Church of St Nicholas, corner of Kuznechny Pereulok and Ul. Marata, ✆ 311 2549, Ⓜ Vladimirskaya/Dostoyevskaya. *Open 10am–4.15pm; closed Mon and Tues.*

Opened in the 1930s, this museum has barely changed in style since, and houses a series of enchanting illuminated dioramas showing life inside Arctic research stations, right down to the portrait of Lenin hanging in the tent. Downstairs there is a collection of stuffed polar wildlife and photographs of the discovery of woolly mammoth remains. Upstairs exquisite handicrafts by the indigenous peoples of the Arctic include fine carving on tusks, embroidery and clothing, some taking the 'Soviet Achievement' as their theme. This is the only museum in the world dedicated to this subject.

Artillery Museum, Arsenal, Kronverk Ditch, Petrograd Side, ✆ 232 4704, Ⓜ Gorkovskaya. *Open Wed–Sun, 11–5, closed Mon, Tues and last Thurs of month.*

Housed in the mid-19th-century horseshoe-shaped arsenal building, with larger rocket launchers in its courtyard, the museum surveys advances in killing technology from the Middle Ages almost to the present.

Botanical Gardens, Ul. Professora Popova 2, Apothecary's Island, north of the Petrograd Side, ✆ 234 1764, Ⓜ Kamennoostrovskaya. *Conservatories open 11–4, gardens open 10–7; closed Fri.*

At the centre of the Botanical Gardens, which started out as a garden for medicinal herbs at the time of Peter the Great, are 10 hectares of hothouses with exotic trees and shrubs. One orchid, called The Princess of the Night, opens only once, on the hottest night of the year (usually in June); the garden stays open for this. There are also rather dusty displays covering herbal medicine and the diet of the dinosaur.

Gas-Dynamics Laboratory Museum, Peter and Paul Fortress, Ⓜ Gorkovskaya. *Open 11–5 (Tues 11–4), last tickets 1 hour before; closed Wed* (*see* p.78).

Museum of Musical Instruments, Sheremetiev Palace, ✆ 272 4074. Instruments throughout the years. *Open 12 noon–6pm; closed Mon and Tues* (*see* p.135).

Museum of Theatre and Musical Art, Ploshchad Ostrovskovo 6, ✆ 311 2195, Ⓜ Gostiny Dvor. *Open 11–6, Wed 1–7; closed Tues* (*see* p.141).

Zoological Institute, Universitetskaya Nab. 1, ✆ 328 0112, Ⓜ Vasileostrovskaya. With a live insect zoo for children. *Open 11–5; closed Fri* (*see* p.168).

Off-beat Alternatives

Museum of Hygiene, Italyanskaya Ul. 25, ✆ 210 8505, Ⓜ Gostiny Dvor. *Open 10–5; closed Sat and Sun.*

Ever wondered about the effect of alcohol on foetuses, or VD on genitalia? Now is your chance to find out, painlessly, with the elucidation of plastic models.

Art Galleries and Museums

The Hermitage, Dvortsovaya Naberezhnaya, ✆ 110 9625, Ⓜ Nevsky Prospekt. One of the world's great collections, started by the tsars and swelled by the wholesale confiscation of aristocratic collections after the Revolution. *Open 10.30–5, 4 on Sun; closed Mon* (*see* **Walk VII**).

Engineers' Castle, Ul. Sadovaya 2, ✆ 210 4173, Ⓜ Gostiny Dvor. *When showing an exhibition from the Russian Museum, open 10–5; closed Tues* (*see* p.79).

Menshikov Palace, Universitetskaya Nab. 15, ✆ 323 1112, Ⓜ Vasileostrovskaya. Its period furniture, pictures, costumes and ornaments give a good idea of the aesthetics of 18th-century St Petersburg interior design. *Open 10.30–5, last ticket 4.20; closed Mon (see p.164).*

The Russian Museum, Ploshchad Iskusstv, ✆ 314 3448, Ⓜ Nevsky Prospekt. A bulging collection of Russian art. *Open 10–5; closed Tues (see p.125).*

Marble Palace, Ul. Millionnaya 5/11, ✆ 312 9196, Ⓜ Nevsky Prospekt. The architectural highlight is the Marble Hall, where a rainbow of different coloured Ural marbles are inlaid in the walls. *Open 10–5; closed Tues (see p.96).*

Tsar Paul I had this castle built and died in it, so it seems only appropriate that the Russian Museum should stage exhibitions connected with him in the few rooms so far restored.

Academy of Arts Museum, Universitetskaya Naberezhnaya 17, ✆ 323 6496, Ⓜ Vasileostrovskaya. *Open 11–6, closed Mon and Tues (see p.162).*

The Academy is still a working art school, and the highlights of any visit are the fantastic wooden maquettes of architects' original work.

Museum of Applied Art, Stieglitz Mansion, Solyanoy Pereulok 13, ✆ 273 3258, Ⓜ Gostiny Dvor. *Open 11–5 daily.*

This extraordinary Renaissance building was commissioned in the late 1870s by the railway magnate Baron Stieglitz as an art school and museum. It has fulfilled the latter function ever since, and entrance to the museum is through the busy art school. Climb the stairs, turn right and walk through until you come to stairs on your left. The museum's dusty collection begins downstairs.

With outstanding examples of European furniture and ceramics, this dark collection, housed in a series of painted, vaulted rooms, is all the more approachable for the fact that its pieces are not all in a perfect, western museum-standard state of repair. The highlight, given the museum's location, is the Russian room, to the right at the back of the central hall, where pride of place is given to 15 glorious ceramic stoves. The white ones at the far end were made in and around St Petersburg, while the earlier coloured tiles were produced in towns around Moscow. The earliest blue and white example, aping contemporary Delft designs, shows naïve representations of different Russian types.

Central Exhibition Hall, Manezh, Isaakievskaya Ploshchad, Ⓜ Nevsky Prospekt. *Open 10–6 when there is an exhibition; closed Thurs.*

This cavernous former riding school houses a changing programme of exhibitions, usually by Russian artists. It has also been known to pulse to the beat of an all-night rave (see p.114).

*For a map showing the area around St Petersburg
see inside back cover.*

Day Trips: Five Palaces

To the south and west of St Petersburg lie a string of jewel-like royal palaces set in rolling parks. Built by the Romanovs in the last 200 years of their rule, those that you can visit today are among the most lavish of their dozens of homes. The continued existence of these palaces, with so many of their original trappings, is a miracle in itself. Contrary to Soviet propaganda, not all the Revolutionary troops in 1917 behaved with decorum as they took control of the former homes of aristocrats and royalty. The first port of call was usually the cellar, and after that paintings and sculptures were often damaged. Large-scale bureaucratic thieving by Stalin's government in the '20s and '30s enriched its own coffers while denuding the country of some of its finest works of art (*see* p.172). Then, in the war, all of the palaces except Oranienbaum were occupied by Nazi troops. Within five weeks of the invasion, the Nazis were shipping 40 or 50 freight cars of furniture, paintings and objects to Germany a day. Paintings that wouldn't easily come off the wall were cut from their frames, imperial dinner services, furniture and marble veneers were mindlessly smashed. Before they left, the Germans set fire to each of the palaces, so that museum directors returning within hours of their retreat found only smouldering carcasses as well as booby-trapped children's toys and brand new pairs of shoes.

Few countries would have attempted to rebuild these palaces, and indeed many people in the Soviet Union regarded it as a thoughtless waste of money in a war-torn country. However the passion of the conservationists won out, partly out of victorious pride, partly because to allow these pre-Revolutionary palaces to die was to give in to the destruction of the war and even to collaborate with a regime (the Soviets) that had wanted to rub out the achievements of the tsarist regime. Remembering Dostoyevsky, they also felt that 'Beauty will save the world'. Rebuilding work continues to this day.

Choosing which palaces to see can be hard. Peterhof is distinctive for its early, clean Baroque architecture and fountain-filled gardens, while for those who like their Baroque more OTT, and gilded to boot, Catherine Palace is the place. Little-visited Oranienbaum was untouched by the Germans, so that its buildings sing with age, while Gatchina is almost unknown to foreigners, with its look of a Renaissance castle. In many ways Pavlovsk is most impressive of all, a classical statement of Russia at its most powerful. Peterhof and Oranienbaum are close, as are the Catherine Palace and Pavlovsk (*see* **inside back cover map**), but to see two of these unique buildings in one day is to risk enjoying neither to the full.

This, the oldest of the accessible royal palace estates, should really be thought of as a park with a number of palaces. It is the enormous formal 18th-century garden, with its straight alleys, cascades and tree-lined vistas on the banks of the Gulf of Finland, that is the main attraction. The **Great Palace**, surveying all from its prominent bluff, is the least atmospheric of all the grandiose residences of the tsars because none of them actually lived in it much; they preferred to stay in Peter's cosy Baroque house, **Monplaisir**, on the seashore.

Peterhof is a good place to come with children, as there are rides to be had in the children's park, and the elaborate waterworks with their golden statues are a thrill for all. More strenuous sightseers will want to wander into the naturalistic 'English' **Alexandria Park** with its quirky Gothic buildings, landscaped in the early 19th century for Nicholas I and named after his wife Alexandra Fyodorovna. Ranged around the entrance to the palace are a number of other **museums**, one tracing the artistic talents of the Benois family, which included 19th-century architects and English comic actors, another recreating the world of an old-fashioned pharmacy.

Deciding when to go can be difficult, as all the buildings have different opening days. The park is *open every day 9am–10pm*, and its fountains work *May–Sept 11am–8pm*. In winter many smaller buildings are shut, though the Great Palace, Marly Palace and Cottage Palace keep their doors open in any weather. The palaces *open variously between 9am and 11am* but *the only time they are all open is at weekends* when the crowds can be obstructive. Call ✆ 420 0073 for information.

Great Palace}	
Benois Museum}	*Closed Mon and last Tues of the month*
Cottage Palace (in winter)}	*Open 10.30–5*
Marly Palace	*Closed Mon*
Monplaisir	*Closed Thurs*
Catherine Wing	*Closed Thurs*
Cottage Palace (in summer)	*Closed Fri and last Thurs of the month*

Getting There and Around

In summer there are two ways of getting to Peterhof: by sea or by rail. From May to Sept, a hydrofoil (*raketa*) leaves the jetty outside the Hermitage at least every 45mins from 9am to 6.30pm, speeding you across the gulf and slowing down to dock at the end of the palace's Marine Canal, giving you a perfect view of the palace as it was designed to be seen. Queues do build up for this as the day wears on, and you can only buy singles. If you want to go back the same way, buy your return ticket as soon as you arrive at Peterhof, as the late afternoon services get fully booked. Year-

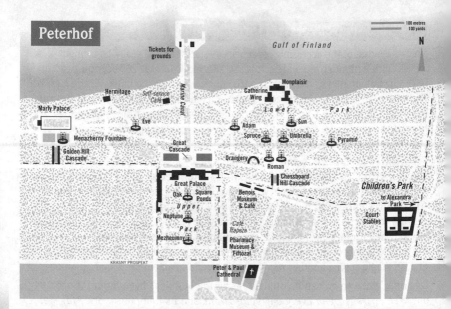

100 metres
100 yards

Gulf of Finland

N

Tickets for
grounds

Marine Canal

Monplaisir

Catherine
Wing

Hermitage

Self-service
Café

Lower

Park

Marly Palace

Eve

Adam

Sun

Menazherny Fountain

Spruce

Umbrella

Pyramid

Golden Hill
Cascade

Great
Cascade

Orangery

Roman

Chessboard
Hill Cascade

Children's Park

Great Palace

Oak

Square
Ponds

Upper

Benois
Museum
& Café

to Alexandra
Park

Neptune

Park

Café
Trapeza

Court
Stables

Mezheumny

Pharmacy
Museum &
Fiftozal

KRASNY PROSPEKT

Peter & Paul
Cathedral

round (but not such fun) you can take the train from Baltic Station (Baltisky Vokzal), get out at Novy Petergof (not Stary Petergof) station, and take any of the nos.351–5 buses for the ten-minute ride to the palace.

lunch/cafés

The most obvious place to eat is in the **bar/café** in the Lower Park, in the 'Illumination Courtyard', named for the firework displays that once took place here (*open 9–9*). An attached VIP restaurant is due to open in autumn 1999. The toilets cost 5 roubles. But better choices are to be found by the Great Palace and the Upper Park. There is a **café** in the Benois Museum (*open 12 noon–6pm; closed Mon and last Tues*); nearby is the **Restaurant Peterhof**, © 427 9096/314 4947 (*open 12 noon–2am*), while the **Café Trapeza** (*open 12 noon–7pm; closed Mon*) is best of all. The **Restaurant Gallery (Galeria)** on the church side of the Palace at the top of the main cascade can get very booked up.

The site of Peterhof (Peter's Court) was dictated by Peter the Great's obsession with his Russian navy, part of which was based on the island fort of Kronstadt, visible from the palace on a clear day. For much of the year the tsar could reach the island more easily by driving here and making the short sea crossing than by undertaking the longer boat journey from the capital. The first building the tsar commissioned (Monplaisir) was little more than a simple Baroque bungalow. In recognition of the need for somewhere to entertain ambassadors and other guests of state, and goaded by his flamboyant advisor Alexander Menshikov, who was already building an ostentatious palace for himself down the coast at Oranienbaum, in 1715 Peter commissioned Jean Baptiste Leblond to build him a Versailles-on-Sea. This palace was only as wide as the Grand Cascade, and Peter continued to live at Monplaisir, but as his reign wore on the gardens became more and more elaborate. The Great Palace was enlarged by Bartolomeo Rastrelli for Empress Elizabeth in the mid-18th century, and it is this version that we see today. From early in the palace's history there was a great summer fête held here every year, when for one day in the year the population of the city and its environs were invited to share and feast in the emperor's domain, illuminated by millions of candle lamps hung from the trees.

This description assumes you opt for the novelty value and fun of the hydrofoil and therefore starts with the four water's-edge palaces, then ambles through the lower park to the Great Palace, the Upper Park, the Benois and Pharmacy Museums and finally the Alexandria Park.

Monplaisir

The short walk from the jetty allows you to feast your eyes on the impressive canal, which draws your attention to the multitudinous water spouts of the Grand Cascade and above it to the palace. Once you hit land, turn left at the first opportunity and wander towards Peter's first home, Monplaisir, © 427 9129, which you enter from the back courtyard (open May–Oct 10–6; closed Thurs).

The house was originally commissioned from an architect named Braunstein in 1714, but it wasn't long before Leblond arrived to make his mark on this many-windowed brick building. Known as the Dutch House, this waterside home so charmed the pragmatic tsar that he gave it the whimsical name Monplaisir. A simple seven-room house flanked by wings containing picture galleries, it focuses on the central Great Hall which served as both living and dining room. Estimated by the painter Nicholas Ge to have been the site of the infamous interview between Peter and his poor son Alexei (it appears in his painting *Peter the Great Interrogating Tsarevich Alexei* in the Russian Museum, *see* p.131), this room was also the site of many a less sobering occasion. A visiting Frenchman, M. Weber, recounts how after a dinner with plenty of Hungarian wine 'it was impossible to refuse another pint glass offered by the Czarina herself. This reduced us to such pitiful circumstances that our servants chose to throw one of us into the garden'. Peter was renowned for these drunken dinners, at which he would quite often take little himself, the better to enjoy his manipulative bullying. The Danish diplomat Just Jual was reduced to bribery to survive, promising an influential priest that he would finance the building of an entire monastery if only he could stop the tsar insisting he should drink. Most of the room is soberly but precisely adorned in the style Peter liked. The coffered roof is a contrasting jewel. Painted by an Italian, at its centre you can see Apollo with his lyre, surrounded by a Renaissance confection of shells, flowers and figures. The corners of the coffer appear to be supported by sculpted torsos representing the four seasons.

On either side of the hall are three small rooms—a bedroom and two studies in one direction, a kitchen, pantry and the Lacquer Cabinet in the other. As well as fine wooden panelling, a number are adorned with Delft tiles and simple plasterwork chimneybreasts and ceilings. The only extravagance in the entire palace is the Lacquer Cabinet, whose orangy-red and black walls were originally executed by early 18th-century Russian icon painters copying Chinese lacquerware. Today's walls are second-generation copies. When the Nazis occupied the estate, they stabled horses in Monplaisir and all but three of the panels disappeared. Luckily Peter's collection of paintings had been evacuated, and now hangs throughout the palace.

Catherine Wing

Open May–Sept 10.30am–6pm; closed Thurs and last Fri of the month.

During the tricky years of Catherine the Great's gradual estrangement from her husband, which began in the 1750s, the future empress spent much time living in the long-demolished Tea House nearby. After her husband had threatened to divorce her and put her in a convent in 1762, it was here that Catherine's lover Grigory Orlov collected her on the day of their planned *coup d'état*, 28 July 1762. Peter III was living at Oranienbaum with his ugly lover, Elizaveta Vorontsova, and Catherine processed triumphantly into the city, receiving pledges of alliegance from whole regiments of soldiers as she went. When Peter came to dine with her and could not find her, he knew he was doomed, and retreated to Oranienbaum to await his fate (*see* p.228). The Catherine Wing, whose name honours these events, was in fact built by Empress Elizabeth in the 1740s so that she could entertain from Monplaisir in her customary style. It contains a number of large rooms, including the Yellow Hall whose table is laid with places for 45 guests. Opposite the Catherine Wing is the Bathhouse (*separate adm*), with a restored bathroom and *banya*.

Hermitage

To find this small red and white Baroque building, surrounded by a moat and overlooking the sea, return to the Marine Canal, cross it and walk on past the café. It's currently closed for restoration, but usual opening hours were May–Sept 11am–6pm; closed Wed and last Thurs of the month.

Should the situation change, you will find yourself in the private dining room that Peter commissioned Leblond to build, including a table which disappeared through the floor between courses, only to reappear covered with further delicacies. Guests marked their choice of dishes on the menu which lay by each plate. Originally even the guests were winched up and down to their waiterless meal, but after Emperor Paul was stranded between floors it was decided to install a staircase.

Marly Palace

Even if the Hermitage is closed the walk was not wasted, for you can con-tinue past the vast pond, which once kept the Imperial table supplied with fish, to the yellow and white Marly Palace (open 10am–6pm; closed Mon; ticket office in the little wood hut to the right of the house).

Built 1719–20, the Small Seaside House, as it was originally known, is one of the most important buildings in the Lower Park, since the three main alleys fan out directly from it. It became known as the Marly Palace after the nearby water cascade and fountains, which were inspired by Peter's 1717 visit to the French king's hunting lodge, Marly-le-Roi. Peter took a close interest in its construction, instructing Braunstein on the use of wood panelling. The ground floor of the palace is taken up with service rooms—an even more elaborate tiled kitchen than at Monplaisir, a pantry containing 17th- and 18th-century crockery, a bedroom and a couple of studies. Upstairs is more showy, with some of Peter's clothes displayed in the Wardrobe Room, and canvases by one of his favourite artists, Alessandro Grevenbroeck. The dining room has a superb view along the vistas of the Lower Park, its solid English table sitting on a parquet floor exploding with dark stars. In the 18th century, during royal dinners, these would have been matched by the starbursts of fireworks let off from pontoons on the lake outside. The walls of the Oak Study in the corner are elegantly decorated with carving, while the desk in the window is said to have been made by Peter the Great himself. The bronze sundial on it was given to the tsar when he was in England by King William III.

Lower Park

Throughout the Lower Park, fountains and cascades of water form grand punctua-tion marks along the vistas. All of these have been recommissioned since the 1940s, when the park was crisscrossed by Nazi trenches and gun emplacements. Most of the fountains' names (marked on the plan) are self-explanatory. The Menazherny Fountain by the Marly Palace gets its name from the French verb *ménager*, 'to economize', its 40ft jets economizing on water by being hollow. The remarkable Pyramid Fountain creates a solid pyramid from its ever-moving jets. Watch out for the fountains near Peter's palace Monplaisir; the tsar himself designed some of them after his 1717 trip to Paris when the practical-joking monarch became enchanted by trick fountains.

The riotous Great Cascade, oriented down the Marine Canal to the Gulf of Finland and the Kronstadt naval base beyond, was designed to embody Peter's mastery over the Baltic following his rout of Sweden from the Gulf and at the Battle of Poltava (1712). Its centrepiece is a gilded bronze statue of Samson, on whose saint's day the battle took place, wrenching open the mouth of a lion, the heraldic beast of Sweden.

You can now enter Peter I's two-storey **Grotto**, which is within the Great Cascade, hidden behind the water (*open 11–4.30 weekdays, 11–5.30 weekends*). Tickets are available from the main palace at the top of the left-hand staircase of the cascade.

Before you leave the Lower Park to explore the Great Palace, you may want to drop in on the palatial Orangery, a semi-circular orange and cream building with huge windows. Originally used to cultivate the fruits, such as grapes, pineapples and oranges, which were a necessary part of any affluent table, it now houses a Museum of Wax Figures (*open 9am–5pm*).

Great Palace

Open 11am–6pm; closed Mon and last Tues of the month.

Empress Elizabeth's favourite architect Bartolomeo Rastrelli exercised considerable restraint on the exterior of Peterhof when he enlarged it in the 1740s–50s. Rather than adding his customary pillars, porticoes and deeply embellished windows, he respected the look of the smaller palace, built during Peter's time, and continued it in his extensions. Only in the gilded domes of the end pavilions can one see his Italian exuberance breaking through. Entrance to the palace is via doors in the Upper Park façade, and tickets for foreigners are on sale beyond the cloakroom. Inside the palace, however, Rastrelli gave free rein to his taste for gilded Baroque decoration. This can be seen on the first **Ceremonial Staircase**, but many of his other interiors were redecorated under Catherine the Great, whose own neoclassical taste required more restraint. Today's palace, restored from the burned-out hulk left by the Nazis in 1944, is largely as it was before the war, when rooms decorated during the reign of Peter the Great stood side by side with those redecorated in the 1840s. Intricate marquetry floors are a striking feature throughout.

At the top of the Ceremonial Staircase is a series of rooms devoted to an exhibition about the restoration work. These lead to the **Blue Reception Room** where the imperial secretary would greet guests. The first of these is known as the Chesma Room after its covering of canvases depicting moments from the great 1770 naval victory over the Turks at Chesma Bay. It is one of a series of rooms that Catherine the Great commissioned Yuri Velten to redecorate. As well as commemorating the battle it is also a covert compliment to the Orlov brothers who were instrumental in putting Catherine on the throne, for Alexei Orlov was the highest-ranking Russian commander at the battle. When he saw the painter Philippe Hackert's preliminary work for the series, he arranged to have a battleship blown up for him, so that he could capture the dramatic essence of the scene.

The largest room in the palace, the **Throne Room**, was used for balls and official receptions. Redecorated by Velten, it nevertheless betrays touches of Rastrelli in its obsession with windows, mirrors and light. Between the upper windows are bas-relief medallions portraying members of the Romanov family, but the equestrian portrait of Catherine the Great behind the throne, by the Danish painter Vigilius Erichsen, is more impressive. It shows her on the day of her *coup d'état*, riding her favourite horse Brilliant and wearing the green uniform of a colonel in the Preobrazhensky Regiment, which supported the putsch against feeble-minded Peter III. On either side of the portrait the walls have been decorated with bas-reliefs showing Justice, Truth and Virtue. The 12 magnificent chandeliers were coloured amethyst by adding magnesium to the glass.

The neighbouring **Audience Hall**, also known as the Ladies-in-Waiting Room, with its riot of gilded Baroque carving, is pure Rastrelli. To widen this long thin space he hung three mirrors on each of the side walls facing one another, so that vortices of swirling gold are caught in a series of endless perspectives. Beyond it, the White Dining Room was redecorated by Velten. Its long thin table is laid with an English cream and mauve service known appropriately as 'Queen's Ware' and produced by Wedgwood in 1770.

The centre of the suite of rooms overlooking the Lower Park is occupied by a **Picture Hall**, flanked by small studies decorated by Vallin de la Mothe in the chinoiserie style which was fashionable in the 1760s. The floors, particularly of the Western Chinese Study, are the most complex in the entire palace and are made using about a dozen different types of wood. The walls of the Picture Hall, also known as the Room of Fashions and Graces, are completely covered by 368 portraits of Russian women by Pietro Rotari, who travelled in Russia from 1757 to 1762. Foreigners were once told that these beauties represented the cream of Russian women from throughout the empire; in fact they were all modelled by eight of Empress Elizabeth's women courtiers, in a fancy dress frenzy.

Beyond the Eastern Chinese Study, the rooms become rather more intimate. The **Partridge Drawing Room** takes its name from the pattern on the silk material on its walls. Based on an 18th-century silk from Lyons, this stuff was in fact made in the 1960s in St Petersburg. The painting on the ceiling gives a hint as to what went on in the room. It shows *Morning driving away Night*, for it was here that those close to the royal family would gather after breakfast to talk, play and plan the day. The harp is early 19th-century, from the London workshop of the French instrument maker Sebastian Erard. The **Divan Room** next door, originally a royal bedroom, is covered in the most sumptuous painted Chinese silk wallpaper, which has been extensively repaired. Near the Divan, you can see the sculpture of one of Catherine the Great's favourite Italian greyhounds, Zemira. The next-door **Dressing Room** with its loud silk walls contains a number of objects given to the Empress Elizabeth by Louis XV of France. The Empresses' Study next door is thankfully plainer, its white silk walls hung with the portraits of female members of the family who lived in this suite— Elizabeth, Catherine the Great and Paul I's wife Maria Fyodorovna. Among them is one of Catherine's lovers, Stanislaw Poniatowski, later King of Poland.

Leaving the private female quarters, the tour moves on to two rooms connected with palace security, the **Standards Room**, where the resident guards' regiment hung their standards, and the Kavalerskaya. Don't miss the intricate inlaid gaming table in the Standards Room. The next four rooms were used as guest rooms and have yet to be restored. They lead to the defiantly zig-zagged floor of the **Crown Room**, which was redecorated by Velten in the 1770s. A door in the back wall communicates with the Divan Room, the empresses' bedroom, by means of a secret corridor, and it is thought that this was probably the emperors' bedroom. It gives directly on to my favourite wood-lined room, **Peter the Great's Study**, whose panels were decorated to designs by Leblond. Eight of them were evacuated before the Nazi occupation and three of the remaining four have been painstakingly recreated. You leave the palace via the Petrine Oak Staircase, watched by a portrait of the tsar.

Before you leave the palace, check out any temporary exhibitions they may be holding on the Ground Floor.

Upper Park

The formal garden known as the Upper Park, was conceived during the reign of Peter the Great. Early lead statues which cracked under the strain of the northern winters were replaced with bronze ensembles, a number of which had to be recreated after the Nazi destruction. The main group is an extraordinary 17th-century survivor, older than even the idea of Peterhof itself. Depicting Neptune and his watery consorts, it was brought here from Nuremberg by the future Paul I and erected in 1799. During the Second World War it was sent back to Germany, but was found by Russian scouts afterwards and reinstalled. The Square Ponds, which once acted as reservoirs for the fountains in the Lower Park, are now presided over by statues of Apollo and Venus, while the Oak Fountain, originally in the shape of a tree, now centres on a mysterious cupid donning the mask of tragedy. The last fountain is named after its muddled history—Mezheumny means 'indeterminate'.

Benois Family Museum, the Pharmacy Museum and Fiftozal and the Peter and Paul Cathedral

Two small museums occupy buildings within easy reach of the Upper Park. The name **Benois** has been linked for over a century and a half with St Petersburg's artistic life. From the loins of a French confectioner, Louis Jules Benois, who arrived in Russia in 1794, came a dynasty of architects, stage designers, sculptors and writers, the most famous outside Russia being the British actor Peter Ustinov. The pinnacle of the career of Nikolai Benois (1813–98), confectioner's son, was the work he did here for the tsar, which included designing this building. The best known Benois in Russia is his son Alexander, who worked with Diaghilev on the turn of the century art magazine *Mir Iskusstva* and was also a stage designer. The

Benois Family Museum contains work by these and the more recent members of the clan. Ustinov's performance as Hercule Poirot in the film *Death on the Nile* is represented by a poster. *Open 10.30am–6pm; closed Mon and last Tues of the month.*

On a completely different note, the **Pharmacy Museum**, an old-fashioned chemists, and the neighbouring herbarium (*fiftozal*), which once grew medicinal herbs for the royal family, brew a number of soothing infusions. With a less advanced (and less powerful) drugs industry, the Russians still tend to use a lot of natural remedies for minor ailments, and useful herbal infusions to encourage sweating, cure constipation or alleviate shock are common knowledge. It's a nice place to have a cup of herbal tea. *Open 11–6; closed Sat and last Tues of the month.* The **Peter and Paul Cathedral** beyond the pharmacy was built in the 1890s in the neo-Russian style, and became a cinema after the Revolution. Its interior has yet to be completely restored, though services are once again held here.

Alexandria Park

Entirely different in conception from the main palace gardens, the Alexandria Park is a product of the romantic era and the naturalistic English style of landscaping made popular by Catherine the Great. It was developed by Tsar Nicholas I and his wife Alexandra, after whom the park is named, with a number of romantic Gothic buildings, most of which are currently in a ruinous state. However their curious, almost suburban, **Cottage Palace** has been restored and forms the focus of an exploration of the area (*open 10.30am–5pm; closed Fri and last Thurs of the month in summer; Mon and last Tues of the month in winter*). To get to the park you take the road running from the Great Palace past the Benois Family Museum along the top of the Lower Park. On the way, the huge timbered building of the Court Stables, now a retirement home, was built by Nikolai Benois, inspired by English medieval architecture. Both the Farm Palace and the eerie Gothic Chapel in the park have been in ruins since the Second World War, though plans are afoot to restore them soon. Continue down through wooded glades and over the ruined bridge before climbing up to the extraordinary hybrid Cottage Palace, which also has a Benois connection—a leading role in the restoration was taken by Irina Benois. Built in 1826–9 by the architect Adam Menelaws, it was to this unpretentious three-storey house, with its exotic wrought iron and wooden decorative flourishes, that Nicholas I and his German wife would retire to relax with their family. It was enlarged slightly in 1842 by Stakenschneider, as their family outgrew its modest proportions, and part of the interior was also remodelled at the turn of the century when Nicholas II's widowed mother, Maria Fyodorovna, spent some time here. Among the more unusual objects is a clock that shows the time in all 66 of Russia's provinces, which at that point included Russian America (Alaska), which was only sold to the USA in 1867.

Oranienbaum (Ораниенбаум)

This small town, known in the Soviet era as Lomonosov, grew up around the palace complex begun here in Peter the Great's reign by his right-hand man Prince Menshikov. Its exotic name conjures up the ultimate aristocratic luxury in these northern climes—orange trees grown here in heated hot-houses. Later in the 18th century, the outstanding Russian man of science Mikhail Lomonosov built a glass and mosaic tesserae factory nearby, hence its second name.

Oranienbaum never fell into Nazi hands during the Second World War: no architectural complex, however painstakingly restored, could retain its spirit of place, its *genius loci*, after such a thorough gutting. Here, the surprise of discovering intimate, jewel-like pavilions and mini-palaces among the lush and informal gardens is undiminished. Come prepared for a good long walk round the five important buildings and handful of lesser ones, leaving time for some boating before climbing back on the train. *Bear in mind that the five buildings open to the public, all on guided tours, share the same opening hours: 11am–6pm, closed Tuesdays, the last Monday of the month and from early November to May Day. The park is open 9–10 in summer, but closes earlier in winter. © 422 3753.*

Getting There and Around

Trains leave Baltic Station at least every half-hour for the hour-long journey to Oranienbaum, four stops beyond Novy Peterhof on the southern bank of the Gulf of Finland. Get off as soon as you see water. Once here, take the road running straight away from the main station entrance, slightly to the right, and turn right at the T-junction to pass the cathedral on your right. The entrance to the park is further down the road on the left.

lunch/cafés

Oranienbaum is a culinary desert, so the best advice is to bring a picnic and supplement it with delicious fresh pasties (*pirozhki*) bought in the shop near the station (buy either *s'kapoostoi*, with cabbage, or *s'myasom*, with meat). Look for the word 'Пирожковая' (*pirozhkovaya*) to identify the shop. In summer fruit can be bought in the market near the cathedral on the way from the station. In the park itself there is a **café** in the Cavalry Barracks, not far from the Chinese Palace, but it's not up to much.

*The path into Oranienbaum Park leads through wild woods and over a stream to a **lake** on which pedalos and rowing boats wait for hire.*

In good weather the shore is dotted with sunbathers and you can row your way up the lake, round its small island to the high rusticated bridge which crosses its feeder river, gently shattering the beams of sunlight with your bow waves.

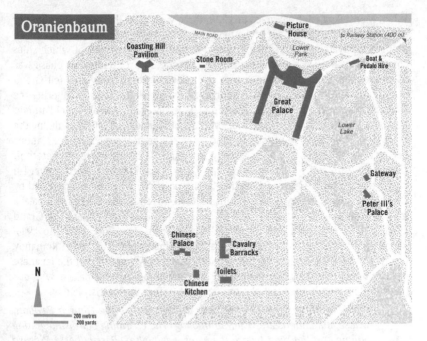

Oranienbaum

MAIN ROAD

to Railway Station (400 m)

Picture House

Lower Park

Boat & Pedalo Hire

Coasting Hill Pavilion

Stone Room

Great Palace

Lower Lake

Gateway

Peter III's Palace

Chinese Palace

Cavalry Barracks

Toilets

Chinese Kitchen

N

200 metres
200 yards

*The copper-roofed pavilion with its lantern top, visible to the side of the lake above the trees, marks one end of the **Great Palace**. Walk along to the gates of the Lower Gardens to find yourself in its full-frontal Petrine Baroque presence. This hemisphere of formal garden contains ghostly memories of the geometric box hedges, knot gardens and topiaried yews which must have focused attention on the formal entrance to the palace.*

Built using a natural rise in the otherwise flat coastal plain, Oranienbaum began life around 1710 as a summer residence for Prince Alexander Menshikov. He was Peter the Great's closest friend and principal political advisor, and had been made governor general of St Petersburg and its environs in 1703. Menshikov already had a grander house than his sovereign in the city, and continued to give full rein to his audacious arrogance here. For while Peter was building the humble one-storey summer palace of Monplaisir at Peterhof, work began on this grandiose palace, with its long semicircle of wings ending in the church pavilion on the right and the Japanese pavilion on the left. In 1713, with the arrival of its principal architect Gottfried Schädel, work got fully under way, though Menshikov bankrupted himself on the project and the interior décor was never finished. Changes to the façade were made by Rastrelli in the 1750s, when he modified the palace wings, and by Rinaldi who classicized the façade for Catherine the Great.

When Menshikov fell from grace in 1728, three years after the death of his master and protector, the palace became a naval hospital. It was served by the canal and harbour excavated by Menshikov just below the Lower Gardens, at which ships could dock from Russia's main naval base opposite on Kronstadt. This phase was short-lived, for Empress Elizabeth gave the palace to her nephew and heir Grand Duke Peter and his German bride Sophia (the future Peter III and Catherine the Great respectively) and work on the complex began again. The architect Antonio Rinaldi took up the interior decoration work where it had been left off, building the Peter III Palace (*see* below) to house the Grand Duke in the meantime. Relations between the young couple were already poor, and Catherine moved to Peterhof, leaving Peter to enjoy Oranienbaum with his mistress Elizabeth Vorontsova. He was living here at the time of Catherine's coup in 1762, when he was arrested by Catherine's lover Grigory Orlov and his brother. Taken inland to the royal palace known as Ropsha, he was strangled by the brothers a few days later. The Grand Duke had never moved into the Great Palace. From the 1760s until the 1917 Revolution, it was constantly in use by various members of the extended Romanov family. Until 1972 it housed government offices but now you can visit the Japanese pavilion in the East Wing and three simply decorated rooms in the palace, with displays of the letters, diaries and photos of a noble (rather than tsarist) family.

> *Walk out of the Lower Gardens by the gate below the Church Pavilion, whose foundations are visibly crumbling. The charming but disintegrating building on the right before the gates was built by Rastrelli as a **Picture House**. Beyond the gate, make your way through an ill-defined car park and up the hill path which leads off to the right behind it.*

This becomes a leafy avenue and passes another small Rastrelli pavilion, the **Stone Room** designed for parties and concerts, on the right, opposite a silted pair of lakes.

The intriguing bell-topped wedding-cake of a building (currently under scaffolding), which seems to grow as you walk towards it at the end of the avenue, owes its curious shape to its even more curious purpose as a **Coasting Hill Pavilion**. The combination of winter snows and a relatively flat landscape means that Russians to this day grow up tobogganing down artificial snow mountains erected for the purpose. The passion for whooshing downhill with the wind in one's face was so ingrained in the Russians' memory of childhood that Catherine the Great commissioned Rinaldi to construct the 18th-century equivalent of a roller-coaster ride here, for the summer pleasure of her guests. The ride was dismantled in the late 1850s.

The building flirts with classicism but, perhaps inspired by its thoroughly frivolous purpose, Rinaldi subverts these with showy touches of whimsy. A forest of pillars, urns and diminishing tiers completes the effect. The interior, through which you will be guided, is even more successful. Much of the paint and plaster on the walls today was applied by the genius of the Barozzi brothers and Stefano Torelli in the

1760s. The ground floor houses an exhibition of fine porcelain pieces, including important early Meissen, and a model of the Coasting Hill at the height of its glory.

The Round Hall was painted and decorated in the height of rococo taste in 1766–7 by the Italians, but its artifical marble floor is the most astonishing feature. It was made by a Signor Spinelli to a design by Rinaldi and is composed of several concentric circles of different colours, laced with garlands and centering on a supremely delicate bird with a twig in its mouth. Very much of its time and a secret of the Italians, such high quality craftsmanship was rarely found again. Indeed it is hard to think of a more perfectly rococo interior anywhere in Russia, informed as it is by the very essence of lightness and *rocaille*. The furniture is Russian-made. The Porcelain Room off to the right was also decorated by the Barozzis, and contains several series of early 1770s Meissen or copies thereof. To compare the real thing with their imitations, bear in mind that Neptune and Thetis, he with his strategically draped green cloak and golden crown, and the Battle Elephant are originals.

The other building which Catherine commissioned at the same time lies beyond the far end of the coasting meadow, set in its own slightly more formal enclave. Known as the **Chinese Palace** because of the rococo chinoiserie inside, it too was built by Rinaldi and decorated by the Barozzi brothers and Stephano Torelli. The rectangular lake and venerable oaks are contemporary with the building, and the sculptures in front of it are 18th-century copies of Apollo Belvedere and Artemis with a doe.

The building, painted in its original bruised pink and deep cream, was originally single-storey, the second floor having been added in the mid-19th century when several of the interiors were also altered. Guided tours begin in the suite designed for Catherine's then 7-year-old son Paul, continue through the small enfilade of state rooms which runs the length of the building and end in Catherine's suite, which balances her son's, both in wings jutting out towards the lake. The Empress used the palace for diplomatic dinners during the White Nights in midsummer, but returned to her official residence at Peterhof at dawn.

The first two ante-rooms in Paul's suite set the tone with their delicate decorative plasterwork set off by pastel-painted walls. The ceiling of the first room shows the muses of the palace, architecture, painting and building, as women armed with their appropriate tools. Look carefully at the French tapestry in the green silk bedroom, which was redecorated in the 19th century; it is sewn on to a background of woven reeds. Entering the prince's boudoir is like walking into a wooden marquetry box, the parquet floor and walls entirely inlaid with different woods.

The State Rooms begin with Stefano Torelli's paintings in the Hall of the Muses, a room shot with light from the windows on either side. Passing through the Blue Drawing Room, which has been invaded by large 19th-century canvases, the Glass Bead Room is decorated on three sides by panels of fantastic birds among burgeoning trees and decorative landscapes, embroidered in silk on to a background of pearly glass beads. Known as buglework, these were made in France, possibly using Russian beads, in the early 1860s, and are divided by ornate gilded floral columns. Wisely, Rinaldi left the fourth wall simple. After that, the Great Hall seems curiously heavy, its walls decorated with artificial marble and relief medallions of Peter the Great and the Empress Elizabeth over the doors. No doubt the room would feel different had its magnificent ceiling painting, specially commissioned for the room from Tiepolo in Italy, not vanished during the Second World War. The Lilac Drawing Room is dedicated to love. The ceiling in the Small Chinese Study beyond is held up at each corner by dragons, traditional Chinese symbols of imperial power, and its walls are covered in a magnificent 20th-century copy of Chinese silk wallpaper. This is merely a prelude to the Large Chinese Hall, in which the Barozzi brothers created inlaid wooden chinoiserie walls, using birch, rosewood, oak and amaranth, with a little green paint and ivory for the faces of the inhabitants of the magical landscape. Apart from the enormous English billiard table, made from Asian redwood and deeply carved, the rest of the furniture is original 18th-century Chinese.

Catherine's Suite, beyond, is an exquisite collection of rooms, decorated with a light Elysian feel; her dressing room is decorated with a series of French allegorical portraits of her ladies-in-waiting symbolizing the seasons of the year and the elements. The penultimate room, known as the Portrait Room, contains 22 portraits by Pietro Rotari, whose more famous portrait series fills every inch of the vast Room of Fashions and Graces at Peterhof. The room was designed around the paintings, so that, as well as being decorative, the portraits add to its physical rhythm by the inclination of their heads, the direction of their glances. The final room was Catherine's Study, its parquet floor an elaborate echo of its painted walls.

To the left of the lake stand the **Chinese Kitchens**, built on the site of the original kitchens in 1870 and painted to match the Baroque exterior.

*Winding your way through the Upper Park towards **Peter III's Palace**, you pass the Cavalry Barracks with its depressing café, and wander through woods, across open spaces and over bridges.*

You should come across an isolated gateway first, its pink arch surmounted by a lantern look-out and a spire leading into nowhere. Once it was the entrance to Peterstadt, a grown-up toy fort built for Grand Duke Peter who, while he waited to succeed his aunt on the throne, channelled his frustrations into a fixation with things military, drilling up to 1,500 soldiers within its 12-pointed star-shaped fortifications. As Archbishop Coxe described it: 'Everything wore a martial appearance: the hours of morning and evening parade were marked by the firing of cannon; a regular guard was stationed; the troops were taught, under his inspection, the Prussian discipline.' All that remains are ghosts of the earth ramparts. Not content with this fantasy toy, Peter also drilled thousands of toy soldiers in his palace, apparently a Romanov tendency that showed itself later in Paul I.

Whatever Rinaldi thought of his patron, he built him a small but perfectly formed home here. Once the servants' quarters, the ground floor now houses an exhibition of the history of Oranienbaum, but is otherwise bare. Upstairs a suite of six small rooms leads from one to the next. They focus on the Picture Hall, where, in the fashion of the time, oils by lesser 17th- and 18th-century west European artists have been disrespectfully cut and reframed to fit the jigsaw that covers the walls. In this particular instance, however, the effect is enhanced by lacquered dados, doors and panels, painted in the Chinese idiom by the highly talented serf lacquer master Fyodor Vlasov. It is the oldest lacquer work of its type in the country.

From here, the walk back to the station via the boating pond is all downhill.

Tsarskoye Selo (Царское Цело)

In its pre-Revolutionary heyday, Tsarskoye Selo ('Tsar's Village') was *the* place to spend the summer. Since the 18th century the royal family and their court had periodically decamped *en masse* from the city to imbibe its fresh country air.

The main attraction for visitors today is the sparkling **Catherine Palace** and its landscaped park. Post-war restoration of this Rastrelli masterpiece continues, but plenty of the palace is open to give an idea of the gilded lifestyle led by its inhabitants. Catherine the Great's preferences, as outlined in a letter to Voltaire, hold true for most of the park: 'I love to distraction gardens in the English style, the curving lines, the gentle slopes, ponds like lakes, archipelagos on dry land'.

It is even truer of the neighbouring **Alexander Park**, which seems like the garden surrounding Sleeping Beauty's castle. Paths, follies and landscaped areas have grown into a nostalgic wilderness, a poignant memorial to the last royal family, who lived in the **Alexander Palace** under house arrest before they were taken east to their eventual execution in Yekaterinburg. The left wing of the palace is now open to the public; and exploring the park can take the form of a seriously long walk.

Some confusion may still arise over the name of the town. During the Soviet era, it was renamed twice, first Detskoye Selo, Children's Village, because of the number of orphanages in the town, and later, to mark the centenary of the poet's death, Pushkin, for it was here that he was educated. Today however, it is once more known as Tsarskoye Selo, though the train station is still called Detskoye Selo. It is best to make the journey on *Wed–Sun*, as the Catherine Palace and the Lycée are *closed on Tues and the last Mon of the month*, the Alexander Palace is *closed on Tues*, and **Pushkin's Dacha** is *closed on Mon and Tues*. If you know you want to see some royal carriages as well, be aware that the Carriage Museum is *closed on Tues and Wed*. If you plan to visit both the Catherine Palace and Pavlovsk in one day, they are both *open on Wed, Sat, Sun and the middle Mondays of the month*. On *Thursdays*, only the state rooms are open at Pavlovsk.

Trains leave Vitebsk Station every 20 minutes or so for the half-hour ride to Detskoye Selo. Before embarking, take in a little pre-Revolutionary atmosphere at the site of Russia's first railway terminus. In 1837 track was laid from here to Tsarskoye Selo, and a model of the inaugural train that took Tsar Nicholas I and his family to their summer palace stands at the end of the platform. The present station was built in 1904, in pure *Style Moderne*, and its waiting room is painted with murals showing the old stations along the route. If you have time, go in the main triple doors and up the steps, turning right into the Royal Waiting Room (*see* p.202).

At Tsarskoye Selo, either walk 15 minutes (*see* map) or take bus nos.370, 378 or 382, all of which drop you near the Catherine Palace and the entrance to the park. Tickets for the park are sold opposite the entrance, and for the palace on its ground floor. Bus nos.370 or 280 will take you from Ul. Kominterna, beside the Orangery, to Pavlovsk.

lunch/cafés

If it isn't a day for a picnic, there are three or four possibilities around the Catherine Palace and Park. In the palace itself there is the expensive **Café Tsarskoye Selo** (entrance on the road opposite the Lycée) serving cold drinks, tea, coffee and snacks, or a cheap local cafeteria at the far end of the ground floor serving *blini* with a variety of fillings. The Admiralty building on the far side of the lake conceals a **restaurant** in its dark interior. There is also a **stand-up café** in the kitchen gates near the Hermitage building. It's best to book at **Podvorie**, Filtrovskoe Shossé 16, © 465 1399, situated between the Pavlovsk and Catherine Palace. It's a tourist trap but the food is delicious. *Open 12 noon–11pm*.

Catherine Palace

© 465 5308; open 10–6, closed Tues and last Mon of month.

This site was first stumbled upon by Peter the Great who gave it to his wife Catherine. During her husband's interminable absences fighting Swedes and Turks, she decided to build a cosy summer palace here (as if they didn't already have enough), and used the architect Braunstein, already busy at Peterhof, to execute the building between 1718 and 1724. Peter was reportedly charmed by the love nest, where he and Catherine had a second honeymoon on his return, but soon went back to his own buildings beside his beloved sea.

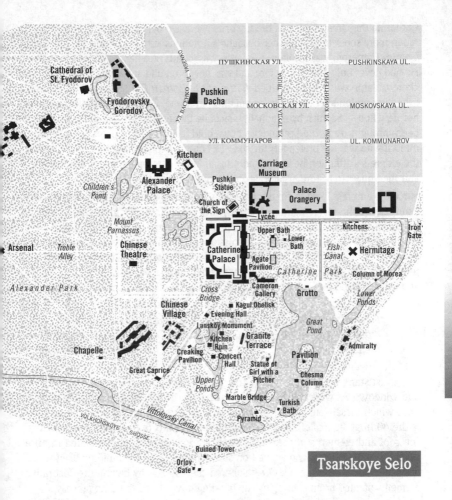

On Catherine's death, the estate passed to her 19-year-old daughter Elizabeth, who named it in memory of her mother; the palace is not, as is so often assumed, named after Catherine the Great. It was during Elizabeth's reign (1741–61) that the palace took its present shape. Having tried no fewer than three different architects to achieve what she wanted, in 1752 she decided that Bartolomeo Rastrelli, who had already completed a number of aristocratic palaces and was in the process of building the Smolny Convent for the empress, should be commissioned to start again. In four years, incorporating parts of the earlier buildings, he had built the longest palace in the world and one of the most opulent interiors.

Tsarskoye Selo   233

Catherine the Great, who was the next ruler to leave her mark on the interior, had much more sober tastes than her husband's flirtatious aunt. Her choice of architect, Charles Cameron, was inspired. Cameron was about 37 when he arrived in Russia. He had never built anything before and was never to build anywhere but Russia. His claim to fame was a book entitled *Baths of the Roman Emperors*, which he published in London after studying the buildings in Rome. Catherine wrote excitedly of her new find—'Scottish by nationality, Jacobite by persuasion'—and of how he had been 'brought up in the Pretender's household in Rome'. In this, it was Cameron himself who was the pretender: the son of a London Scot, a master mason, to attract the empress's attention he insinuated himself into the romantic tale of the Jacobites and their quest to restore a Catholic Stuart to the British throne.

Since the empress liked to conduct her life at Tsarskoye Selo as far as possible away from the public glare, hating ceremony and even fining women who stood up when she walked into the room, Rastrelli's endless succession of state rooms were of little use to her. Cameron was commissioned to turn a number of them into cosy suites, creating a series of Adamesque neoclassical interiors that were completely new to Russia. Most original of all was his bathhouse, the Agate Pavilion. Those you can see stand out as simple and intelligent beside those of the flouncy Rastrelli.

> *Before paying and entering the park, notice the nearest corner of the palace, crowned by a clutch of five gilded cupolas, each dressed with a cross, rising over the palace chapel beneath. Once in the park precincts, the deep turquoise façade of the palace, with mesmeric white and bronze embellishments, unfolds endlessly.*

You must stand back to appreciate this 1,000ft symphony of columns, porticoes and windows. As with many of Rastrelli's façades, its success hangs on the rhythm with which these elements are distributed. One astounding feature of the building is the 60 huge figures of Atlas supporting the columns of the upper storey. They, the roof and elements of the window decoration were originally gilded in pure gold, dazzling visitors who arrived on sunny days, while the building itself was a greyish green. Catherine the Great sobered the exterior by having the decorative elements painted bronze, bringing the building down to earth in the process.

> *The entrance is some two-thirds of the way along the façade. As an independent foreigner you will not be consigned to a group tour but will be able to wander through the palace at leisure.*

Begin with the **State Staircase**, one of the few rooms redesigned since the 18th century. In 1860 Ippolito Monighetti created this pure white space, decorated only by a collection of Chinese and Japanese plates, vases and pots standing on modelled wall brackets built into the walls. The monogram over the doors, MA, belongs to Maria Alexandrovna, wife of the tsar reigning at the time, Alexander II.

> *Turn right at the top of the stairs.*

The next two rooms cover the history and restoration of the palace, with prints and plans of the palace as it was, photos of the destruction wrought by the Nazis and an exhibition of tools and methods used in the restoration. The first restored room you find yourself in is the largest in the entire palace, the **Great Hall**. Designed by Rastrelli for Elizabeth, its opulence seems entirely fitting for a woman who is said to have owned 15,000 dresses: the effect of the windows and gilded mirrors is like being inside a crystal box on a glorious sunny day. On the ceiling, set among *trompe l'œil* architectural details, is a painting of the Triumph of Russia. It is one of the few ceiling works not to have been irreparably damaged, and some of the painting, particularly round the edges, is still the original 18th-century Italian work.

Beyond the Great Hall lie state rooms and Catherine the Great's chambers, the **Fifth Apartment**. The last set of exquisitely decorated rooms were created for her by Cameron and are said to be his finest work; one is so jewel-like that it became known as the tabatière, due to its similarity to the richly encrusted snuff-boxes carried by the aristocracy of the period. Tantalizingly, they are still closed to the public, though restoration of their neoclassical interiors, which also include columns of mauve glass in the bedroom and specially commissioned Wedgwood plaques, is under way. Instead the tour now swings round to explore the length of Rastrelli's great **Golden Enfilade**, which leads down the courtyard side of the building. From the windows you can see the single-storey wings in which court officials were housed, built by Savva Chevakinsky, Rastrelli's contemporary and the builder of the palace chapel. Sadly, nothing has yet been made of the garden within their embrace.

In the original palace the only staircase was beyond the Great Hall, so that visitors invited to the court chapel had to walk the entire length of this gilded corridor to get there. The first room they reached was the Knights' (Kavalerskaya) Dining Room, with its massive corner stove covered in Dutch tiles and reaching to the ceiling. Only special dinners, such as those honouring one of the Orders of Knighthood, were held here, illuminated by Rastrelli's great twisting branched wall lights.

Passing through the State Staircase again you come to the **Main Dining Room**, where guests ate between its gold and white walls overlooked, ironically, by a series of monumental German paintings of birds and beasts. The table is laid with the Hunters' dinner service, made in St Petersburg in 1760, of which only 50 pieces are left out of a set of 1,000.

Searching for novel interior decoration, in the next two rooms, the Raspberry and the Green Pilaster Rooms, Rastrelli made pilasters from crumpled coloured foil behind glass. They are perhaps the least satisfying rooms in the palace, though the gilding and the recently woven silk covering the walls are very fine. The corner stove in the red room is covered in delightful Russian 18th-century tiles. It also contains a delicate Chinese ivory chess set, while the green room has been decorated with French furniture from the Hermitage.

The **Portrait Hall** contains paintings of all of the Romanov women involved in the 18th-century Catherine Palace. On your right as you enter you will find the likeness of Catherine I, wife of Peter the Great. Then comes a portrait of Catherine the Great before her ascent to the throne and a picture of Peter the Great's favourite sister, Natalya. Last of all, on the far wall, comes Elizabeth, the patron of Rastrelli.

The most famous room was the **Amber Room**, decorated with a number of huge panels made entirely of Persian amber. Peter the Great had fallen for them when visiting Friedrich Wilhelm I of Prussia in 1715, and had dropped such mighty hints that the monarch felt obliged to give him them on his departure. They were used here by Rastrelli in 1755, having been carried by hand all the way from the capital by veteran soldiers. There were not enough to cover the walls entirely, but Rastrelli did his usual trick of dividing them with gilded mirrors and painting imitation amber panels at the top of the room. Today, the entire room is being remade, with new painstakingly crafted panels, as the whereabouts of the original panels has been uncertain since the Second World War. Rumours claim that they were discovered buried beneath a former Soviet army base in Ordruf in Germany in the autumn of 1991. No move has been made to excavate the panels, and conspiracy theorists even link a number of recent mysterious deaths to the affair. For years it was thought they were hidden deep in a German salt mine, possibly still guarded by descendents of the dwarfs who greeted amazed Allied art experts after the war. Their families had lived and worked in the mine for generations and spoke a medieval form of German. Others insist that the amber was destroyed.

After the Amber Room, visitors are swept into the vast magnificence of the **Picture Hall** which is plastered, walls and ceiling, with 17th- and 18th-century French, Italian, Dutch and Flemish canvases. No 18th-century Russian palace was thought complete without a hall decorated in this manner, for which paintings were summarily cut to size. Before the Nazi occupation 114 of the 130 pictures were evacuated. During the restoration, paintings were taken from the unseen stores at the Hermitage. The next room, the **Small White Dining Room**, contains a ceiling mural of the Birth of Venus and a breathtakingly intricate inlaid wooden desk, made by one of the serfs of the Sheremetiev family. In the Reception Room of Alexander I, which heralds a series of rooms often used by the emperor and his wife Elizabeth, hang a number of portraits. Alexander I stares out from the far wall as you enter the room, with Catherine the Great opposite him. On the wall to the left of the door is the young Alexei, whose death was brought about by his father Peter the Great, and opposite is his half-sister Anna, mother of Catherine the Great's short-lived husband Peter III.

A couple of small ante-rooms lead on to the beginning of the First Apartment, decorated by Charles Cameron, a test Catherine set him before letting him loose on her own rooms. Sadly, most of the time only the **Green Dining Room** is open to view but it shows the contrast between this style and that of Rastrelli. The powdery green walls are covered in white classical reliefs. To suit this more rigid style, even the parquet floor is laid in more formal patterns, and for the first time we find fireplaces and carved marble mantelpieces entering the vocabulary of Russian interior design. When it was only half done, Catherine was already crowing that 'so far only two rooms are finished, and people rush to see them because they have never seen anything like them before'. If you are allowed further into the apartment, in which Elizabeth, the wife of Alexander I, lived for many years, the highlight is her bedroom, with its forest of porcelain pillars, painted doors and false Wedgwood medallions. Beyond lies the superb, deep blue Baroque chapel designed by Savva Chevakinsky, and its ante-room, the Predkhornaya, whose walls are covered with its original silk wallcovering from Lyon, an extra roll of which had been waiting patiently in the cellars and was luckily evacuated. Hand-embroidered by Russian serfs in the 18th century, the intricate still lifes took several years to finish. Most likely however, you will find yourself channelled into the rooms decorated in the Russian Empire style for Alexander I by Vasily Stasov.

Created after Alexander's defeat of Napoleon, these rooms are suffused with a martial theme and a sense of empire. The walls of both the **Arched Room** and the **State Study** are made of smoothest *scagliola*, false pink marble, painted with *grisaille* murals of war trophies and allegorical scenes. The furniture here, designed by Stasov specially for the room, has been recently copied from a 19th-century watercolour. The other feature of the room, boldly offset against the pale pink walls, is its plethora of rich green malachite objects.

This begins the **Small Enfilade**, which runs along the park side of the palace. It has proved impossible to restore the rest of its rooms, as the records are insufficient, so they are used as exhibition space.

The exhibition, and the tour of the palace, ends by the State Staircase. Leaving the palace turn right and walk to the Agate Pavilion and the Cameron Gallery, which contains an extensive exhibition of pre-Revolutionary Russian costumes and materials.

Markedly more restrained than the main palace, Cameron's yellow stucco **Agate Pavilion**, studded with niches, sculptures and reliefs, stands on a monumental rusticated ground floor. It contained the Russian imperial *banya*, the baths; Catherine was able to get into them from her private rooms in this wing of the palace, via the so-called Hanging Garden on the first floor above the arches beyond the pavilion. Unfortunately, though the first floor rooms survived the Nazi occupation well, despite being used as an officers' mess, the ground floor baths were used as stabling and have not been restored. The entire building is closed to the public.

*Walk beneath the arches beyond the Agate Pavilion, and down towards the lake with the towering **Cameron Gallery** on your left.*

The long line of decreasing arches behind you was built by Cameron as a gentle ramp so that the Empress, now in her mid-50s, could walk easily in and out of the garden with her favourite greyhounds. Towards the end of her life Catherine, who was tone deaf, admitted that 'the only sounds I recognize are those of my nine dogs…each one of whom…I can recognize by his voice.' The ramp leading up to the gallery on the far side was also built for Catherine.

Cunningly using the slope of the land to echo the hilltop position of temples in the ancient world, Cameron built this gallery on a massive foundation of rusticated stone. Courtiers could dine in the glazed gallery on the top floor in bad weather, taking constitutionals on the covered walkways which surrounded it. In summer, these were punctuated by 53 bronze busts, mostly copies of antique sculptures of philosophers and writers in the Hermitage.

Taking the first of the two magnificent staircases at the far end of the gallery, the door between the embrace of the next flight leads into the **Museum of Court Dress** (*open 11am–5pm; closed Mon and Tues*). Here the world which greeted the author of the 1914 Baedeker's Guide, in which 'nearly one-tenth of the male population of St Petersburg wear some kind of uniform, including not only the numerous military officers, but civil officials, and even students, schoolboys, and others', comes to life. As well as official dress, there are also some civvies—including magnificent women's wedding dresses of fine lace.

Catherine Park

The Catherine Park graphically illustrates the two opposing schools of 18th-century landscape gardening—the formal and the naturalistic. In front of the palace precise beds of black and red arabesque shapes made from chips of lignite and brick, symmetrical ponds, hedges and rows of trees lead into a wilder area of woodland paths around the cross-shaped **Hermitage**. This alluring structure, if you can see it for scaffolding, was built by Rastrelli as a secluded spot in which Elizabeth could entertain small groups to dinner. It is currently closed to visitors. Rastrelli's other garden pavilion, the so-called **Grotto** by the lake's edge, is about as far from most definitions of the word as you can get. The only concessions made to its organic forebears appear high up, where fish heads and sea-gods take the place of acanthus leaves in the 'Corinthian' capitals and mock stalactites drip in place of triglyphs.

The romantic, naturalistic park surrounding the various ponds was created later, by Catherine's English gardener John Bush. It is dotted with monuments, statues and follies; the **Chesma Column** in the middle of the lake, a rostral column in the classical tradition, celebrates the naval victory over the Turks, while the **Column of Morea** celebrates a successful land victory in the same year, 1770. A number of the buildings, the Gothic **Admiralty**, the neoclassical **Evening Hall** and the **Marble Bridge**, a copy of the Palladian bridge at Wilton, were designed by V. I. Neyelov and son, whom Catherine sent to England to study landscape architecture.

The **Pavilion** on the island, now entirely screened by a stand of mature trees, was built by Quarenghi as a shelter for musicians, who would accompany royal boating outings. You can still hire dinghies from the prettiest of all the follies, the faded apricot and pink **Moorish Baths**, which were only added in the mid-19th century.

On the other side of the Great Pond, a wide gravel path and a narrower road are separated by a host of small ponds and pavilions, including a number of buildings in the Chinese style. While in England, V. I. Neyelov and his son would have come across Sir William Chambers, who had visited China, published a book on the *Designs of Chinese Buildings*, and built the ten-storey pagoda in Kew Gardens. They were responsible for the **Creaking Pavilion**, so called after an apparently humorous appreciation of specially designed creaking floorboards, and the **Great Caprice**, a scaled-down copy of the vast arch at Fukien, through which ships had been able to pass. The great artificial rock pile of the Caprice, topped by its pagoda-style summerhouse, spans the narrow road.

Not far beyond the road is the Neyelovs' colourful **Chinese Village**, an agglomeration of cottages with splayed roofs focused on a central courtyard building. Until the Revolution, courtiers lived here during the summer months while the royal family was in residence; the buildings are now being restored and sold as houses once more.

Alexander Park and Palace

Beyond the Chinese Village you stray into the Alexander Park, with its wooded paths and occasional Gothic buildings (the Arsenal and the Chapelle). Following the Cross Canal past the now overgrown formal area of the park, you arrive at the Children's Pond and beyond it at the **Alexander Palace** (*open 10–4.30; closed Tues; © 466 6669*). Built by Giacomo Quarenghi on the orders of Catherine the Great, this archetypal Palladian building was given to her much-loved grandson, the future Alexander I, on the occasion of his marriage. Lived in by both Nicholas I and Alexander III, its most famous inhabitants were Nicholas II, Alexandra and their family, who were imprisoned here between the tsar's abdication in March and August 1917, when they were transported, not to a port and then to England, as they had been led to believe, but in a closed train to Siberia, where they lived until they were transported to Yekaterinburg where they were shot the following July. The building was badly damaged in the war but 12 rooms have been reopened, in which personal belongings, artwork and icons of the late Tsar are on display. Most moving are the children's clothing and toys. The tsar's apartments were on show before the war, complete with the empress's medicine chest and the rose oil left in the icon lamp in the imperial bedroom. Its then director described how 'one had the impression that the people who had lived there had just gone into another room a minute ago.'

Lycée and Carriage Museum

Unless you speak Russian, you may want to miss the reverential conducted tours of the **Lycée** where Alexander Pushkin studied for six years (*open 10.30am–5.30pm; closed Tues and last Mon*). He was among the first intake at the school, which began in 1811. As the poet describes it in Eugene Onegin, these were:

> *Days when I came to flower serenely*
> *in lycée gardens long ago...*

Tours begin on the second floor with the Empire-style examination room, and then move on to a semi-circular classroom with built in wooden desks, the music room and the physics laboratory. Fencing masks, accomplished drawings and musical instruments given an idea of the skills a young nobleman was expected to master. Upstairs the long pale corridor of the dormitory is lined with the small rooms of the pupils. Alexander Pushkin's name plate hangs over the door of No.14. On the first floor, an exhibition sets the Lycée in its social context.

The **Carriage Museum**, in the old royal stables, is *open 11am–5pm; closed Tues and Wed.*

Pushkin's Dacha (Dom Kitaeva)

Not far from the Alexander Palace, you can visit the delightful, light and airy corner house that Pushkin rented with his wife for the summer of 1831. During that summer, visitors would go into the park on purpose to meet the poet, once it was established that he walked there in the early evening. In the company of Gogol and the poet Zhukovsky, Pushkin passed many an evening of readings and gentle literary banter. An English-language text in each room explains the short but charming exhibition (*open 11am–6pm; closed Mon and Tues*).

On your way to the *dacha*, look at the statue of the poet (1900) staring off into space seated on a bench in the garden near the **Church of the Sign**. The church is the oldest building in the town (1734), and is in a terrible state of disrepair.

Pavlovsk (Павловск)

There is something about Pavlovsk which, more than any other palace round St Petersburg, exudes a sense of the aspirations of those who created it in the late 18th century. The palace was one of the first to undergo restoration after the war; both it and the park have been largely recreated, and are even beginning to show signs of maturity again. Paint peels off the façade of the palace, and looking down one of the endless avenues it is hard to believe the devastation wrought on its 150-year-old landscape only 50 years ago, when over 70,000 trees were felled or irreparably damaged. The Slavyanka River, its bridges, woods, pavilions and open meadows are once more an idyllic rural vision, while the interior of the imperious yellow and white palace has once more become an exquisite mixture of Empire grandeur and cosy proportions. Thanks to feverish activity in the months leading up to the Nazi occupation, some 14,000 pieces of furniture and fittings were evacuated, all of which have been returned to their original places, and copied where only one of a set was taken. As a monument to both 18th-century Russia and Soviet restoration, Pavlovsk has no equals. *The palace, ✆ 470 6536, is open 10.30am–5.30pm; closed Fri and first Mon of every month. On Thurs only the first floor, containing the state rooms, is on view. If you are going to combine a visit to Pavlovsk and Tsarskoye Selo come on a Wed, Sat, Sun or one of the middle Mondays of the month.*

Getting There and Around

It takes 40 minutes to get to Pavlovsk by train from Vitebsk Station. It is the stop after Detskoye Selo, the station for Tsarskoye Selo, and it's either a 15-minute walk or a bus ride from there to the palace. Buses nos.317, 370, 383 and 383a leave from the square in front of the station, going right to drop you at the palace in five minutes. Alternatively walk straight across the road and, buying a ticket at the gate, set off straight across the park. Turn right when you can no longer go straight, cross the River Slavyanka on your left and walk up to the palace on the hill. To get to Tsarskoye Selo, take the 370 bus from the stop beside the palace, back to the railway station and on. It will drop you a block from the Catherine Palace.

lunch/cafés

There is a very good restaurant in the recently restored hall in the south wing, serving soup of the day, sandwiches, pastries and more substantial hot dishes. In the right weather Pavlovsk's park is crying out for picnickers to settle down on its sloping meadows or to place themselves strategically on one of its sylvan perspectives. Try living up to this description of mid-19th century pleasure-seekers 'who resort hither daily in such numbers to enjoy the country, to dine, and to drink punch and champagne'. There is also **Podvorie** (*see* p.232).

The Palace

As Pavlovsk's name suggests, the palace originally belonged to Emperor Paul (Pavel in Russian) and his wife Maria Fyodorovna. Catherine the Great gave them the land, undulating on either side of the lazy bends of the Slavyanka river, to commemorate the birth of their son and heir Alexander in 1777. It was Paul's talented and energetic German wife who left a greater mark on the place. Once Paul had been given the fortress-like palace at Gatchina in 1784, he preferred to spend his time there, taking out his lust for power on a benighted regiment of soldiers.

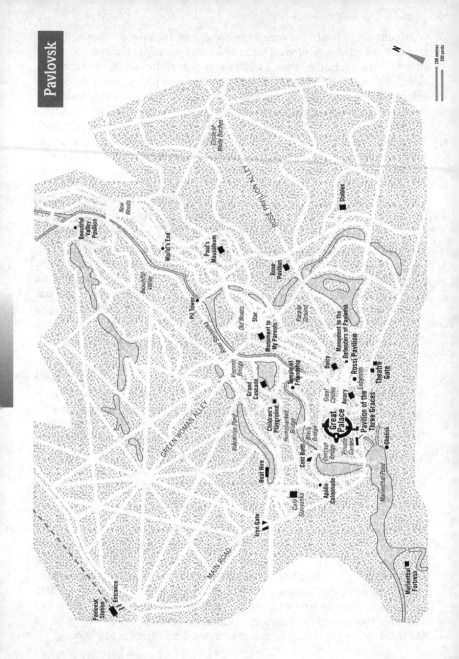

N

200 metres
200 yards

Circle of
White Birches

New
Woods

Beautiful
Valley
Pavilion

World's End

Beautiful
Valley

Paul's
Mausoleum

ROSE PAVILION ALLEY

Stables

Rose
Pavilion

Pil Tower

Red Slavianka

Old Woods

Star

Parade
Ground

Monument to
My Parents

Viscont
Bridge

Grand
Cascade

Temple of
Friendship

Dairy

Monument to the
Defenders of Pavlovsk

GREEN WOMAN ALLEY

Vokzalnye Pond

Children's
Playground

Humpbacked
Bridge

Black
Bridge

Great
Circles

Rossi Pavilion

Aviary

Labyrinth

Theatre
Gate

Boat Hire

Cold Bath

Centaur
Bridge

Great
Palace

Pavilion of the
Three Graces

Private
Garden

Café
Slavianka

Apollo
Colonnade

Obelisk

Iron Gate

Marienthal Pond

MAIN ROAD

Marienthal
Fortress

Pavlovsk Station

Entrance

There are three architects whose names are linked with Pavlovsk—Charles Cameron, Vincenzo Brenna and Andrei Voronykhin. The initial design belonged to Cameron, who was Catherine's favourite architect and had been 'lent' to her son and daughter-in-law as a double-edged favour. Though he was an inspired architect, he was an arrogant and stubborn man who liked to dictate the look of his buildings, right down to the last door handle. Maria Fyodorovna had strong ideas of her own, while her husband was prejudiced against any favourite of his mother's. When Catherine summoned Cameron to the Crimea in 1786, the palace was not finished, and the young couple took the opportunity to get rid of his services and handed the work to the assistant they had chosen for him, Vincenzo Brenna.

In 1803 a fire damaged most of the central section of Pavlovsk. By this time Brenna had left the country and Paul had been murdered. His widow, who retired more and more to Pavlovsk, hired the Stroganovs' serf-architect Andrei Voronykhin to oversee the restoration, and he continued to work at Pavlovsk until his death in 1814. Having outlived her husband by 27 years and seen two sons crowned emperor, Maria Fyodorovna finally died in 1828. After her death the palace passed to her son Mikhail, who neglected it. The park took on a life of its own however, once the railway had been built in the 1830s and the station building (Vokzal, named after the pleasure gardens at Vauxhall in London) became the most exciting concert hall in the St Petersburg area. For ten years Johann Strauss was the principal conductor, and the public flooded to picnic in the park before and after performances. After the Revolution, Pavlovsk opened as a museum, though Stalin managed to sell a number of its most valuable treasures. In 1957 the first of its restored halls was reopened.

Arriving in the embrace of the courtyard, you come face to plinth with a statue of Paul I, a copy of the one at Gatchina placed here in 1872. Tickets are on sale in the pavilion at the centre of the right wing.

On entering the palace you will find yourself in the **Egyptian Hall** and will immediately be aware of many of the distinguishing features of the palace. Magnificent crystal lanterns hang from a painted ceiling, while a *trompe l'œil* fresco beneath the stairs gives an extraordinary sense of illusion. The 12 Egyptian sculptures were designed after the 1803 fire by Voronykhin, for Napoleon's 1790s campaign in Egypt had introduced a fashion for the aesthetics of the ancient Egyptians. To the right of the ground floor is the suite of Maria Fyodorovna when she was Dowager Empress. It faces her private rose garden and can be visited for an extra charge.

*Taking the staircase to the first floor, you will find yourself in the state rooms, which centre on the round **Italian Hall**.*

Under the soft natural light of the Pantheon-like dome, the false marble walls are covered in medallions, caryatids, and friezes, but the joy of the room is the Roman statues, copies of Greek originals, which fill the niches. These were too fragile to be evacuated, so in 1941 they were taken down to the vaulted cellars and packed together behind a specially built false wall. The Nazis never discovered them.

To the right of the Italian Hall, through a small dressing room and study, is **Paul's Library**, designed by Brenna in 1790 and divided by a tall arch. Books are relegated to small low bookcases and the walls are divided by tall thin tapestries illustrating La Fontaine's fables and given to the Grand Duke and Duchess by Louis XVI when they visited him in 1782. This trip, made while Cameron was building their palace, was one of the causes of Paul and Maria's quarrel with the architect. He was disgruntled when he heard his patrons were buying quantities of European furniture and objects without consulting him. Brenna on the other hand was quite happy to design a room around fine objects owned by the couple. A number of the ivory and amber objects in this room were turned and decorated by Maria Fyodorovna, who you can see in the full-length portrait. More interesting than the circular temple beneath her portrait is the square one on Paul's large mahogany desk. Maria painted a cameo of her husband on the pediment, whilst each face of the octagonal altar is adorned with the cipher of herself or one of her children, like a shrine to the family. She even made the twelve ivory columns supporting the desk. The firescreen, also thought to have been painted by Maria Fyodorovna, has a more morbid history. It was behind this that Paul tried to hide from his assassins on the night of his murder in the Mikhailovsky Castle (*see* p.98).

Next to the library is the **Tapestry Room** in which, for the moment, the valuable Gobelin tapestry on the curving wall, from the extremely popular Don Quixote series, is flanked by two Belgian tapestries on the same subject. Restorers at Gatchina are putting immense pressure on Pavlovsk to give them back the French tapestry, since it originally hung with two others in a recently reopened room. However, Pavlovsk's own magnificent set of Gobelins, again given by Louis XVI, were sold by Stalin, and as Pavlovsk was one of the earliest restored palaces, they had first choice of suitable antiques to replace gaps in the collection. The highly decorated mahogany writing desk was made in St Petersburg for Paul I, while the gilded furniture came from the workshop of the famous Henri Jacob in Paris.

> *A suite of three grand rooms at the end of the building looks straight out over the garden to the Apollo Colonnade on the far side of the Slavyanka.*

The Halls of War and Peace, flanking the Grecian Hall, were decorated by Brenna in gold and white marble. Contrasting decorative themes are used in each, in the plaster mouldings, gilded door panels and even the ceramic stoves. In the **Hall of War**, shields, armour and weapons celebrate Russia's increasing success on the international battlefield. The **Hall of Peace** is contrastingly lyrical, a sea of cornucopias overflowing with fruit, garlands of flowers and musical instruments. The blue vase with bronze chasing is known as the Tsar's Vase. Between them lies the palatial **Grecian Hall**, surrounded by fluted deep green columns painted to look like grand *verde antico* marble. Designed by Cameron, it is decorated with special carved wooden gilt furniture by Voronykhin.

> *From the Hall of Peace you enter the state suite of Maria Fyodorovna, starting in her Library.*

Like the Tapestry Room opposite, its wall is hung with a French tapestry. Much of the furniture was designed by Voronykhin, including the magnificent chair behind the desk, whose back supports are shaped like cornucopias to hold flowers. The desk was made by David Roentgen, the Prussian furniture maker who had so impressed Catherine the Great with his gift of an incredible mechanical cabinet that he became the *ne plus ultra* of cabinet makers at the late 18th-century Russian court.

Next you find yourself in the empress's narrow, highly decorated **Boudoir**. The marquetry floor is inlaid in a complicated arabesque design to mirror the painted ceiling. As many as 50 different shades of wood might be used by Russian marquetry craftsmen, including material imported from every continent. The pilasters are painted with a series of patterns copied from Raphael's Loggia in the Vatican, and the grand porticoed fireplace is laden with jasper and porphyry objects.

The **Empress's Bedroom** was designed by Brenna, though not to be slept in: Versailles was responsible for the absurd concept of the state bedroom, which the Russians took to even greater excess. The bed and furniture were made in Paris for this room by the Jacob studio. The exquisite Sèvres toilet set was commissioned by Marie Antoinette for her friend Maria Fyodorovna; its 64 pieces include cups with portraits of the doomed French king and queen as well as eye-baths and numerous pots for potions. Furniture in the **Empress's Dressing Room** was made by the Tula metalworkers, whose fame traditionally rested on their weaponry.

> *Leaving the empress's suite, turn right into the curved **Picture Gallery**, built by Brenna in 1797 as a grand corridor leading to the Throne Room.*

The collection of mediocre 17th- and 18th-century European paintings, acquired by the royal couple on their tour of Europe, is not as interesting as the handsome brown porphyry vases, which are among the earliest to have been carved from the newly discovered veins in the Ural Mountains.

The **Throne Room** is impossibly grand, and its restored ceiling is actually closer to what Brenna envisaged than the plain white surface that went before. By a stroke of luck Soviet researchers found part of the original design, by the brilliant theatrical designer Pietro di Gottardo Gonzaga, which had been eradicated over 100 years earlier. The principal restoration painter, Anatoly Treskin, steeped himself in Gonzaga's work in order to reinvent the missing three-quarters of the ceiling, creating a tottering edifice of crumbling architecture reaching to the open sky. The only furniture in the room is three tables loaded with dinner services. In the centre is an 18th-century French creation known as the Paris Service, while the rest is the St Petersburg Gold Dinner Service, made in the early 19th century.

Beyond the Throne Room, Paul asked Brenna to add a room known as the Hall of the Knights, in which he could entertain in his newly-found position of protector of the Knights of St John of Malta. Since his youth, Paul had been fascinated by the antiquated chivalry of this crusading order and, as it faced expulsion from Malta, he gave the order temporary sanctuary, though his Orthodoxy prevented full personal membership. On his death it faced inevitable eclipse. Against the pale green walls with their white plaster reliefs are Roman copies of Greek original sculptures. You will also be able to peer into the palace chapel beyond from the royal balcony.

> *Returning to the staircase, the tour continues downstairs, in the marginally less opulent private living quarters of the royal family.*

The first room is the so-called **Raspberry Room**, Paul's private study dominated by views of his favourite park at Gatchina by Shchedrin. The **General Study**, with its portraits, was where the family used to gather. A number of the amber and ivory objects were made by Maria Fyodorovna, as were some of the miniatures in Paul's **New Study** next door. Above them hangs the group family portrait, with their daughter Olga, who died at the age of three, represented by a bust. The startlingly different **Corner Drawing Room** was an early design by Carlo Rossi in 1803. Rossi's time was to come under Maria Fyodorovna's son Alexander I who, perhaps mindful of this simple yet powerful and dignified mauve and yellow silk creation, chose him to give architectural voice to Russia's moment of triumph over Napoleon. Rossi also designed the furniture, made from Karelian birch, whose distinctive patina derives from its slow tortuous growth in the permafrost. Cameron designed the simple white and green **Dining Room**, though the frieze and cornice were redesigned by Voronykhin after the fire of 1803. This room, opening straight out on to the sloping lawn, was always popular, and it was here that Maria Fyodorovna chose to entertain her guests, who included many of the musical and literary luminaries of St Petersburg. The Dowager Empress was also known for her good works; with extraordinary foresight she not only set up orphanages, schools and hospitals, but in the town of Pavlovsk she inaugurated inoculation programmes and built the first school for the deaf and dumb.

The corner **Billiard Room**, long ago deprived of its billiard but not its card tables, is adorned with 12 18th-century Venetian copies of Canaletto. Try out the acoustics. The neighbouring **Old Drawing Room** is hung with three more tapestries given to the royal couple by the ill-fated Louis XVI. This time, they belong to the New Indies series, showing the fecund exoticism of the flora and fauna of newly 'discovered' lands. The four paintings by Hubert Robert in the small **Ballroom** were specially commissioned from the highly fashionable French painter for Pavlovsk. The rest of the room is as it was when Cameron designed it.

The main tour of the palace ends here, since the suite of rooms on the ground floor of the southern wing are currently under repair. However on the second floor you will find an exhibition of 19th-century Russian domestic interiors.

The Park

The creation of Pavlovsk Park, which at the time of its creation at the end of the 18th century was twice the size of New York's Central Park and the largest landscaped area in the world, was undertaken by successive architects at the palace under the direction of Maria Fyodorovna. The widespread but unfounded suggestions that Capability Brown, the paramount English designer, was responsible for the overall plan merely attest to its success, greatly helped by the natural charm of the undulating landscape. The more formal areas around the palace were planned by Cameron and Brenna, while it was the stage designer and muralist Gonzaga who had the more profound effect on the outer reaches of the park, in the early 19th century. Seeing the landscape as a series of interlinking canvases, Gonzaga became more and more involved in judiciously pruning, felling and planting trees so that they became like brush-strokes on his landscape. As visitors walked through the park, he felt, every so often an entirely new, perfect and yet natural-looking view should open up.

The Italian was a genius with form and artifice, and his *trompe l'œil* arcade beneath the Rossi Library, now barely visible, was so successful that dogs were known to run straight into the wall hoping to get into the room beyond. He orchestrated a number of elaborate *fêtes champêtres* for Maria Fyodorovna, including one to celebrate the triumphant return of her son Alexander I after the war with Napoleon. But his most extraordinary performance took place in 1798, when for three hours he entertained the royal family with an endless series of changing theatrical sets on an otherwise empty stage.

Apart from commissioning some 37 monuments in the park, Maria Fyodorovna's role seems to have been that of plantsman, sending seeds back from Europe, ordering bulbs from Holland and England and trees from Finland and the Baltic states. Her fame as a connoisseur was such that George III sent her 126 exotic species from Kew Gardens, with their own personal gardener.

The **Private Garden** by the palace is separated from the rest by a wrought-iron fence and can only be visited from the palace. Its formal beds were designed by Cameron, who was also called back to the palace in 1800 to complete the garden with the addition of the **Pavilion of the Three Graces**. The statue by Triscorni that it shelters, in homage to Canova, shows Joy, Flowering and Brilliance stretching to hold a vase aloft. During the 1941 evacuation, the statue was buried nearby at a depth of five metres by a team of women. When the Nazis arrived, they noticed that the earth was disturbed and dug down three metres before deciding that the Russians were just trying to waste their time.

Looking from the palace, two pavilions divide the space to the right of the Triple Lime Alley. First comes Cameron's romantic **Aviary**, draped in vines. Royal parties would eat here to the accompaniment of birdsong. Beyond it and surrounded by a labyrinth is the **Rossi Pavilion**, which though designed by Rossi was only erected in 1914 to house a statue of Maria Fyodorovna. The alley culminates in a **Monument to the Defenders of Pavlovsk**, all those people who lost their lives clearing the park of mines after the war (see p.150).

Beyond the monument the **Rose Pavilion** has been rebuilt to Voronykhin's original plans, unfortunately not including the Aeolian harps that were built into the window frames, allowing the wind to play music to the assembled company. Silk roses and laurels hang in garlands across the ceiling of the main ballroom. Beyond it one of Gonzaga's most ambitious pieces of landscaping, the **Circle of White Birches**, was replanted after the war and is now thriving. Closer to the monument is the rustic looking **Dairy**, with its tiled inner sanctum. In Maria Fyodorovna's day there was always a samovar of cold fresh milk awaiting passers-by.

Beyond the dairy is an old farm stable from which horses can be 'rented' for an hour or two, or, if you want to feel more à la Russe, you can be driven around the park in a horse and cart. The Old Woods and New Woods on the banks of the Slavyanka are dotted with monuments erected by Maria Fyodorovna to her parents and to her husband. The star at the centre of the Old Woods is presided over by bronze statues of Apollo and the Muses. Back towards the palace from the Dairy, the **Great Circles** were laid out by Brenna, who also built the long staircase sweeping down towards the river. The sculptures at the centre of the formal parterre represent Peace, with a lion, and Justice, brandishing a sword.

Some of the most accessible park architecture sits on the banks of the Slavyanka close to the palace. Both the **Apollo Colonnade** and the **Temple of Friendship** were designed by Cameron, while the Visconti and the Centaur Bridges were built by Voronykhin. With its towering sculpture of Apollo and the tumble-down cascade beneath it, the colonnade was perfected by nature in 1817, when a landslide took part of the round portico with it, leaving the structure in a state of romantic ruin. It was Maria Fyodorovna's good judgement that it should not be repaired. The monumental round Temple of Friendship was the first building Cameron erected in the park, in 1782. Both Maria Fyodorovna and Paul intended the beautiful Doric building as a thank-you to Catherine the Great, for lending them her architect, and hoped that its theme might encourage a rapprochement between mother and son. However Catherine seems to have been oblivious to their intentions, and though she admired the building she thought it rather dark inside.

Forty-five kilometres southwest of St Petersburg, Gatchina is the furthest and least visited of all the restored royal palace estates. With its fortress-like exterior, it has been associated with the military since Grand Duke Paul, emperor-in-waiting, took out his frustration drilling a private army of 2,000 soldiers here in the late 18th century. After the Nazi destruction of the palace, the building was shored up and occupied by the Soviet military who did little to help the fabric of the building. They were finally dislodged in 1977, though there are still barracks in the neighbourhood. Restoration of the enormous and rather forbidding structure, containing a total of 500 rooms, began at once, but so far only seven rooms have opened to the public, though a handful of others are nearing completion. *Open 10am–6pm; closed Mon and first Tues of the month.*

Gatchina's park is vast and delightfully dishevelled, with paths weaving between its Silver, White and Black Lakes. Its principal designers were a pair of Englishmen, who went by the fitting names of Mr Bush and Mr Sparrow. Two garden pavilions to look out for are on or near the White Lake. The round Temple of Venus, on the Island of Venus, is sometimes used as a venue for summer concerts. Above it, not far from the Dubok Café, is the deceptive Birch Cabin (Beryozovy Domik). Behind a classical portico stands what looks like an enormous pile of logs with a door in it. Once inside, you find yourself in a room almost as grand as those in the palace.

Getting There and Around

Hourly trains leave Baltic Station (Baltisky Vokzal) for Gatchina. The palace is five minutes' walk down an avenue of trees behind the station building. The town of Gatchina lies on the far side of the park, beyond the Dubok Café, and is served by a no.26 minibus which runs to and from Ⓜ Moskovskaya on Moskovsky Prospekt.

lunch/cafés

The only place to eat on the estate is at the **Dubok Café**, Prospekt Oktyabr 2A, ✆ 8-271 15959. To get there take the bridge between the Black and Silver Lakes (to the right as you look from the palace out over the garden), walk past a green wooden building and up through the trees past a series of dry ponds. The food is well-prepared and tasty, and just as hearty as you would expect from a country inn. Ask for the speciality *myasa Gatchini*, a tender piece of beef in a kind of Stroganoff sauce. *Open 12 noon–11pm; closed 5–6pm.*

Sitting on the banks of Black Lake, the village of Khotchino was first mentioned in the 15th century. After Peter the Great created St Petersburg, he granted the obscure farmstead now known as Gatchina to his favourite sister, Natalya. In the

1760s Catherine the Great bought it for her lover Grigory Orlov, who was delighted with its rural setting, surrounded by good hunting ground and a considerable distance from the ceremony and intrigues of the court. On a high bluff above Silver Lake, he commissioned Antonio Rinaldi, author of Catherine's Chinese Palace at Oranienbaum, to build him a castle in the European idiom, far removed from the brick and stucco porticoed buildings that had become the Russian norm. Rinaldi, who had worked on similar buildings in Italy, and studied English castles during his travels, created an austere central block from local yellowish limestone, broken only by slim pilasters and rectangular windows and ornamented on two corners by towers. Curving single-storey arcades ran on either side of the building to kitchen and stable blocks. The building was completed in 1781, two years before the death of Orlov, whereupon Catherine bought it back from his family for one and a half million roubles and gave it to her 30-year-old son and heir Paul. He usually hated any place associated with his mother's lovers; but though Orlov had killed Paul's father, he had always been careful to treat Paul with sympathy and to spend time with the lonely young man. Paul fell immediately for the solid charms of Gatchina. By the time he had established his own mini-empire on the estate, guarded by sentries and shot through with militarism, Paul felt the palace was not grand enough to serve as the royal palace, and brought the Florentine architect Vincenzo Brenna over from his palace at Pavlovsk. As well as adding a second storey to the curved wings of the palace and a third to the central block, Brenna also raised the height of the two towers and dug a moat round the building. Inside, rooms decorated with rococo flourishes by Rinaldi, fine for the empress's lover, were not serious enough for her heir, and Brenna redecorated many in the weighty self-important style of Imperial Rome. Sadly Gatchina drove Paul further from his loyal wife Maria Fyodorovna, who loved Pavlovsk, the palace they had created together, better.

Apart from Alexander III, Paul's successors were not keen on Gatchina, though Nicholas I commissioned new building on the wings and a new suite of living rooms in the right-hand wing (as you look at the palace from the train station). It was here that Alexander III and his family, including the last tsar, came to live immediately after the assassination of his father had thrust him on to the throne. Alexander III, an arch-reactionary, was terrified of the revolutionary elements that he felt were running wild in society, and felt secure behind the quasi-fortified walls. For the first two years of his reign he lived here almost continuously, venturing to St Petersburg only for receptions and balls, and sometimes dressed like a peasant, stalking deer with his children in the park, chopping wood and shovelling snow.

Only the 18th-century state rooms of the palace are currently open to the public, and most of what you see dates to Brenna's redecoration, though glimpses of Rinaldi's decorative touch are visible in most rooms too.

*Arriving at the great, brooding palace from the train station, you find your-
self dwarfed in its gravel courtyard.*

Here, Paul used to drill his troops, with the aid of a cane with a watch embedded in
its handle. His two thousand strong private army was dressed in Prussian uniforms
and wigs, so that with the European-looking castle in the background visitors often
remarked that Paul's Gatchina felt nothing like Russia. A snub-nosed sculpture of
the monarch surveys his domain to this day. On the ground floor, Gatchina's
famous collection of weaponry is once again displayed in one of the curving wings.

If you are lucky you may be allowed to visit the long underground tunnel which
runs from the castle to a grotto on the edge of Silver Lake. Use was famously made
of it by the Prime Minister of the provisional government in 1917, Alexander
Kerensky, who escaped to Gatchina from the Winter Palace on the night of the
October Revolution, only to avoid a revolutionary mob here six days later by fleeing
down the corridor disguised as a sailor.

*The other rooms which have been restored are the state rooms used by
Paul and his family on the first floor.*

At the top of the stairs you enter the empty green and white space of the **Ante-
room** in which guests would sit waiting a summons from Paul. The military
symbolism of the reliefs on the walls and the ceiling were added by Brenna, but the
floors and doors are the designs of Rinaldi, executed again during the post-war
restoration. In their task, Gatchina's restorers were greatly helped by an intricate
series of watercolours of the interiors executed by Luigi Premazzi and Edward Hau
in the 1870s and early 1880s. A small lobby off the Ante-room acquaints you with
images of the palace's two creative spirits—Rinaldi and Brenna—to personalize the
competitive harmony between their two styles which seems embodied in the place.

To the left of the Ante-room the geometric world of Imperial Rome is evoked in the
Dining Room, with its pairs of white Carrara marble columns topped by full
Corinthian capitals and classical reliefs. Everything, including the stern doors and
floor, was designed by Brenna to provide a suitable environment for Paul's serious
pre-parade breakfasts. The cooks would bring the dishes from the kitchen and lay
them out behind the low marble balustrade, now occupied by a statue of Eros.
From here guards bore the dishes to their boss in a time-honoured and pompous
ritual. Musicians played from the area round the balustrade and if anyone made a
slip, woe betide them. Paul's punishments were summary and brutal. On a bad day
an officer could be exiled to Siberia for wearing his hat at the wrong angle.

Also looking out over the palace garden to the lake is **Paul's Throne Room**, rather
small considering the emperor's pretensions, but heavily gilded to make up for its
lack of size. Brenna designed the room around three of the many French tapestries
that Louis XVI had presented to the Grand Prince in Paris in 1782. Opposite one
another are portrayals of the animals and people of Asia, and over the mantelpiece,

itself set with semi-precious stones, the fertility goddess Ceres represents summer. Notice how the swags in the tapestry have been continued in the relief decoration in the rest of the room, and how the motif of the dog is repeated in the clock beneath.

The most recently opened room is the **Raspberry Parlour**, whose name and décor are based on the magnificent French tapestries that adorn its walls. In 1782 Louis XIV gave Paul and Maria Fyodorovna three tapestries from a cycle illustrating *Don Quixote*, all of which originally hung here. Probably the most valuable Gobelins in Russia, they were evacuated before the war, but so far only two have been returned, causing internecine war in the normally respectful conservation world. The third hangs in the library at Paul's other palace, Pavlovsk, whose own tapestries were sold by Stalin's government in 1929–30 and are now in the Getty Museum in California. Maria Fyodorovna's **Throne Room** is also sometimes known as the Picture Hall, for obvious reasons. An imperial dictat from her husband ruled that, while his throne could rest on a platform with three or eight steps, hers must be no more than a single step off the ground.

The last room is the **White Ball Room**, the largest in the palace, with an exceptional toffee-coloured floor. Beneath its floral patterns, the restorers have used the grain of the wood and its variety of tones to give an illusion of depth to the surface. Rinaldi's *scagliola* architraves and the plaster high-reliefs over the doors are boldly exuberant, as is his moulding round the ceiling, while Brenna's relief-strewn walls work to calm the room down. Together, their work is the embodiment of the transition between Baroque and neoclassicism—classical pilasters are surrounded by swags and other Baroque details.

> *The last part of the tour of the palace takes place on the second floor, which was turned into exhibition rooms as early as the 1880s.*

The second room contains portraits of a number of Gatchina's inhabitants. Grigory Orlov is resplendent in a foppish pink embroidered silk top, beside his mistress the Empress Catherine who often visited him here, calling him her 'Gatchina landlord'. On the second wall you will find Paul's wife, Maria Fyodorovna.

In the third room you can get acquainted with the family of Nicholas I. His favourite daughter Alexandra, who died of tuberculosis, lives on in a posthumous portrait which shows her in a white lacy dress holding a pink rose. In the background you can see the Alexander Palace at Tsarskoye Selo where she died. Highlights from the rest include marble relief portraits of Catherine the Great and snub-nosed Paul by Marie Collot, and a room of art inspired by or made specially for Gatchina, including a magnificent bureau inlaid with views of the palace. The doll, called Pandora, gives a clue as to how St Petersburg's first ladies kept abreast of European fashions in the 18th century. It was one of many sent to Maria Fyodorovna from the couture houses of Paris, modelling a dress which she could then order if she liked it. The entire transaction was carried out by post.

Food and Drink

The outside world gets a confused picture of the Russians and their food. The Japanese even made a diplomatic *faux pas* over it, initially citing the fatness of the average Russian as a reason for refusing the country food aid in 1992. The queues outside the shops, tales of meagre supplies and the *matrioshka*-shaped matriarchs simply don't add up, until you realize that an unhealthy 70% of the average Russian diet comes from starch and sugar. Cholesterol is taken to be an eccentric western obsession, odes are written on the virtues of *sala*, pure pork fat, few people believe that vodka could possibly be fattening, and once you reach 40 it is thought perfectly healthy to put on a couple of stone. This cultural climate, combined with the geographical one, adds up to an unhealthy diet.

Intourist, the former tourism monopolists, provided barely adequate meals for the groups of foreigners they herded through the country, and certainly left no room for choice. Christopher Hope described the restaurant scene in 1990 as 'the unspendable in pursuit of the inedible'.

He wouldn't know the place today. You can eat Georgian or Korean, cheaply or at great expense, quickly or at leisure, with or without music. There are literally hundreds of eateries to choose from, and with careful planning you need not eat a bad meal in the city.

Restaurants

It was the legalization of co-operative restaurants back in 1986 that began the surge in good food outside the home in the Soviet Union. In the less commercial establishments it can be hard deciphering the menu when you get there, though it is well worth the effort. Ignore the fact that many of them are called 'café'—the word for a place that majors in coffee is normally *kofeinaya*.

If you are not feeling adventurous you will fall victim to overpriced hotel restaurants. In the new joint ventures these offer world-class imported seafood, the very best in Russian *nouvelle cuisine* and American steak-house fare. Lesser hotels still have mediocre 'soviet'-style restaurants for the nostalgic, and often rent out space to private restaurants too. A number of the huge state restaurants lumber on, serving a well-worn combination of a Russian menu, a 'live' band and a more or less tasteful floor-show. Where groups of ordinary folk would once spin out an evening amid a growing forest of bottles to celebrate a birthday or anniversary, today only tourists and the hoods and *biznissmeny* of the new Russia can afford it.

Fast food and genuine cafés tend to be listed, where appropriate, in the walks. Some of their signs are instantly familiar—McDonald's and Pizza Hut—others have to be carefully deciphered. Look out for those advertising the following:

блинная, serving sweet and savoury *blini* (pancakes); пельменная, offering *pelmeni* (meaty dumplings with a dollop of sour cream or tomato sauce); пирожковая, with its stock of meat and vegetable-filled pasties; or мороженое, where welcome Russian ice cream is dispensed.

New restaurants are still opening, so for a full and up-to-date list you should get hold of the latest edition of the *Travellers' Yellow Pages*. Those listed below are a personal selection.

Russian, Caucasian and Central Asian Food and Menus

Despite the poverty of the Russian diet, exacerbated during the Soviet period by a piecemeal distribution system across a neglected network of roads, the Russians certainly know how to eat. A birthday celebration entails months of saving up sugar, meat, fish and alcohol, found at cheap prices earlier in the year, and turning it all into a traditional four-course feast, which also serves as the basis for menus in Russian restaurants. First come the *zakuski*: cold meats and fishes, caviar, cheese, salads and pickles, warm pancakes and mushrooms baked in sour cream. For centuries foreigners have been caught out thinking that this is the whole meal, indulging to the hilt and then being faced with soup, a main course accompanied by potatoes, and a pudding. The secret, tried and tested in the long dark northern winters, is to take your time, a practice at which the Russians are masters.

Within the ex-Soviet Union, the Georgians were renowned for their hospitality and the profusion of their feasts. True to this reputation, a lot of the very best food in St Petersburg is served in Georgian restaurants. While the menu follows the same basic four-course form, the *zakuski* are more elaborate, involving spicy aubergine and sheep and goats' cheese; soups are mutton- and bean-based, and often highly spiced. Meat, particularly poultry, is set off by sauces made with nuts and coriander, or stuffed with rice into peppers and vine leaves, and puddings are laced with nuts and honey. The Central Asian republics of the former Soviet Union also have their restaurants, a mixed bunch at best, distinguished by quantity rather than quality of *plov* (a rice, meat and vegetable paella) and *shashliki*, kebabs.

A full list of items you are likely to find on restaurant menus can be found in Language (*see* pp.299–302). If you are offered any of the following do not refuse.

Russian delicacies: *gribi so smetanoy* (mushrooms in sour cream), *blini s'ikroy* (pancakes and caviar), *okroshka* (cold summer vegetable soup made with *kvas*, a fermented bread drink), good *borshch* (beetroot soup), *kulebiaka* (salmon pie), *pelmeni* (meat dumplings) and *pirozhki* (pies—often cabbage or, ideally, mushroom).

Georgian delicacies: *khachapuri* (cheesy bread), *satsivi* (walnut and coriander sauce), *khinkali* (juicy meat dumplings with a spicy tomato sauce), and any *zakuska* with *baklazhan* (aubergine).

Prices

Payment in restaurants is safest in cash, though most of the smarter establishments accept credit cards. Prices range from outrageous to ludicrously little. The price categories below apply to three- or four-course evening meals (depending whether you are eating from a western or Russian menu) with alcohol, per head.

very expensive	∞∞∞∞∞	over $70
expensive	∞∞∞∞	$40–$70
moderate	∞∞∞	$20–$40
inexpensive	∞∞	$10–$20 (closer to $20)
cheap	∞	under $10

Note that many establishments offer a set lunch, which they call a 'business lunch', at a set price, often around $12 a head.

Reserving Tables and Opening Hours

Always make a reservation for the evening. Even if the restaurant is not full you may be turned away without one. You should also reserve tables in the more popular places for lunch. Many restaurants only accept evening reservations from noon on the day. Where booking policy is even more idiosyncratic it is spelled out below. The majority of places are open from about noon to midnight, with an hour's break somewhere between 4 and 6pm. Again, only variations on this are noted below.

tipping

Many restaurants now add a 10–20% service charge to their bills, leaving it for you to decide if the service merited something on top. If a service charge is not included, good service should be generously rewarded.

Vegetarians

It is not easy avoiding meat and fish in Russia, and to be certain that flesh doesn't pass your lips you will be restricted to a monotonous diet of bread, tomato and cucumber salads and mushrooms in sour cream. What is billed as *salat* never has a lettuce leaf in it, and *stolichny salat* is a concoction of potatoes, mayonnaise and chicken. Almost all soups, except summer *okroshka*, are based on a meat stock, and only in the most expensive restaurants will you find an alternative vegetarian main course. Two pieces of advice: choose Georgian restaurants and concentrate on their vegetable *zakuski*, and visit the cities in summer when vegetables are more plentiful and you can buy raspberries and other fruits on the street. Those who eat fish will be better off. *Bliny* with caviar and pickled herring are offered as *zakuski*, and there is usually a fish main course, often sturgeon, to follow.

Despite their reputation for drinking, Russian bar culture is surprisingly undeveloped. In winter, the search for oblivion takes place at home, round the kitchen table, and in summer cans of beer and bottles are consumed on park benches and in other open spaces. Bars are either stygian dumps where regulars bring their own fold-up milk cartons to drink from, or hotel piano bars serving French champagne at some $100 a bottle. At the former (normally signed БАР or РЮМОЧНАЯ) cozy, vinous friendships often lurch rapidly into punch-throwing, and the only women to be found are haggard alcoholics. Unless you're with a local, these haunts are probably best avoided, except by novelists researching a Dostoyevskian opus. Recently, a number of better-quality watering holes have opened up, independent of the hotels. The list below concentrates on these, and highlights the better hotel bars, though you will find somewhere to drink in all of the cities' hotels.

What to Drink?

Vodka (*see* pp.56–7) is nothing like as exclusive as you might think. As well as the 'little water', you will regularly be offered Russian and imported beer, wines from Georgia and Moldova, Armenian and Azerbaijani cognac, sweet wines known as *portvein* and a colourful host of imported liqueurs. Be very wary if you buy on the street or in kiosks—mercantile morality is non-existent and lethal home-made spirits (*samogon*) find their way into bottles, disguised behind innocuous labels. Buy familiar brands, check that tops are secure and look through the bottle to see how the label has been stuck on. Straight, horizontal lines of glue tend to mean factory production. More elaborate patterns should be avoided. Another obvious tell-tale sign is Spanish wine labels on bottles with plastic (*i.e.* Georgian or Russian) tops.

Long before the vine found commercial purchase on French soil, it grew on the slopes of the Caucasus, and the Georgian wines can be delicious. Discard the prevailing western prejudice for dry wines, since the most rounded Georgian wines are rich, red and semi-sweet—look out for *Kindzmarauli*, with its deep velvety fruit, or *Akhasheni* which is less rich but much easier to find. The former holds the dubious distinction of being known as Stalin's favourite. Of Georgia's dry table wine the white *Tsinandali* is drinkable and oaky, while *Mukuzani*, *Napareuli* and *Saperavi* are all dependable reds, the latter slightly rougher. Russian, or Soviet as it is still often labelled, champagne is readily available and cheap. It comes brut (*brut*), dry (*sukhoye*), semi-dry (*polu-sukhoye*), semi-sweet (*polu-sladkoye*) and sweet (*sladkoye*). Stick to the first two or three, and don't expect finest Epernay at these prices.

No drinking session is complete without a handful of Russian toasts. Give full rein to wishful thinking and sentimentality and you will get along fine. The most common toast is a simple *Na Zdaroviye*, 'your good health', which given the amount you are likely to drink is only the shadowiest hope.

Listings

Restaurants and bars are listed geographically. In the main part of the city south of the Neva they are split between those inside the Fontanka River and those beyond it. The rest of the city divides into Vasilievsky Island, the Petrograd Side and the Islands, and the Vyborg Side.

Breakfast

Angleterre, Isaakiyevskaya Ploshchad (entrance closest to St Isaac's Cathedral), ✆ 210 5032. Hotel restaurant offers an all-you-can-eat buffet, including delicious *aladi* pancakes. *Open from 7.30.* Ⓜ Sennaya Ploshchad

Astoria, Ul. Bolshaya Morskaya 39 (entrance on Isaakiyevskaya Ploshchad), ✆ 210 5757. Another hotel restaurant next to the Astoria, above, also offering a sumptuous buffet to start the day. *Open from 7.30.* Ⓜ Sennaya Ploshchad

Evropeisky Restaurant, Grand Hotel Europe, Ul. Mikhailovskaya 1/7, ✆ 329 6000. Serves a much more expensive buffet breakfast in its elegant hall. *Open 7–10 Mon–Sat; jazz brunch Sun 12–3.* Ⓜ Nevsky Prospekt

Inside the Fontanka

ꙮꙮ **Evropeisky Restaurant**, Grand Hotel Europe, Ul. Mikhailovskaya 1/7, ✆ 329 6000, is reckoned to be the best in town by those who can afford it. Proceedings are very formal beneath the towering glass ceiling of its Art Nouveau dining room; the service is exemplary, the fillet of salmon stuffed with cream cheese melt-in-the-mouth. *Open 7pm–11pm, Sun 10–4 for an extravagant champagne and jazz brunch.* Ⓜ Nevsky Prospekt

ꙮꙮ **Dvorianskoye Gnezdo (The Noble Nest)**, Ul. Dekabristov 21, ✆ 312 3205, ✉ 312 0911. To make a real night of it, try this restaurant in a restored garden pavilion. The food and surroundings are outstanding but the service is slow. There is live classical music from 8pm. Book in advance, and dress smartly. *Open 11am–midnight.* Ⓜ Sennaya Ploshchad

ꙮꙮ **Taleon Club**, Nab. Reki Moiki 59, ✆ 315 7645, *open 12noon–6am* (bar), 3am (restaurant). The fantastically restored Eliseyev House has become St Petersburg's most expensive restaurant, the haunt of the city's élite, with great wine and food. Ⓜ Nevsky Prospekt

ꙮꙮ **Kochubey**, Konnogvardeysky Bulvar, ✆ 210 9615; *open 1pm–midnight.* Good German-style food. Ⓜ Nevsky Prospekt or Sennaya Pl.

ꙮꙮ **Restaurant St Petersburg**, Nab. Kanala Griboyedova 5, ✆ 314 4947. A spotless tourist restaurant, with unusually imaginative Russian cuisine and a historic (and histrionic) cabaret from 7pm, followed by Russian folk music. Candle-light helps to disguise the artificiality of the wooden-boothed intimacy. Well-behaved staff, if a bit slow, but very touristy. *Open noon–4am. Business lunch served until 5pm.* Ⓜ Nevsky Prospekt

ꙮꙮ **Rossi's**, Grand Hotel Europe, Ul. Mikhailovskaya 1/7, ✆ 329 6000, is an Italian restaurant serving good continental food, from steaks and hamburgers to seafood and pasta. Good service. *Open noon–11pm.*

◍ Nevsky Prospekt

∞∞∞ **Caviar Bar**, Grand Hotel Europe, Ul. Mikhailovskaya 1/7, ✆ 329 6000, has delicious food accompanied by a balalaika group from 8pm. A real treat, if expensive. *Open 5pm–11pm.*

◍ Nevsky Prospekt

∞∞∞ **Chopsticks**, Grand Hotel Europe, Ul. Mikhailovskaya 1/7, ✆ 329 6000, serves the best Chinese food in the city, and by far the most expensive, prepared by the Hong Kong-trained chef. *Open daily noon–11pm.*

◍ Nevsky Prospekt

∞∞∞ **Graf Suvorov**, Ul. Lomonosova 6, ✆ 315 4328. Five-star Russian-European cuisine, with a good choice of seafood, at one of the best little restaurants in the city. *Open 12 noon–2am.* The attached café is cheaper. ◍ Gostiny Dvor

∞∞∞ **Tandoor**, Voznesensky Prospekt 2, ✆ 312 3886, is an Indian restaurant in the centre of town, a godsend for vegetarians, specializing in tandoori-cooked dishes. *Open 12 noon–11pm.*

◍ Nevsky Prospekt

∞∞∞ **Bistro Le Français**, Ul. Galernaya 20, ✆ 315 2465. Parisian-style café-restaurant with red checked tablecloths, a bar and mouth-watering French food, including a good cheeseboard. The chef is actually French. *Open 11am –1am.* ◍ Nevsky Prospekt

∞∞∞ **Sakura**, Nab. Kanala Griboyedeva 12, ✆ 315 9474, is a good Japanese restaurant in a terrific location. *Open noon–11pm.* ◍ Nevsky Prospekt

∞∞∞ **Adam Ant**, Nab. Moiki 72, ✆ 311 5575; *open 1pm–midnight.* European cuisine for smart post-*perestroika* Russians. ◍ Nevsky Pr./Sennaya Pl.

∞∞∞ **Federico Fellini**, Ul. Malaya Konyushennaya 4/2, ✆ 311 5078; *open 12 noon–1am.* St Petersburg's first and only cinema restaurant: each room is decorated in a different cinematic theme, with the waiting staff dressed accordingly.

◍ Nevsky Prospekt

∞∞∞ **Kioto**, Naberezhnaya Reki Fontanki 77, ✆ 310 2547. Japanese cuisine including a full sushi bar, cooked by a Russian chef who trained in Japan. Business lunches served until 4pm. *Open 1–midnight.*

◍ Sennaya Ploshchad

∞∞∞ **1001 Nights**, Millionnaya Ul. 21/6 (entrance on Zaporozhsky Pereulok), ✆ 312 2265. A fun, recently redecorated Uzbek restaurant which serves belly-dancers and snake charmers with your *plov* and *manti*. *Noon–11pm.*

◍ Nevsky Prospekt

∞∞∞ **1913**, Ul. Dekabristov 2/13, ✆ 315 5148, is a clean, air-conditioned Russian restaurant with reliably good food like potato pancakes with sour cream. *Open 12 noon–1am.*

◍ Nevsky Pr./Sennaya Pl.

∞∞∞ **Nevsky 40**, Nevsky Prospekt 40, ✆ 311 9066. Two restaurants in this German establishment serve the same microwave menu, but for aesthetics choose the recently restored turn-of-the-century chinoiserie tea room, with its fine silk embroidered panels of birds. Bizarre menu stretches itself too wide, with herring and sauerkraut competing with Malaysian *nasi goreng*, and tastes of nothing much as a result. *Open 12 noon–12 midnight.*

◍ Gostiny Dvor

∞∞∞ **Metropol**, Sadovaya Ul. 22, ✆ 310 1845. If you absolutely must have a Soviet nostalgia trip do it here, in the oldest restaurant in the city, which first opened its doors in 1898. Stick to *zakuski* and be warned, it has the worst food in the city and you can't talk when the music gets going.

Ⓜ Gostiny Dvor

∞ **Milano**, Karavannaya Ul. 8, ✆ 314 7348, is a rather nice typical Italian restaurant run by a charming Milanese. Daily specials available. *Open 12 noon–midnight.*

Ⓜ Gostiny Dvor

∞ **Senat Bar**, Galernaya Ul. 1–3, ✆ 314 9253. A cavernous basement joint with low lighting, decorated with freshly commissioned paintings of the 18th-century city and plaster busts. Mostly a drinking haunt; there is a small restaurant although eating here feels rather claustrophobic. Business lunch 1pm–5pm. *Open noon–5am.*

Ⓜ Nevsky Prospekt

∞ **Winter Garden**, Astoria Hotel, Isaakiyevskaya Ploshchad (entrance furthest from cathedral), ✆ 210 5815. There is an old-world charm about this conservatory restaurant, where a grand piano tinkles in the background and traditional Russian food is served on pre-war plates. A great place to while away the afternoon over buttery *blini*, *borshch* and beef Stroganoff. Business lunch Mon–Fri 12pm–3pm, brunch served on Sundays. *Open noon–11pm.* Ⓜ Sennaya Ploshchad

∞ **Nikolai**, Dom Arkhitektorov, Ul. Bolshaya Morskaya 52, ✆ 311 1402. The restaurant in this grand town house was once the exclusive preserve of the Union of Architects. Since opening its doors to all comers, it has become one of the most popular dining-rooms in the city. It's not the food that attracts, nor the erratic supply of alcohol or the lack of English spoken by the staff. It's the ambience

in the two rooms—one plastered with dark embossed leather wallpaper and quasi-historical paintings, the other airy and lightly painted. The menu is short and verbal, and the main courses usually include a choice of meat or fish, both of which often turn up *pod mayonaisom*, baked under mayonnaise. *Open Mon–Fri 12 noon–11pm.* There's also the **Bar Matador** downstairs, *open Fri and Sat 3pm–11pm.*

Ⓜ Sennaya Ploshchad

∞ **Literaturnoye Café**, Nevsky Prospekt 18, ✆ 312 6057, is ideal for those who like rowing with waiters. Whether by surly service or over-charging, they are sure to infuriate you in their frilly shirts and 19th-century frock-coats. Only the endless wave of tourists, drawn by the fact that Pushkin set out for his fatal duel from a completely different establishment on this spot, allows them to get away with it. Saving graces? Delicate metal tree chandeliers and live classical music downstairs. *Open 11am–1am.* Ⓜ Nevsky Prospekt

∞ **Assambleya**, Ul. Bolshaya Konyushennaya 13, ✆ 314 1537, serves good and unpretentious Russian food very slowly in its coldly decorated interior. *Open noon–11pm.*

Ⓜ Nevsky Prospekt

∞ **Mezzanine Café**, Grand Hotel Europe, Ul. Mikhailovskaya 1/7, ✆ 329 6000, is a good meeting place serving tea and cakes and offering a bar. *Open 10am–10pm.*

Ⓜ Nevsky Prospekt

∞ **Sadko**, Grand Hotel Europe, Ul. Mikhailovskaya 1/7, ✆ 329 6000, has a simple blackboard menu which changes daily, offering a choice of three dishes for each course. By day the view of life on Nevsky Prospekt, just a pane of glass away, cannot be bettered. In the evenings they have live music and the joint gets considerably more lively. *Open noon–midnight.* Ⓜ Nevsky Prospekt

∞ **Le Chandeleur**, Ul. Bolshaya Konyushennaya 1, ✆ 314 8380, has pleasant French cuisine with good salad and crêpes for lunch. The live music (between 8pm and 11pm) gets loud, but it attracts a good crowd. *Open 11am–midnight.*

Ⓜ Nevsky Prospekt

∞ **Ket**, Karavannaya Ul. 24, ✆ 315 3900; *open 12 noon–11pm.* Good value and delicious Russian-European restaurant, popular with locals.

Ⓜ Nevsky Prospekt

∞ **Komandor**, Millionnaya Ul, 3, ✆ 325 7132/314 3256, offers European food in a good location, although the restaurant is a bit dark. There's live music in the evening, from 7 to 11. Business lunch for around $5. *Open 11am–2am.* **Café Anna** does fast food and snacks close by.

Ⓜ Gorkovskaya/Nevsky Prospekt

∞ **Patio Pizza**, 30 Nevsky Prospekt (next to Nevsky metro), and 182 Nevsky Prospekt, ✆ 271 7792. Great salad bar in a pizza parlour. *Open 12 noon–midnight.* Ⓜ Nevsky Prospekt

∞ **City Bar Kapella**, 2nd floor, Moika 20, ✆ 314 1037; *open 11am–midnight.* A fun, popular hang-out with a mixed crowd of students and musicians. An amusing American cook prepares good salads and other European dishes. Some outside tables for a sunny day. Ⓜ Nevsky Prospekt

∞ **Tchaika**, Kanala Griboyedova 14, ✆ 312 4631, is a German pub serving cold beer and snack food: burgers, frankfurters and so on. *Open 11am–3am.* Ⓜ Nevsky Prospekt

∞ **01**, Ul. Karavannaya 7, is a tiny restaurant serving plentiful food and alcohol. Soups and stews are particularly recommended, often laced with the southern flavour of coriander. Gets full and you can't reserve, so you just have to try your luck. Afternoon and early evening are best. *Open 12 noon–4pm,5–11pm.* Ⓜ Gostiny Dvor

∞ **Idiot Café**, Nab. Reki Moiki, 82, ✆ 315 1675, offers Russian food and good vegetarian options: naturally, it's a popular hang-out for foreign students, with a wide selection of English books lying around for casual reading. Brunch is served at weekends. Unusually, there's a non-smoking room. Ⓜ Nevsky Prospekt

∞ **Old Café**, 108 Nab. Reki Fontanki, ✆ 316 5111; *open noon–11pm.* A tiny, atmospheric Russian restaurant with only a few tables, so book in advance if you can. Ⓜ Nevsky Pr.

∞ **Sevillia**, Ul. Malaya Morskaya 7, ✆ 315 5371. Spanish restaurant close to Nevsky Prospekt, serving delicious food, with an authentic Latin feel to the décor. There's Spanish dancing in the evenings but it costs more.

Ⓜ Nevsky Prospekt

◊ **Café St Petersburg**, Kanala Griboyedova 5. Round the side of the restaurant of the same name (above), this very popular small café serves decent homemade food, most of it laid out on the counter so you can choose. there's outdoor seating in summer. *Open noon–9pm.*

Ⓜ Nevsky Prospekt

◊ **House of Scholars Café**, Dvortsovaya Nab. 26. A convenient café for a quick breather from the Hermitage. Walk across the hall, past the huge chinoiserie urns, and through the door beyond the grand staircase. Before the Revolution, this Renaissance-style palace belonged to the Grand Duke Vladimir, and it was here that members of the Romanov family gathered to write a letter of warning to Tsar Nicholas II in 1916.

Ⓜ Nevsky Prospekt

Bars

Most of the places to drink have been mentioned above since they also offer food. Any café which is not specifically described as without alcohol will also serve you a drink. In addition however, there is a very dull, expensive bar in the Astoria Hotel (St Isaac's Cathedral entrance) and a more lively, more expensive one in the Grand Hotel Europe.

Shamrock, 27 Dekabristov Ul., ℗ 219 4625; *open 12 noon–2pm*. A Russian take on the Irish pub!

Beyond the Fontanka River

∞∞ **Afrodite**, Nevsky Prospekt 86, ℗ 275 7620, has the strange feeling of being part of a chain of seafood restaurants, perhaps because of the colourful menu. Its location in the basement of what was once one of the many Yusupov palaces and is now the actors' union, means that at weekends you can continue the evening dancing upstairs. *Open 12 noon–1am.*

Ⓜ Mayakovskaya

∞∞ **Izmailovsky Dvor**, 13-aya Krasnoarmeiskaya g.1, ℗ 251 3076, is a restaurant-café with an intimate interior decorated in white, serving European and Russian food. *Open noon–midnight.*

Ⓜ Tekhnologichesky Institute

∞∞ **Club Ambassador**, Nab. Reki Fontanki 14, ℗ 272 3791. Extremely expensive, clubby restaurant with an ever-changing short menu and one of the most romantic mock 17th-century vaulted Russian interiors, with live music from 7pm to add to the atmosphere. Service in the candle-lit rooms is immaculate. *Open 1pm–midnight.*

Ⓜ Nevsky Prospekt

∞∞ **Troika**, Zagorodny Prospekt 27, ℗ 113 5343, the self-proclaimed 'Moulin Rouge of St Petersburg', is the more traditional place to go for a slap-up meal and opulent floor-show. There's live music from 8.30. *Open noon–1am.* There's also the **Beer Bar** next door, *open 4pm–5am.*

Ⓜ Pushkinskaya

∞∞ **Imperial**, Nevsky Palace Hotel, Nevsky Prospekt, 57, ℗ 275 2001, situated on the second floor of the hotel, with a view onto Nevsky Prospekt. The restaurant offers a 'Swedish table' (smorgasbord) in the evenings and an orchestra from 7pm till 11pm. There's a very good Sunday brunch served 12–4. *Open for breakfast 7am–10.30am and dinner 7pm–midnight.* Ⓜ Nevsky Prospekt

∞ **Café Ambassador**, Nab. Reki Fontanki 14, ℗ 272 9181. Deservedly popular thanks to its imaginative menu, huge main courses (including a good selection of salads) and unusually late hours. You may have to queue for a table. Place your order at the bar, pick up your own cutlery and cold dishes. The rest will be brought to you. Staff speak some English. *Open 1pm–5am.* Ⓜ Nevsky Prospekt

∞ **Pizza House**, Ul. Podolskaya 23, ℗ 316 2666, will do you grilled steak or Weiner Schnitzel as well as one of its 17 varieties of pizza (including some vegetarian options). As you might have gathered from this eclectic menu, they are not part of the huge American chain, but a Finnish-Russian joint venture. Call them on this number to order a delivery. *Open 12 noon–12 midnight.*

Ⓜ Tekhnologichesky Institute

Stroganov Dvor, courtyard of Stroganov Palace, ☏ 311 7297, offers a variety of snacks, soups, quiches and Russian and European main dishes, served rather slowly in a pleasant atmosphere with live music accompaniment. There's a crèche. *Open 10am–2am.* Ⓜ Nevsky Prospekt

Smolnensky Hotel, Tverskaya Ul. 22, ☏ 276 6217; *open 8am–10pm.* The Soviet-style décor of this well-located hotel directly opposite the Smolny complex will be familiar to fans of Cold War spy movies, but its clean restaurant offers a typical Russian menu. Ⓜ Chernyshevskaya

Café Rioni, Shpalernaya Ul. 24, ☏ 273 3261. Family-run restaurant serving the best Georgian food in the city. *Open weekdays 11am–11pm, Sat, Sun 1–11pm.* Ⓜ Chernyshevskaya

Zvezdachot, Ul. Marata 35, ☏ 164 7478. Down a few steps off busy Ul. Marata, you walk into this café-restaurant whose name means 'astrologer'. Book an astrological reading and get a personal horoscope along with the European-style cuisine. *Open 12 noon–11pm.* Ⓜ Vladimirskaya

Metekhi Café, Ul. Belinskovo 3. A good choice for vegetarians, this cheap Georgian restaurant often has salted cheese (like the Greek *halloumi*) called *sir suluguni*, and *lobio* (beans in a spicy tomato sauce). Add more heat with a judicious sprinkling of *adjika*, the pepper mix you will find on each table. If *khachapuri* is not on the menu, you can always buy it and bring it with you from **Vodi Lagidzi**, the café next door. *Open 11am–9pm.* Ⓜ Gostiny Dvor

Carrolls, corner of Ul. Rubinshteina and Nevsky Prospekt, is St Petersburg's first homegrown fast-food hamburger bar. It has the typical fast food menu (burgers, chicken, coleslaw), interior and smell. *Open 9am–11pm.*

Ⓜ Nevsky Prospekt

Three Bears, Ul. Furshtadtskaya 35, ☏ 272 3533. Small basement café with a wood interior, not far from the German and American consulates, serving Central Asian and Georgian food to the sometimes over-loud beat of MTV. The best place in this book to eat *plov*, the only thing to avoid is the sometimes overly greasy soup. Look over fellow diners shoulders to check. *Open 12 noon–11pm.*

Ⓜ Chernyshevskaya

Route 66, Stremyannaya Ul. 11, ☏ 311 2217, is a typical American diner located behind the Nevsky Palace Hotel. *Open 10am–8pm.*

Ⓜ Nevsky Prospekt

Café/Bar (unnamed), Ul. Saltikova-Schedrina 36, ☏ 272 0935; *open 12 noon–11pm.* For speedy service and a traditional Russian menu, try this courtyard bar with a choice of indoor or garden tables. Ⓜ Chernyshevskaya

Café Sunduk, Furshtadtskaya Ul. 42, ☏ 272 3100; *open daily 10am–11pm.* An atmospheric little café-bar with a couple of tables outside, serving food and freshly squeezed juices.

Ⓜ Chernyshevskaya

Bars

John Bull Pub, Nevsky Prospekt 79, ✆ 164 9877, is much as it suggests, an 'English pub' where you can consume draught beer in familiar saloon bar surroundings. Also serves a cold snack menu. *Open 12–12.* Ⓜ Mayakovskaya

Mollie's Irish Bar, Ul. Rubinshteina 36, ✆ 319 9768/314 9768. The drink, not the food, is the point of this busy and popular watering hole. *Open 11am–3am.*

Ⓜ Dostoyevskaya/Vladimirskaya

Beer Garden, Nevsky Prospekt 86, in the courtyard, is open 1pm–3am daily in the summer, serving snacks with beer.

Ⓜ Mayakovskaya

Vasilievsky Island

∞∞∞ **Academia**, 1st Birzhevoy Proezd, ✆ 327 8949; *open 12 noon–5am, with disco 9pm–12.30am; credit cards accepted.* Huge trendy delicious pizza restaurant, some tables outside.

∞∞∞ **Staraya Tamozhnya (The Old Custom House)**, Tamozhenny Per 1, Vasilievsky Island, ✆ 327 8980, offers 'French cuisine, English management'. It's situated in one of Peter the Great's bonded warehouses, under bare brick arches, with bar staff in customs uniform. The French chefs produce such classics as pea soup, sole meunière and 'surf and turf' as well as red or black caviar and oysters. There are two bars and a great choice of wines. Credit cards accepted. *Open 1pm–3am.*

Ⓜ Vasileostrovskaya

∞∞∞ **Kalinka**, Syezdovskaya Linea 9, ✆ 323 3718; *open 12 noon–11pm, no credit cards.* A fairly expensive, good three-star Russian/Georgian restaurant, warm and atmospheric with good service but very popular. There's a wolf at the door and a bear at the bar (stuffed, of course).

Ⓜ Vasileostrovskaya

∞∞∞ **Hotel Ship Peterhof**, Naberezhnaya Makarova, ✆ 325 8888, has a Russo-European restaurant, the **Svir**, whose chef delights in regular food festivals, featuring food from different countries. Ordering à la carte is distinctly expensive, but there is a good inexpensive set lunch. In the height of summer, the best place to eat is outside, at the grill bar on deck. Credit cards accepted.

Ⓜ Vasileostrovskaya

∞∞∞ **New Island Restaurant-Ship**, berthed at Rumyancevsky spusk (near where Universitetskaya Nab. meets the 1-aya Liniya of Vasilevsky Island), ✆ 963 6765. An unusual dining experience: French and Russian cuisine, featuring lots of seafood, served over the course of a 1½hr cruise along the Neva, with splendid views of much of historic St Petersburg including the Hermitage and St Isaac's Cathedral. In winter a free skating rink is established around the ship. Prices are wide-ranging: you could eat for under $10. Leaves at 2, 4, 6, 8 and 11pm; the 8pm dinner cruise is longer.

Ⓜ Vasileostrovskaya

∞∞ **Venetsia**, Ul. Korablestroiteley 21, ✆ 352 1432. If you happen to be nearby, patronize the rouble pizzeria here but leave the overpriced and under-imaginative Italian restaurant alone. Ⓜ Primorskaya plus tram (11 or 63) bus (41, 42 or 47) or trolleybus (10,10a and 46).

∞∞ **The Great Wall**, Sredny Prospekt 11, ✆ 323 2638. Reliable Chinese.

Ⓜ Vasileostrovskaya

Café Fregat, Bolshoi Prospekt 39/11-aya Liniya 14, is a long, thin, dark restaurant, with a plain Russian menu enlivened by daily specials and the rare opportunity to drink the late lamented Russian favourite, *kvas.*

Ⓜ Vasileostrovskaya

Petrograd Side

∞∞ **Russki Moderne**, Ul. Lenina 32, ✆ 230 8830. Russian/Georgian food served in a cosy interior. Food and service are fine and there's a piano player from 7pm. *Open 12 noon–11pm.*

Ⓜ Petrogradskaya and a 15min walk

∞∞ **Café Tet-a-Tet**, Bolshoi Prospekt 65, ✆ 232 7548, is best described as the most suitable restaurant in St Petersburg to make a proposal of marriage. The small Empire tables barely seat more than two, the tinkly piano music is just loud enough to camouflage your conversation from the other diners, the lighting is perfect. It serves Russian/European cuisine and offers a selection of Georgian wines. Best to book in advance. *Open 1pm–11pm.* Ⓜ Petrogradskaya

∞∞ **Pirosmani**, Bolshoi Prospekt 14, ✆ 235 6456. For a once in a lifetime experience, ask if you can dine at the table in the middle of the pond, and order a selection of starters. As is so often the case with Georgian food, these are better than the main courses. Even if you think you don't like semi-sweet wine, try the Georgian red, Kinsmarauli, Stalin's and everyone else's favourite. There's live music from 8pm. *Open 12 noon–11pm; reservations (a must) 2–5pm.*

Ⓜ Petrogradskaya
(The metro is at the far end of Bolshoi Prospekt, a considerable walk; we recommend a taxi.)

∞∞∞ **Austeria**, Peter and Paul Fortress, ✆ 238 4262. Set in the defensive outravelin of the fortress, this good Russian restaurant takes its name from the first hostelry that opened nearby in St Petersburg. The recent refurbishment reflects the high quality of the place. Wonderful views. *Open 12 noon–12 midnight.* Ⓜ Gorkovskaya

∞∞ **Zebra**, Kronverksky Prospekt 55, ✆ 232 9802, opposite the zoo, serves Russian food with a strong animal theme—ideal for children. *Open 10–10.* Ⓜ Gorkovskaya

∞∞ **Tbilisi**, Ul. Sytninskaya 10, ✆ 232 9391. This Georgian restaurant, with its elderly doorman in Georgian dress, is dark and well-designed for secret rendezvous and caucasian cabals in its nooks and crannies. Order *kharcho* and *khachaphuri* to start, and anything after that will be pure profit. The service is excellent and friendly and the food is very good. Reserve.

Ⓜ Gorkovskaya

∞∞ **Café Fortetsia**, Ul. Kuybysheva 7, ✆ 233 9468, is a small, louchely-upholstered Belgian joint venture serving good Russian food, seafood and salads. The private room and its perennial celebration is intriguing. *Open 12–11pm.* The café next door serves standard grilled chicken and so on (*open 11am–10pm*).

Ⓜ Gorkovskaya

∞∞ **Grand Café Antwerpen**, Kronverksky Prospekt 13/2, ✆ 233 9746, *open 1–11pm.* This sparkling clean restaurant is a good lunch option with Russian-European food, and a café next door for snacks and drinks, *open 12 noon–12 midnight.* There are tables outside in summer, and live music from 7pm.

Ⓜ Gorkovskaya

∞ **Demyanovaya Ukha**, Kronverksky Prospekt 53, on corner with Ul. Markina, ✆ 232 8090, hides behind windows of stained-glass fish. Though variable, this fish restaurant can serve some of the best value food in the city. You can start with caviar or fresh crab in mayonnaise, follow it with the eponymous *ukha* (fish soup) and continue with delicately stuffed *sudak* (pike). The owner has a boat on Lake Ladoga, which off-loads fish for the restaurant twice a week in summer. There's also a guitarist and sometimes a balalaika trio. Either book, or ring persistently at the door. *Open 11–11 weekdays, till 8pm weekends.*
Ⓜ Gorkovskaya

◇ **Troitsky Most**, Ul. Malaya Possadkaya 2. It is left to devotees of Hari Krishna to provide St Petersburg with its only vegetarian restaurant; the soya-based food is good. *Open 24 hours.* Ⓜ Gorkovskaya

Bars

Kazemat Bar, Peter and Paul Fortress, ✆ 238 4541. Attached to the Austeria (*above*), this bar is done up to look like a prison cell, in keeping with its fortress location. *Open 11am–4am.*
Ⓜ Gorkovskaya

Vyborg Side

∞∞∞ **Nevsky Melody**, Sverdlovskaya Naberezhnaya 62, ✆ 227 1596 or 222 5180. Night-time complex combining restaurant, casino, bowling alley and nightclub plus erotic shows at midnight and one. Not surprisingly, this is a good place if you want to find bandits. The food in the smart chrome interior is fine and there's a business lunch at a set price. Save yourself hassle and take a taxi. *Open 12 noon–1am, nightclub until 4am.*

∞∞∞ **Schwabski Domik**, Krasnogvardeisky Prospekt 28/19, ✆ 528 2211. No-nonsense German food, wurst and schnitzel, served either at tables or in a stand-up bar where it is considerably cheaper. *Open 11am–midnight.*
Ⓜ Novocherkasskaya (Krasnogvardeiskaya)

Where to Stay

For those for whom enjoying the ambience of a hotel is part of the fun of a holiday, St Petersburg is not a highly-starred destination, unless you are willing to pay heavily. Although the hotel scene has improved, there is still something of a gap between astronomical, expense-account hotels and dreary, gargantuan Soviet-style places. The few hotels that do fit the bill tend to fill up, so book early to avoid disappointment. This is particularly true at certain times of the year, during the White Nights festival for example, when there never seem to be enough beds.

If you are paying through the nose you can expect Burberry, American Express and neo-Fabergé boutiques nestling on the ground floors (or the first floor as they call it here), while lobster and caviar bars, Italian trattorias, and business and health centres cater to other needs. In the cheaper hotels, security may not be great and you should leave your valuables in the hotel safe.

For those on a low budget, there are a number of good, cheap hostel options. The following listings have been divided by price, but within each band hotels nearest the centre are listed first, getting further out as the list continues.

Most hotels will accept all major credit cards (and to a lesser extent travellers' cheques) as payment. For a double room occupied by two people, reckon on:

luxury	∞∞∞∞∞	over $300
expensive	∞∞∞∞	$150
moderate	∞∞∞	$60–$150
inexpensive	∞∞	$40–$60
cheap	∞	under $40

Renting a room in a flat, bed and breakfast, will cost you from $35 a night; a whole flat that much more.

Hotels

∞∞∞∞∞ **Grand Hotel Europe**, Ul. Mikhail-ovskaya 1/7, ⓒ 329 6000, ⓐ 329 6001. The renovation of this central hotel overlooking Nevsky Prospekt and the Russian Museum has put it at the heart of St Petersburg tourism, even if you can only afford to pop in for the occasional coffee or a meal in its cheapest restaurant, Sadko. It is a pity that the Swedish hotel group

Reso have reinvented much of the Art Nouveau interior, and not very well at that. The rooms, decorated in pastel shades with spotless tiled bathrooms, can be stuffy—ask for an outside room or one overlooking the covered atrium.

Ⓜ Nevsky Prospekt

∞∞∞ **Nevsky Palace**, Nevsky Prospekt 57, ✆ 275 2001, ✉ 301 7323. From the Austrian Marco Polo group comes this slightly soulless offering, a renovation of the former Baltiskaya Hotel building on Nevsky Prospekt. There are two floors of rooms for non-smokers, and all the amenities, including a pool and sauna.

Ⓜ Mayakovskaya/Pl. Vosstaniya

∞∞∞ **Astoria** and **Angleterre**, Ul. Bolshaya Morskaya 39, ✆ 210 5757, ✉ 210 5059. Once two hotels, now bashed together into one. Fears for their fabric during renovation prompted a challenge by conservation pressure groups. Though the exterior was saved, from the interior it would seem their fears were justified, with just the dining room in the glass-ceilinged Winter Garden left to remind you how it must once have been. That said this is an efficient, modern hotel at the heart of the city, with clean rooms and a fabulous breakfast.

Ⓜ Nevsky Prospekt

∞∞∞ **Hotelship Peterhof**, Naberezhnaya Makarova, by Tuchkov Bridge, Vasilievksy Ostrov, ✆ 325 8888, ✉ 325 8889. Cabins are small, except on the more luxurious Boat Deck. The staff are helpful, the à la carte dining room expensive but good.

Ⓜ Vasileostrovskaya

∞∞∞ **Neptun**, Nab. Obvodnovo Kanala 93a, ✆ 315 4965, ✉ 113 3160 . This 70-room hotel includes everything you would expect from a recently built establishment of this price, but nothing can change the industrial location.

Ⓜ Pushkinskaya
15 minutes' walk away

∞∞∞ **Pulkovskaya**, Ploshchad Pobedy 1, ✆ 123 5122, ✉ 264 6396. Behind its dark glass front this Finnish-Russian hotel looks and feels like a nightclub. Built with the business traveller in mind, halfway to the airport, facilities include a business centre, a sauna and tennis courts.

Ⓜ Moskovskaya
10 minutes' walk away

∞∞∞ **Askur**, Pervy Berozovaya Alleya 7, ✆ 234 4588. Though it is fun staying in this small hotel, formerly for high-ranking Communist officials, housed in a *dacha* on pretty Kamenny Ostrov, there's a funny atmosphere in the former corridors of power. Rooms are huge but echoingly empty.

Ⓜ Chyornaya Rechka
or Petrogradskaya
bus 46 or 65 to the island
and then by foot

∞∞∞ **Pribaltiskaya**, Ul. Korablestroiteley 14, Vasilievsky Ostrov, ✆ 356 0263, ✉ 356 0094. Miles from the centre of St Petersburg, on the edge of the Gulf of Finland, this 1,200-room, concrete ship of a hotel may be fine for large groups with their own buses but it makes no attempts to be attractive to the individual tourist—unless, that is, (s)he has a particular *penchant* for early 70s psychedelic interior design, Russian-style. To get there you'll need to allow a lot of time: head for Ⓜ Primorskaya and take tram 11 or 63, bus 41, 42 or 47 or trolleybus 10, 10a or 46.

∞∞∞ **Sankt Peterburg**, Pirogovskaya Naberezhnaya 5/2, ✆ 542 9411, 📠 248 8002. The best choice in this category has to be this hideous 1970s building on the Vyborg side of the River Neva, on the principle that if you're in it you can't see it. You can, if you ask for a river view, see the wide expanse of the Neva slipping past, between you and the showy Palace Embankment. The hotel is feeling its age a bit, and the top floors still haven't been repaired after the 1991 fire, but you'll want for nothing important here, as long as you don't mind the uninspiring walk to the metro.

Ⓜ Ploshchad Lenina

∞∞∞ **Matisov Domik**, Reki Prynzhki Nab. 3/1, ✆ 219 5445, 📠 219 7919. That rare thing, a small family-run hotel tucked away on a quiet backwater 10 minutes' walk from Theatre Square.

Ⓜ Sennaya Ploshchad

∞∞∞ **Mercury**, 39 Ul. Tavricheskaya, ✆ 275 8745, 📠 276 1977. This tiny hotel tucked away in one of the city's nicest residential areas originally hosted regional party members only. The English-speaking manager, Alexander Leonov, is keen to lure foreigners to its clean, quiet rooms, and bar/buffet. Rates are a bit stiff at the moment but try negotiating by fax beforehand.

Ⓜ Chernyshevskaya

∞∞∞ **Moskva**, Ploshchad Aleksandra Nevskovo 2, ✆ 274 3001, 📠 274

2130. Close to the metro station and St Petersburg's most important monastery is about the most one can say about this drab, brown hotel. Its also got a reasonable shop selling imported goods on the ground floor.

Ⓜ Pl. Aleksandra Nevskovo

∞∞∞ **Okhtinskaya-Viktoria**, Bolsheokhtinsky Prospekt 4, ✆ 227 4438, 📠 227 2618. If it wasn't for the isolated location on the Vyborg side of the river opposite the Smolny Cathedral, this would undoubtedly be St Petersburg's best value hotel. Rooms are small but clean and service really exists, though the restaurant retains an exclusively group-tourism feel. Ask for a room overlooking the river, which will give you a view of Rastrelli's sublime cathedral.

Ⓜ Novocherkasskaya
and tram 7, 23 or 46

∞∞∞ **Karelia**, Ul. Tukhachevskovo 27, ✆ 226 3515, 📠 226 3511. As an independent traveller, resist being put here at all costs. Though the staff are friendly it is in an endlessly depressing area of town and the local transport takes hours.

∞∞∞ **Hotel Russ**, Artillereyskaya Ul. 1, ✆ 273 4683, 📠 279 3600. Former party hotel in a bizarre building offering good facilties for businessmen at moderate rates.

Ⓜ Vasileostrovskaya
and tram 11 or 40

∞∞ **Akademicheskaya**, Ul. Millionnaya 27, ✆ 315 8696, 📠 315 3368, go straight through the courtyard. If you can talk your way into this hotel which used to be reserved for guests of the Academy of Sciences you are laughing. The rooms are rather shoddy, there isn't always water, let alone hot water, but you are on millionaire's row, the road leading from the Hermitage, in which the cream of St Petersburg society lived until the Revolution.

Ⓜ Nevsky Prospekt

∞ **Oktyabrskaya**, Ligovsky Prospekt 10, ✆ 277 0016, ✉ 315 7501. This cheap and central option offers no decor to look forward to and a smelly warren of endless corridors to negotiate. An uninviting room is fine for a city like this in summer however—you should want to be outside all the time.

Ⓜ Ploshchad Vosstaniya

∞ **Mir**, Ul. Gastello 17, ✆ 108 5166, ✉ 108 5165. Small low-rise Russian hotel right next to one of St Petersburg's most original pieces of architecture, the Chesme Church. Staff are friendly considering that foreigners are a rarity, but rooms are small.

Ⓜ Moskovskaya

Cheaper Options

Youth Hostels

◇ **Holiday Hostel**, Ul. Mikhailova 1, ✆/✉ 542 7364. Sits right on the River Neva, next door to the infamous Kresty Prison. Prices include breakfast, though other meals are also served in the café.

Ⓜ Ploshchad Lenina

◇ **St Petersburg Youth Hostel**, Ul. Tretaya Sovyetskaya 28, ✆ 329 8018, ✉ 329 8019. Pioneered by an American, who came here to learn acting and became a businessman, the hostel has 50 beds and more in the summer. It also has an excellent travel agent/tourist information set up on the ground floor.

Ⓜ Ploshchad Vosstaniya

◇ **Sputnik**, Morisa Tereza Prospekt 34, ✆ 552 5632, ✉ 552 8084. Cheap student hotel, particularly if you have a student identity card.

Ⓜ Chyornaya Rechka

Campsites

Of the two campsites on offer, the **Retur Motel-Camping**, Bol. Kupalnaya Ul 28, Sestroretsk, Alexandrovskaya Village, ✆ 437 7533, ✉ 434 5022, 29km from the city on Primorskoye Shosse towards Finland is infinitely preferable to the crime-ridden **Olgino Motel-Camping**, Primorskoye Shosse, ✆ 238 3671, ✉ 238 3463, only 18km out on the same road. It is a long ride to both from Chornaya Rechka metro station, on buses 110, 411 or 416. You can also get to the Retur by train from Finland Station: go to Sestroretsk and get off at Aleksandrovsky.

Renting Rooms and Flats

If you are in this bracket you will probably have already booked your accommodation through one of the operators listed on pp.9–10. However, if you do want to rent on the ground ring the following:

Nadia Ribinitskaya, ✆ 393 6965, 📠 272 8295 (no English spoken).

Host Families Association, Tavricheskaya Ul. 5–25, ✆ and 📠 275 1992, *hofa @usa.net*, can provide both bed and breakfast and full board accommodation with Russian families in St Petersburg and some 40 other cities across the CIS.

St Petersburg Bed and Breakfast, ✆ and 📠 219 4116, and ask for Katya Cherkasova.

Entertainment and Nightlife

Theatre, classical music, ballet and opera have long been the mainstay of evenings in St Petersburg, but with liberalization a healthy rash of music clubs and discotheques and a dubious dose of casinos have emerged. Rock music used to be rationed and used cynically by the regime to keep young people away from church on Good Friday—the only televised rock concert coincided with the most important Orthodox service of the year. Today top Russian bands like Zvuky Moo and Liuki fill vast auditoriums and sports stadiums, and less well-known talents play in rock clubs in both cities.

Jazz too has its own space, though it tends to be traditional or Dixieland. It's come a long way from its hooligan reputation under Communism, when Maxim Gorky claimed that 'from saxophone to the knife is just one step'.

But if the days of political censorship are over, those of economic censorship have only just begun. After years of state subsidies, the government has turned off the tap and theatres, the film business and even one of the world's most famous ballet companies, the Kirov, now known as the Mariinsky, have been forced to confront the realities of the free market. As a result, the Mariinsky is now on tour abroad, earning foreign currency, for a large part of the year, and film production has dropped from over 800 films a year to around 60. Though ballet performances continue, you are as likely to see the stars of the company in New York, Sydney or London as you are here.

Most cinemas now show a staple diet of cheap American films. Films are always dubbed into Russian rather than subtitled, often by one man playing men, women and children. They are advertised on huge posters which list all the films showing in the city. Keep your eyes open near cinemas.

Something that hasn't changed is the summer break which most theatres take between mid-July and mid-September. Beware that if you come during that time your options will be severely diminished. For listings, consult the Friday edition of the *St Petersburg Times*, or the monthly *Pulse* magazine.

Tickets

To buy tickets (at a price!) use the service bureau in your hotel. For cheaper tickets try the box office at the venue or buy from touts operating outside. For a good choice get there half an hour before and try for tickets in the *parterre* (stalls) or *amphiteatr* (circle). Unless you know the theatre well, beware of *balkon* (balcony) tickets, as you may find yourself with a limited view.

There are also a number of theatre ticket kiosks, Teatralnaya Kassa (marked either Театральная Касса or simply Театр, theatre), all over the city, which you will identify by the chaos of printed tickets stuck to the windows. The system by which they receive tickets is random, but it is worth checking the windows for anything you might fancy in the central ones. In St Petersburg the most helpful are the Central Ticket Office, sandwiched between cafés at Nevsky Prospekt 42, the office in the detached Portik Rusca where Ul. Dumskaya meets Nevsky Prospekt and in the ticket hall of the Hermitage Museum, where you should look out particularly for tickets to performances in Catherine the Great's Hermitage Theatre. The Mariinsky Theatre will insist that you buy a 'foreigner's ticket' at twenty times the price for a local, and there is no use trying to get around it.

Bridges

One vital factor governing your decisions between April and November, when the Neva runs through the city free of ice, is the bridges. To let shipping into the network of rivers, lakes and canals that leads right through Russia to the Black and Caspian Seas, they are opened for nearly three hours in the middle of the night. If you get stuck on the wrong side you face either a long, cold wait or, if you are lucky, an extortionately expensive boat ride. There are respites over various bridges around 3am:

Dvortsovy Most	1.55–3.05 and 3.15–4.45
Birzhevoy Most	2.25–3.20 and 3.40–4.40
Troitsky Most	2–4.40
Most Leytenanta Shmita	1.55–4.50
Tuchkov Most	2.20–3.10 and 3.40–4.40
Liteyny Most	2.10–4.40
Kamennoostrovsky Most	2.15–3 and 4.05–4.55
Bolsheokhtinsky Most	2.45–4.55
Alexandra Nevskovo Most	2.35–4.50
Sampsonievsky Most	2.10–2.45 and 3.20–4.25
Bolshoykrestovsky Most	2.05–2.55 and 4.45–5.20
Grenadersky Most	2.45–3.45 and 4.20–4.45

White Nights

Though touted as a major event in St Petersburg's calendar, it is quite easy to miss the cultural events which mark the longest days of the year over the summer solstice on June 21. Ask your hotel service desk or Russian friends to give you the low down. To appreciate nature's performance, which keeps the skies light from 5am to 3am and the city ghostly in its silvery grip, take a walk on the banks of the river. There is a light-headed, 24-hour party atmosphere of guitar playing and drinking, as boats buzz up and down, music blaring, champagne bottles held aloft.

Rock concerts are held at Palace Square, the Peter and Paul Fortress and Yelagin Island, together with other outdoor events. Those on for a marathon with the Russians can catch a boat at midnight at Anichkov Most which sails round the canals and rivers until 5am. The one-hour trip from in front of the Hermitage leaving at 10pm is too sedate, and it is too early to see the bridges going up. Best of all, arrange during the day for a private boat near Nevsky Prospekt on the Moika Canal to meet up with you later and scud beneath the opening bridges.

Ballet and Opera

Mariinsky Theatre, Teatralnaya Ploshchad 2, ✆ 114 5264 or 114 4344. Known as the Kirov ballet during the Soviet period, this charming building with its delicate blue and gold interior has been home to some of the greatest dancers of all time—Nureyev, Baryshnikov and Pavlova among them. It premiered Tchaikovsky's *Sleeping Beauty* in 1890. It is a measure of quite how traditional Russian ballet is that the very same choreography is danced today. The main company tours a great deal but is most likely to be at home in winter. Excellent secondary companies perform during the rest of the year, except July and August when the theatre closes. The Mariinsky is also currently the best place to see opera.

Ⓜ Nevsky Prospekt and bus 22 or 27

Mussorgsky Theatre of Opera and Ballet, Pl. Iskusstv 1, ✆ 219 1949 or 219 1978, is St Petersburg's second ballet and opera stage, on which everyone descends in July and August when the Mariinsky is closed.

It is well worth keeping an eye open for performances in both the **Hermitage Theatre**, Dvortsovaya Naberezhnaya 34, ✆ 110 9030, and the **Yusupov Palace Theatre**, Naberezhnaya Reki Moiki 94, ✆ 314 8893 or 314 9088. Both are small, private affairs. Performances tend to be extracts, but the buildings themselves and their intimate proportions make the occasions a treat.

Yubileyny Sports Palace, Pl. Dobrolyubova 18, Petrograd Side, ✆ 119 5601, often stages ballet on ice in winter.

Classical Music

St Petersburg State Capella, Nab. Reki Moiki 20, ✆ 314 1058, used to produce the choir for the tsar's chapel in the Hermitage, and classical choral music is what it is still best at though you can hear folk music too.

Shostakovich Philharmonia, Ul. Mikhailovskaya 2, ✆ 110 4257. Tickets for concerts in both the featureless big hall, with its entrance on Pl. Isskustv, and the small (Glinka) hall at Nevsky Prospekt 30 can be bought at this address. Large posters outside advertise the programme; inside is a good secondhand music, record and compact disc emporium.

Rimsky-Korsakov Conservatoire, Teatralnaya Ploshchad, ✆ 312 2519, *bookings 11am–7pm; matinée performances noon, evening 6.30pm*. Classical concerts attached to St Petersburg's renowned musical teaching establishment.

Oktyabrskaya Concert Hall, Ligovsky Pr. 6, ✆ 275 1273, is used equally for important Russian and foreign classical and rock.

Rimsky-Korsakov's Flat, Zagorodny Prospekt 28, ✆ 113 3208 or 210 5226, continues the composer's tradition of musical evenings on Wed/Sat.

Theatre

Bolshoy Dramatichesky Teatr, Nab Reki Fontanki 65, ✆ 310 0401. St Petersburg's premier theatre is largely known for it traditional staging of traditional Russian plays.
Ⓜ Gostiny Dvor

Alexandrinsky Theatre, Pl. Ostrovskovo 2, ✆ 110 4103 or 311 1533. A beautiful neoclassical theatre, part of one of Rossi's ensembles built to aggrandize the city after the victory over Napoleon. The theatre stretches occasionally to ballet in the summer. Productions are very traditional.
Ⓜ Gostiny Dvor

Maly Dramatichesky Teatr, Ul. Rubinshteyna 18, ✆ 113 2094. Of all the mainstream theatres, this is the place to come to see more experimental staging and controversial new Russian plays.
Ⓜ Vladimirskaya/Dostoyevskaya

Baltisky Dom, Aleksandrovsky Park 4, ✆ 232 4490 or 6244. Known as a youth theatre, attracting the more innovative but lesser known St Petersburg companies who perform raw plays appealing to a younger audience.
Ⓜ Gorkovskaya

Circus and Puppetry

The Circus, Naberezhnaya Reki Fontanki 3, ✆ 210 4198. The oldest extant circus in Russia, which still uses animals to a greater extent than circuses in the west. Closed mid-July to mid-Sept.

Bolshoy Puppet Theatre, Nekrasova Ul. 10, ✆ 273 6672, originally started as a travelling company in 1931. There are matinée and evening performances, both aimed squarely at children. The theatre also has its own troupe of clowns.

Cinema

Dom Kino, Karavannaya Ul. 12, ☎ 314 8118, is the club of the union of cinema workers, and you are supposed to be a member to enter, but try your luck. They show classic Russian films, dubbed foreign films and retrospective seasons by geniuses of the order of Paradzhanov. At the same address is **Rodino**, ☎ 314 5667, largely a children's cinema. Ⓜ Gostiny Dvor

Anna Akhmatova Museum, Nab. Reki Fontanka 34, ☎ 272 2211, *open 11am–5.30pm* (*see* p.136). The museum includes a literary video club, with a catalogue of films about Russian literary figures, in both English and Russian.
Ⓜ Mayakovskaya

Spartak, Ul. Saltikova-Shchedrina 8, ☎ 272 7897. This converted church shows dubbed foreign films. Ⓜ Chernyshevskaya

Dostoyevsky Museum, Kuznechny Pereulok 5, ☎ 311 4031, arranges showings of film adaptations of the novelist's work, in Russian, at around midday most Sundays.
Ⓜ Vladimirskaya/Dostoyevskaya

Aurora, Nevsky Prospekt 60, ☎ 315 5254, has screenings of the latest Hollywood movies in Dolby stereo but dubbed into Russian.

Crystal Palace, Nevsky Prospekt 72, ☎ 272 2382, costs about $5 but has frequent widescreen showings of recent Hollywood films in the original language

Comedy

If your Russian is sufficiently advanced, try the **Chaplin Club**, Ul. Tavricheskaya 59, ☎ 272 6649. Reservations recommended.
Ⓜ Chevnyshevskaya

Jazz and Indie Clubs

St Petersburg was the fount of underground rock in the 1970s and 1980s. Big names include Boris Grebinshikov and his famous St Petersburg band *Akvarium*, and DDT, a rock band led by the poetic lyricist Yuri Shavchuk. Bands of this stature are likely to fill auditoria like the **Oktyabrsky** and **Yubileyny** (above) or the **Sport and Culture Complex**, Prospekt Yura Gagarina 8, by Ⓜ Park Pobedy.

Jazz Club, Zagorodny Prospekt 27, ☎ 164 8565, invites you to book a table and listen to jazz star David Goloshchukhin and his band. If you want to listen to modern jazz, the only chance is during the late night sets on Fri and Sat *Open 8–11, later on Fri and Sat*. A good night out but rather sedate and no dancing. Ⓜ Vladimirskaya

JFC Jazz Club, Ul. Shpalernaya 33, ☎ 272 9850, is a less formal venue with music from across the jazz spectrum, avant-garde to traditional. Ring to make a reservation. *Open daily 7–10*. Ⓜ Chernyshevskaya

Rok Klub, Ul. Rubinshteyna 13, was the only officially sanctioned rock club in the city for a long time, hence its imaginative Soviet-style name. Still open and fronting a wide range of indie bands, but ignored by the hardcore St Petersburg music scene. *Open 8–3*.
Ⓜ Mayakovskaya

Zoopark, in the zoo, Alexandrovsky Park 1, ✆ 232 3145, is a small club specialising in live rock and folk for singer/songwriters. Get there between 6.30 and 7pm or you won't get in. ⓜ Gorkovskaya

Indie Club, Lenin House of Culture, Pl. Obukhovskoy Oborony 233. Foreign and out-of-town groups share the stage with locals in this heavy metal hang out. *Open 2nd and 4th Friday of the month.*

Roksi, Ul. Tushina, attracts a number of popular and more famous bands with its big hall. *Open Sat from 7.* ⓜ Ligovsky Prospekt

There are a number of really nice café/clubs in the city, bohemian hangouts with occasional live acts:

Manhattan/Kotyol, Nab. Reki Fontanki 90, ✆ 113 1945, offers anything from rock through blue to jazz, plus billiards. ⓜ Nevsky Prospekt

Fish Fabrique, Pushkinskaya Ul. 10, is one of the city's best art cafés with background rock and progressive dance music, DJs and funky local bands. ⓜ Ploshchad Vosstaniya

Poligon, 65 Lesnoi Prospekt, ✆ 245 2720, holds occasional hardcore punk, rock and heavy metal concerts. ⓜ Lesnaya

Tinkoff, 7 Kazanskaya Ploshchad, ✆ 314 8485, is the city's first brewery bar, offering excellent beer plus jazz Wed–Sat, Latin music on Sunday 9–11 and rock from 11.30pm on Fri and Sat. ⓜ Nevsky Prospekt

Moloko, Perekupnoi Pereulok 12, ✆ 274 9467, is a cosy rock club for the arty student. Cheap and cheerful.
ⓜ Ploshchad Vosstaniya
ⓜ Ploshchad A. Nevskovo

Nightclubs

The urge to rave in Moscow was imported from St Petersburg where a number of companies, Tanzpol and MX among them, have been set up specifically to organize one-off parties in bizarre locations. For a while the place to dance was in a swimming pool on the Petrograd Side, and during the White Nights festival in 1993 those who could get in got down among the military hardware in the courtyard of the Artillery Museum. Watch out for posters advertising such events.

The Mafia now runs nightlife, whether in casinos, strip clubs or just one-off events. But as long as you've paid your entrance fee and are having a good time, this won't affect your evening. All of these clubs charge an entrance fee of around $15.

Griboyedov, Voronezhskaya Ul. 2a, ✆ 164 4055, is the liveliest place in the city, operating a strict policy of 'face control'. Cool dance music, art happenings, exhibitions and live concerts all take place in this converted bunker. Dress up and look cool. *Open 5pm–6am, closed Thurs.*
ⓜ Ligovsky Prospekt

Dom Aktyorov, the actor's club, at Nevsky Prospekt 86, ✆ 273 3189, hosts dancing Wed–Sun from 12–5. ⓜ Mayakovskaya

Mama, Malaya Monetnaya Ul. 3B, ✆ 232 3137, plays a wide range of techno music on Fridays, drum 'n' bass and jungle on Saturdays. Open 11pm–6am.
ⓜ Gorkovskaya

Hollywood Nites, Nevsky Prospekt 46, ✆ 311 6077, is a disco, club and bar, with a variety of music on offer depending on the evening. It's centrally located and open all hours.

Port Club, Antonenko Pereulok 2, ✆ 314 2609, is open daily 3pm–6am and holds techno parties from 10pm on Fri and Sat. It's also the venue for occasional pop and rock concerts. Ⓜ Sennaya Ploshchad

Nevsky Melody, Nab. Sverdlovskaya 62, ✆ 227 1596. Discotheque attached to an expensive restaurant and casino, attracting a richer mix of businessmen and molls. *Open 9–4.*

Ⓜ Novocherkasskaya plus tram 7, 23 or 46

Spartak, Ul. Saltikova-Shchedrina 8, ✆ 275 7739. This popular arts cinema also hosts concerts and dance parties in its auditorium.

Ⓜ Chernyshevskaya

Erotic Shows

Astoria Hotel, Ul. Bolshaya Morskaya 39 (entrance on Isaakiyevskaya Ploshchad), ✆ 210 5757, provides a number of scantily clad girls wriggling around poles, which spectacle they advertise as a 'fashion show'.

Golden Dolls, Nevsky Prospekt 60, ✆ 110 5570, has flashing lights and girls in see-through shifts enticing passers-by at all hours. In the evenings the pumping bass carries to the street. Entrance fees can be up to $100.

Folk Dance Shows

Nikolayevsky Palace, Ploshchad Truda 4, ✆ 312 5500 or 312 1913, holds a short but fiery display of traditional and Cossack dancing.

Gay Clubs

Club 69, 2-aya Krasnoarmeiskaya Ul. 6, ✆ 259 5163, is the city's premier male gay venue, with striptease and drag shows. Dress up. Women pay double to get in.

Ⓜ Tekhnologichesky Institute

Casinos

The city's best casinos are operated by the Conti group and include:

Olympia, Liteyny Prospekt 14, ✆ 275 0407. *Open noon–6am.* Ⓜ Nevsky Prospekt

Taleon Club, Nab. Reki Moiki 59, ✆ 315 7645, 312 5373. *Open noon–6am.*

Ⓜ Nevsky Prospekt

Nevsky Melody, Neberezhnaya Sverdlovska 62, ✆ 227 2676. *Open 9pm–3am.*

Ⓜ Novocherkasskaya plus tram 7, 23 or 46

Shopping

Gone are the days when you had to bring everything you might conceivably want with you to Russia. Everything is now available somewhere, though often at a price that few Russians can afford. The phenomenon of the kiosk is legendary. Over a period of months hundreds of thousands of these metal boxes appeared on the streets, filling the gaping hole in state supply with everything from condoms to clothes. On top of these there is a healthy sprinkling of shops, both home-grown and foreign, selling western goods (food, clothes and electrical items) in an environment you would recognize.

The more demanding shopper and those on a low budget, like the majority of the Russian population, face trickier terrain. The difficulty lies in finding something interesting and good-looking at a reasonable price. To be successful you should learn a number of Russian habits. Pop into shops as you pass for a quick look and glance into kiosk windows. Always keep an *avoizka*, a 'just-in-case' bag, traditionally a string one, somewhere about your person, as you never know when you are going to find what's needed. There is nothing more satisfying than coming back from an excursion with the very thing of which the city is currently in *defitsit*. Never think you will come back and buy something later. Quality flies out of the shops.

As for handing over the money and getting the goods in return: if you are in a Russian shop this too has its own logic. Take pencil and paper with you if your Russian is not strong. First identify what you want and how much it will cost. If it entails weighing, have the assistant do so, so that you know the exact price. Next, bearing in mind also the number of the counter (*otdel*), go to the cashier at the till (*kassa*) and tell her (it usually is) the price and counter. Pay and take your receipt back to the counter where you hand it over in exchange for your purchase. This may entail three separate queues. One final piece of advice—think laterally if you are determined to find something in the Russian shops. Logic like selling loo paper in stationery departments defeats most western minds.

Art and Antique Exports

You should be aware that it is illegal to export anything pre-1930. They may simply be taken from you at the airport on your departure. On top of this you are *supposed* to get permission from the Ministry of Culture to export more recent painting and sculptures. So many tourists do so without permission that it is hard to believe the process of getting a letter from the artist and two photographs of the work and greasing the palm of the bureaucrat is worth it. If you are buying a serious piece, however, the artist or gallery owner will help you.

Opening Times

Russian shops are mostly closed on Sundays, and universally take an hour's lunch break somewhere between 1 and 3. They open between 8 and 10 and do not close until 8 or 9. Supermarkets and shopping centres run in partnership with western firms tend to eschew the lunch hour and open for 12 hours: 8–8 or 10–10. Times have only been given where they do not correspond to these outlines, or where shops are also closed on Saturdays or Mondays.

Antiques

As well as the export difficulties mentioned above, watch out for fakes, particularly icons. The antiques market is not large. Families treasure the one old teacup or chair to have survived the upheavals of the last 80 years, while the rest of the set is being cherished by the descendants of KGBisti who helped themselves during the wholesale confiscations that accompanied arrests before the war. However, incomprehensible inflation is causing people to surrender their valuables to *kommissionny*, shops which sell them for a small percentage. This is where the fun is to be had, as long as you think of the money you are providing the owners with, not their sentimental loss.

Harmony, Ul. Mokhovaya 32, ✆ 273 6610; *open 11–7 with lunch between 2 and 3*. Set up like a domestic museum, with friendly staff who may be willing to negotiate over prices. Good for linen and antique clothes.
Ⓜ Nevsky Prospekt

Sankt Peterbourg, Nevsky Prospekt 54, ✆ 312 6676, is the city's most exclusive *kommissionny*, selling fine objects, and less good paintings and furniture, at inflated prices.
Ⓜ Gostiny Dvor

Kommissionny, Kamenoostrovsky Prospekt 4, is worth keeping an eye on as well, especially for china and glass.
Ⓜ Gorkovskaya

Staraya Kniga, Nevsky Prospekt 18, ✆ 312 6676, is better known for books but also sells bric-a-brac and fine old prints of bizarre subjects. Prints of St Petersburg are infinitely easier to find on the Portobello Road.

Art

There is a danger of killing your aesthetic sense with an overdose of mediocre painting in the streets and galleries. Since the idea of the starving 'underground' artist first gripped the tourist imagination in the early 80s, those of dubious talent have been encouraged to expect good money for their efforts on Nevsky Prospekt and near the Cathedral of the Saviour of the Blood (*see* 'Souvenirs'). The following list highlights the better galleries in which you can regain a sense of perspective.

Gallery 10–10, Ligovsky Prospekt 53, was originally located at the heart of the vibrant St Petersburg underground art scene, attached to a huge artistic squat. Pushkinskaya 10, where the gallery started, held an iconic position in the history of Underground St Petersburg, for it was here that many of the leading painters, poets and thinkers of the early 1980s came together to live. *Closed Sat and Sun.*

Ⓜ Ploshchad Vosstaniya

Dostoyevsky Museum, Kuznechny Pereulok 5/2, ℰ 311 4031, houses a number of galleries in its building, including one that specializes in characterful naive painting. *Open 10.30–5.30; closed Mon.*

Ⓜ Vladimirskaya

The Exhibition Centre for St Petersburg Union of Artists, Naberezhnaya Reki Moiki 83, ℰ 314 4734, attempts to represent the city's artistic traditions from realism to avant-garde. The gallery also intends to buy important pieces of Petersburg art to serve as the foundation for a Museum of Modern Art.

Ⓜ Nevsky Prospekt

National Centre Gallery, Nevsky Prospekt 166, ℰ 277 1216, exhibits a mixed bag of painters in its peaceful courtyard rooms. The directors have a good eye, the gallery a good café. Ⓜ Ploshchad Aleksandra Nevskovo

Lavka Khudozhnikov, Nevsky Prospekt 8, ℰ 312 6193, concentrates less on paintings than on ceramics, jewellery and even printed silk. Ⓜ Nevsky Prospekt

Books

Well-printed colour art books are still one of the bargains to be had in Russia, and you will find them for sale outside any of the major tourist sights. Second-hand bookshops sometimes turn up old English-language books and magazines that have arrived there by their own mysterious routes and could end up being taken back to the land of their birth by you. They often share space with yet more *kommissionny*.

Bukinist, Lityeiny Prospekt 57/59, ℰ 273 2504, contains yards of dusty old books on all manner of subjects, plus a few antique objects.

Ⓜ Mayakovskaya

Kniga, Nevsky Prospekt 16, ℰ 312 8535, and the shop in the **Russian Museum**, Ploshchad Iskusstv, share the best selection of art books and postcards.

Ⓜ Nevsky Prospekt

Anglia, Nab. Reki Fontanki 40, ℰ 279 8284, is a bookshop dedicated to English-language books.

Ⓜ Nevsky Prospekt

Staraya Kniga, Nevsky Prospekt 18, ℰ 312 6676, sells a small, high-quality selection of books, displaying the most valuable in glass-fronted mahogany bookshelves from a bygone age.

Ⓜ Nevsky Prospekt

Clothes

If fashion is what you are after on holiday, you've chosen the wrong place to come. If something vital is missing from your wardrobe, and you have the stamina, you could scour the Russian department stores for items, but you are far more likely to find what you want at the expensive boutiques selling imported clothing. That just leaves fur hats and coats, a Russian speciality. Hats appear wherever tourists congregate. Coats can be found, if your conscience allows, at the fur shops below.

Burberry, Grand Hotel Europe, Ul. Mikhailovskaya 1/7, has a selection of the label's classic clothing range.

ⓜ Nevsky Prospekt

Rot Front, Ul. Soyuz Pechatnikov 23, ✆ 114 7451, and the **fur shop** at Lena Nevsky 50, ✆ 311 7169, are stuffed with fur coats and hats. ⓜ Petrogradskaya

Lenwest, Nevsky Prospekt 119, ✆ 277 0635, *open 10–7, Sun 11–5*, is the best shoe shop in the city, and tries to ensure it stocks good warm boots in winter.

ⓜ Ploshchad Vosstaniya

Department Stores

Known as *univermag* and mostly built in the 19th-century as emporia for the sale of piles of exotic goods, Russia's department stores became a showcase for the dreary state consumerism of the Soviet Union. Today the bright colours of Benetton are pitched next to the increasingly competitive offerings of Russian manufacturers. The more traditional still offer a 'universal' range of goods from clothes and shoes, household goods and stationery to musical instruments and souvenirs.

Gostiny Dvor, Nevsky Prospekt 35. An absolutely endless series of concessions and departments fill this 18th-century warren of a building, which is a source for some of the cheapest souvenirs in town. ⓜ Gostiny Dvor

Passazh, Nevsky Prospekt 48, is undergoing a piecemeal modernization. Highlights include a small *kommissionny* section, bed linens on the top floor and the odd stall of imported clothing.

Apraksin Dvor, Ul. Sadovaya, is another 18th-century umbrella covering separate shops. For a modern-day descent into the world of a Dostoyevskian market seek out the arched entrance to *Veschovy Rynok*, the penny-pinching, underworld flea-market which takes place inside the courtyard. *See* p.142. ⓜ Nevsky Prospekt

Food and Drink

There are three ways of buying food in St Petersburg: in the state shops, at the markets and in the supermarkets, mostly owned by foreign companies. The easier the experience, the more expensive the produce. Queues still form at cheap state shops, no longer so much because of poor supply but simply because they are all most people can afford. The one Russian shop you should not miss is the bread shop. Russian bread, the normal brown rye loaf, is delicious, and if you are lucky you will find an aromatic (*aromatny*) loaf in stock, the king of which is known as 'Borodinsky'. There is a bread shop in every neighbourhood, simply called хлеб (*khleb*—bread).

More affluent Russians, foreigners and—on special occasions—everyone else, head for the markets, where fruit and vegetables, dairy products and better, more varied cuts of meat are available in abundance. They are exclusively Mafia-controlled, often by gangs from the southern borders between Russia, Azerbaijan and Georgia.

The rule here is to bargain. Even if you manage to talk your way out of the foreigners' premium, the salesman will still be making a healthy profit.

There is a rash of foreign-run supermarkets in St Petersburg. Each has its own strengths and weaknesses, and labelling can be an initial problem (is this Finnish for flour or sugar?). Russian food shops, the best of which are called 'Gastronom', are open 8–9, the markets are open 9–5 and the supermarkets 10–8. Most are open 7 days a week. Some supermarkets only accept credit cards and you must have your passport with you as identity.

Gastronoms and Specialist Russian Shops

Yeliseyev's, Nevsky Prospekt 58, is the original branch of the 19th-century grocery empire. The décor is uplifting, the crowds queuing for the mediocre stock less so.

Gastronom, corner of Ul. Millionnaya and Zaporozhny Pereulok, is very crowded, but on good days you can find smoked salmon and caviar here.

Pirozhnoye Ul. Bolshaya Konyushennaya 7, ✆ 314 1558, *open 10am–10.30pm*, sells a delicious selection of cakes and biscuits.

Markets

Kuznechny Rynok, Kuznechny Pereulok 3, is the city's best market and sells healthy fat chickens, vegetables, fruit, delicious honey and mouthwatering pickled garlic and cucumbers. *Closed Mon.*

Depending where you are, you may prefer to buy veg and fruit from: **Nekrasovsky Rynok**, Ul. Nekrasova 52, **Sytny Rynok**, Sytninskaya Ploshchad 3/5, Petrograd Side, **Vasileostrovsky Rynok**, Bolshoy Prospekt and 4/5 Liniya on Vasilievsky Ostrov.

Supermarkets

Stockmann's, Finlandsky Prospekt 1, ✆ 542 2297, is a Finnish joint venture with by far the best selection of imported food in the city. *Open daily 10am–10pm.*

Babylon Super, Maly Prospekt 54–6, Petrograd Side, ✆ 230 8096, includes fresh fruit and vegetables, fresh bread, frozen foods and an extensive delicatessen counter. *Open 24 hours.*

Music

Keep your eyes constantly skinned for cheap classical CDs on the Melodiya label, as their normal outlets are increasingly unreliable. You are as likely to have them sold to you in the streets or in a bookshop as you are in record shops.

Philharmonia Ul. Mikhailovskaya 2. Fight your way past the ticket office for the concert hall to discover a secondhand record, tape and CD emporium with surprising finds for the connoisseur. Ⓜ Nevsky Prospekt

Saigon, Nevsky Prospekt, next to the Aeroflot building, sells good-quality pirate CDs and tapes very cheaply.
Ⓜ Nevsky Prospekt

Gramplastinka, 7-aya Liniya 40, Vasilievsky Ostrov, has stacks of classical LPs and as good a selection of CDs as you will find in the city.
Ⓜ Vasileostrovskaya

Souvenirs

Unless you are fussy there is no need to plan your shopping in this department. The stock items will find you—again and again. The delightful wooden Russian nest-dolls, *matrioshkas*, are so numerous they become nightmarish, but they are great when you get them back home. If you are serious about quality look for one in which all the figures are slightly different, with a wealth of detail in their costume. Themes include political leaders, fairytales, or women carrying different icons or aspects of domestic life. You can pay the equivalent of hundreds of dollars for the best. Other items that turn up consistently at tourist sites include old Soviet flags, banners and badges, gem-like painted Palekh (and fake Palekh) boxes, tin trays, floral scarves and brooches.

Outside the **Church of the Saviour on the Blood** is an open-air market of paintings and souvenirs where you will find everything on offer in one place, *open daily 9–dusk.*
Ⓜ Nevsky Prospekt

Naslediye (Heritage), Nevsky Prospekt 116, ✆ 279 5067, ✉ 219 2129, *open daily 10am–7pm*, sells good quality *matrioshkas*, painted trays, *khokhloma* (painted cups and spoons) and scarves as well as enamelled eggs and the occasional inviting piece of one-off craftsmanship.
Ⓜ Ploshchad Vosstaniya

Khudozhestvenny Promysli, Nevsky Prospekt 51, is a cheap shop sometimes selling embroidered linen, traditional Russian shirts and socks. **Ⓜ** Nevsky Prospekt

Ananov, Grand Hotel Europe, Ul. Mikhailovskaya 1/7. You have to be seriously rich to consider buying the exquisite jewellery or *objets d'art*. Andrei Ananov has taken up the mantle of Carl Fabergé, the famed jeweller who made his name creating intricate Easter eggs for European royalty before the Revolution. Ananov claims many of his best customers are also royal. Fine enamelled Easter eggs (small enough to hang on necklaces) are made by a skilled team of retrained veterans disabled in the Afghan war. **Ⓜ** Nevsky Prospekt

Polar Star, Nevsky Prospekt 158, sells basic gold rings and necklace chains but of more interest are the pretty necklaces threaded with semi-precious stones.
Ⓜ Ploshchad Aleksandra Nevskovo

Sports Gear

Planet Fitness, Nab. Robespierre 12, ✆ 275 1384, *open weekdays 7am–10.30pm, Sat 9am–9pm, Sun 9–10pm.* Gym that also sells trendy outfits for working out.
Ⓜ Nevsky Prospekt

Sporttovary, Nevsky Prospekt 122, has an erratic supply of Russian sporting equipment, particularly for fishing.
Ⓜ Ploshchad Vosstaniya

Kondratievsky Market, Polyustrovsky Prospekt 45, is St Petersburg's pet market, where they logically if inconsiderately do a huge line in fur hats as well. *Sat best for pets; closed Sun.* Ⓜ Ploshchad Lenina plus trolleybus 3, 12 or 43.

Pet Boutique, Entrance 13, Ulitsa Bucharestskaya 23, ✆ 105 3974, specializes in winter clothes for cats and dogs. *Open daily 12–8.*

Chronology

862	Swedish Vikings under Rurik found state of Rus at Novgorod
880	Oleg makes Kiev the capital of the Rus
988	Under Vladimir I, Kievan Rus adopts Christianity
1223	First Mongol raid
1240	Kiev sacked by Mongols
1242	Alexander Nevsky defeats Teutonic Knights on Lake Peipus
1327	Metropolitan of Russian Orthodox Church moves to Moscow
1328	Ivan I is created Grand Prince of Muscovy
1380	Dmitry Donskoy leads the first victory against the Mongols at Kulikovo
1480	Ivan III stops paying the annual tribute to the Mongols
1547	Ivan IV adopts the title 'tsar'
1563–7	Ivan IV's terror, carried out by the *oprichniki*
1571	Crimean Tartars raid Moscow for the last time
1588	Russia is granted her own Patriarch
1605–13	The Time of Troubles
1613	The Romanovs ascend the throne of Russia
1649	Russia's gets her first rationalized law code, the *Ulozheniye*
1660	Patriarch Nikon is deposed
1697–8	Peter the Great visits Europe
1700–21	Great Northern War
1703	Foundation of St Petersburg
1712	St Petersburg becomes capital of Russia
1722	Table of Ranks adopted
1772	First Partition of Poland
1773–4	Pugachev Uprising
1783	Potemkin annexes the Crimea
1792	Second Partition of Poland
1795	Third Partition of Poland
1805–7	First war with Napoleon
1812	Napoleon invades Russia and is driven out
1814	Congress of Vienna
1825	Decembrist Uprising

Chronology, Glossary & Street Names

1853–6	Crimean War
1861	Emancipation of the Serfs
1881	Assassination of Alexander II, the 'Tsar-Liberator'
1903	Pogroms against Russia's Jewish communities
1904–5	Russo-Japanese War
1905	The 1905 Revolution
1906	Russia's first elected *duma* meets

1911	Prime Minister Stolypin assassinated in Kiev
1914	First World War begins
1916	Rasputin is murdered
1917	Nicholas II abdicates in February
	Bolsheviks seize power in October Revolution
1918	Russia bows out of First World War at Treaty of Brest-Litovsk
	Romanovs murdered
	Government returns to Moscow
1918–20	Civil War
1922	Formation of the Soviet Union
1924	Lenin dies
1928	First Five Year Plan introduced
1934	Murder of Kirov; the purges begin
1939	Nazi-Soviet Pact
1939–40	War with Finland
1940	Soviet Union annexes Baltic Republics and Bessarabia
1941	Germans attack the Soviet Union
1941–4	Siege of Leningrad
1945	Second World War ends: Yalta and Potsdam conferences
1956	Khrushchev denounces Stalin in secret speech at 20th Party Congress
	Hungarian Uprising crushed
1961	Contruction of Berlin Wall
1962	Cuban Missile Crisis
1968	'Prague Spring' put down by Soviet troops
1979	Invasion of Afghanistan
1985	Gorbachev introduces *glasnost* and *perestroika*
1986	Chernobyl nuclear reactor blows up
1989	Soviets pull out of Afghanistan
	East European satellite states declare independence of Soviet Union, culminating in fall of Berlin Wall
	Yeltsin tears up Communist Party card on TV
1990	Baltic Republics gain independence
	Yeltsin voted President of Russian Republic
	Conservative August coup fails
	Ukraine, Belarus and Georgia declare independence
	Gorbachev resigns as head of a non-existent Soviet Union
1992	Radical PM Gaidar replaced by more conservative Chernomyrdin
1993	September: Yeltsin dissolves parliament
	October: he defeats his parliamentary opposition, led by Khasbulatov and Rutskoi, in bloody Moscow shoot-out
	December: parliamentary elections yield high nationalist vote
1994-6	Chechen War
1996	Yeltsin reelected as President
1998	Russian economic collapse

Selected List of Russian Rulers

The Rurik Dynasty

Rurik	862–879	Vasily II	1425–62
Oleg	879–912	Ivan III ('the Great')	1462–1505
Vladimir I	978–1015	Vasily III	1505–33
Vladimir Monomakh	1113–25	Ivan IV ('the Terrible')	1533–84
Alexander Nevsky	1252–63	Fyodor I	1584–98
Daniil	1276–1303	Boris Godunov	1598–1605
Ivan I ('Kalita')	1328–40	Fyodor II	1605
Dmitry Donskoy	1359–89	The Time of Troubles	1605–13
Vasily I	1389–1425		

The Romanov Dynasty

Mikhail	1613–45	Elizabeth	1741–61
Alexei	1645–76	Peter III	1761–62
Fyodor III	1676–82	Catherine II ('the Great')	1762–96
Ivan V & Peter I	1682–98	Paul	1796–1801
(Sophia regent to 1689)		Alexander I	1801–25
Peter I ('the Great')	1698–1725	Nicholas I	1825–55
Catherine I	1725–27	Alexander II	1855–81
Peter II	1727–30	Alexander III	1881–94
Anna	1730–40	Nicholas II	1894–1917
Ivan VI	1740–41		

Prime Ministers of Provisional Government

Prince Lvov	Feb–May 1917
Alexander Kerensky	May–Oct 1917

People's Chairman

Vladimir Ilich Lenin	1917–24

General Secretaries of the Communist Party

Joseph Stalin	1924–53	Yuri Andropov	1982–84
Georgi Malenkov	1953–55	Konstantin Chernenko	1984–85
Nikita Khrushchev	1955–64	Mikhail Gorbachev	1985–91
Leonid Brezhnev	1964–82		

Presidents of the Russian Republic

Boris Yeltsin	1991–

Glossary of Terms

atlantes	male human figures supporting architectural features in place of columns
banya	communal Russian steam bath
boyar	senior Russian nobles below princes (the class was abolished by Peter the Great)
caryatids	female human figures supporting architectural features in place of columns
Cheka	earliest name for Bolshevik secret police (1917–21)
constructivism	Soviet name for the Modernist architecture of the 1920s
cupola	dome above a church or belltower, often onion-shaped in Russia
dacha	wooden country house
drum	cylindrical base on which a cupola sits
dvorets	palace
futurism	avant-garde movement in art, which sought to incorporate technological imagery
grisaille	mural in shades of grey and white, resembling plaster relief
icon	religious painting, traditionally encaustic on wood
iconostasis	wall of icons dividing nave from sanctuary in Russian churches
KGB	Soviet secret police between 1954–91, short for the Committee for State Security
kokoshniki	ornamental gables on the roof of Russian churches and palaces, often semi-circular or ogee shaped
kremlin	medieval fortress at the heart of traditional Russian town
krepost	military fortress
lavra	highest level of monastery
Metropolitan	The primate of an ecclesiastical province or see, similar to a bishop or archbishop
muzei	museum
NKVD	name given to the secret police in 1934–46
ogee	arch or gable shaped like the top part of a spade in a pack of playing cards
sobor	cathedral
Style Moderne	Russian word for Art Nouveau style in architecture and design
tent roof	steep sided, almost conical roof, as seen on Russian churches; known as a *shatyor* in Russian
terem	women's quarters in traditional palace, at the top of the house
tserkov	church
zakomar	semi-circular gable on top of wall

Street Name Changes

The dissolution of the Soviet Union has led to the reversal of one of its absurder policies: the renaming of streets, squares, metro stations and indeed whole cities after Communist heroes and work-forces. The process of reversal began in June 1991, when the citizens of Leningrad voted to change the name of their city back to St Petersburg, and has been going on, not without controversy, ever since. Some of the names chosen by the Communists included Pushkin Square and Chekhov Street: indignant citizens are now asking why dishonour should be done to these respectable Russian heroes in order to change back to a name commemorating a church which no longer exists. A definitive list of name changes has been announced by the city government, but their use is distinctly piecemeal, and the putting up of new street signs even more so. The list below features the names in common use on the left, followed by their alternatives on the right. In most cases the 'new' (that is, pre-Revolutionary) names have caught on, and you will find the old Communist name on the right. The lines indicated by an asterisk indicate that the old Communist names still prevail, and the 'new' names are given on the right, in case they come into use soon. Bear in mind that whatever the common usage, when talking to people, particularly taxi drivers, you may need to know that what is Tverskaya Ul. to one citizen is still Ul. Gorkovo to another.

Streets and Squares

Angliskaya Nab.	Nab. Kraznovo Flota
Birzhevaya Pl.	Pushkinskaya Pl.
Bolshoy Sampsonievsky Pr.	Pr. Karla Marksa
Bolshaya Konyushennaya Ul.	Ul. Zhelyabova
Pl. Dekabristov	Senatskaya Pl.*
Furshtadtskaya Ul.	Ul. Petra Lavrova
Galernaya Ul.	Krasnaya Ul.
Bolshaya Morskaya Ul.	Ul. Gertsena
Malaya Morskaya Ul.	Ul. Gogolya
Kronverksky Prospekt	Prospekt Maxima Gorkovo
Gorokhovaya Ul.	Ul. Dzerzhinskovo
Italyanskaya Ul.	Ul. Rakova
Kamennoostrovsky Pr.	Kirovsky Pr.
Karavannaya Ul.	Ul. Tolmacheva
Konnogvardeysky Bulvar	Bulvar Profsoyuzov
Malaya Konyshennaya Ul.	Ul. Sofi Perovskoy
Ul. Mikhailovskaya	Ul. Brodskovo
Millionnaya Ul.	Ul. Khalturina

Pl. Ostrovskovo	Aleksandrinskaya Pl.*
Ul. Pestelya	Panteleymonovskaya Ul.*
Pochtamtskaya Ul.	Podbelskovo Per
Ul. Saltykova Shchedrina	Kirochnaya Ul.*
Sennaya Pl.	Pl. Mira
Shpalernaya Ul.	Ul. Voinova
Troitskaya Pl.	Pl. Revolutsii
Pl. Truda	Blagoveshchenskaya Pl.*
Ul. Truda	Blagoveshchenskaya Ul.*
Pl. Vosstaniya	Znamenskaya Pl.*
Voznesensky Pr.	Pr. Mayorova

Bridges

Troitsky Most	Kirovsky Most
Most Leytenanta Shmidta	Nikolayevsky Most*
Birzhevoy Most	Stroiteley Most
Politseysky Most	Narodny Most
Lityeiny Most	Aleksandrovsky Most*
Panteleymonovsky Most	Most Pestelya

Metro Stations

Ⓜ Sennaya Ploshchad   Ⓜ Ploshchad Mira

Ⓜ Devyatkino   Ⓜ Komsomolskaya

Ⓜ Novocherkasskaya   Ⓜ Krasnogvardeyskaya

There is no point pretending that Russian is an easy language, with its strange alphabet, nouns and adjectives declining in seven cases, and verbs of motion with perfective and imperfective aspects in all tenses. However, you will get an immense sense of satisfaction, not to mention great orientational benefit, if you learn to read the Cyrillic script. Cosmopolitan Russians will always applaud your efforts to actually speak a few words, though country folk can be remarkably unsympathetic about your communication difficulties. St Petersburg is full of English-speakers, and one will nearly always appear when you need one.

If you are going to be in the country for some time and want to do rather better, you will find lists of Russian language courses in the classified ads in the *St Petersburg Times*. A good teach-yourself course is to be found between the covers of *The Penguin Russian Course*, for which cassettes are also available. Langenscheidt produce both a pocket and a mini English–Russian, Russian–English dictionary, one of which you may wish to take with you as well.

Note on Transliteration

This book largely follows the transliteration set out overleaf, except for a few proper names, the standard English spelling of which has been established by the media: *e.g.* Gorbachev, not Gorbachov.

The common masculine adjective endings -ый, -ий have both been rendered into English with a single -y, as the nuances of sound are not important to a new Russian speaker.

Many masculine and neuter adjectives in the genitive singular end in -ого (ogo) and -его (ego), but are confusingly pronounced -ovo and -evo. They have been transliterated with a 'v' as they are pronounced, but in these cases, which often occur in street names, there will be a discrepancy between the written Russian and the transliteration, *e.g.* Площадь Островского = Ploshchad Ostrovskovo.

Language

The Russian Alphabet

		Transliteration	Pronunciation
А	а	a	as in 'car'
Б	б	b	as in 'book'
В	в	v	as in 'van'
Г	г	g	as in 'good'
Д	д	d	as in 'day'
Е	е	ye/e	as in 'yes'
Ё	ё	yo/o	as in 'yonder' (often not accented)
Ж	ж	zh	like 'g' in massage
З	з	z	as in 'zone'
И	и	i	like 'ee' in 'feet'
Й	й	y	as in 'boy', but silent at end of word
К	к	k	as in 'kin'
Л	л	l	as in 'lamp'
М	м	m	as in 'man'
Н	н	n	as in 'nut'
О	о	o	as in 'pot' when stressed; like 'a' in 'aloud' when unstressed
П	п	p	as in 'pen'
Р	р	r	as in 'red' (rolled)
С	с	s	as in 'sing'
Т	т	t	as in 'top' (sometimes written as *m*)
У	у	u	like 'oo' in 'fool'
Ф	ф	f	as in 'fat'
Х	х	kh	like 'ch' in Bach
Ц	ц	ts	as in 'lots'
Ч	ч	ch	as in 'chair'
Ш	ш	sh	as in 'ship'
Щ	щ	shch	as in 'fresh cheese'
Ъ	ъ	{none}	unpronounced hard sign
Ы	ы	y/i	like 'ey' in 'chop suey', pronounced from the back of the throat
Ь	ь	{none}	unpronounced soft sign
Э	э	e	as in 'set'
Ю	ю	yu	like 'u' in 'use'
Я	я	ya	as in 'yard'

Essential Phrases

English	Pronunciation	Russian
yes	da	да
no	nyet	нет
please	pazhálsta	пожалуйста
thank you	spasíba	спасибо
not at all	nyé za shto	не за что
hello	zdrávstvuitye/privét	здравствуите/привет
goodbye	da svidániya	до свидания
see you later	poká	пока
good morning	dóbroye útra	доброе утро
good evening	dóbry vyécher	добрый вечер
glad to meet you	óchen priyátno	очень приятно
how are you?	kak delá?	как дело?
fine/good	kharashó	хорошо
bad	plókha	плохо
Do you speak English?	vy govorítye pa-anglísky?	Вы говорите по-английски?
I don't understand	ya nye ponimáiyu	Я нс понимаю
I don't speak Russian	ya nye gavaryú pa-rússky	Я не говорю по-русски
Slowly, please	máidlyenna, pazhálsta	Медленно пожалуйста
I am English (m/f)	ya anglichánin/anglichánka	Я англичанин/англичанка
American (m/f)	ya amerikánets/amerikánka	Я американец/американка
Canadian (m/f)	ya kanádets/kanádka	Я канадец/канадка
Australian (m/f)	ya avstrályets/avstralíka	Я австралец/австралийка
Please help me	pamagítye mnye pazhálsta	Помогите мне пожалуйста
Go away!	von otsúda!	Вон отсюда!
Help!	pamagí!	Помоги!

Common Signs

entrance	vkhod	вход	closed	zakríta	закрыто
exit	výkhod	выход	for repairs	na remont	на ремонт
toilet	tualyét	туалет	out of order	nye rabótayet	
men	múzhi	мужи			не работает
women	zhhení	жены	no entry	vkhóda nyet	входа нет
open	otkríta	открыто	no smoking	nye kúrit	не курить
			ticket office	kássa	касса

Buying and Selling

How much is it?	skólka stóit?	Сколько стоит?
Too expensive	éta dóroga	Это дорого
I would like	ya khachú	Я хочу
This one	éta	Это
more/less	yeshchó/ménshe	ещё/меньше
(very) big	(óchen) bolshóy	(очень) большой
(very) small	(óchen) mályenky	(очень) маленкий
old/new	stáry/nóvy	старый/новый
hot/cold	goryáchy/khalódny	горячий/холодный
What is it?	Shto éta?	Что это?
Please show me	Pakazhítye mnye pazhálsta	Покажите мне пожалуйста

Numbers

0	nol	ноль	21	dvádtsat adín	двадцать один
1	adín	один	22	dvádtsat dva	двадцать два
2	dva	два	30	tréedtsat	тридцать
3	tree	три	40	sórok	сорок
4	chetíry	четыре	50	pyatdecyát	пятьдесят
5	pyat	пять	60	shestdecyát	шестьдесят
6	shest	шесть	90	dyevyenósta	девяносто
7	syem	семь	100	sto	сто
8	vósyem	восемь	200	dvyésti	двести
9	dévyat	девять	300	trísta	триста
10	décyat	десять	400	chetírysta	четыреста
11	adínnadtsat	одиннадцать	500	pyatsót	пятьсот
12	dvyenádtsat	двенадцать	600	shestsót	шестьсот
13	treenádtsat	тринадцать	1000	týsyacha	тысяча
14	chetírnadtsat	четырнадцать	5000	pyat týsyach	пять тысяч
15	pyatnádtsat	пятнадцать	1,000,000		
20	dvádtsat	двадцать		millión	миллион

Directions

(on the) left	(na) lyéva	(на) лево	square	plóshchad	площадь
(on the) right	(na) práva	(на) право	lane	pereúlok	переулок
Straight on	Pryáma	прямо	boulevard	bulvar	бульвар
street	úlitsa	улица	avenue	prospékt	проспект

Transport

train	póyezd/elektríchka	поезд/электричка
bus	avtóbus	автобус
metro	metró	метро
trolleybus	trolléibus	троллейбус
tram	tramvái	трамвай
taxi	taksí	такси
car	mashína	машина
Where is…?	gdye…?	Где…?
…the bus stop	…avtastántsiya	…автостанция?
…the tram stop	…tramváinaya stántsiya	…трамвайнная станция?
…the trolleybus stop	…trolleistántsiya	…троллейстанция?
…the train station	…vokzál	…вокзал?
When is the next train?	Kogdá slyéduyushchy póyezd?	Когда следующий поезд?
Ticket, please	Bilyét, pazhálsta	Билет, пожалуйста
return	tudá i abrátna	туда и обратно

Food and Drink

restaurant	restorán	ресторан	supper	úzhin	ужин
café	kafé	кафе	knife	nozh	нож
bar	bar	бар	fork	vílka	билка
food shop	gastronóm	гастроном	spoon	lózhka	ложка
market	rýnok	рынок	glass	stakán	стакан
breakfast	závtrak	завтрак	cup	cháshka	чашка
lunch	abéd	обед			

Useful Phrases

I am vegetarian (m/f)	Ya vegetariánets/ vegetariánka	Я вегетарианец/ вегетарианка
I don't eat meat or fish	Ya myása i rýbu ne yem	Я мясо и рыбу не ем
Please bring me…	Prinesítye pazhálsta…	Принесите пожалуйста…
…the bill	…schot	…счёт
…an ashtray	…pépelnitsu	…пепельницу
…more…	…yeshchó…	…ещё…
I would like…	Ya khachú	Я хочу

Basic Foods

хлеб	khleb	bread	сахар	sákhar	sugar
масло	másla	butter	соль	sol	salt
молоко	malakó	milk	перец	pyérets	pepper
яйцо	yáitsa	egg	сметана	smyetána	sour cream
яйчница	yáichnitsa	omelette	кефир	kefír	drinking
мясо	myása	meat			yoghurt
рыба	rýba	fish	сыр	seer	cheese

Fruits

яблоки	yábloky	apples	клубники	klúbniky	strawberries
сливы	slivý	plums	малины	malíny	raspberriesv
вишны	vishný	cherries	ягода	yágada	berries
апельсин	apelsín	orange			
лимон	limón	lemon	картофель	kartófel	potato
винограды	vinogrády	grapes	риз	riz	rice

Vegetables

помидор	pomidór	tomato	свёкла	svyókla	beetroot
огурец	agouryéts	cucumber	грибы	gribý	mushrooms
лук	luk	onion	баклажан	baklazhán	aubergine
перец	pyérets	pepper			
капуста	kapusta	cabbage			
морковь	markóv	carrot			

Meat and Fish

говядина	govyádina	beef	сельдь	seld	herring
свинина	svínina	pork	лососина/	lososína/	salmon
курица	kúritsa	chicken	сёмга	cyómga	
телятина	telyátina	veal	щука	shchúka	pike
баранина	baránina	mutton/	осетрина	osetrína	sturgeon
		lamb			

Drinks

(минепальная) бода	(minerálnaya) vodá	(mineral) water
чай	chai	tea
кофе	kófye	coffee
сок	sok	fruit juice
напиток	napítok	fruit drink
вино	vinó	wine
пибо	píva	beer
водка	vódka	vodka
коньяк	kanyák	cognac
шампанское	shampánskoye	champagne

Dishes from the Menu

Супы	**Supi**	**Soups**
щи	shchi	cabbage soup
борщ	borshch	beetroot soup
окрошка	akróshka	cold vegetable soup
уха	úkha	fish soup
харчо	kharchó	spicy mutton soup
солянка	solyánka	soup with pickles

Закуски	**Zakuski**	**Appetizers**
икра (красная/ чёрная	ikrá (krásnaya/ chórnaya)	caviar (red/ black)
баклажанная икра	baklazhánnaya ikrá	cold baked aubergine
блины	bliný	pancakes/blini
грибы со сметаной	gribý so smetánoi	mushrooms in sour cream
ассорти мясное/ рыбное	assórti myásnoe/ rýbnoe	assorted cold meats/ fish
столичный салат	stolíchny salát	cold chicken & vegetables in mayonnaise
салат из огурцов	salát iz ogúrtsov	cucumber salad
салат из помидоров	salat iz pomidórov	tomato salad
хачапури	khachapúri	cheesy Georgian bread
лаваш	lavásh	flat Georgian bread

Вторые Блюда	Vtoriye Bliuda	Main Courses
антрекот	antrekót	entrecote steak
бефстроганов	befstroganóv	beef stroganov
бифштекс	bifshtéks	beef steak
бастурма	bastúrma	cured meat
цыпляата табака	tsiplyáta tabáka	flat, grilled chicken
долма	dólma	vine leaves stuffed with rice & meat (Central Asian)
сосиски	sosíski	frankfurter-type sausages
биточки	bítochki	meatballs
ачма	achmá	noodles & cheese (Georgian)
голубцы	golubtsý	cabbage leaves stuffed with mince
котлеты	kotléty	meat croquettes
кулебяка	kulebyáka	pie with cabbage or fish
пхали	pkháli	aubergine with walnut sauce (Georgian)
манти	mánti	giant meat dumplings (Central Asian)
жаркое	zhárkoye	beef stew
шницель	shnítsel	schnitzel
шашлык	sháshlik	kebab
плов	plov	pilaf (Central Asian)
люла-кебаб	liúla-kebáb	spiced, minced kebab
пельмени	pelméni	meat-filled dumplings
пирожки	pirozhkí	pies
сациви	satsívi	walnut & coriander sauce, with poultry (Georgian)

Десерт	Dessert	Dessert
мороженое	morózhenoye	ice cream
пирожное	pirózhnoye	pastry
вареники	varéniki	jam or fruit dumplings

Maps and Useful Local Reference Books

Northern Cartographic/Russian Information Services currently produce the most up-to-date maps of St Petersburg, available from hotels in the city and by ordering from a good bookshop abroad.

The **St Petersburg Times** is an excellent twice-weekly English-language paper, and **Pulse**, a more culturally slanted magazine, appears monthly. Pulkova Airoprt produces a good monthly magazine, the **St Petersburg Review**, with listings of theatres, restaurants and museums and relevant articles in English.

The Traveller's Yellow Pages to St Petersburg has been produced by the gargantuan efforts of an American-led team. Aside from bars, restaurants, hotels and airlines, they list addresses and phone numbers for a host of other potentially useful services, such as television repair shops, local government offices and food radioactivity testing. These are on sale in hotel shops and supermarkets. If you don't see them around, get in touch with their office at Naberezhnaya Reki Moiki 64, ✆ 315 6412, ✉ 312 7341. Their US phone number is (516) 549 0064.

Russia Survival Guide, published by Russian Information Services Inc., is a regularly updated guide to doing business and travelling in Russia. They also publish a number of other useful fact sheets. For more information call them in Vermont, USA on ✆ (802) 223 4955, ✉ (802) 223 6105 or Moscow on ✆/✉ (095) 254 9275.

You will find **maps** showing the routes of overground public transport for sale on the street or in kiosks. They come only in Cyrillic and are called Маршрути Городского Транспорта (Marshruty Gorodskovo Transporta).

Travel

Duncan Fallowell, *One Hot Summer in St Petersburg* (Vintage 1995) Endearing gay romance which captures with enthusiasm the unexpected web the Russians and their city weave around a first-time visitor.

Colin Thubron, *Among the Russians* (Penguin 1985). Thubron's book, a perceptive description of travels in Russia and the Caucasus in the early 1980s, is a testament to how much can change in 15 years, and yet how much the Russians remain the same.

Lawrence Kelly, *St Petersburg: a traveller's companion* (Constable 1981) traces the history and social mores of the city through excerpts from contemporary documents, from the earliest accounts to the Revolution.

Susan Richards, *Epics of Everyday Life* (Viking 1990). An English woman's encounters in Moscow and other cities of the Soviet Union, capturing the enduring charm of the Russians during a period of constant change.

Further Reading

Marquis de Custine, *Letters from Russia* (Penguin 1991) is the classic 19th-century account of Moscow and St Petersburg through the eyes of a conservative Frenchman.

John Steinbeck and Robert Capa, *A Russian Journal* (Paragon House, NY 1989). In 1948 this renowned US writer/photographer team recorded their impressions of Russia during the austerity of the post-war Stalinist period.

Truman Capote, *The Muses are Heard* (from *A Capote Reader*, Hamish Hamilton 1987). A wickedly amusing piece of reportage describing the journey to Russia and reception of a 1956 American touring production of Porgy and Bess.

History

Tibor Szamuely, *The Russian Tradition* (Fontana 1988) traces the roots of revolution in Russia back to medieval times in an engrossing account of the country's social history.

Orlando Figes, *A People's Tragedy: The Russian Revolution 1891–1924* (Vintage 1999). Massive and minutely researched, this view of the revolution tries to understand why it succeeded by concentrating on its less well-known participants.

Geoffrey Hosking, *A History of the Soviet Union* (Fontana 1990). The second edition of this comprehensive survey of Soviet history runs well into Gorbachev's term as General Secretary.

Hedrick Smith, *The New Russians* (Vintage 1991). Absorbing study of Russian society on the eve of *glasnost* and of the momentous political, social, economic and psychological changes of 1985–1991.

David Remnick, *Lenin's Tomb* and *Resurrection* (Vintage Crime/Black Lizard 1998). One of the best western commentators on Russia's recent changes, the then Washington Post correspondent wrote the first book on the collapse of the Soviet Union, the second on Russia's efforts to find her future.

Biography and Autobiography

Robert K. Massie, *Peter the Great* (Abacus 1993) is a Pulitzer Prize-winning 850-page masterpiece of historical biography. The pages fly by as the giant epileptic tries to haul Russia out of a vividly-portrayed Middle Ages and into the modern world.

John T. Alexander, *Catherine the Great* (OUP 1989). Unlike many of her biographers, Alexander's analysis of Catherine the myth takes an intelligent probing attitude which only adds to his portrayal of Catherine the empress.

Christine Sutherland, *The Princess of Siberia* (Robin Clark Ltd 1988) is the breathy, romantic account of Princess Maria Volkonskaya's journey to and life in Siberia in the 1820s, to join her husband who was exiled for his leading role in the Decembrist Uprising.

Robert K. Massie, *Nicholas and Alexandra* (Atheneum 1967) is the standard, very readable portrait of the last of the Romanovs, now somewhat overtaken by the opening of archives and discovery of the bodies of the family near Yekaterinburg.

Michael Glenny and Norman Stone, *The Other Russia* (Faber & Faber 1991). Takes the form of a series of interviews with members of the greatest Russian diaspora, those who fled their native land in the aftermath of the Revolution.

Michael Ignatieff, *The Russian Album* (Penguin 1988). In this endearing volume, Ignatieff digs back to reveal the anti-Semitic skeletons in his family cupboard and to provide a vivid depiction of the Revolution and exile from an aristocratic perspective.

Osip Mandelstam, *The Noise of Time* (in **The Prose of Osip Mandelstam**, Quartet Encounter 1988). Memoirs of life in St Petersburg by the poet who died a victim of Stalin in the Gulag in 1938.

Isaac Deutscher, *Stalin* (Penguin 1976). The classic biography, its relatively sympathetic analysis ever more questionable in the light of new revelations.

Evgenia S. Ginzburg, *Into the Whirlwind* and *Within the Whirlwind* (Collins Harvill 1989). A terrifying account of life in the gulag in the 1930s and '40s by one of the survivors.

Joseph Brodsky, *In a Room and a Half* and *A Guide to a Renamed City* (essays from *Less than One*, Farrar Straus Giroux 1986). Fascinating, evocative memoires of life in Leningrad in the 1950s and '60s.

Nadezhda Mandelstam, *Hope against Hope* and *Hope Abandoned* (Collins Harvill 1989 & 1961) together chronicle a life of internal exile in constant opposition to the Soviet system, during which the author's primary concern was the preservation of her husband, Osip Mandelstam's poetic works and his rehabilitation. Nadezhda is a writer of brilliance in her own right, and has produced the definitive chronicle of life under Stalin.

Art and Architecture

Christopher Marsden, *Palmyra of the North* (Faber and Faber 1942). An enthusiastic and intimate account of the architectural and artistic birth of St Petersburg in the 18th century.

George Heard Hamilton, *The Art and Architecture of Russia* (Pelican History of Art 1992). A full analysis of the development of Russian art and architecture from medieval times to the early 20th century.

Camilla Gray, *The Russian Experiment in Art 1863–1922* (Thames and Hudson 1993). Exhaustive survey of the 'great experiment' which profoundly influenced the course of 20th-century painting world-wide.

Geraldine Norman, *The Hermitage* (Pimlico 1999) is an engrossing, panoramic history of the museum and its collections by a British art critic.

Suzanne Massie, *Pavlovsk—The Life of a Russian Palace* (Little Brown 1990). By tracing the two-hundred-year history of one of Russia's most perfect palaces, the author has managed to write not only an architectural history but also a social history, embracing everyone from the 19th-century royal inhabitants to the 20th-century restorers. Brilliant.

Dmitry Shvidkovsky, *The Empress and the Architect* (Yale 1996) tells of the relationship between Catherine the Great and her favourite architect, the enigmatic Charles Cameron, and sets their achievements in the context of late 18th-century European architecture.

George Galitzine, *Imperial Splendour* (Viking 1991). Compact history of Russia with breath-taking photographs and stunning gatefolds.

Katya Galitzine, *St Petersburg—The Hidden Interiors* (Hazar, 1999). A thorough history of the city up to the present day, told by photographs of lesser-known buildings as well as text.

Sociology and Culture

Francine du Plessix Gray, *Soviet Women—Walking the Tightrope* (Virago 1991). Taking as its central paradox the official equality yet unofficial inequality of the country's women, these interviews paint a grim picture of ignorance and social injustice.

Suzanne Massie, *Land of the Firebird: the beauty of old Russia* (Touchstone 1982) is a wonderful, evocative, colourful account of the culture of pre-Revolutionary Russia—its literature, painting, dance, jewellery, music, sculpture, gardening and much, much more.

Solomon Volkov, *St Petersburg: a cultural history* (Sinclair-Stevenson 1996). A brilliantly written cultural biography of the city concentrating on the 20th century and such greats as Shostakovich, Akhmatova and Brodsky.

Thomas Lahusen (ed.), *Late Soviet Culture* (Duke University Press, 1993) gives a taste of post-perestroika academic thinking, in fields as diverse as 'Saint' Alexander Pushkin, Soviet film and women's studies.

Russian Cuisine

Anya von Bremzen and John Welchman, *Please to the Table* (Workman Publishing, NY 1990). This enchanting book covers the whole of the former Soviet Union and is more a bible of domestic mores than a cookbook. Peppered among the recipes are mouth-watering quotes from Russian literature, notes on favourite dishes, menu suggestions and host of other enlightening culinary trivia.

St Petersburg in Literature

Anna Benn & Rosamund Bartlett, *Literary Russia: A Guide* (Papermac 1997) will guide you round the places associated with Russia's great writers.

Alexander Pushkin, *The Bronze Horseman* (Bristol Classical Press 1992) is Pushkin's epic poem of the 1824 flood which helped to create the mythos of the city.

Lev Tolstoy, *Anna Karenina* (Penguin Classics). Tolstoy's take on the corrupt society of St Petersburg.

Fyodor Dostoyevsky is the classic 19th-century St Petersburg novelist, with *Crime and Punishment* (Penguin Classics) perhaps the most evocative of his *œuvre*.

Andrei Bely, *Petersburg* (Penguin 1983) is not just a taste of Russian symbolism and an evocation of the turbulence beneath the surface of St Petersburg in 1905: Bely's novel is one of the great experimental works of this century.

Andrei Bitov, *Pushkin House* (Harvill 1990) tells the story of Soviet youth lived out in post-Stalin Leningrad.

Sacheverell Sitwell, *Valse des Fleurs* (Sickle Moon 2000) is a whimsical evocation of a ball at the Winter Palace in St Petersburg in 1868, complete with court runners delivering invitations and Ethiopian palace guards.

Daniil Kharms, *The Plummeting Old Women* (Lilliput 1989) is a collection of short pieces by one of the great absurdist modernists of the early Soviet period. Kharms died under Stalin; though well known as a writer for children, his other works are only now receiving the attention they deserve.

Anna Akhmatova, *Selected Poems* (Collins Harvill 1989). Pained, strained and painfully moving, even in translation, Akhmatova's is the voice of St Petersburg speaking through the period of Leningrad.

Glas is a quarterly of new Russian writing in translation, available from Dr Arch Tait, Dept. of Russian Literature, University of Birmingham B15 2TT.

Main page references are in **bold**; page numbers of maps are in *italic.*

Index

Also Available from Cadogan Guides...

Country Guides

Antarctica
Belize
Central Asia
China: The Silk Routes
Egypt
France: Southwest France;
     Dordogne, Lot & Bordeaux
France: Southwest France;
     Gascony & the Pyrenees
France: Brittany
France: The Loire
France: The South of France
France: Provence
France: The Côte d'Azur
Germany: Bavaria
India
India: South India
India: Goa
Ireland
Ireland: Southwest Ireland
Ireland: Northern Ireland
Italy
Italy: The Bay of Naples and Southern Italy
Italy: Italian Riviera
Italy: Lombardy, Milan and the Italian Lakes
Italy: Tuscany and Umbria
Italy: Venetia and the Dolomites
Japan
Morocco
Portugal
Portugal: The Algarve
Scotland
Scotland's Highlands and Islands
South Africa, Swaziland and Lesotho
Spain
Spain: Southern Spain
Spain: Northern Spain
Syria & Lebanon
Tunisia
Turkey
Western Turkey
Yucatán and Southern Mexico
Zimbabwe, Botswana and Namibia

City Guides

Amsterdam
Brussels, Bruges, Ghent & Antwerp
Edinburgh
Florence, Siena, Pisa & Lucca
Italy: Three Cities—Rome, Padua, Assisi
Italy: Three Cities—Rome, Florence, Venice
Italy: Three Cities—Rome, Naples, Sorrento
Italy: Three Cities—Venice, Padua, Verona
Japan: Three Cities—Tokyo, Kyoto, Nara
London
London-Brussels
London-Paris
Madrid
Manhattan
Moscow & St Petersburg
Paris
Prague
Rome
Spain: Three Cities—Granada, Seville,
     Cordoba
Venice

Island Guides

Caribbean and Bahamas
NE Caribbean: The Leeward Islands
SE Caribbean: The Windward Islands
Jamaica & the Caymans

Greek Islands
Crete
Mykonos, Santorini & the Cyclades
Rhodes & the Dodecanese
Corfu & the Ionian Islands

Madeira & Porto Santo
Malta
Sicily

Plus...

Southern Africa on the Wild Side
Bugs, Bites & Bowels
Travel by Cargo Ship
London Markets

Available from good bookshops or via, in the UK, **Grantham Book Services**, Isaac Newton Way, Alma Park Industrial Estate, Grantham NG31 9SD, ☎ (01476) 541 080, ✆ (01476) 541 061; and in North America from **The Globe Pequot Press**, 246 Goose Lane, P.O. Box 480, Guilford, CT 06437-0480, ☎ (800) 962 0973, ✆ (203) 458 4603.

The Metro

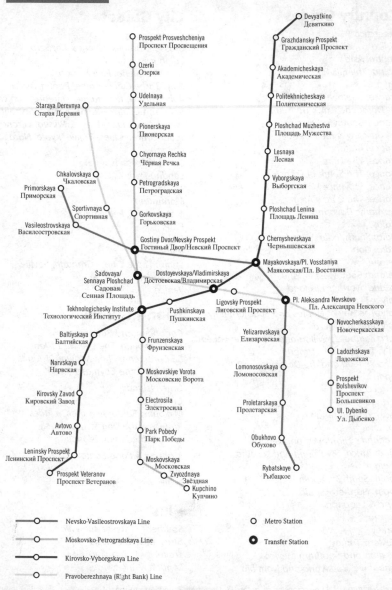

Devyatkino
Девяткино

Grazhdansky Prospekt
Гражданский Проспект

Prospekt Prosveshcheniya
Проспект Просвещения

Akademicheskaya
Академическая

Ozerki
Озерки

Politekhnicheskaya
Политехническая

Udelnaya
Удельная

Ploshchad Muzhestva
Площадь Мужества

Staraya Derevnya
Старая Деревня

Pionerskaya
Пионерская

Lesnaya
Лесная

Chyornaya Rechka
Чёрная Речка

Vyborgskaya
Выборгская

Chkalovskaya
Чкаловская

Petrogradskaya
Петроградская

Ploshchad Lenina
Площадь Ленина

Primorskaya
Приморская

Sportivnaya
Спортивная

Gorkovskaya
Горьковская

Chernyshevskaya
Чернышевская

Vasileostrovskaya
Василеостровская

Gostiny Dvor/Nevsky Prospekt
Гостиный Двор/Невский Проспект

Mayakovskaya/Pl. Vosstaniya
Маяковская/Пл. Восстания

Sadovaya/
Sennaya Ploshchad
Садовая/
Сенная Площадь

Dostoyevskaya/Vladimirskaya
Достоевская/Владимирская

Pl. Aleksandra Nevskovo
Пл. Александра Невского

Ligovsky Prospekt
Лиговский Проспект

Novocherkasskaya
Новочеркасская

Tekhnologichesky Institute
Технологический Институт

Pushkinskaya
Пушкинская

Yelizarovskaya
Елизаровская

Ladozhskaya
Ладожская

Baltiyskaya
Балтийская

Frunzenskaya
Фрунзенская

Lomonosovskaya
Ломоносовская

Prospekt
Bolshevikov
Проспект
Большевиков

Narvskaya
Нарвская

Moskovskiye Vorota
Московские Ворота

Proletarskaya
Пролетарская

Ul. Dybenko
Ул. Дыбенко

Kirovsky Zavod
Кировский Завод

Electrosila
Электросила

Avtovo
Автово

Park Pobedy
Парк Победы

Obukhovo
Обухово

Leninsky Prospekt
Ленинский Проспект

Moskovskaya
Московская

Rybatskoye
Рыбацкое

Prospekt Veteranov
Проспект Ветеранов

Zvyozdnaya
Звёздная

Kupchino
Купчино

Nevsko-Vasileostrovskaya Line

Metro Station

Moskovsko-Petrogradskaya Line

Transfer Station

Kirovsko-Vyborgskaya Line

Pravoberezhnaya (Right Bank) Line

314